TH.
VATIC
CONSPIRACY

Intrigue in
St. Peter's Square

Peter Kross

Adventures Unlimited Press

To:
Bill Wertheim,
my long time, college friend

Books by Peter Kross:

American Conspiracy Files
Tales From Langely
The Secret History of the United States
JFK: The French Connection
Spies, Traitors and Moles
The Encyclopedia of World War II Spies
Oswald, the CIA and the Warren Commission

THE
VATICAN
CONSPIRACY

Intrigue in
St. Peter's Square

Peter Kross

The Vatican Conspiracy

ISBN 13: 978-1-939149-87-9

Published by:
Adventures Unlimited Press
One Adventure Place
Kempton, Illinois 60946 USA

auphq@frontiernet.net

www.adventuresunlimitedpress.com

Seal of the Vatican.

Coat of Arms of the Vatican.

TABLE OF CONTENTS

I like the dreams of the future
better than the history of the past.
—Thomas Jefferson

INTRODUCTION

What we know of the inner workings of the Vatican is shredded in mystery, with people seeing conspiracies at every turn. The complex web of the Vatican has been seen in both fiction and non-fiction, the previous being the hit movies by Dan Brown from his novels, *The Divinci Code* and *Angels and Demons,* in which the Vatican is under siege from old nemesis like the Freemasons, Opus Die and other sinister groups.

Vatican City is the smallest country in the world. It is encircled by a two-mile border with Italy, covers just 100 acres and is smaller than Central Park, in New York. The pope is the head of state, prints its own money, stamps, and issues its own passports. St. Peter's Basilica sits atop a city of the dead, a fact that is not well known today. In ancient times, the Pope ruled as an absolute monarch, sometimes leading armies in battle and executing their enemies without blinking an eye. Over the years, the various Popes had a running feud with Italy and they ruled Vatican City and the papal-states without regard to Italian law. It wasn't until the country was united in 1870 when that all changed. In fact, Pope Pius IX said he was a "prisoner of the Vatican" and for almost 60 years, the Popes refused to leave its confines.

The dispute between the Church and the Italian government came to an end in 1929 with the signing of the Lateran Pacts, which allowed the Vatican to exist as its own sovereign state and Italy paid the Church $92 million for the Papal States.

During World War II, Italy was on the side of the Axis powers but did little to actually aid them in the fight against the allies. After Italy fell to allied powers, its influence on the world scene began to diminish. Throughout the war, the Pope failed to stand up to Hitler and did even less to help the majority of Italian Jews to leave Italy for safety. It has been verified over the years, the Vatican helped certain high-ranking Nazi officials to flee Italy, using false passports and travel documents issued to them by the Church. This so called Ratline allowed some of the highest-ranking Nazis to flee to South America and Egypt, sometimes right under the noses of American intelligence officials. This is not a pretty story but one that must be told in order to understand how our post-World War 2 history was conducted.

American and Italy go back hundreds of years with each side doing each other's bidding. What is little known in American-Italian relations is that John Surratt Jr, one of the conspirators in the plot to kill President Lincoln, fled the country and wound up in Italy as part of the Popes personal Zuave guards until he was unmasked and fled to Egypt where he was captured. At the time of the Lincoln assassination, persistent rumors abounded in the United States that the Vatican had somehow played a role in the president's death, something that was never proven, but was a common theme in certain circles.

This book, *The Vatican Conspiracy: Intrigue in St. Peters Square,* will try to tell that story.

The book will tell the story of the US-Italian-Vatican Connection from World War II to the 1980s under the Reagan administration.

You will learn of a little known story of an American military officer who was killed (some say by his own men) in Italy during the war, culminating in a congressional investigation when the war ended. I will tell the story of James Angleton's work as an American spy in Italy during the war and his relationship with the Church and how the OSS infiltrated certain of its agents into the Vatican to aid in the efforts to oust Hitler. Also in that chapter, I will tell of Angleton's covert efforts to aid the Pope in its covert activities to overthrow the government of Adolf Hitler. I will then go extensively into the so-called Ratline that allowed Nazi leaders to flee Germany at the wars end. I will also delve into Operation Paperclip and Operation Safehaven in which Switzerland laundered money from Germany in order to pay that nations cost of the war. The last three chapters delve into the most recent intrigues in the Vatican, including the attempted assassination of Pope John Paul II in Rome and who might have been behind it, the Mysterious death of Pope John Paul 1st in Rome, only serving just 33 days in the Papacy. I'll also cover the Vatican Bank scandal involving Roberto Calvi and an American Bishop of the Vatican bank, Paul

Marcinkus. The last chapter involves the murders of two members of the Swiss Guard by one of the Pope's own men.

This is not a pretty story, but most stories like this never are. This is a tale that most readers of history do not know, but one that must be told. History is never what we are told to believe, not cut and dry, not exactly what we were led to believe. So, here is the story, warts and all.

—Peter Kross
North Brunswick, N.J.

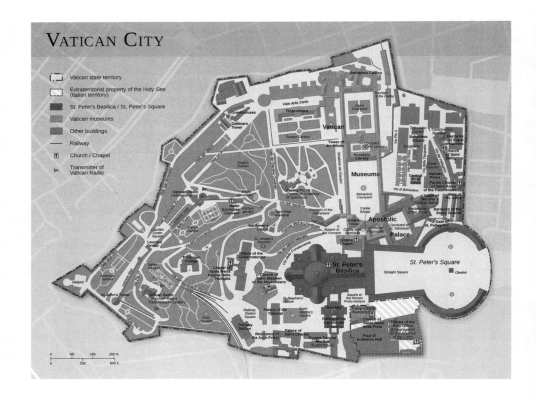

Chapter 1

A Death in Wartime:
Who Killed Major Holohan?

In the latter part of 1944, the OSS, the Office of Strategic Services, mounted a plan called Operation Chrysler in Italy to "act as a liaison with partisan commanders, attempt to guide and control developments in northern Italy, and create unified partisan command under the direction of the supreme allied commander." This seemingly simple order was just the start of one of the most controversial and mysterious events to come out of the war, affecting the OSS directly, and leading to a congressional investigation.

The genesis of Operation Chrysler (also referred to as the Mangoseteen Mission) was laid out by William Donovan, director of the OSS, and Colonel William Suhling, chief of Special Operations in Italy. Throughout the war, the OSS had been supplying the various resistance groups, including some of the communist forces, with military and communications equipment. Toward the end of the war, the OSS decided to suspend these airdrops because of intense quarreling between the various groups. However, other items such as food, clothing, and medical supplies continued to be parachuted in for the rebels.

Donovan and Suhling decided to send an American team to Italy to sort out the troubles that had been brewing among the various factions of the resistance. The Americans wanted a non-Italian officer to lead the mission because he would not be unduly influenced by the factions. The man chosen to lead Operation Chrysler was Major William Holohan. Bill Holohan was a Roman Catholic, a graduate of Manhattan College in New York and later Harvard Law School. Prior to the war, he had worked as a lawyer for the Securities and Exchange Commission. When Donovan approached Holohan about taking over the mission, he immediately volunteered his services.

The units that had overall responsibility for running Operation Chrysler were the Fifteenth Army Group, under the command of British General Harold Alexander, and the National Committee of Liberation Headquarters in Northern Italy, located in Milan. During the height of the war, the Po Valley, where this mission was to take place, was under German control. However, by 1944, the various resistance groups were in charge, vying with each other for superiority in the region. It was the job of Major Holohan and his team to rein in the competing entities and make sure they took orders from the Fifteenth Army Group.

Holohan's team was dropped behind the lines on September 26, 1944. Their jumping off point was the Maison Blanche Airport in Algiers, and their destination was an area near Lake Orta, north of Milan. The unit was comprised of Major Holohan, Lieutenant Victor Giannino, second in command, Lt. Aldo Icardi, the intelligence officer, Sergeant Carl Lo Dulce, the wireless operator, Gianni, an Italian partisan agent, Tullio Lussi, an Italian partisan agent also known as Captain Landi, who belonged to the Di Dio resistance organization, Sgt. Arthur Ciamicola, a weapons expert, and "Red," an Italian radio operator.

Lt. Icardi, 23, Major Holohan's immediate deputy, was a graduate of the University of Pittsburgh with a degree in political science. He was a professional intelligence officer whose job was to oversee the dangerous crossing of Americans into enemy-held territory. He was also in charge of a special intelligence training school in southern Italy. He was fluent in Italian; Holohan did not speak the language.

Upon landing, the Americans were met by members of the resistance and taken to their camp. They spent the next month hiding from German patrols in the town of Coiromonte. At one point, the Germans sent out scouting parties looking for the Chrysler team.

The OSS headquarters in Switzerland had been operating agents in the Ossola Valley of Italy for some time. This rugged region was controlled by the partisan brigades, and served as a natural boundary that prevented all but a frontal attack. OSS-Switzerland encouraged these partisans to launch hit-and-run raids against German fortifications in the area and promised arms and equipment. But by the time the Chrysler team landed, the Ossola Valley had been liberated of German activity, a fact that was not passed on to them.

To add to the confusion, the Chrysler team was met by Vincenzo Moscatelli, the leader of the communist faction in the area. Moscatelli's communist brigades had been attacking German units in the region for some time, inflicting heavy casualties. With the Germans now cleared out, Moscatelli in effect began to operate what he called the "Republic of Ossola" with himself as its leader.

In this highly charged mix, Major Holohan and his men had to deal with the appearance of Alfredo Di Dio, leader of the Christian Partisan Brigade. Di Dio harangued the Americans for not supplying his group with the promised weapons and material. He said, "I have been abandoned by the traitorous Communists, and the Americans too, have abandoned me after encouraging me to create the situation." The Di Dio group lost 4,000 partisan fighters due to what its leader believed was OSS malfeasance.

Major Holohan carried with him a sum of money that was to be used to finance espionage operations headed by a man called Giorgio, whose real name was Aminta Migliari. He was head of a partisan group called SIMNI, or Military Information Service of the Partisan Forces in Northern Italy. He was also head of security for the Chrysler mission. A woman named Marina Duelli was also assigned as a courier to Major Holohan. One secret mission funded by Major Holohan was called Salem and was run out of the headquarters of the National Committee for Liberation in Milan.

Before leaving Algiers, Major Holohan was given funds by Tullio Lussi, a partisan leader code named "Captain Landi." As mentioned above, Captain Landi belonged to the Di Dio resistance organization. A high school teacher in Milan, Landi joined the OSS in Bari, Italy, and was assigned to the Chrysler mission. He gave both Major Holohan and Lt. Icardi gold coins, comprising 100 marengos to each roll, for a total of 2,100 marengos. They also carried $16,000 U.S. and $10,000 in Italian lira. The disposition of the money would play a part in the tragic events that followed.

Major Holohan used some of this money to pay the expenses of Georgio's men, until it was decided that they wouldn't be able to carry the heavy gold bars with them. Georgio made a deal with Major Holohan to sell the gold at market prices and return the cash to him. A business deal was worked out between Georgio, Lt. Icardi, and a few local Catholic priests in the Lake Orta area. The money, about $15,000, would be used to finance the purchase of buildings, machinery and land to be used after the war ended.

In the third week of November 1944, the Chrysler team captured four men in civilian clothes who were operating in their area. They turned out to be three German soldiers and a Swiss citizen. On them were detailed scale maps of the area, as well as direction finding equipment.

Shortly before the incident, the Chrysler team suffered its first major setback. A large airdrop of guns, ammunition, and supplies, code named "Pineapple-1," headed for the Di Dio-Christian Partisan Brigade, was intercepted. The supplies were taken by a communist group called the Sixth Nello Brigade. After all was divided up, the Di Dio group got one third of the supplies, while the communists claimed two thirds.

The question was how the communists knew of the airdrop. Was there a traitor in the Chrysler group or among their allies? Major Holohan met with the leader of the communist group in that part of Italy, Vincenzo Moscatelli, to clear the air. The Major told Moscatelli that there would be no further airdrops until his men agreed to work directly under American supervision and stop the internal fighting. Major Holohan butted heads on several occasions with Moscatelli, who believed that the Americans were not willing to share all they knew with the communists and did not trust them. At one point during the mission, Major Holohan, with Aldo Icardi working as a translator, had a meeting with Moscatelli to further clear the air. Moscatelli complained that most of the supplies that the Allies were giving them were going to the Christian Democrats, a rival group. Holohan told Moscatelli that "his mission was not to establish a communist regime in Italy but to kill as many Germans as possible."

For some time, the Chrysler team had been holed up at the town of Villa Castelnuovo. Sympathetic locals told them that a fascist patrol was looking for them. The Major decided to leave the area, and as the team made their way through the dense, cold forest, a number of shots broke out. Men scattered for cover. In the ensuing battle, Major Holohan was killed.

It took Allied intelligence a long time to figure out what happened to the Chrysler team that fateful night. OSS headquarters in Sienna, Italy did not hear from the Chrysler team for the first two weeks of December. On December 14, they received a message that the Chrysler team had been attacked and in the ensuing engagement, Major Holohan had disappeared. An OSS report from that period of time, between December 1 and 15, said, "This team was recently forced to suspend contacts because of enemy action in the zone. It is believed that the mission is moving to a safe zone." Since OSS HQ did not hear from the Chrysler team, they asked an unnamed Italian secret agent who was operating in the area to find out what really happened. He reported back that "the mission was fraught with danger because its presence was known to the residents of the nearby villages, its transmissions could be heard by the enemy, and its movements were hampered by the fact that its personnel was operating in U.S. Military uniform."

While the OSS tried to figure out what was going on regarding the death of Major Holohan, on January 18, 1945, a large amount of supplies comprising twenty-four tons of weapons was dropped to the various resistance groups, including the communists and the Christian Democrats near Lake Orta. Shortly after this event took place, Aldo Icardi and Carl Lo Dolce left the area and moved to the town of Busta Arisizio, near the town of Milan and Lake Orta. They now blended into the area and began establishing an intelligence network that ran until the war was over. But while Lo Dolce and Icardi were winding down their operations, another investigation into the mysterious death of Major Holohan was just beginning.

In February 1945, the Army declared that Major Holohan was "Missing in Action" and notified his family in Brooklyn, New York. What the family did not know was that the Army's Criminal Investigation Division had begun an investigation into the Major's death. In 1947, CID agents arrived in the Lake Orta area and began to question locals who had lived there during the war. One interesting development they found was that Aldo Icardi had invested in an operation with Aminta Migliari, who was part of the Chrysler mission, and went by the nickname of "Giorgio." Investigators wanted to know where Icardi got the money and who gave it to him.

In August 1947, CID investigators tracked down Icardi, who

was then attending the University of Pittsburg law school, for an interview. They put him through a polygraph test which lasted almost an entire day regarding the events relating to the murder of Major Holohan. The report cleared Icardi of any illegal dealing with Migliari and also said that he was not lying about his knowledge of what happened to the major.

It was now time for the Italian government to begin its own investigation of the Holohan murder and they appointed a police detective named Elio Albieri as the lead investigator. He went to Lake Orta and began talking to people who lived in the area during the time in question. He found a woman named Marina Duelli who gave him the names of two ex-partisans, Giuseppe Manini and Gualtiero Tozzini, who were in the region at the time. Both men were part of Holohan's bodyguard during the war and, it seems, had a lot to say.

Albieri talked to both men and he then turned over the investigation to an American, a CID agent named Major Henry Manfredi who was stationed in Trieste, Italy. During his interrogation of Tozzini and Manini, both men told Agent Manfredi that they were part of the murder plot against Major Holohan and that their accomplices were none other than Aldo Icardi and Carl Lo Dolce at the Villa Castelnuovo on the night of December 6, 1944. "They stated that Holohan had been poisoned with cyanide in his minestrone, and when that seemed not to have worked, he was shot twice in the head by Lo Dolce, using Manini's 9-millimeter Beretta, as he lay sick, from the cyanide, on his bed. His corpse was then taken on Icardi's instructions and placed in the deepest part of Lake Orta."

Lake Orta was then dragged and the body of Major Holohan was pulled out. The corpse revealed two 9-millimeter slugs in his head. Tests were done to see who owned the gun and it turned out that Manini was the original owner.

William Donovan, the head of the OSS during the war, got involved in the probe of Major Holohan's death and he contacted U.S. Attorney General Howard McGrath and General George C. Marshall, then Secretary of Defense. He reviewed the case with then, and told them that the evidence pointed to the culpability of Icardi and Lo Dolce. Donovan told his colleagues that he did not believe that the United States had jurisdiction in the murder of

Major Holohan but might be able to conduct an investigation in the case of Icardi's possible embezzlements of funds.

As the OSS investigation was going on, they began looking at intercepted German signal traffic that was gathered during the time of the Holohan murder. The intercepted decrypts in the area of Villa Castelnuovo reported no mention of the capture or death of Major Holohan. OSS radio officers did, however, learn from their intercepts that the Germans mentioned the disappearance of an "officer." not an "agent."

After the death of Major Holohan, Lt. Icardi took over command of the Chrysler team and was later awarded the Legion of Merit. In February 1945, Lo Dolce suffered a nervous breakdown and was sent to Switzerland to recover. But the case was still not closed.

Secretary Marshall decided to intervene and he ordered two U.S. agents to look into the case. They were H. Rex Smith and Harry Gisslow of the Criminal Investigation Division Department. They questioned Carl Lo Dolce in Rochester, New York and during their talks, Lo Dolce wrote an eight-page confession, backing up the account of Tozzini and Manini. Lo Dolce said that he did not believe that Major Holohan had complete control of the Chrysler mission and tensions between the major and his team were growing day by day. He wrote in his statement that, "Icardi would tell me about what the mission was supposed to do and Icardi would tell me continuously that things were going wrong and how operations should have been conducted and I began to feel that we were all in a situation from which we would not survive."

Lo Dolce further stated that Manini brought something that looked like a piece of paper and said that it was poison that could be used to kill Major Holohan. Lo Dolce also said that sometimes the Chrysler team members talked about killing the major, but only in a light-hearted manner. But the light-hearted manner obviously turned deadly, since the major's body was found at the bottom of Lake Orta.,

On the night of December 6, 1944, continued Lo Dolce, Manini put poison in Major Holohan's soup as the men began dinner. The major then left the table feeling sick and returned to his room. Lo Dolce said to Icardi, "that if he (Holohan) lives through this he will send a message to Headquarters, so we'll have to make sure he doesn't live." Lo Dolce asked both Manini and Tozzini if they would kill the major, but they refused to do so.

Lo Dolce said that a coin was tossed to see who would kill the major, and that Icardi won the toss and subsequently killed Major Holohan. Lo Dolce said that after the major's death, he, Icardi, Manini, and Tozzini brought the major's body in a boat and dumped him in Lake Orta. He said that all of the men began firing their weapons to make it look like a firefight had broken out between themselves and the Germans.

In 1951, after a change of heart, Lo Dolce wrote a letter to William Donovan, refuting his confession regarding the circumstances of Major Holohan's death. Part of his letter reads as follows: "I didn't kill Major Holohan and I do not know who did. I didn't plot with any Italians or with Lt. Icardi to kill or rob him of huge sums of money which didn't exist. I am innocent of these charges."

The CID's investigation into Major Holohan's death continued and a new figure in the case, Special Agent Frederick Gardella, took over. He traveled to Italy and interviewed many of the players, including an important partisan leader by the name of Georgio Aminta Migliari who called Holohan, "an upright man and a true soldier, just but firm." He also interviewed a woman named Marina Duelli on September 18, 1946 (she had been interviewed by Italian authorities in the past regarding the Holohan case). Marina had served as a messenger between the partisans and Holohan and liked the major very much. She said that "partisans, not the Germans or the fascists, had been responsible for Holohan's death, and there had been friction between Icardi and Holohan, and when she felt that Captain Leto, the real name of Recapito Pasquale, was working against Holohan on behalf of Moscatelli, she had gone to Switzerland to warn the OSS of her suspicions concerning Holohan's disappearance."

After a long investigation, Agent Gardella found out many incriminating facts, including the following:

Icardi and Lo Dolce made many statements about wanting to "get rid of the Major": Icardi was organizing business deals for the future and not letting his superiors know about it; any new information provided by the partisans was to be given only to Icardi, not Major Holohan; the disappearance of Major Holohan was a political move started by the Communists headed by Moscatelli; and... both Icardi and Lo Dolce did not cooperate with Major Holohan. Icardi was more interested in personal affairs, and of elevating his position with the mission than carrying out his required duties. In the ensuing years, Major Holohan's body was found floating in the cold waters of Lake Orta, wrapped in a sleeping bag, with two bullets in his head.[1]

Aldo Icardi was called before a congressional committee looking into the Holohan affair. Icardi said that upon hearing shots coming from the villa and the surrounding area, he fired back, not seeing if he hit anyone. Icardi would write about his part in the Holohan case after the war in a book called *American Master Spy.*

Icardi turned for legal assistance after he was indicted in August 1955 (but not Lo Dolce) on eight counts of perjury to one of the most talented attorneys in the country, and a man who would play an important role in American politics and law for many years, Edward Bennett Williams. Williams was then thirty-five years old and had previously represented Senator Joseph McCarthy, who came to power in Washington seeking out communists in the United States government. In later years, Mr. Williams would also represent teamster bosses like Dave Beck and Jimmy Hoffa, Bobby Baker, one of President Lyndon Johnson's long-time friends, the fugitive, Robert Vesco, among others.

A person Williams called on for help in Icardi's case was an ex-FBI and CIA officer, and Howard Hughes associate, named Robert Mahue. Mahue came to fame in the early 1960s, when he was a go-between in the Eisenhower administration and the American mob's plot to murder Fidel Castro. One of the men whom Mahue contacted for the Castro hit was mobster Johnny Rosselli, along with two other mobsters who were also involved in the Castro plots, Santos Trafficante and Sam Gianciana.

In March 1956, Williams and Mahue traveled to Italy to do their own leg work and met with various people around the Lake Orta area including Giuseppe Manini and Tozzini. They also met with

---

[1] Kross, Peter, *The Encyclopedia of World War II Spies*, Barricade Books, Fort Lee, N.J., 2001, Pg. 109.

Vincenzo Moscatelli in Rome. Moscatelli had by now, become a member of the Italian parliament and he was very frank with the two men regarding what happened to Major Holohan. "He readily conceded that the Communist partisans had eliminated Major Holohan, and he defended it as a necessary act. Moscatelli's position was that Holohan was an obstructionist who had to be removed. There was no way to remove him except by murder. He absolved Icardi and Lo Dolce of any knowledge or involvement in the killing, and was ready and willing to testify in court." [2]

At the congressional hearing, Williams brought out the Army's finding that, "The disappearance of Major Holohan was a political move engineered by the Communist group headed by Moscatelli, a man of few scruples who was capable of weakening the opposite party to enrich his group." He also told the committee that he believed that Moscatelli was the person responsible for killing the Major for his own, personal reasons.

One of the witnesses whom Williams called was Congressman Cole who was a member of the congressional panel that investigated Major Holohan's death. Williams got Rep. Cole to admit that "he had discussed with his staff the possibility of perjury charges against Icardi even before they invited him to testify."

In the end, the magistrate, Judge Keech, found for the defendant, Aldo Icardi. The trial was now over, but the controversy over what really happened to Major Holohan has never ended.

The United States government took no further action against Icardi and Lo Dolce. Since the Italians couldn't get jurisdiction over the two Americans, nothing more was done.

Convicted for the murder of Major Holohan in absentia, Manini and Tozzini were ultimately acquitted.

---

[2] Lulushi, Albert, *Donovan's Devils: OSS Commandos Behind Enemy Lines-Europe, World War 11,* Arcade Publishing Co., New York, 2016, Page 329.

William J. Donovan.

Major William Holohan, center.

James Jesus Angleton as a young man..

Pope John Paul II.

Chapter 2

James Angleton,
the OSS and the Vatican

James Angleton was one of the most controversial members of the Central Intelligence Agency and his hunt for suspected moles inside the CIA cost many distinguished men their professional reputations and lives. By the time of his dismissal from the Agency in the 1970s, his hunt for a suspected mole would even cast doubt on his own loyalty to the CIA— some people even believed he was the mole that everyone was looking for. During World War II, Angleton served in London and Rome for the X-2 division of the OSS and played an important role in running agents inside Italy; he even had sources inside the Vatican who reported to him on the political and military situation going on in the Holy See. He had contact with a ranking member of the Vatican who would later become the Pope of Rome.

James Angleton was born in Boise, Idaho in 1917. His father served in World War I and was on an expedition that ran down the famous Mexican outlaw, Pancho Villa, after his raid in Columbus, New Mexico. His father, Hugh Angleton, worked in later years for the National Cash Register Company, in Boise until 1927, and later in Dayton, Ohio. In 1931, the family moved to Milan, Italy where his father ran his own franchise of the National Cash Register Company before selling it back to the firm in 1964, when he retired. Hugh Angleton married a striking Mexican woman and they named their son James Jesus, due to his mother's strict Catholic upbringing. As a child, James Angleton lived in Arizona and suffered from tuberculosis. The climate of Arizona did not appeal to him and it was a relief when the family moved to Italy. From a young age, Jim had two loves in his life: fly fishing and poetry. These were not common interests of most of his contemporaries, but he didn't care what other people thought and he continued these pursuits for the rest of his life.

While living in Italy, he attended school but he soon returned to the United States and enrolled in Yale University in New Haven. His roommate was Reed Whittemore, who would later become a well-known poet in his own right. At Yale, Angleton and Whittemore founded a literary journal called *Furioso*, which published such notable poets as Pound, Cummings, Archibald MacLeish, and others. After graduating from Yale, Angleton was accepted to Harvard Law School. His father wanted him to join him in the National Cash Register Company, but young Jim had other ideas. Private business did not make him happy and whatever he did in the future would be of his own choosing.

In 1943, two years after the war began, James Angleton entered the Army in New Haven. He was just twenty-five years old but wanted to serve his nation in time of war. By the summer of 1943, he was asked to join the infant OSS (Office of Strategic Services), headed by William Donovan. Two important people pulled strings in order for Angleton to enter the OSS: his father Hugh Angleton, who would also serve in the OSS and be posted to Italy at the same time that his son was also in that country, and his one-time English professor at Yale, Norman Holmes Pearson. After his training at a military camp in the mountains in Maryland, Angleton was shipped off to London where he was to join the fledgling American wartime unit called X-2, or counterintelligence. One of Angleton's fellow recruits, a man named Dr. Bruno Uberti, would later write of Angleton, "I considered him extremely brilliant but a little strange. I met a lot of important Americans from General William Donovan on down. But Angleton was the personality which impressed me the most. He had a strange genius, I would say—full of impossible ideas, colossal ideas."

The United States did not have any intelligence service to speak of, except those of the military services, the Army, the Office of Naval Intelligence, and the FBI. J. Edgar Hoover was leery of any other branch of the American government taking espionage responsibilities and he made it clear to President Roosevelt that he did not like anyone else taking over his turf. The President, however, told Hoover that if the United States was to win the war, we needed to have a verifiable intelligence service to act in coordination with the British who had a monopoly of hundreds of years in the intelligence business. The United States was to learn from the British, who were eager to help the Americans get up to speed as far as intelligence collection was concerned.

Angleton arrived in England at the time of the blitzes from German bombers who were pounding London at will. The headquarters of the infant OSS team that Angleton joined was located at the West End Ryder Street location, where he took up shop. The Ryder Street site combined counterintelligence operations of the OSS and Britain's MI6. He soon learned all the tricks of the espionage trade, including how to run agents in foreign lands, the art of counterintelligence, and how to penetrate the enemy's own intelligence services. While in England, Angleton and the rest of his team were informed that the British had broken the German military code via the Enigma machine and were able to read all secret communications sent from the various German military units to their headquarters in Berlin. The breaking by Enigma was the most important espionage coup of the war and was instrumental in the ultimate defeat of Germany by the Allies. They also learned that the British had captured all the agents sent to that country by the Germans, and were now using them to send false information back to Berlin. This was called the Double Cross system. One of the electronic sources the British undertook was called Ultra.

One of the men most responsible for the success of the Double Cross system was the noted historian Hugh Trevor-Roper. Trevor-Roper worked for an organization called MI8-C, which monitored German wireless traffic. All the information gathered by Roper was turned over to the huge decoding branch of British intelligence called GCHQ, the Government Communications Headquarters responsible for Enigma intercepts.

The man who was most responsible for recruiting Angleton into the OSS was a scholar from Yale University named Norman Holmes Pearson. Pearson was one of the most brilliant men at Yale and he soon took a liking to his pupil, James Angleton. Pearson was a specialist in American literature and was the department chairman at Yale University. While attending Yale, Pearson and a fellow student by the name of William Rose Benet published a two-volume *Oxford Anthology of American Literature* and later co-edited five volumes on *Poets of the English Language*. For Angleton, who had a life-long interest in poetry, his introduction to Norman Holmes Pearson was a life changing moment.

Norman Holmes Pearson was recruited into the OSS by Donald Downes who worked for the OSS in London. The London X-2 branch was established in March 1943 under the direction of James Murphy and Noman Pearson. They started out with a staff of three people but it soon blossomed to many more. When James Angleton arrived in January 1944, the staff had expanded to seventy-five people. Angleton had his own secretary named Perdita Doolittle. The office was always in chaos with people running in all directions, trying to do two things at once. One of the men who was assigned to Angleton's London headquarters was a bright young Englishman named Harold "Kim" Philby. Angleton and Philby's paths would cross many times while they both were at OSS X-2, and soon a friendship would grow. What neither Angleton nor any of his fellow X-2 members knew at the time, was that Philby was a double agent who was working for the Russians for a number of years.

Six months after arriving in London, Angleton was promoted to second lieutenant and soon thereafter became chief of the Italian Desk for the European Theater of Operations.

As mentioned before, the United States did not have its own organized intelligence system, let alone any counterintelligence organization. The creation of Bill Donovan's infant intelligence organization, COI (Coordinator of Information), was the initial step in bringing about the centralized espionage unit called X-2.

The United States turned to the British Security Coordination (BSC) based in New York to plan its initial steps in counterespionage. The basis of the British counterespionage success was its comprehensive security register of enemy personnel or suspected agents. They agreed to turn over this motherlode of information to the Americans, only on the condition that the Americans train their own personnel in how to handle the security of this material.

In an unprecedented security arrangement between the United States and Great Britain, the Americans established a civilian counterespionage organization (CE)within the OSS, similar to the

British MI6 and MI5. The first American representative arrived in London in November 1942 as the special liaison to British intelligence.

For its own part, the OSS set up its CE headquarters in New York, in the same building housing Bill Stephenson's BSC. At first, all CE material coming from OSS London and elsewhere were handled by the BSC then given to the OSS for its own use.

On June 15, 1943, the CE department was given autonomous status as part of the OSS's SI, or Secret Intelligence system. This was the infancy of the latter day counterintelligence division of the Central Intelligence Agency.

Throughout the war, London served as the headquarters for all X-2 operations in Europe. With the growth of the London operation, the need for the New York office diminished, and most of its work was sent overseas. In September 1943, the research work at New York was ended. The OSS set up an X-2 Registry in Washington, and most of its records from New York were transferred to that facility.

By far, the most important part of CE was it Central Registry in Washington. A spy agency, no matter how big or small, is only as good as the knowledge it accumulates from various sources, and OSS X-2 was no exception. By having an extensive filing system on all aspects of enemy operations, X-2 was able to prepare its agents for their own CE duties.

X-2 had its first big role following the Normandy landings in June 1944. A small, covert detachment arrived in Paris on August 15, 1944, before all German troops had left the city. This group set up the first X-2 headquarters for all of France. Their biggest victory was the capturing of a number of Germans who had infiltrated American territory, wearing GI uniforms, performing sabotage behind the lines. In time, X-2 was able to "turn" six of these men into their own CE assets.

X-2 also worked closely with other departments within the OSS as in combating German intelligence activities in Switzerland. The Safehaven Project (more about this in the next chapter), as it was called, worked under the direction of the SI that was responsible for intelligence gathering in neutral countries, as well as German occupied Europe. According to a report on Allied activities in

Switzerland "Safehaven thus emerged as a joint SI/X2 operation shortly after its inception, especially in the key OSS outposts in Switzerland, Spain, and Portugal, with X-2 frequently playing the dominant role." By January 1945, a number of X-2 agents were working in Switzerland, monitoring the passage of looted gold and cash.

Angleton took basic training in the OSS in the Catoctin Mountains of Maryland, at a secret location known only to the recruits and their superiors. One of Angleton's fellow recruits, a man named Dr. Bruno Uberti, would later write of Angleton, "I considered him extremely brilliant but a little strange. I met a lot of important Americans from General William Donovan on down. But Angleton was the personality which impressed me the most. He had a strange genius, I would say—full of impossible ideas, colossal ideas."[1]

One of the trainers at headquarters was the British agent Harold "Kim" Philby, who took on the job of helping to train his American counterparts. One of his jobs was to train the Americans in the art of using double agents in the field. One American said of Philby's talk on the subject, "I do remember being very impressed. He really knew what he was doing."

Whoever said that was right on the money, for it would turn out in later years that Kim Philby was a double agent for the Russians for many years, and was part of the so-called "Cambridge Five" Russian spy ring that was recruited at Cambridge University almost a decade earlier. Over the years, as Angleton began his rise in the OSS and later in the CIA, the betrayal of Kim Philby was taken as a personal affront, as the two men were very close, and Angleton thought of Philby as his intelligence mentor.

For the reader who is not familiar with the background of Kim Philby, the writer needs to explain who Philby was and how he and James Angleton became intertwined.

Harold "Kim" Philby was born in 1912 in Ambala, India. He was given the nickname of "Kim" after the character in one of Rudyard Kipling's novels. His father was the noted spy and adventurer Harry St. John Philby, assistant commissioner in the Punjab district of India, when that country was part of the British

[1] Martin, David, *Wilderness of Mirrors,* Harper & Row Publishers, New York, 1980, Page 13.

Empire. The elder Philby married in 1910 while stationed there. It was during his stint in India that his first son, Kim, was born.

Kim Philby attended the Westminster School and graduated in 1928. He then went to Trinity College at Cambridge, where he was to meet some of his fellow traitors: Anthony Blunt, Guy Burgess, and Donald Maclean. During their time at Cambridge, they were recruited by the NKVD, the Russian espionage service.

His first marriage was to Alice Friedman in Vienna, Austria, on February 24, 1934. His new wife was a communist who was on the run from the police. By marrying Philby, she became a British subject and was given a passport which allowed her to legally leave the country. Philby did not tell his bride of his pro-communist connections, one of the first betrayals in a life of deceit he was to become used to.

During the Spanish Civil War, Philby worked for the *Times of London* covering the conflict, allowing his pro-Franco sympathies to show. In 1939, he and Alice were divorced. He was transferred as *Times* correspondent and spent most of his free time spying for the Russians against the Germans.

When the British entered World War II, Philby joined the British Expeditionary Force as a reporter and was sent to France. After the fall of France, Philby returned to England, and it was then, according to him, that he was approached by MI6 to become one of their own. Other sources in the know said that St. John Philby pulled strings to get his son into the secret service. Whatever the case, young Kim was now inside the bowels of the British Secret Service, an unsuspected double agent who would remain in that role until the early 1960s.

Philby's first posting was with Section V, the counterintelligence section of the SIS. He would become the leader of the Iberian subdivision of Section V, responsible for running agents in such countries as Spain, Portugal, Italy, and North Africa.

Philby, however, had more important chips up his sleeve, and the plan he devised was sanctioned by his controllers in Moscow. As the war grew to a close, both the U.S. and England feared Russia as a potential enemy once the conflict was over. The intelligence services of both countries wanted to keep a close watch on Russia. Philby asked that he be allowed to set up a sub-section within Section

V, whose primary duties were to monitors Soviet intelligence. This was immediately agreed upon, and Philby was now in a position to funnel highly informative intelligence emanating from the British SIS to Anatoli Lebedev, his Soviet controlling officer. The name given to this desk by Philby was called "Section 5." In order to show his progress, Philby unmasked for British intelligence the name of a long-time Soviet spy operating in England, Boris Krotov. By the time of Philby's report, Krotov had departed for Moscow and was unreachable. What Philby did not say in his missives was that Boris Krotov was not only his handler but controlled Guy Burgess and Donald Maclean, as well.

Philby's treachery was also seen regarding the anti-Hitler plots then being hatched inside Germany. He was aware of the plots being planned by Admiral Canaris, the head of the Abwehr (the department that carried out German intelligence operations), to overthrow Adolf Hitler, as well as their negotiations with the West to secure a separate peace. This turn of events sent shockwaves inside the Kremlin. The last thing the Soviets wanted was a non-Hitler country allied with the United States and Great Britain against the Soviet Union.

Philby began plotting against Admiral Canaris, even going so far as to devise a scheme that he proposed to "C" (Stewart Menzies, who was, in effect, Britain's super-spy) to have the admiral killed while he was in Spain. Philby's pathological desire to see Canaris removed sprang from his fear of an entente between Britain and Germany. This, Philby vowed, would not happen.

In August 1945, just as the war was ending, Philby's cover was almost blown. A Russian named Konstantin Volkov, working as vice counsel in Istanbul, Turkey, defected. He said that he had information about a number of Soviet moles inside British intelligence, one of whom worked inside the London counterespionage section (Philby).

Philby got wind of the Volkov defection and personally took over the file on him. Philby told his British controllers about Volkov's allegations and the SIS allowed Philby complete discretion in the case. Under mysterious circumstances, Volkov disappeared, never to be heard from again (it is believed that he was killed by Russian assassins).

In 1949, Philby was posted to Washington, where he took over the job of liaison between the SIS, the FBI and the CIA. Philby's cover in Washington was that of first secretary at the British embassy. Philby had first met James Angleton during World War II, but their paths did not cross again until he arrived in the States. His official duty was to act as executive assistant to the Assistant Director of Special Operations, whose primary responsibility was to act as the liaison officer between the various international intelligence services, like those of Israel and France. Philby's deception cost the CIA the lives of a number of undercover agents who were parachuted into Albania in a futile attempt to overthrow the communist government.

Philby's undoing began in 1951 when he learned that MI5 was going to arrest Guy Burgess and Donald Maclean, who were part of the Cambridge Spy Ring. After Philby alerted them, both men made a quick escape to Moscow on May 21, 1951. Philby received the news of their flight from Geoffrey Paterson, who worked in the British embassy in Washington. Philby, trying to sound shocked, offered his services in whatever way he could to help. In an elaborate game of chess, Philby informed his contacts at the FBI of the flight of Burgess and Maclean, hoping to deflect their interest in him. But sounder heads in the Bureau realized that at one point Burgess lived with Philby in Washington and it did not take too long to suspect that Philby was not only the traitor in their midst, but certainly the person who tipped his friends off.

Philby's private prayers were answered when, on June 5, 1951, the head of British intelligence wrote to Philby telling him that his special emissary, John Drew, would be arriving in Washington the following day with orders that he return home. In England, he was confronted by accusations made by another defector named Ismail Akhmedov-Ege, a Turk who had been a colonel in the KGB. Akhmedov-Ege was now working for the CIA, and he told them that Philby was a Russian mole. After a long investigation during which Philby denied he was a Russian agent, he decided to retire from government service. He denied any relationship with either Burgess or Maclean (a lie), and his story was believed by many top men in the British government.

However, the reaction was different in Washington as the

CIA and the FBI began their own investigation into the possible intelligence blunders that Philby might have caused. Shortly after Philby's recall to London, Walter Bedell Smith, the CIA Director, ordered both Angleton and William Harvey to initiate inquiries into the possibility that Philby was a Russian spy.

Both men studied the same evidence but came up with two very different conclusions. Harvey's five-page report detailed Philby's relations with both Burgess and Maclean and ended by saying that Philby was a Russian spy. In Angleton's four-page narrative, which was not as detailed as Harvey's, he concluded that his old friend was not a Soviet agent. Angleton went on to say that Philby was being duped by Guy Burgess and that Burgess was acting on his own as a Soviet spy. Angleton further told DCI Smith that he should not accuse Philby of working for the Russians.

The Philby affair had now pitted the CIA and the British SIS in direct opposition to each other. If Philby had planned all along to drive a wedge between the two services, it worked out perfectly. In the summer of 1956, Kim Philby was sent to the Middle East by the SIS under journalistic cover. He moved to Beirut, Lebanon where he spied for the British in that city. While in Beirut, he was finally unmasked by the Station Chief and before he could be arrested, fled to Moscow in January 1963. While in Moscow, he wrote his memoirs called *My Silent War* (1968). He was still trailed by his erstwhile partners and died in 1988, never truly appreciated by the nation he strived so hard to serve.

The Philby affair had a profound effect on James Angleton and how he would view other defectors who came calling in the years ahead. Angleton had a deep and profound affection for Philby, a man he called a friend. He now had to face the irrefutable fact that the man whom he gave the deepest secrets of the West to was indeed a Russian mole. Philby's treachery left a personal mark on Angleton's psyche; he felt bitterly deceived that he had gone out on a very long limb for him, and did not want to accept the fact that he had been duped.

Philby's treason would be a body blow to Angleton in every respect. Every decision he made regarding the Russians and their spy war against the United States was made with Philby at the back of his mind. Biographer Michael Holtzman wrote, "The revelation his British friend Kim Philby actually worked for Moscow would propel Angleton in the sixties from garden-variety suspicion of the Soviets to a state that some in the CIA have compared to clinical paranoia. That was a shattering experience for Angleton, (CIA) psychiatrist John Gittinger recalled. From that period on he was the most suspicious man in the agency. My own feeling is the emotional wreckage of that close friendship, made him distrust everybody and colored his life from that point on." [2]

Angleton's initial assignment in in 1944 in Rome X-2 was supposed to have lasted only six weeks but as time went on, he became so adept at his new job that the assignment stretched to three years. According to George Chalou in The Secret War, "in the last year of World War II, Angleton rose from chief of the X-2 unit in Rome to chief of all OSS counterespionage operations in Italy. By the age of 28, as bureaucratic initials and superiors were changing in Washington, he became chief of all secret activity, intelligence and counterintelligence in Italy for the Strategic Services Unit (SSU), the successor of the OSS."

Through his counterintelligence work, Angleton and his team "amassed over 50 informants and had penetrated seven foreign intelligence services, including Tito's Otsek Zascita Naroda, the French Service de Documentation (SDECE), and the Italian Naval Intelligence Service, also called the SIS," according to Chalou.

The intelligence product that Angleton and his Allies at X-2 put together came from intercepts from various sorts of intelligence operations, called ISOS. This information mainly came from intercepts from the German Abwehr, headed by Admiral Canaris. ISOS was part of the wide-ranging catch of intelligence gleaned from ULTRA, in which the Allies were able to read German military messages without them knowing about it.

Before James Angleton was sent to Rome, his father, Hugh Angleton, had done quite a bit of work there. The elder Angleton was the man to see in Italy when he ran the NCR business. He

---

[2] Holtzman, Michael, *James Jesus Angleton: The CIA & the Craft of Counterintelligence*, University of Massachusetts Press, Amherst, MA. 2008, Page 206.

became the president of the U.S. Chamber of Commerce in Italy, and had a close association with the U.S. Ambassador in Rome, William Phillips. From his business connections, he met and cultivated many important Italians of all walks of life, and he soon was reporting all he leaned to Ambassador Phillips. From the contacts he made across Europe, he found out information on German arms manufacturing, and information regarding the capabilities of German engines. He also made frequent trips to such nations such as Germany, Poland, Romania, and Hungary, establishing what he called "an internal spy trade." He was friendly with the German naval attaché in Rome, and as a member of the Masons, he was able to use his contacts in that group to keep tabs on the Italian Foreign Minister, Count Ciano. He also learned from his sources that his phone had been tapped and he had to use other means of getting his information to Allied sources in Italy.

With war on the horizon, Hugh Angleton took his wife and two daughters to Switzerland and then by boat, headed to the United States, arriving on the day that Pearl Harbor was attacked—December 7, 1941. Hugh Angleton soon joined the army and after his initial training, joined the OSS, under the direction of William Vanderbilt, who was the former Republican Governor of Rhode Island. Vanderbilt served as the executive officer for Special Operations at the OSS and he had little quarrel in getting Hugh to join the club. He arrived in Italy on OSS business in October, 1943, but contrary to stories that he and his son served together in Italy, that was not the case. While riding in a jeep, he was injured, shattering his leg, and was then posted to the headquarters of General Mark Clark's staff. When the war ended, Hugh Angleton and his family returned to Rome where they lived until 1964. He died in Idaho in 1973.

It is interesting to note that there are some similarities between the fathers of Kim Philby and James Angleton. They were both successful men in their own right, serving their respective countries in time of war. Harry St. John Philby, was one of the most noted men of the World War I era, a man whose exploits were front page news during that time. He was one of his day's most fascinating personalities and was primarily responsible for the choice of a profession his son would later take. He served in Mesopotamia during World War I for British military intelligence, in time, forming a strategic and personal relationship with King Ibn Saud. Another personality of the time who had a similar pedigree was T.E. Lawrence, "Lawrence of Arabia," who also worked for British intelligence in the deserts of Arabia.

In his book on Kim Philby and his father called *Treason in the Blood,* author Anthony Cave Brown writes about the relationship between Lawrence and St. John Philby. "Within the week Philby was with Lawrence in Amman. Lawrence began to hand over to Philby a piece of the Arabian Desert and the Fertile Crescent that everybody wanted but none knew what to do with. The process took ten days, and Lawrence transferred, with much else his personal, initialed files, which covered 1914 to 1921. All related to high British policy in the Middle East in the period before, during and after the Arab Revolt and included a record of the British government's dealings with Hussein, Feisal, Abdullah, and Ibn Saud and matters concerning the Balfour Declaration and the Sykes-Picot Agreement."[3]

From 1943-44, the London X-2 station where James Angleton worked was a beehive of activity. It was from this location that all western European intelligence operations were run, prior to the D-Day invasion of France in June 1944. A number of men who would later play an important role in the CIA came to London to work with men like James Angleton. Among them were David Bruce, Arthur Goldberg, William Casey, and Thomas Karamessines. Arthur Goldberg would serve in the cabinet of President Kennedy as Labor Secretary. William Casey would become the director of the CIA under President Ronald Reagan and would become embroiled in the Iran-Contra Affair in which arms were sold to the Contra rebels in exchange for the release of American hostages being held in Lebanon. Thomas Karamessines would serve in the CIA and played a role in the American-led efforts to assassinate Fidel Castro in the early 1960s. Another man who was in the London OSS station was Edward Weismiller, a friend of Norman Holmes Pearson. Years later, Weismiller wrote an espionage novel called *The Serpent Sleeping.* He was a graduate of Cornell College

---

[3] Cave Brown, Anthony, *Treason in the Blood: H. St. John Philby, Kim Philby, And The Spy Case of the Century,* Houghton Mifflin Co., Boston, MA. 1994, Page 71.

in Iowa and wrote a book of poetry called *The Deer Come Down.*

On July 17, 1943, a scant two weeks before he took up his London posting, James Angleton married Cicely d' Autremont whom he had met while in Boston. On August 18, 1944, she gave birth to their first child, James Charles. Angleton was not able to be there for the birth of his son, but his wife kept him up to date on the baby's progress.

As the British began teaching their American cousins the art of counterespionage, Angleton received help from a number of top British agents he worked alongside at OSS headquarters. Some of these men were Colin Roberts, Dick Brooman-White, Felix Cowgill, and of course, Kim Philby.

While Angleton, Casey, Phillips, and Goldberg, among others. were the nucleus of the London station, they still had to contend with the constraints put on them by their colleagues. SIS and SOE (British Special Operations Executive) tried to limit the means by which OSS operated in theater Europe by controlling the means of transport for OSS men, stymieing OSS movements in Britain as far as training was concerned, and limiting OSS contacts with the many exiled governments that called London home.

With the help of William Donovan and the intervention of General Dwight Eisenhower, this hard-nosed British attitude toward the OSS gradually changed. Ike went to bat for the OSS, sending forceful messages to British intelligence officers and cajoling them into seeing the value of shared work by both parties. OSS London chief William Phillips met several times with Eisenhower, and it was agreed that Phillips would submit all projected operations for approval. With pressure put on by Eisenhower, the SOE decided that it was easier to cooperate with the OSS than to combat them.

In 1942, OSS London got their first breakthrough when the SOE agreed to make available to Donovan's men their agent chain from Spain to Gibraltar regarding escaped POWs. They also let the OSS have access to their radio networks and allowed men on the ground to use British radios for their own communications process.

The man who did the most to make solid the new cooperation between OSS and SOE was Ellery Huntington. Huntington was promoted to command worldwide special operations, and he arrived in London to view the scene firsthand. With his British counterparts in tow, Huntington toured SOE bases and worked out arrangements whereby OSS men were assigned to those units. OSS London established a large Geographic Desk which worked closely with their counterparts. This section was responsible for transport, operations and communications. OSS officers were also permitted to attend SOE training schools.

Huntington and Brigadier Colin Gubbins, a high-ranking officer in the SOE, set the stage for OSS operations in various parts of Europe. Gubbins arranged for the OSS to mount operations in the areas of France and Switzerland, where the British presence was the weakest. In return, OSS provided the necessary supplies to the SOE in France and the Low Countries, including planes, boats, and radio sets. SOE units were also given assignments in Sweden and Finland via the penetration of agents into both of those countries.

SI London also played a pivotal role in the planning of the Torch invasion of North Africa. SI agents made extensive links with French groups, including the Free French, as well as some members of the Vichy government in North Africa. Their heaviest involvement centered on French Resistance Groups trained and equipped by the Allies.

When James Angleton moved his OSS operations to Italy, he was in the thick of the secret fight against Nazi Germany. Italy was the cornerstone of a myriad of OSS operations in southern Europe, a proving ground for military forays into France and North Africa. The strategic position of Italy in the war was not lost on the Allies when they were establishing their intelligence services.

Italy served as an important OSS bastion for covert missions in Europe. From Italy, OSS men made contact with a number of Italian resistance movements and set up a clandestine radio communications network of agents reporting on German activities. They infiltrated German lines using returned POWs, linked up with anti-German emissaries in Switzerland, and provided needed supplies for Allied attacks in North Africa. Among the secret contacts that Angleton made while stationed in Italy were certain high officials in the Vatican who would prove to be of great help to him as the war continued to its end (more about the Vatican in this chapter).

The Italian section of the OSS began operations in 1941, under the direction of David Bruce. Bruce was then chief of the SI branch of COU. Bruce asked his friend Earl Brennan, who once worked for the State Department, to take over the Italian SI. Brennan and his staff began intelligence collection preparations for the expected American invasion of Sicily.

The SI Branch sent its own agents to the newly created OSS stations around the globe. Vincent Scamporino went to North Africa to work with Colonel William Eddy and would later play a role in the "Vessel" case a blown intelligence operation involving the Vatican, in which Angleton would play a major role.

In May 1943, Max Corvo was sent to Allied Headquarters to head up SI operations in Italy. Corvo and William Eddy began in earnest to prepare for Operation Husky, the attack against Sicily. For the OSS, Operation Husky was a model of success. This was the first time that they were able to use their expertise under wartime conditions. OSS teams provided General Patton's 7th Army with vital intelligence on German positions. The SI division made long-term contacts with local people who were willing to aid the American cause. Intelligence gathered in Husky was invaluable for the later invasion of Salerno, and more important—the OSS was finally recognized as a reputable fighting force.

The OSS received a shot in the arm with the surrender of Italy to the Allies. The Italian army general staff moved its base of operations to Brindisi and immediately made contacts with the SI. Their intelligence branch, SIM, loaned a large intelligence contingent of its own men and resources for missions slated for northern Italy. The OSS also made deals with two large Italian resistance groups, the ORI (Organization for Italian Resistance) led by Raimondo Craveri, and CLNAI (Committee of National Liberation for Northern Italy).

In August 1944, William Donovan made another personnel move, shaking up the Italian OSS branch. Colonel Edward Glavin replaced Colonel William Eddy. Glavin brought all OSS branches in Italy under one umbrella, moving his new military headquarters to Siena and then to Florence. OSS forces were also put under the command of Company D, 2677th Regiment, under the leadership of Captain William Shilling. Captain Shilling would head the OSS in

Italy until the war ended.

Throughout the war, the Italian Navy had a good relationship with the OSS and with Angleton in particular. The Italian Navy, via a man named Captain di Fregata Carlo Resio, who was a chief of intelligence, asked Angleton if he would like to use two of his Italian officers for intelligence help. He also offered Angleton the use of four radio operators for future penetration operations that might come up in the future. He also asked that the OSS Marine Unit take over the Italian "GAMMA" frogman school, located at the port of Taranto, which was scheduled to be closed down. Resio told Angleton that the OSS could use the Taranto port to train its own Marine Unit for sabotage operations that could be used in the Pacific theater of operations.

In messages to and from Angleton and OSS headquarters, Resio was given the code name "SALTY," and his information soon came in spades. SALTY-Resio began sending back vital information "beginning in January 1945, including such information as the pending threat of communist insurgency and Soviet support for the same; the other, the existence of a Fascist residue that had to be wiped off the Italian slate." [4]

When Angleton began sending his SALTY information to OSS headquarters, he was given a less than an ecstatic welcome. The top brass said that Angleton had exceeded his mandate as far as Resio was concerned, and that some of the information Resio was sending back might be planted. OSS headquarters were particularly upset at Angleton because they believed the SALTY intelligence was putting the Russians in a bad light. This was still 1945, and the European war would not be over for another five months; and it was not our place to detract from our Russian allies. All that would change once the war was over, but for now, only nice things could be said about our Russian friends. One OSS report on SALTY'S material said, "In its first assessment of Resio's information, X-2 headquarters lectured young Angleton on the possibility that his information was politically inspired. The SIS, they cautioned, had long been considered royalist and anti-Soviet: therefore, it seems that this information may well be in the nature of a propaganda plant." Angleton took the criticism hard and he decided not to

[4] Artifice: James Angleton and X-2 Operations in Italy, CI Reader, Volume 2 Chapter 3.

forward any more information gleaned from SALTY to OSS headquarters.

Another plan that was run by Angleton that had better results was dubbed IVY, which was a collaborative effort between X-2, the SIS and Carlo Resio (yes, SALTY). The plan was to use Italian naval agents to penetrate enemy units in northern Italy. Resio presented Angleton with a source called IVY who lived in Florence, who had previously worked in secret with the Nazi collaborators and was now ready to come home. IVY targeted a man named Borghese, a Fascist who ran an operation called XMAS in northern Italy. IVY told Angleton that he'd use the services of a number of men under his control who would provide six radio sets for Allied use. These men would be dressed in US military uniforms and be assigned to teams in such places as Genoa, La Spezia, Trieste, and Venice. "These scouts were to assist X-2 in tracking down Borghese's stay-behind network."

While plan IVY was a partial success in linking up with anti-Fascist groups in northern Italy, the credit for the success of IVY went to British and Italian intelligence who were able to better penetrate Borghese's organization. It seems that the IVY network was penetrated by enemy agents and a number of team IVY were later executed.

With SALTY and IVY now history, Angleton got a chance to use his undercover skills in another operation, this one called SAILOR. SAILOR was part of Carlo Resio's intelligence network who offered, on his own, to supply James Angleton with top-secret intelligence that was not regularly coming from the Italian Royal Navy. Angleton had a warm relationship with the members of the Italian Navy and they, in turn, supplied him with much needed information about conditions in that nation. Angleton called his naval contacts "the stronghold of Monarchism." Unlike other agents whom Angleton ran during his time in Italy, SAILOR was not out to advance his own career. Only eight months after he began sending information to Angleton, SAILOR talked about leaving the Navy and going back to South Africa where his brother lived.

"In the year for which there is evidence of his work for X-2, SAILOR strengthened Angleton's ability to monitor Italian efforts to rebuild an intelligence capability. Notably, on three occasions, he revealed secret Italian intelligence activities and then maneuvered himself into a position from which he could act as X-2's eyes and ears."[5]

In his first assignment for Angleton and the OSS, SAILOR, in effect, became a double agent on behalf of the OSS. He made covert contact with certain members of Soviet intelligence after the Italians left the war. SAILOR contacted his Soviet counterpart in Istanbul, Turkey a man named Akim Nihailov, and offered to turn over all his intelligence files. As their relationship grew, the Soviets tried hard to recruit SAILOR into their midst, and after some time, they tried to reconnect with him in Rome in the fall of 1945. While all this was going on, SAILOR kept X-2 apprised of all that was happening, vis a vis, the Russians.

Another of SAILOR's major accomplishments was to warn the Americans that certain anti-Communist Albanians had approached the Italian Royal Navy for money and guns to attempt the overthrow of the Albanian government run by Enver Hosha. It was decided at the highest levels at OSS that SAILOR should become the intermediary between the Royal Navy and the anti-Communist Albanians. For over one year, the OSS was able to monitor the talks via SAILOR.

One of Angleton's duties in the OSS/X-2 hierarchy was to work with the various Italian resistance groups that dotted the landscape in the war against the Nazi regime. There were many divergent groups under the resistance umbrella and the OSS, and Angleton in particular, had to make all of them happy, in one form or another.

Of all the countries on the European continent from which the OSS mounted secret operations, none was more important than Italy. The use of the Italian landscape in military operations against the Germans was extensive, exploiting many different political parties for the common end.

The decision to use Italy as a jumping-off point for American raids was opposed in Washington by the Joint Chiefs of Staff. The Chiefs wanted as much control over military policy as possible, and they distrusted the use of clandestine operations over force.

After the Quebec Conference of August 1943, where American policy for the invasion of Europe was formulated, President Roosevelt decided to use Italy as a base for OSS operations.

[5] Ibid.

American military planners decided that an invasion of Italy would begin from Sicily. The main obstacle was the lack of spy networks in Italy. In order to utilize it as a funnel into Germany, underground groups had to be organized.

The officer in command of American forces in Italy was Col. Edward Glavin, the OSS commander of the central Mediterranean theater of operations. As Glavin took over the Italian operations, he was to find that there were two competing OSS intelligence services operating in Italy. The first was the Italian SI (Secret Intelligence) led by Vincent Scamporino, and the second, the OSS SI detachment associated with the U.S. Fifth Army. As the two groups became operational, it became obvious there would be no cooperation between them. Each wanted its own share of the intelligence pie, causing confusion and bitter differences between them.

Some of Scamporino's men became bogged down in internal Italian politics, especially among partisan groups. In order to get a firmer hand on the Italian partisans, Colonel Glavin moved his headquarters from Algiers to Caserta, Italy.

In late 1943, the Allies captured Naples and set in motion a large Allied/Italian partisan resistance alliance. OSS teams made contact with many different partisans, including communists and socialists. One of the main Allied military units to run covert operations teams was Company D, of the 2677th Regiment. Colonel William Schuling, who ran Company D, had no sooner taken over, than he ran into problems with some of his communist agents. They wanted to use American radio transmitters to relay messages to communist cells, as well as instruct their men to disregard orders by the OSS.

Throughout the war, the OSS had to work with numerous extremist patriot bands, whose goals were diametrically opposed to its own. Declassified OSS records show many of these partisans to have been cold-blooded killers and crooks.

The two most active resistance parties in Northern Italy were the Party of Action and the communists. Another important group was ORI, headed by a man named Raimondo Craveri, or "Mondo." Mondo's ORI worked closely with the OSS, having established a number of large courier systems in northern Italy and a messenger service in Switzerland. At this time, ORI was completely controlled by the OSS. OSS documents reveal that Mondo decided not to work with the British, but to remain with the OSS, which provided his band with all necessary supplies. ORI's job was to destroy all railroad stations in the Bologna and Florence areas. The communists were very active in the area, vying with the ORI for supplies. Of the patriot situation in the country, Colonel Glavin said, "There are disadvantages to our getting involved in this matter. OSS should not exclusively tie itself up with any one organization."

Despite bitter political differences between various Italian patriot bands, as well as the unsavory nature of some of their leaders, the work done by these cliques helped ensure victory in the war.

If SAILOR, SALTY, and IVY were strictly military intelligence penetrations set up by X-2 and supervised by Angleton, the next case he was to become involved with had both political and military undertones that might have altered how long the war lasted. This was the so-called Vessel case which involved the use of the Vatican to try to end the war as soon as possible. Angleton played a large role in the Vatican intrigue, which will be dealt with later on in this chapter.

The earliest cooperation between the OSS and the Vatican began in 1941, when Bill Donovan established an informal working relationship with a Father Morlion, the leader of an anti-Nazi group called the European Catholic anti-Comintern. This organization was also an intelligence service named Pro Deo. Donovan gave funds to Pro Deo, which supplied him with insight into the political thinking of Vatican officials.

The OSS had numerous undercover operations with the Vatican during World War II, trying to use the Holy See as in intermediary in negotiating peace terms. In 1944, the OSS was immersed in Vatican intrigue in the case known as Vessel, whose information reached the upper levels of the American government, right into the Oval Office of President Roosevelt. By the time the Vessel case was over, it would prove to be one of most embarrassing and unproductive affairs conducted by the OSS during the war.

The Vessel case began when Vincent Scamporino, the OSS SI chief stationed in Rome, obtained intelligence coming from inside Pope Pius XII's palace. After receiving this information that he called "Z," he sent it on to Washington for evaluation. Scamporino had been a veteran of the State Department, served in the New Hampshire legislature, and was an expert on Italy.

Upon reading the news imparted by Scamporino, most of which concerned Japanese foreign policy, it was deemed of great value, and the OSS X-2, counterintelligence unit was called in to protect the source, now called Vessel. Vessel was paid up to $500 a month. The Vessel case was overseen by Brigadier General John Magruder, the director of all OSS intelligence services.

As Donovan and his men studied the information coming in from Vessel, they could only wonder at their good fortune. They read the minutes of meetings from the branches of the Vatican, including the Secretariat, the Department of Extraordinary Affairs (the foreign affairs branch), the Propaganda division, and the writings of the pope himself.

The first time that Donovan received any information on what was to become the Vessel case, it came from OSS headquarters in Washington via a message from a man named Charles Cheston who was about to send a vital piece of information to President Roosevelt from one of his important sources inside the Vatican. This source proved to be Vessel. The information that Cheston was going to send to FDR was a summary of a talk that Pope Pius had only a month earlier with Father Norbert de Boyne, who was his vicar general of the Jesuits. The talk concerned the possibility that the Vatican was interested in mediating a peace agreement between Japan and the Allied powers. The Pope then asked his ambassador to Japan to feel out the government in Tokyo to see if there was any validity in this prospect.[6]

If Donovan was enamored by Vessel, James Angleton, then the head of OSS X-2 in Rome, saw it differently. Angleton was generally wary of sudden influxes of intelligence, especially from people whose bona fides he did not know. If we want to see how wary of sudden intelligence bonanzas Angleton was, we have only to look at how deliberately he worked on the three cases mentioned above. Angleton did, however, check out the middleman who brought the Vessel material to the OSS, a Russian named Dubinin.

[6] Waller, Douglas, *Wild Bill Donovan: The Spymaster Who Created the OSS and Modern American Espionage*, The Free Press, New York, 20II, Page 297-98.

Angleton's investigation showed that Dubinin was working for the British and the French, and that did not approve of the Vessel affair.

Later on, more information came in regarding the Pope and a possible end to the war on the part of the Japanese. At that time, Vessel sent another intelligence bonanza to the OSS of conversations between the pope and Cardinal Fumasoni-Biondi. In them, it was said that the Japanese agreed that in return for peace, they would give up claims to all the territory they conquered except Hong Kong and Hainan; that Japan wanted to regain lands controlled before the Sino-Japanese war of 1894—Japan believed they were the "victor" in the war, and the Allies should consider them as such; and finally, that the Philippines should become an "independent regime."

Future news reports from Vessel began to shift from political to military matters. In one month, it was learned that the Japanese had put a new, heavily fortified battleship into service, and that it was heading to Nagasaki in December. Later communiques referred to the fact that the U.S. air raids caused many injuries to factory workers and that there were rumblings that the government was responsible for making defeat inevitable.

As certain defeat on the part of Japan became apparent by 1945, the government in Tokyo began to make secret overtures to the Allies to see if any accommodation on leaving the war was even possible. The role played by American code breakers in translating military and diplomatic codes was hidden from the Japanese during the Pacific war. From listening posts in Hawaii, California, and other parts of the Pacific, navy cryptologists translated messages from Tokyo to their military and diplomatic embassies. The name for this secret endeavor was "Magic."

One of the earliest Japanese peace feelers decoded by the Magic intercepts was a summary from the War Department's Office of Assistant Chief of Staff, G-2, dated March 25, 1943. The message was a March 19 letter to Tokyo from the Japanese Ambassador to Moscow, Sato. Part of the letter is as follows:

> You (Morishima) informed me that there may be strong opposition to maintaining the status quo and that many advocate lashing out at the Soviet Union. Therefore, when this question comes in the Foreign Office, I want you to

be present and take part in deliberations and use every conceivable means at your command to drive home our arguments.[7]

It is not entirely clear from the forgoing note whether Sato thought the whole question of war or peace with Russia was to be debated in Tokyo in the near future, or whether the phrase "when this question comes up" was a reference to some narrower issue.

Another War Department document of June 1945 concerns the role of the Vatican in peace talks. In a message dated June 3, Ken Harada, the Japanese Envoy to the Vatican, advised Tokyo that he has rejected the request of an unidentified American to discuss peace terms. Part of Harada's message reads as follows:

Mgr. Vagnozzi, who was formally a counselor of the Apostolic Delegation in the United States (1942-43) and is now in the Department of Foreign affairs, paid a visit on the 27th to the priest Tomizawn, who is a non-career employee of our office. Vagnozzi made the following statement.

An American who has been in Rome several months, wants to get in contact with Japan in connection with the question of peace and has requested that I act as in intermediary. I am not ready to reveal his position or name, but his father occupies a rather influential place in society, and he himself is a Catholic, and a sincere person. He says that he has no official status and that if plans are made to carry on further discussions, it will naturally be necessary for someone with official standing to handle it.[8]

What is obvious from these Magic letters is that by 1945, the Japanese government was convinced that victory was impossible and peace feellers from the Emperor were looking for the best terms available to Japan. The government leaders decided to fight on to the end. This decision ultimately resulted in the dropping of two atomic bombs on Nagasaki and Hiroshima in August 1945.

While Vessel was providing the Roosevelt administration with

---

[7] Kross, Peter, *The Encyclopedia of World War II Spies,* Barricade Books, Page 125.
[8] Ibid. Page 126.

what seemed to be serious material, a rift between the X-2 and SI developed regarding the handling of Vessel. At the same time that Vincent Scamporino was receiving his reports, James Angleton was getting similar stories from his own source in the Vatican, Fillippo Setaccioli, code named Dusty. It seemed clear that Dusty was a middleman for Vessel. For his part, Angleton wanted to control all Vessel information, not wanting to share it with his colleagues in SI. The rift between the two espionage branches of OSS finally received the attention of the Roosevelt administration. They now decided to double check the Vessel material, and what they found was nothing less than a hoax being perpetrated.

The material that this secret source inside the Vatican was providing was nothing less than spectacular, but was it legitimate? The OSS was getting material from this person relating to the trip planned by FDR to meet with Russian Premier Joseph Stalin and British Prime Minister Winston Churchill in the city of Yalta. Certain high-level Japanese businessmen were proposing to the government in Tokyo that it see about making a peace treaty with the United States. The source had information on the extent of the damage an American air raid had made on an Osaka armored car plant. When Bill Donovan stopped over in Italy he was briefed on the Vessel case by Angleton and Scamporino, but he really didn't think the information he received worthy of interest. James Magruder, who was Donovan's senior deputy for intelligence at the OSS, sent Scamporino a letter asking how credible the source in the Vatican was. He answered his own question by saying that his information was "too good to be true."

In February 1945, Vessel sent a report to Washington regarding a meeting attended by Myron Taylor, the president's personal envoy to the Vatican, and Ken Harada, the Japanese ambassador to the Vatican. When asked to confirm his meeting with the Japanese ambassador, Myron Taylor denied having met him. The minutes of this meeting supplied by Vessel had the Japanese saying that they would not negotiate on any Allied terms and that they saw no likelihood of an early end to the war. Another part of the news report had the Russians telling the Japanese that they would put pressure on the Allies to negotiate a separate peace treaty.

These Vessel documents finally sent up red flags in both the

OSS and the White House, and soon, the president ordered a full-scale investigation of all things Vessel to proceed at once.

For his part, Angleton tried very hard to "control" all of the intelligence coming out of the Vatican from all his sources. He asked his superiors if he could cut loose all of his middlemen except, for one, Dusty. When Angleton tried hard to persuade his OSS superiors to have him turn Dusty into a double agent he was denied the request. This all happened at the time when President Roosevelt suddenly died in April 1945 and any further requests from Angleton to OSS HQ, died with the president. What the White House did not know (among others in the OSS in Italy, including Angleton), was that the information being supplied to Washington was all fake. Vessel proved to be a fake, pulling the ears off of anyone who'd pay the price he was demanding for his "fake news."

Vessel, it turned out, was the Italian writer and confidence man, Virgilio Scattolini. Scattolini, the author of a number of pornographic books, was a reporter for the Vatican newspaper *Osservatore Romano.* After being fired by the paper when they found out about his pornographic work, he took to creating and selling bogus information on Vatican affairs to anyone who would pay his high fees. Scattolini was tried in an Italian court for crimes against the Vatican, found guilty, and served seven months in jail. After leaving prison, he disappeared.

It was later learned from an investigation into the Scattolini affair that he left the Vatican with a huge treasure trove of information. In order to make money, he wrote all sorts of Vatican documents and reports, purporting to be the genuine article. Many reporters who worked in the Vatican knew Scattolini, and he sold these bogus reports to such media outlets as *The New York Times,* Agence France-Presse and TASS, the Russian news service. He also sold his false information to ambassadors from such countries as England, Poland, Argentina, and Spain.[9]

The Vessel case was an embarrassment to the OSS. Scattolini not only had fooled American's spymasters, but taught them a powerful lesson in how a source should be handled and how the vetting process of prospective agents should be dealt with creating secret, counterintelligence operations.

____If Angleton thought he'd seen the end of his participation in

[9] Waller, Douglas, *Wild Bill Donovan,* Page 302.

secret intelligence work after these four cases were closed, he was highly mistaken. As the war was slowly but surely coming to a close with Allied victory in sight, Angleton and the OSS were to be thrust inside the bowels of a secret conspiracy hatched by dissident German military officers who were hell bent on overthrowing Adolf Hitler. In this secret plot, they had an ally inside the highest circles of the Vatican, a man who was in touch with the plotters inside Germany, and whose participation in this plot was not be learned until years after the war ended. It was Pope Pius XII, Eugenio Pacelli.

On the night of April 8, 1945, a prisoner who was being held at the infamous Flossenburg concentration camp in the mountains of Bavaria, 40 miles east of Nuremberg, was taken at night to the gallows where he was to be hung for acts against the German state. Flossenburg was opened in May 1938, and held, what was called "asocial" persons, Jews, some political prisoners and foreign POWs. Between 1938 and April 1945, more than 96,000 prisoners went through the barbaric gates of the prison. By the time the prison was liberated by the Allies, almost 30,000 had died. Among those who were murdered at the camp were 1,000 Soviet prisoners, as well as 1,500 Polish detainees.

The man who was being led to his death was called "the best agent of the Vatican Intelligence in Germany." His name was Josef Muller, a Bavarian book publisher and avid stamp collector. He was anti-Hitler in his politics and gave certain Jews whom he was Allied with fake papers and money, to flee the country. Over time, the German Gestapo had gotten wind of Muller's supposed treachery and had him under constant surveillance. The Gestapo charged Muller in a plot to kill Adolf Hitler, along with other members of the German military staff, "using the spy service of the Catholic clergy."

Going through his papers at Flossenburg, a German military officer found some in Muller's possession that were quite revealing.

One of these missives said that Muller was "an unusually intrepid man of the Jesuit school," through whom dissident German generals maintained contact with the pope.

Thinking that the end was near, the guards escorted Josef Muller to the awaiting gallows. As he was about to be put to death, his hanging was suddenly postponed, and he was returned to his cell. His liberator was Johann Rattenhuber who was the head of Hitler's bodyguard and a friend of his. Rattenhuber pleaded with the German High Command to spare Muller's life and that request was granted.

The sudden sparing of his life was the culmination of a very secretive and highly illegal activities on Muller's part to overthrow the government of Adolf Hitler and end the war on better terms than if the war went on unchecked. It also marked his covert dealings with some of the major leaders in the Vatican, including Pope Pius XII, and the Pope's efforts to aid the anti-Hitler generals in the plot to overthrow the German government.

In order to understand the full picture of Josef Muller's participation (among the many other players in the drama that lay ahead), it is necessary to go back to the start of World War II, and the military and diplomatic events that took place during that time.

Historians have called the period of time between the German invasion of Poland and the opening of hostilities with France and England the "Phony War." This was the time in which the Germans solidified their rule in Poland and waited for a response from the Western powers. This was also a time when the internal German resistance movements, especially those generals who were opposed to Hitler's invasion of Poland, had time to contemplate what actions to take. What the anti-Hitler officers hoped for was the aversion of a full-scale European war. To that effect, they began covert contacts with different Western factions to block further bloodshed.

The prime mover in these intrigues was Abwehr chief Wilhelm Canaris. Canaris, aware of the atrocities that had been inflicted by German troops during the invasion of Poland, made sure that members of the High Command were made well aware of what had transpired. He and his deputy, Hans Oster, brought the evidence of mass murders of both civilians and armed troops to officers in the SD and SS. These Hitler loyalists brushed off Canaris's news, leaving him in the lurch.

Canaris had served in the German military in World War I, dabbling in espionage. He was in the submarine and surface fleets, and set up a spy network in French occupied Morocco. Using a false passport, he arrived in New York in 1916 to sabotage American armaments factories.

In April 1915, Canaris's ship, the *Dresden,* was sunk near the Chilean coast. Her entire crew was captured and put in chains. Canaris somehow managed to escape, and walked across the snow-capped Andes toward Argentina with forged papers.

He boarded a ship bound for Holland via Falmouth, England and landed in Berlin in October 1916. He immediately reported to the German military; they saw great potential in Canaris and sent him off to Spain. Using the code name "Reed-Rosas," Canaris then made contact with anti-Spanish, North African tribesmen whom he tried to entice into revolt.

British intelligence agents in Spain were watching Canaris, and it has been reported that British Army Captain Stewart Menzies vetoed plans to assassinate Canaris, proposed by none other than British double agent Kim Philby. In later years, when speaking about this incident, Stewart Menzies admitted, "He did give me assistance. I liked and admired him. He was dammed brave."

In 1920, Canaris took part in a plot to overthrow the German government organized by Wolfgang Kapp. Its goal was to return Germany to her pre-World War I status. Canaris served a brief time in jail after the unsuccessful coup.

While he was working as a military intelligence officer for the Third Reich, Canaris was mistrustful of Hitler's military leadership and, more importantly, his conduct in the war. While it has never been fully confirmed, it's widely believed that Canaris met with representatives of British intelligence during the war.

Canaris was playing a dangerous game of double-dealing against his superior officers. On one occasion, Heinrich Himmler, Hitler's main deputy and the man who was put in charge of the "Final Solution" to the Jewish question, sent him to Spain to persuade Francisco Franco to cooperate in an attempt to take over the British Rock of Gibraltar. Canaris got the Spanish dictator to refuse to allow German troops on Spanish soil, and to bar Spanish participation on any attack on the "Rock." The Abwehr chief also tipped off Franco to the impending German attack on the Soviet Union.

Canaris was also playing with fire with his most ardent foe, Reinhard Heydrich. The men knew each other from their navy days but a rather hostile relationship was formed when they began vying for the top spot in German intelligence circles. Canaris had a secret file on Heydrich consisting of rumors that Heydrich had Jewish bloodlines.

What is known about Canaris's clandestine meetings with the British SIS is that he gave intelligence information via a Switzerland contact. Her name was Madame Szymanska, a Polish national who had a relationship with the SIS.

During the time of the plots to remove Hitler from power, Canaris met secretly with Josef Muller in Italy to discuss the conspirator's latest moves. A later CIA assessment of Muller's clandestine meetings, stated that during the first three years of the war, Muller visited the Vatican at least 150 times, "always with the consent of the government he wished to overthrow."[10]

Unknown to many Nazi leaders, was that Canaris was part of a group of conspirators called the Schwarze Kapelle (Black Orchestra) that had many followers in the German armed forces. Schwarze Kapelle members planned to take over the government, oust Hitler, and seek an end to the war. One of Canaris's underground links was to sympathetic ears in the Vatican.

One of the first moves made by Canaris was to inform his sources in the pope's palace of a plan to attack Norway and Denmark. The man who received the notice was the Belgian Ambassador to the Vatican. The high official who provided this information was Hans Oster, Canaris's deputy. Oster, in turn, passed this intelligence to Josef Muller, a Catholic lawyer in Munich, and a personal friend of Pope Pius XII. Muller was also on good terms with other men in the Vatican, such as Father Robert Leiber, and Monsignor Ludwig Kass, a Vatican official. Father Leiber was in contact with members of the OSS, as well as a courier of documents to and from Rome (more on Father Leiber in this chapter). Oster approached Muller and asked him if he would serve as an intermediary between the

[10] Riebling, Mark, *Church of Spies: The Pope's Secret War against Hitler,* Basic Books, New York, 2015, Page 66.

Schwarze Kapelle and the British government, via the Vatican. Muller quickly accepted.

As mentioned above, Hans Oster (1888-1945), was a top deputy to Admiral Wilhelm Canaris in the Abwehr and a prime participant in the back channel plots to kill Hitler.

When World War II broke out, Admiral Canaris picked Oster to be his deputy at Abwehr headquarters. In Oster, Canaris found a like-minded man when it came to seeing the horrors being inflicted upon Germany at the hands of Hitler. In short order, Oster became a leading figure along with his boss, Canaris, in high-ranking German military officers' far ranging plots to remove Hitler from power.

The spark igniting Oster's treason was the unfair trial brought by Hitler against General Werner von Fritisch, the chief of the army command. General Fritisch withdrew his support of Hitler during the Czech crisis of 1939, in which Germany annexed territory. In retaliation, false charges that Fritsch was a homosexual were brought up, and the much-decorated general was indicted. After a three week trial in which the defense proved the charges against General Fritisch were a fabrication, Hitler summarily dismissed him as the country's military chief. The Fritisch affair put officers who were opposed to Hitler's policies on notice that the same thing could happen to them. Among them were Wilhelm Canaris and Hans Oster.

The removal of General Fritisch was the catalyst that made both Oster and Canaris begin planning for the Fuhrer's end. Oster held meetings with Colonel Ludwig Beck, who was general chief of staff of the army. Beck, a World War I veteran, was an early supporter of Hitler until the Czech crisis. Beck told his fellow officers that if Germany found itself at war with both England and France, Germany would lose.

With Beck and other staff officers on their side, Canaris gave Oster the go-ahead to plan the dismissal of Hitler. To that end, Oster began contacting many of the organized resistance groups who were anti-Hitler. He provided them with secret intelligence from Abwehr files on Hitler's plans and his whereabouts during his trips. Commander Fritz Leidig, head of the Abwehr's naval intelligence branch, later wrote about how important Oster was in the war against Hitler. He was "the center of gravity for resistance within the Germany military."

In April of 1940, German plans to attack Norway were put in motion, with the code name "Operation Weser-Excerise." When Oster found out about the impending operation, he took immediate steps to inform the Norwegian government. He contacted an old friend, Colonel Gijsbertus Jacobus Sas, the Dutch military attaché in Berlin, informing him that hostilities against the nation were going forward. To Sas's ultimate discredit, Oster's information was not sent to Oslo, the Norwegian capital. In days', the Nazi's attacked Norway, taking a large number of casualties before ultimately overrunning the country.

By March 1943, Oster had brought into his cabal another ranking German officer, 42-year old General Henning von Tresckow, chief of staff to Field Marshall von Kluge. When it was learned that Hitler was planning an inspection trip to Kluge's headquarters at Smolensk, von Tresckow devised a plan to assassinate Hitler by blowing up his plane. Upon the successful completion of the plan, a coup would be staged at General Kluge's military headquarters, at which point the army would come under his command. (By this time, Hitler had appointed himself as commander-in-chief of the German armed forces, taking that responsibility away from his generals.)

The bomb was clandestinely placed on Hitler's aircraft by a Colonel Brandt, one of his aides, and was hidden in two brandy bottles. Unfortunately for the plotters, the bomb failed to go off. In a scramble to remove the evidence before anyone on the plane could find it, one of the plotters, Lt. Fabian von Schlabrendorff, a lawyer by trade, managed to get on board and take it away.

Oster and Canaris were also responsible for saving the lives of many Jews, whom they took under Abwehr control. Oster gave them jobs as his personal agents, and sent them to Switzerland with the knowledge that they would then seek political asylum. In time, the Oster-Canaris connection helped more than 500 Dutch Jews escape to points in South America.

In April 1943, Oster and Canaris's treachery was finally unmasked by the Gestapo. Gestapo agents found documents linking Oster to the smuggling of Jews out of Germany. In what turned out to be a lucky break for Oster, he was spared harsh punishment and was only given a slap on the wrist, convicted on charges of "inefficiency." Oster was removed from his Abwehr post; his loss a terrible blow to the resistance.

One final attempt on Hitler's life took place on July 20, 1944, in what came to be known as Operation Valkyrie. While Hitler was at his headquarters at Rastenburg, East Prussia, the plotters, led by Chief of Staff Colonel Claus von Stauffenberg, placed a bomb in the room where Hitler was conducting a meeting. The bomb went off, but Hitler survived. In the immediate purges that followed, many of the conspirators including Hans Oster and Wilhelm Canaris were arrested. In the wake of the abortive assassination attempt, nearly 5,000 people connected in any way to the plot were killed, including Oster and Canaris. (The plot to kill Hitler was portrayed in the movies many years ago in *Valkyrie,* starring Tom Cruise as Claus von Stauffenberg.)

However, before their death in the Valkyrie plot, Wilhelm Canaris and Hans Oster were two of the principal players in the Vatican connection to overthrow Adolf Hitler.

———————

The one man who was at the center of the Vatican intrigues during World War II and who was an intermediary between the Schwartz Kapelle and certain high-ranking Vatican officials, was none other than Pope Pius XII, Eugenio Pacelli. There has been a long-running controversy regarding the role played by Pope Pius XII during the war. His detractors say he didn't do enough to save the Jews during the war and denounce the anti-Jewish laws that were being promulgated in Germany during that time, while his backers say he took concrete steps to save numerous Jews from certain death.

Over the past several years, new research has come to light about the secret role that Pope Pius XII played during the war, especially in regard to the anti-Hitler plots. The author who brought this information to light was Mark Riebling, in his book *Church of Spies: The Pope's Secret War Against Hitler.* I will delve into the new research in this chapter, but first, the reader should be given some detailed background on Pope Pius XII in order to understand who he was and the time he lived in.

✴ Eugenio Pacelli was born on March 2, 1876 in Rome, Italy. His family were part of the so-called "black nobility" at that time and were devoted to the church. His great-grandfather served as minister of finance under Pope Gregory XVI, and his grandfather served as the undersecretary of the interior under Pius IX. His grandfather was also the founder of the newspaper called *L'Osservatore Romano*. His father was a high-ranking Vatican official and had the title of "chief of Catholic Action as well as the dean of the Consistorial College of Advocates which prepared cases for beautification." The future pope's brother, Francesco was a Papal Marquis, and had the distinction (or not) of having Benito Mussolini crown him as a prince.

Pacelli entered the priesthood at a young age and attended the Appilinare Institute of Lateran University and the Gregorian University, getting degrees in law and theology. In 1899, he was ordained as a priest and in 1901 was appointed to the papal secretariat of state. He also taught international law and diplomacy at the school for papal diplomats in Rome. In 1914, he was named secretary of the Congregation for Extraordinary Affairs.

In 1917, during World War I, Pacelli was appointed to the post of ambassador to the German state of Bavaria by Pope Benedict XV. He remained in Bavaria after the war ended and had a run in 1919 when a mob of communists crashed into his office carrying pistols. Thereafter, he had a hatred of communism that he harbored during World War II. In 1920, the Pope sent him on a diplomatic mission as the papal nuncio (ambassador) to the newly elected German Weimar Republic.

Pacelli was elected as a cardinal of the church in 1929 and the next year, he was elected Secretary of State. In 1935, he received another top post in the church hierarchy, when he was appointed papal chamberlain (camerlengo) and was thus the administrator of the church.

It was in this period of time (the middle 1930s) that the Vatican was able to negotiate with the government of Italy the so-called Lateran Accords, which allowed the Vatican to become an independent state, called Vatican City.

On March 2, 1939, Eugenio Pacelli was elected the new Pope and became the 261st leader of the Roman Catholic faith. Upon his election, he chose to be called Pius.

Three days after becoming pope, Pacelli was shocked when Germany attacked Czechoslovakia, thus, starting World War II. He did not immediately denounce Hitler's actions. He did however, meet with four leading German cardinals, but did not attack Hitler's actions. For whatever reason, the new pope did not want to antagonize Hitler and did not want to break relations with that nation. He did however, "give the cardinals a personal affirmation, in German, to take back the Reich."

With war now a fact of life, the new pope tried his best to act as impartially as possible. For reasons of his own, he did not want to annoy either Hitler or fascist Italy when it came to European politics, hoping that in time, he could act as in intermediary to settle the conflict. As time went on, and Germany attacked Poland on September 1, 1939, the pope still did not verbally attack Hitler for his actions. The pope gave an encyclical in which he said the church was not one of neutrality, but one of impartiality.

While the pope's diplomatic game was going on, he took the first steps to try to end the war by making covert overtures to the British government in 1940, telling them that certain anti-Hitler generals were willing to overthrow him (the plots led by Stauffenberg and others) if they could be assured that they could receive an "honorable "peace from the Allies (mainly Britain).

One of the men whom the pope called on when it came to Vatican finances was Bernardino Nogara, who had good contacts inside the Vatican and who had been a special advisor first under Pope Pius XI and now, Pope Pius XII. He was adept at hiding and investing Vatican funds, and new information coming from the National Archives in London says that he spirited thousands of dollars out of the Vatican during the war to the United States for re-investment and safekeeping. The work that Bernardino Nogara did at the Vatican soon gleaned the attention of the OSS under William Donovan and his ace agent in Italy, James Angleton. In an investigation that the OSS conducted on Nogara's business dealings, there was even talk that he might have been a Nazi spy working out of the pope's inner circle.

Bernardino Nogara was the financial advisor to the Vatican between 1929 and 1954. He was the first Director of the Special Administration of the Holy See, in effect, serving as the chief financial officer at the Vatican. As Director of Special Administration, Nogara made large-scale investments of Vatican money, opening accounts in various countries in the world, including Nazi Germany. The money that Nogara invested was hidden from the Allies via interlocking companies that couldn't be traced.

According to the newly released records from the National Archives in London, the Vatican moved large amounts of its gold reserves which were under threat of seizure by the Nazis to the United States in order to fight the Nazi horde then conquering Europe. This new information was based on records coming from British intelligence interceptions of Vatican financial transactions dated 1941-1943, which was published in a December 2012 article entitled *"New Perspectives on Pius XII and Vatican Financial Transactions during the Second World War,"* written by Patricia McGoldrick of London's Middlesex University.[11]

According to the article written by Professor McGoldrick and printed in the Italian newspaper *L'Osservatore,* the guiding force behind all these Vatican money operations was none other than Bernardino Nogara. The article in the newspaper says in part, "Nogara, in consultation with Curia officials, was the protagonist of the Vatican's financial strategy which was fundamentally important to the Allies' victory over the Nazis and Fascists in World War II. This strategy concerns millions of dollars invested in the largest banks of the US and Great Britain, by which persecuted Churches and exhausted peoples were given aid." The documents say that the origin of these reports came from the Vatican's main financial department, the Special Administration of the Holy See of which Bernardino Nogara was the director.

Under the auspices of the Vatican, at the start of the war, large amounts of Vatican gold and securities were moved to accounts in the United States for safekeeping. These were worth a total of $10 million dollars and were used to finance different church activities. Nogara, it was said, made arrangements with such high-profile

[11] No author, *How Pius XII' Dollars Helped Defeat the Nazi's, National* Catholic Register.

American banks such as JP Morgan and the National City Bank of New York to take in the Vatican's cash. The Vatican also had money in accounts in banks in England. At one point, the British government tried to block an account, but pressure was put on the Americans and the transaction went through without any problems.

Professor McGoldrick wrote in her article, "These activities provide clear evidence that the Vatican systematically sent its securities for safekeeping to the United States. Furthermore Washington was not only aware of the move, but exempted the Vatican from restrictions to related operations in enemy countries (US Freezing Orders), and even offered greater flexibility to requests from Rome. The securities consisted of donations, bonds, revenues from dioceses and gains from investments." The documents show that Nogara's money was invested in US Treasury Bills, and in such companies as Rolls Royce, United Steel Corporation, Dow Chemical, Westinghouse Electric, Union Carbide, and General Electric.

Into the mix of the Vatican Bank and Bernardino Nogara, enters the familiar figure of Allen Dulles who was the OSS chief spy during the war. Allen Dulles was the Director of the CIA during the Eisenhower administration and part of the Kennedy administration. He was highly involved in the plots to kill Cuba's strongman, Fidel Castro, in the early 1960s, and was fired by JFK after the failed Bay of Pigs invasion of Cuba in 1961. He also served as a member of the Warren Commission that looked into the assassination of JFK, and held back vital information such as the CIA plots to assassinate Fidel Castro from that body.

Dulles began his career in the secret world of spying in World War I when he was stationed in neutral Switzerland. After the war was over, he served in the State Department's Near East Department and attended various important international conferences. In 1926, he quit the Department and returned to New York where he entered the influential law firm headed by his brother, John Foster Dulles, called Sullivan and Cromwell.

After the U.S. entered World War II in 1941, Dulles resumed his career in intelligence that would last the rest of his life. He joined the Office of the Coordinator of Information, the predecessor of the OSS and ran its New York office. Dulles's agents specialized in collecting information from German emigres to the U.S., and worked closely with the head of the British Security Coordination in the U.S., William Stephenson. With the advent of the OSS, the U.S. needed an espionage outpost in the heart of Europe where it could collect intelligence on the warring parties. Dulles was asked to establish a spy operation in Bern, Switzerland and he quickly accepted. Once settled in Bern, Dulles immediately began to develop a covert network of anti-Hitler German military officers who wanted to see the Fuhrer dead. His number one German contact was a diplomat named Fritz Kolbe, code named "George Wood." Over the next several months, Kolbe provided Dulles with thousands of pages of diplomatic material coming from the German Foreign Ministry. The British never trusted the information provided by Kolbe and expressed their misgivings to Dulles. One of the men who gave derogatory comments to Dulles and Bill Donovan, the head of the OSS, was the Russian double agent, Kim Philby. But despite (or because of) Kolbe, Dulles was able to achieve an intelligence bonanza vis-a-vis anti-Hitler activities in Bern.

One of the major pieces of intelligence that Kolbe gave to Dulles concerned the fate of Hungary's Jews. He told Dulles that the Jews were going to be rounded up and sent to the concentration camps then being built across Nazi-occupied Europe. This material that found its way to the desk of FDR who was most interested to learn what was going on. To his discredit, as news of the large scale killings of Jews and other minorities by the Germans came to light, the president never ordered that the rail lines going into and out of the concentration camps be bombed in order to stop the mass killings. The rationale of the United States at the time was that the killings would stop once Germany had lost the war. But how many more innocent victims had to die before that happened?

In his 2015 ground-breaking book on the life of Allen Dulles called *The Devil's Chessboard: Allen Dulles, the CIA, and the Rise of America's Secret Government,* writer David Talbot takes a stark look at Dulles's lack of interest in the fate of Hungary's Jews. Talbot quotes a World War II historian named Neal Pearson who edited a collection of Dulles's OSS intelligence reports saying, "Whatever his reasoning, his reticence on this subject is among the most controversial and least understood aspects of his performance in Bern."

The Dulles brothers, John Foster and Allen, were no strangers to the profits that could be made from their long-standing relationships with high-powered German industries developed after World War. Through their international law firm, Sullivan and Cromwell which was headquartered in New York, the Dulles brothers made major investments in Germany and knew all the important players in international finance in that country, as well as in the rest of Europe.

During their legal work in Europe after the end of World War I, the Dulles law firm represented many German industries like I.G. Farben, a large German chemical company which, among other things, produced Zyklon gas which was used to kill concentration camp inmates. Also, the Krupp steel firm and armaments maker which helped build up the German war machine. Sullivan and Cromwell also aided in the economic rehabilitation of Germany after the war and when Hitler came to power, they were reluctant to say anything nasty about Hitler, lest it annoy their powerful German and European clients who paid them lavishly for their services.

John Foster Dulles was of the same mold as his brother when it came to dealing with Hitler as he came to power in Germany. Under pressure from his brother and other members of his firm, Foster Dulles was forced to cut relations with the office in Germany where lawyers were forced to sign every letter with the words, "Heil Hitler." Foster Dulles was also a contemporary and friend of Charles Lindberg, whose "America First" committee wanted to keep the U.S. out of World War II and who was personally pro-Hitler in his politics.

More evidence of just how cleverly Sullivan and Cromwell were tied to the Nazis is in the person of Dulles's former Berlin law partner, Gerhart Westrick. When Westrick came to the United States in August 1940, he had a number of social calls with people he knew. He threw a party at the Waldorf-Astoria Hotel in New York on June 26, 1940 to celebrate the Nazi victory over France. Instead of repudiating what Westrick did, Foster Dulles instead went to his friend's defense by saying that he had "a high regard for his integrity."

When Allen Dulles was stationed in Switzerland during WWI,

he made it his business to try to arrange a separate peace deal with the German military who were then in Italy. This back channel was called Operation Sunrise and its ingredients were not sent to Washington for review.

In March 1933, Allen Dulles went to Europe on a mission for President Roosevelt and he stopped off in Berlin to meet with Hitler. After meeting with Hitler, he told his brother Foster that he did not see the German leader as a bad person and that he was "rather impressed" with Joseph Goebbles, Hitler's propaganda minister.

As the decade of the 1930s ended, Allen Dulles had a partial change of heart when it came to German-American relations. He was now more of a critic of Hitler and his regime, but his law firm continued to do business in Germany.

Allen Dulles' Nazi connections were under review by the Roosevelt administration when Dulles entered the OSS in 1941. When Dulles began his duties with the OSS out of its Rockefeller Center Headquarters in New York, he was under close surveillance by the men who worked in Donovan's bailiwick.

The OSS office that Dulles worked in was part of the secret British intelligence operation then operating out of the same building called BSC—British Security Coordination—headed by William Stephenson, also known as "the Man Called Intrepid." From its headquarters at Rockefeller Center, BSC's men and women were tracking down agents in South America and other parts of the Western Hemisphere, as well as establishing a working relationship with the OSS and the FBI.

By the time Stephenson arrived in New York, his proposed activities had caused a great deal of dissension among the president's advisors. FDR had given Stephenson carte blanche to use America in his counterespionage activities. The president failed to notify Congress about Stephenson's dealings on American soil. But if the Congress didn't know about Stephenson, two other men who would play an important part in the Stephenson-BSC story surely did.

They were J. Edgar Hoover, and the newly appointed head of the Office of the Coordinator of Information (COI), William Donovan. Donovan and Stephenson, called "Little Bill" and "Big Bill," worked closely together to their mutual advantage. Hoover, on the other hand, saw Stephenson's role in America as conflicting directly with his own domination over all U.S. intelligence functions.

Stephenson directed his cadre of spies throughout North America, setting up a secret training facility dubbed "Camp X" in the Canadian wilderness, where agents were schooled before setting off for missions in Europe. Personally supervising the rigorous training schedule, Stephenson prowled the grounds of Camp X, overseeing radio communications techniques and operating stations in Bermuda, where code breakers intercepted transmissions. Stephenson, according to legend, brought his friend and fellow agent Ian Fleming with him on his tours of Camp X.

But other objective historians take a somewhat different view of Stephenson's importance in the running of the BSC. They point that the BSC was really operated by Britain's sabotage organization, SOE or Special Operations Executive. SOE was responsible for "setting Europe ablaze," and sending sabotage teams throughout Nazi occupied Europe to disrupt German military activities. Stephenson's BSC, these skeptics say, was used to recruit agents for SOE's use for its own clandestine activities. To Stephenson's credit, he did have a close, working relationship with Bill Donovan, with information jointly shared. Stephenson's major backer was FDR, who was kept abreast of BSC's work.

After the war, Stephenson retired to Bermuda where he spent the rest of his life. Whether Stephenson's role in espionage activities was as definitive as he hoped is still a subject of debate among scholars of the war. What is not debatable, however, is the continuing "Intrepid legend."

Besides Donovan's OSS which was keeping an eye on Allen Dulles, so was Bill Stephenson's BSC. Stephenson's spies were well equipped to watch over Dulles' activities and report back to Washington if either Allen or Foster continued to do back channel activities with Hitler and his regime. The organizations shared a small space in their Rockefeller Center headquarters and so it was not that hard for both Donovan and Stephenson to keep tabs on Allen.

One of the reasons FDR did not trust Allen Dulles and put him under surveillance was his business links with Nazi Germany and his lenient attitude toward Hitler's regime.

Another top advisor to FDR who took notice of Allen Dulles' activities was William O. Douglas, a personal friend of the president's and a future Supreme Court Justice. FDR appointed young Douglas to the position of head of the Securities and Exchange Commission, whose duties were to monitor the financial dealings of companies and banks in the United States. Through his position at the SEC, Douglas could see if the Dulles brothers were doing anything illegal or improper in their business dealings, especially if it related to business with Germany. At one time, Douglas applied for a job with Sullivan and Cromwell but was so taken aback by his interview with John Foster Dulles' attitude that he turned the job down. As Douglas later said of the interview, "I was so struck by Foster's pomposity that when he helped me on with my coat, as I was leaving his office, I turned and gave him a quarter tip."[12]

The president was not the only one who was dubious of Allen Dulles' loyalty. That feeling was shared by his wife, Eleanor, who took a dim view of Dulles' work in Bern due to his somewhat pro-Hitler ideas. John Loftus, who was a former Nazi war crimes investigator for the U.S. Justice Department and a writer on intelligence history of World War II, said of Allen Dulles's time spent in Bern, "He was a dangle. The White House wanted Dulles in clear contact with his Nazi clients so they could be easily identified."

And now, we return to Bernardino Nogara and his relationship with the OSS and Jim Angleton.

The aforementioned John Loftus wrote of Sullivan and Cromwell, "Its clients needed the Vatican bank to launder their profits under the watchful eyes of both the Nazis and their own governments, while the Vatican needed the Dulles brothers to protect its own investments in Hitler's Germany."[13]

New research by author Gerald Posner in his book *God's*

---

[12] Talbot, David, *The Devil's Chessboard: Allen Dulles, the CIA, and the Rise of America's Secret Government*, Harper Collins, New York, 2015, Page 24.

[13] Posner, Gerald, *God's Bankers: A History of Money and Power At the Vatican*, Simon and Schuster, New York, 2015, Page 132.

Bankers, A History of Money and Power at the Vatican, makes the case that Nogara, besides being the pope's financial banker, was possibly a spy for the Germans. In a new documents found by Posner in the National Archives, there is a 1945 OSS intelligence report concerning Nogara's possible Nazi ties. While he was chief of the Rome OSS desk for the X-2 organization, Angleton compiled a dossier on Nogara and his tenuous Nazi ties, which was marked "Secret" on every page.

How Angleton and the OSS learned about possible Nogara-German ties was from a one-page appendix to a summary of an interrogation of Reinhard Karl Reme, an Abwehr intelligence officer. Reinhard Karl Reme used an alias as a partner in a German insurance company called Jauch Hubener. In this report, Angleton created a chart of the Abwehr's top men in Italy and Reme's "remote branch" of the Abwehr was listed. One of Reme's cells was headed by a man who was called "Nogara" (no first name was mentioned).

Karl Reme downplayed his espionage activities, but Angleton said that Reme had traveled widely in Europe to such places as Spain and Greece, spoke English, German, and Italian, and had a law degree. All of this does not necessarily mean anything out of the ordinary, but it seems that Reme was not your ordinary soldier. With this information on hand, Angleton believed that Reme was working for the Abwehr before the war started. Angleton spoke with Reme and concluded that he "was head of the recruiting center in Milan for the Abwehr."

Posner writes, "Reme gave his interrogators the names of fifty-eight agents he and his Italian-based unit had recruited during the war. Nogara is not among them. But he provided the name to Angleton on the supplementary Abwehr chart, meaning the Nogara on that chart was almost certainly recruited before 1943, and likely before the war." [14]

Another place where Bernardo Nogara possibly recruited Nazi spies was Constantinople, Turkey when he was there on Vatican business prior to World War I. While he was in that city, Nogara was influential in getting Italian companies business contracts with large Turkish businesses and soon had a team of informers and agents at his disposal. Walter Schellenberg, a high-ranking German intelligence chief, told Angleton that the Abwehr had recruited a

[14] Ibid. Page 134.

number of foreigners who were then working in Constantinople, but he could not name them. These events, as Walter Schellenberg described, were at the time that Nogara lived in that city.

In the late 1920s, before Nogara began working for the Vatican, he spent many years working in Germany as the Italian representative operating the division of the Inter-Allied Commission "charged with rebuilding German industry." It is not out of the question that sometime during that period Nogara was recruited by the Germans as some sort of agent, for some unspecified reason.

As for Reme, he was transferred to the Combined Services Detailed Interrogation Center (CSDIC) for "further interrogation." CSDIC was a secret prison run by the British military intelligence, MI5, located in Bad Nenndorf, Germany. In an interesting development, Posner writes that no further U.S. probe into a possible Nogara-German link was made after Reme's initial chart with the name of Nogara on it. We don't know if Nogara was a double agent working for the Germans. But what is indisputable is the fact that the pope's number one banker had worldwide business relationships while he was working for the Vatican. Since there is no paper trail linking any more possible ties between Nogara and the Germans, one cannot definitely prove one way or another if these ties were just circumstantial or otherwise.

The reader has been informed of the links between Hans Oster, Admiral Canaris, and the pope, in the efforts to overthrow Hitler. But the story is much more complicated, involving the Allied governments, mostly Great Britain, and to a lesser extent, the United States. After the beginning of the pope's efforts to oust Hitler using the members of the Schwartz Kapelle, he then made certain covert efforts to reach the British government in London to sound them out as far as what peace deals he may have been able to facilitate. One of the men the pope used in his British connection was Father Ludwig Kass, a confidant of the pope and a friend of Josef Muller. Father Kass was the former chairman of the now banned German Catholic Center Party and the pope's trusted advisor on anything related to Germany. Muller informed Father Kass of the German resistance's need for the Vatican's help and he then passed on that information to the pope.

Father Kass was now given the responsibility of negotiating

secretly with London in the plots to oust Hitler, and the first person he met with was the British ambassador to the Holy See, D'Arcy Osborne. During the early anti-Hitler plotting, Father Kass met with Ambassador Osborne and told him how much the resistance leaders hated Hitler but also told him that the chances for overthrowing him were less than good. When he reported back to London of his talks with Father Kass, he asked that in correspondence to him Kass's name not be written down in order to keep his identify from getting into the wrong hands. The ambassador also told his superiors in Whitehall that the government would be wise to keep open any and all channels to the Vatican in the efforts to overthrow Hitler.

However, there were some in the British government who took a skeptical view on what Father Kass was saying. Undersecretary Alexander Cadogan said that Father Kass's story was "the ridiculous stale story of a German opposition ready to overthrow Hitler, if we will guarantee we will not take advantage." He said it was about the 100th time he had heard that story. "We have reason to believe that the Gestapo have a hold on Mgr. Kass." The Foreign Office then sent a note to Ambassador Osborne that they believed that Father Kass might have been under Nazi influence through German priests in Rome.

The pope received the message from London and in it were the conditions that they laid out: any post-war German government must include the elimination of the National Socialists Regime (Hitler's party). For all intents and purposes, the pope was now knee deep with the resistance against the Hitler regime.

The pope now imposed certain conditions if he was going to take the plot any further. If and when the German regime fell, he wanted Josef Muller to become the Vatican's special envoy to the new German government. He also wanted to seek a separate peace with the Western Allies, something that they were not willing to do. As far as the Allies were concerned, Germany had to be defeated at all costs in order to insure an effective peace after the war ended. The British decided not to go along with the pope's plea for a separate peace deal, and were not notified when a spy in their midst sent a copy to the Russians notifying them of the British-Vatican correspondence. That spy was none other than Kim Philby.

The Americans were notified about this correspondence via

a confidant of the pope's, Father Robert Leiber (more about him coming up). Father Leiber gave this information to a Jesuit in Rome named Father Vincent McCormick, who then gave it to Harold Tittmann, who was a U.S. diplomat in the Vatican. Another person Muller gave this information to was Allen Dulles who was then stationed in Bern, Switzerland. After the war was over and many documents from that period were declassified, a note concerning Josef Muller said, "he (Muller) was our agent and informant during the war with Germany." The declassified records also state that both Allen Dulles and William Donovan were in contact with Muller during the war.

It was part of Muller's job at this time to hide the role of the pope in the anti-Hitler plotting. At one point he wrote the following, "We could not portray the pope as a direct accessory to an assassination plot." He also wrote the ensuing note in that regard, "But we had to consider what we would do if such a thing was aborted (the proposed overthrow of Hitler). The pope couldn't just immediately be standing by, visibly ready for a regime change—he'd look like a guilty schoolboy. At that moment, much would depend on the demeanor of the pope."[15]

Soon, the pope had a direct meeting with Ambassador Osborne in Rome. The pope told him that he had a meeting with a "German representative" whom he would not name. He told Osborne that he learned that the Germans were preparing an attack thatwould take place through Holland and that, "It would be violent, bitter and utterly unscrupulous."

Osborne later informed London of this meeting by saying in part, "His Holiness had said that he could answer for the good faith of the intermediary, but he could not guarantee the good faith of the principals." Osborne said that if London wanted to connect with the pope, he would be the back channel. He also said of the pope, "he begged me to regard the matter as absolutely secret. If anything should become known the lives of the unnamed generals would be forfeit."

Ambassador Osborne cabled London concerning the pope and the anti-Hitler plots saying, "I think His Holiness' urgent insistence on the most absolute secrecy is a measure of his own belief in the bona fides of his informants." The pope was now up to his eyeballs

[15] Riebling, Mark, *Church of Spies*, Page 150.

at the center of the Vatican conspiracy to get rid of Adolf Hitler. *Pius XII*

The British ambassador made contact with the resistance leaders and listened to what they had to say, but was unconvinced. Osborne told His Majesty's government that he'd recommend continued contacts only if the Hitler regime was gone and the Germans promised to return lands conquered in recent cross-border raids, and only if Germany agreed to return the Sudetenland to Czechoslovakia.

In another communication to Osborne from the pope, His Holiness said that he learned that certain elements of the German army were poised to stage a coup, but only on the condition that the merger of Austria and Germany would be guaranteed. Foreign Secretary Halifax responded by saying that France and Britain would not be party to any blackmail, and more importantly, that the Austrian populace should later have self-determination in their future.

The so-called X Report, drafted by Canaris and Hans Oster, which laid down British conditions for a peace treaty with Germany, now made its way to the resistance leaders. Others who were adding clauses to the X Report were Josef Muller, Hans von Duhnanyi, a Ministry of Justice official, and Generals George Thomas and Franz Halder.

These men told the British that the foundation of any plan was the prompt removal of Hitler. General Halder, in a move that he later regretted, gave a copy of the X Report to Walter von Brauchitsch, the commander in chief of the German army. Halder was shocked when General von Brauchitsch all but labeled him a traitor and warned him to ignore the report. For the Schwarze Kapelle, the cold shoulder given to them by General von Brauchitsch was the last straw in any possible deal involving the Vatican trying to end the war. Hitler was now prepared to invade France, Norway, Denmark, and possibly England.

While the Schwarze Kapelle was working with the Vatican, Reinhard Heydrich's SD was following matters intently. The mole was a Benedictine monk named Herman Keller who lived and worked in an abbey called Beuron, high in the Swabbian Mountains. Keller was Heydrich's informant, and through intrigue on Keller's part, was able to oust the Arch Abbot of the monastery,

Rafael Walser, and virtually rule on his own terms.

Josef Muller was ordered to investigate Keller, and he proved that the monk had initiated trumped-up charges against the Arch Abbot. Keller was sent to Jerusalem, where he was once again put under the command of the SD.

Keller traveled to Basel, Switzerland in October 1939, and it was there that he met a Berlin lawyer, Dr. Hans Etscheit. Etscheit was then working for Admiral Canaris's Abwehr, and had no idea that the monk was working for the rival SD. After hours of conversations, Etscheit told Keller about the Vatican connection, believing that his secret was safe with the monk. Keller had learned from Etscheit that Muller was the middleman with the Vatican, and Keller traveled to Rome where he confronted Muller about his Vatican contacts.

Canaris and Oster wrote their own versions of the Muller-Etscheit allegations, playing down any conspiracy and leaving out the most critical names of those involved. Canaris personally brought the report to Hitler, who, after reading it, called it "nonsense."

The Schwarze Kapelle-Vatican connection failed. However, as one part of the conspiracy ended, other people close to the pope would enter the fray, and get the Holy See more involved in the plots than ever before. One of those men was a close associate of Pope Pius, Father Robert Leiber.

The Vatican was a hotbed of espionage during World War II, with agents from all sides seeking out information on each other. The OSS had its own sources of information inside the walls of the pope's palace, and these men passed on valuable tidbits of knowledge from their sources. One of the men the Americans used as a conduit was Jesuit priest Robert Leiber, a confidant of the Papal Nuncio in Germany, Cardinal Eugenio Pacelli, later, Pope Pius XII.

Father Leiber, Bavarian by origin, during the war was a teacher of theological studies at the University of Munich. Cardinal Pacelli knew of Leiber's work and had him come in for an interview. He was so impressed with the young man that he asked him to become his private secretary. Father Leiber accepted the offer immediately and became privy to decisions relating to the outcome of the war. By accepting the Cardinal's offer of a job, he would later be thrust into the middle of the Vatican intrigues. Father Leiber worked alongside Cardinal Pacelli when the future pope held the position of Secretary of State at the Vatican. Like many men of the Catholic Church, Father Leiber was anti-Nazi, seeing in the Hitler regime a country bent on destroying the Jews and other minorities, bent on subverting religious freedom in Germany. He worked behind the scenes with a number of anti-Hitler plotters, including Josef Muller, and was privy to their plans.

It was not clear how and when Father Leiber came to the attention of the OSS, but by August of 1944, he was having confidential meetings with Bill Donovan's representatives.

Father Leiber had left Germany in 1932 to move to Italy, but he still had unusual sources of information on the plans to kill Hitler. Between 1939 and 1943, Father Leiber's main contact with the German opposition was a Catholic lawyer, the aforementioned Josef Muller. Muller worked in the Abwehr beginning in 1939 and soon became disenchanted with Hitler's Third Reich. Over time, Muller made contacts with men inside the Abwehr who took active steps in trying to eliminate Hitler. One of the men whom Muller reached out to was Hans Oster, whose story was told earlier in this chapter. Another source of intelligence for Father Leiber was Hans Bernd Gisevius. Gisevius worked at Abwehr headquarters and was also a leading member of the opposition group. He later operated out of Switzerland and was also had secret contact with Allen Dulles who was OSS station chief in Bern.

Throughout the behind-the-scenes plotting against Hitler, the conspirators kept Father Leiber up to date on all their plans. He knew of the winter 1939-40 plot against Hitler led by General von Halder. It was hoped by these men that the German offensive against Norway would fail, thus giving the opposition ammunition to supplant Hitler. To their dismay, the Norwegian campaign was a success, and the plan was called off.

Leiber was also knowledgeable concerning a plot that was scheduled to take place in September-October, 1943. He received fragmentary details of this proposed action by a colonel in the Germany Embassy in Rome. The attempt was to take place no later than October 15, but it was all contingent on the stabilization of the Russian front. Since the military situation was still fluid, the plot did not go off. In his discussion with OSS representatives in Rome, Father Leiber attributed the failure of the plots to the following: first, many of the conspirators were not sincere in their efforts to topple Hitler, and second, they did not want to imperil the overall safety of the Reich.

Father Leiber discussed matters then going on in Germany with his OSS listeners. He said that in his opinion, as long as Hitler governed, the Catholic youth of the country was lost. Once the war was over, the Church had to place its trust for religious renewal on the very young and the present, older generation.

Father Leiber also had ties with the OSS in the person of one of its agents, Raymond Rocca, who was then working for X-2 (counterintelligence). One day, Ray Rocca went by car to the Vatican to meet with an American Jesuit, Father Vincent McCormick. The men had a history before this meeting, when Rocca supplied information to Father McCormick on the Gestapo infiltration of the Gregorian, a Jesuit university where McCormick served as rector. Inside the bowels of the Vatican, the two men met with Monsignor Ludwig Kass who was doing excavations below ground. Monsignor Kass was a personal confidant of the pope, and the leader of the Catholic Church trusted Kass with the most important of church affairs. One of the secret missions that the pope asked Kass to perform was to go down to the underground vaults of the Vatican in search of the bones of St. Peter, one of the twelve apostles and the founder of the Catholic Church. Along with Kass in this most secret endeavor were four members of the Papal Institute for Christian Archeology. Catholics had a special place in their history for St. Peter. He came to Rome from the Middle East and became the first pope, and was then crucified for his faith. Emperor Constantine built the original St. Peter's Basilica in 333 over what was thought to be St. Peter's burial place. The search for St. Peter's tomb was one of the most highly guarded secrets of the Vatican and the pope paid the expenses for the dig from his own pocket.

Sometime after the excavation began, Monsignor Kass excitedly told the pope that they believed they had made a momentous discovery. Under the high altar of St. Peter's, where old maps told of the exact site of St. Peter's burial, the team found

250 bone fragments that filled three small lead boxes. In an unusual move, after the excavation was completed the pope ordered the site closed forever and had the bones placed in his private apartment. The only other person besides Kass and his team who was aware of the find was the pope's personal physician, Riccardo Galeazzi-Lisi. The doctor, who had no training in physical anthropology, told the pope that the bones belonged to one person, who was, at death, about sixty to seventy years old. That finding was enough for the pope to decide that the bones found underneath the Vatican were indeed those of St. Peter.[16]

Rocca told Kass that the OSS had information that certain captured German officers told interrogators that they were anti-Nazi, and that he was also there to verify claims by "Albrecht von Kessel, the deputy Reich ambassador to the Holy See that the entire embassy had been in on the plot against Hitler. If deported to Germany, they would be as good as dead as soon as they re-entered the territory of the Reich."

After much haggling, arrangements were made for Rocca to meet with Father Leiber, and the father did not pussyfoot around when it came to his knowledge of the church's role in the anti-Hitler plots. He told of three plots that preceded the July 20th attempted assassination of Hitler by Stauffenberg and his co-conspirators. He mentioned that General Franz Halder, the former Wehrmacht chief of staff, was one of the plotters and that General Halder might have shared his information with the pope.

Rocca had many questions to ask Father Leiber but the priest was circumspect when it came to answering them. One question always bothered Rocca when it came to what Father Leiber really knew. He always speculated as to why the plotters trusted Father Leiber with their most sensitive information. Was it because they knew he'd inform the pope of what they were telling him?

Father Leiber wasn't the only person the OSS had contact with in the Vatican during the war. On the day that FDR died, James Angleton sent one of his most trusted agents, James Plaut, to the Vatican to see Albrecht von Kessel, who was the first secretary in the German embassy at the Vatican. In peacetime, Plaut worked at the Fogg Museum at Harvard, and served as director of the Orion Project (or the Monuments Men), whose responsibility it was to

[16] Posner, Gerald, *God's Bankers*, Page 94-95.

recover stolen art looted by the Nazis. The purpose of the meeting was so that Kessel could give Plaut a copy of a manuscript that he'd written concerning his role as Stauffenberg's Vatican agent.

The story of the Monuments Men is a little known but important story in the tale of World War II, one that is not touched upon much in the teaching of the war. The story of the Monuments Men was popularized in the movie of the same name starring George Clooney, Matt Damon, and others.

On March 22, 1945, two months before Germany surrendered to the Allies, the U.S. Third Army, led by Lt. Col. George Patton, crossed the Rhine River and on April 6th, two military policemen from Patton's command received information from two displaced women who said that certain amounts of gold were hidden in the Kaiser's mine.

A half-mile below ground, Patton's men found 550 sacks of German paper currency, totaling a billion Reichsmarks stacked along the walls of the main passageway. General Dwight Eisenhower, the Allied commander in chief decided that the money had to be moved to a safer place. On April 14, 1945, the treasury of the Third Reich was taken to the Reichsbank in Frankfurt, which was now in American hands.

Information relating to the Merkers mine was relayed to the members of the Monuments Men. Two members of the Monuments Men, Robert Posey and Lincoln Kirstein, arrived at Merkers to make an inspection. As they approached the mine—it was guarded by a ring of steel—hundreds of soldiers carrying automatic weapons, tanks and machine guns formed a huge circle near the mine. As the elevator took them deeper in the mineshaft, they were subjected to a sight that startled them to the bone. Beyond the blasted door, they a found Nazi treasure room about 150 feet long and 75 feet across. Inside was a railroad track that the Nazis used to bring and remove gold from the mine.

On the floor of the mine lay thousands upon thousands of bags of gold. Inside the shaft was Room 8, another treasure trove of stolen Nazi loot and what was inside was even more extraordinary. Inside was box upon box of stolen art works, some of the most important and valuable pieces of art that were stolen from the homes of victims of the Holocaust. Also discovered were ancient Egyptian papyri in metal cases, Greek and Roman decorative art, ancient rugs and mosaics. They also found 8,198 gold bars, 7II bags of U.S. $20 gold pieces, 1,300 bags of other gold coins, hundreds of bags of foreign currencies and $2.76 billion German Reichsmarks.

In a massive undertaking, the U.S. began the removal of the looted gold and artwork; it was taken away for cataloging and safekeeping. Not all of the gold was removed, as some enterprising U.S. soldiers decided to take for themselves the spoils of war, albeit illegal.

In their brief talk, Kessel lamented the loss of his friends in the war, especially those who worked against Hitler. It was more of a talking session on Kessel's part and when he was finished, Rocca left with a heartfelt respect for one of his most important Vatican agents.

In the 1960s, Ray Rocca would investigate, along with the CIA, another high-profile case: the assassination of President Kennedy. The lessons that he learned while working for the OSS in the Vatican case did him well when it came to his new task.

The two areas the CIA looked into were Lee Harvey Oswald's trip to Russia (any possible Soviet intelligence involvement with him) and the possible Cuban connection to the president's death. At that time, Rocca was the chief of research and analysis for the CIA's Counterintelligence Staff. As head of R&A, Rocca worked closely with James Angleton, who was in charge of the mole-hunting unit at the CIA, the CI branch. It would later be learned that the CI branch had a huge file on the "defector" Lee Harvey Oswald, and the Oswald paper trail that was later to be unearthed via the JFK Records Act led directly to Angleton's office.

Rocca was suspicious of Oswald's two-year stint in the Soviet Union saying of Oswald's time there, "because the people he (Oswald) was in touch with in Mexico had traces, prior traces, as KGB people. They were under consular cover and obviously could have been doing and were undoubtedly doing a consular job in those earlier contacts."

Rocca, Angleton, and Richard Helms, who would later become the director of Central Intelligence, were all concerned about possible Cuban involvement with Oswald in the assassination. But Helms said years later that it was virtually impossible to develop factual leads concerning this aspect of the case.

By late December 1963, Angleton's CI staff was given responsibility in assisting the Warren Commission in its investigation. Rocca's team coordinated all cable traffic concerning the assassination, studied it, and passed it on to the Warren Commission. Even though Rocca's R&A staff did most of the paperwork, it was still Richard Helms who called the shots and Rocca had to divert to Helms if there were any major questions or problems that needed to be addressed.

Rocca was also involved in the minute details of Oswald's trip to Mexico City in September 1963, two months before the president's assassination. Fifty years later, there is still much speculation of just what Oswald was doing in Mexico City and the CIA took that problem very seriously.

During its investigation of the Kennedy assassination, the CIA refused to provide the Warren Commission its sources and methods on Oswald's trip to Mexico City, but in order to get some written report to them, provided them with a narrative minus this vital information. On February 10, 1964, a lawyer for the WC, J. Lee Rankin, sent a letter to the CIA asking them if Oswald was in direct communications with anyone at the Soviet Embassy in Mexico City based on any sensitive sources. The agency failed to give Rankin a satisfactory answer. Later, Rocca would state that in the January-February 1964 time frame, several representatives from the Warren Commission were shown some information gleaned from these sensitive sources at CIA headquarters. But Rocca insisted that he personally did not make this material available to the staff.

Rocca was also involved in the CIA's probe of the Kennedy assassination when it came to what was referred to as the "unidentified man" story. This was a photo of an unidentified man in Mexico City whom the CIA mistakenly took for the real Lee Oswald. This man, whose picture has been known to researchers for years, is still a mystery (maybe not to the CIA), and what, if any, his relationship might be to Oswald and the assassination is still in doubt.

The origin of this unidentified man photograph goes back to November 23, 1963, when the FBI, after getting it from the CIA, showed it to Marguerite Oswald, Lee Oswald's mother. This photograph was thought to be the real Lee Oswald but it is clearly not. This man was beefy, with broad shoulders, a receding hairline and older than the 24-year old Oswald. When she testified before the Warren Commission on February 10, 1964, Mrs. Oswald said that the man in the photograph was Jack Ruby (not true).

When the "unidentified man photograph" became known to the Warren Commission they began immediate steps to ascertain who the man was and how the CIA had obtained the photo. On February 12, 1964, Lee Rankin wrote to Thomas Karramesiness, the assistant deputy director for plans (DDP) asking for the identity of the man and the circumstances of how the CIA came to possess it. On the same day he also sent a letter to DCI John McCone requesting CIA materials that the agency had sent to the Secret Service but not the Warren Commission concerning the unidentified man photo.

Rocca was up to his neck in the unidentified man investigation and tried to keep information on the subject in house, and out of the WC's hands. Rocca stated in a memo James Angleton's desire not to respond to the WC's request for information on the photo:

> Unless you feel otherwise, Jim would prefer to wait out the Commission on the matter covered by paragraph 2 [letter to John McCone]. If they come back on this subject he feels that you, or someone from here, should be prepared to show the Commission the material than pass it to them in copy. We have either passed the material in substance to the Commission in response to earlier levies or the items refer to aborted leads, for example, the famous six photos, which are not Oswald.

From this passage it obvious that the CIA knew that the man in the photo was not Lee Oswald. But did they know who he really was? Years later, the later CIA Director William Colby would comment on the unidentified man, "To this day we don't know who he is."

One of the most pivotal events of the war, as far as Italy and the pope were concerned, came when the Allies invaded Sicily. This was the beginning of the end for Italy in the war and soon after the invasion, events began to move at a fever pitch. Soon thereafter,

King Victor Emmanuel had Benito Mussolini arrested and named Marshal Badoglio as his successor. After the Armistice was declared and Italy left the war, an infuriated Adolf Hitler decided to invade the Vatican and kidnap the pope. Hitler went so far as to have a number of his troops take up positions around St. Peter's Square in preparation for action. The only defense the Vatican had was the ill-equipped Swiss Guard, who were no match for the German's who were poised to strike when ordered. As the standoff went on, the Vatican received a report that the Germans were prepared to put the pope under their "protection." Protection meant arrest and that was not an option that the Vatican relished. This tip came from Albrecht von Kessel who stated that Hitler blamed the pope for the defeat of Italy "because the pope had long talked by phone with Roosevelt." At the news of an impending attack on the Vatican, Father Leiber, at the instruction of the pope, began moving the pope's most important documents under the floors of the Apostolic Palace.

Hitler had long planned to invade the Vatican and take Pope Pius XII hostage. In talks with his top generals, Hitler ordered detailed plans to occupy the Vatican. In talking with Walter Hewell, a top German general, Hitler said, "I'll go right into the Vatican. Do you think the Vatican embarrasses me? We'll take that over right away. For one thing, the entire diplomatic corps are in there. It's all the same to me. The rabble is in there. We'll get that bunch of swine out of there. Later we can make apologies. That doesn't make any difference." When asked about what documents they might find inside the Vatican, Hitler said, "There, yes. We'll find documents. The treason will come to light."[17]

After a successful takeover of the Vatican, the plan was to spirit the pope and his entourage (including the King) away to Germany. However, in heated talks with his top brass, the plan to seize the pope was scrubbed. They decided it was not worth the huge risks that would be taken if such an event took place. The Nazis decided that world opinion would be so much against them that the effort was not plausible.

Despite the decision to not invade the Vatican, Hitler had put in motion a secret plan to kidnap the pope during the war. The man he tasked for the job was Lt. General Karl Wolff. Wolff served in

[17] Riebling, Mark, *Church of Spies,* Page 176-177.

the dreaded Waffen SS, and as a deputy to Reichsfuhrer Himmler. He was put in command of German troops located in rear combat areas in early 1945. He was the strong man in Hitler's staff, as well as one of a number of high-ranking officers involved in making a separate peace with the Allies.

One day, Hitler invited Wolff to his headquarters for a private meeting. He ordered General Wolff to take a number of highly trained troops, head to the Vatican, and take Pope Pius XII out of the country. Hitler was aware of the pope's actions in trying to save a number of Jews from certain death by hiding them in safe houses around Rome. He also knew that a number of his high-level commanders had made covert contacts with the pope in order to end the war. General Wolff had no choice but to draw up plans to kidnap the pope, including designs to take him to Liechtenstein. Unknown to Hitler, Wolff had no intention of carrying out his mission.

Wolff contacted two trusted emissaries in his search for a peaceful end to the war: Dr. Rudolf Rahn, the German Ambassador to Italy, and Ernst von Weizacker, the envoy to the Vatican. He told them of Hitler's plan and reassured them that he would never give the order for the mission to proceed. He also sent a letter to the pope describing the kidnapping plot, and his reaction to it.

In December 1943, General Wolff met with Hitler regarding the current status of the mission. For hours, he pressed the point, saying that if the pope was kidnapped, all of Italy would be aflame, and that worldwide Catholic repulsion against Germany's actions would result in a huge propaganda defeat. A reluctant Hitler finally canceled the project.

With the Vatican plot now out of the way, Wolff turned his attention to making contact with the OSS representative in Switzerland, Allen Dulles. When he arrived in Bern, Dulles agreed to meet with Wolff but on one condition" Dulles wanted Wolff, the commander of German forces in Italy, to release two top Italian partisan leaders allied with the U.S., Antonio Usmiani and Ferruccio Parri. Within a week, both men were freed.

Under strict secrecy Wolff was taken to Dulles's home by Professor Max Hausmann, who hid the general and his men while they were in the city. Wolff got right to the point. He said that it was time for the war to come to an end, and told Dulles that he was going to try to persuade Albert Kesselring cooperate with him. Wolff told Dulles that he had operational control over all German forces in the strategic areas of Western Austria, the Tyrol, and the Brenner Pass. Dulles wrote, "Wolff feels that joint action by Kesselring and himself would have a vital repercussion on the German army, particularly on the Western front, since many Generals are only waiting for someone to take the lead. Wolff made no request concerning his personal safety or privileged treatment from the war criminal viewpoint."

He told Dulles that if Kesselring agreed, he would attempt to get him to join him in Switzerland to coordinate surrender terms. In order to show further good faith, Wolff told Dulles that he would stop hit-and-run raids on Italian partisans by German troops, would release a number of imprisoned Jews, and would further assure the safety of 350 American POWs, including a number of sick and wounded held in Italy. Dulles listened intently to General Wolff and assured him that he would study the offer and get back to him in the near future.

General Wolff's discussions with Dulles got the attention of Ernst Kaltenbrunner, the head of the Nazi security police, the SD. Kaltenbrunner warned Wolff not to interfere with the course of the war. What Wolff did not know was that Himmler too was in covert contact with the Western Allies via Carl Burckhardt, the president of the International Red Cross.

In March 1945, Wolff was again in contact with Dulles saying that Kesselring had agreed to the surrender of German forces in Italy. He also told Dulles that his family was being "guarded" and that he feared for their lives if he continued meeting with the OSS.

While all these secret dealings were going on with General Wolff, Bill Donovan cabled Dulles telling him to break off talks with Wolff before the situation got out of hand. It seemed that Soviet leader Joseph Stalin was having a fit concerning a possible separate peace treaty between the Allies and Germany that might affect Russia. Stalin angrily spoke to President Roosevelt about the situation but he finally came to his senses and the situation calmed down.

In the midst of all this, Donovan went to Paris for talks with

American officials and was surprised that Dulles was in town. They held their meetings at the Ritz Hotel in Paris, where among other things, they talked about the sudden death of FDR just two days before. Donovan told Dulles that Wolff had returned to Berlin to meet with Hitler and Himmler and that he might not be allowed to return to Italy. Donovan further told Dulles that the operation they were conducting with Wolff, code named Operation Sunrise, was now shut down and that things would have to take their own shape as the war came to an end.[18]

Donovan was right. Wolff was indeed in Berlin, trying to get out of the mess he had gotten himself into. Hitler told Wolff that his actions were tantamount to treason. Wolff countered by telling Hitler that he was acting on his own, and that he was trying to persuade the Americans to make an alliance with Germany against the Russians. In the end, Hitler took no punitive action against Wolff, and he was free to proceed with his plans for the surrender of German troops in Italy.

General Wolff was contacted by Marshal Rodolfo Graziani, the Italian Minister of War, who assigned him the task of conducting the surrender of his armies. The ceremony took place on April 29, 1945 at Allied HQ in the Summer Palace in Caserta, Italy. The men who signed the capitulation orders were Lt. Colonel Viktor von Schweintz and Major Max Wenner, General Wolff's spokesperson. More than a million German troops gave themselves up, in a ceremony that allowed the troops a sense of dignity. Karl Wolff escaped certain death with Hitler's suicide in his bunker. His heroic actions in the Italian surrender saved thousands of lives and contributed to the end of the war.

In this narrative, we've seen a number of OSS agents who played prominent roles in the secret dealings surrounding the papal quest for peace: James Angleton, Raymond Rocca, and James Plaut (not to mention Father Leiber and Ludwig Kass). Now, another OSS operative would weave his way into the secret labyrinth, Martin Quigley.

Martin Quigley was an OSS agent sent to Vatican City in 1944 on the personal orders of William Donovan. His mission was to sound out Japanese diplomats about the possibilities of negotiations

---

[18] Srodes, James, Allen Dulles: Master of Spies, Regnery Publishers, Washington, D.C., 1999, Page 346.

for an end to the war in the Pacific.

Martin Quigley was a long-time friend of Bill Donovan, and when the war began, Donovan asked him to take on certain confidential work for the United States. Quigley also counted among his contacts President Roosevelt and Francis Cardinal Spellman, Archbishop of New York, one of the most powerful Catholic leaders in the country.

Quigley worked in the Hollywood movie industry, and had contacts among the producers and actors. In January 1943, after a meeting with OSS officer Frederic Dolbeare, on Donovan's instructions, Quigley provided certain information to the OSS. He said that he still maintained indirect communications with persons in European countries who might be of help to the OSS. "People who have connections with men of political interest in this country [the US], individuals who might be willing to serve abroad, wholly untrustworthy characters, and people who might know, in definite terms, matters of scandal relating to official people in enemy countries."

Mr. Dolbeare wrote to Donovan regarding his meeting with Quigley. The message reads in part," I see no possible harm in attempting a survey of the possibilities of that area, provided the name of OSS is left out of it." Donovan however, had another, more important mission for Quigley to perform.

In the fall of 1944, Donovan met with Quigley in Washington and, over lunch, gave him his new orders. He was to go to the Vatican and make contact with the Japanese via his connections with the Holy See, to sound out the Japanese about ending the war. His Vatican assignment was not Quigley's first work for the OSS. He had previously served in Ireland in 1943 under the cover as a representative for the American film industry. In reality, he was an agent in that neutral country, spying on any possible German penetration of the Emerald Isle.

Using the same commercial cover in Italy, he sailed for Europe in December, departing from Newport News, Virginia on a 14-day voyage to Naples, arriving in Rome a few days later. He found an expensive apartment owned by Dr. Ing Giovianni Pasani, located at 162 Via Po. His formal instruction from the OSS were to "establish and maintain the commercial cover and acquire intelligence of direct or indirect military or strategic value." He had access to a local taxi driver who would take him on his rounds, and had two locations for his "dead drops" of dispatches and other correspondence. As soon as Quigley was settled in Rome, he began developing his American and Vatican contacts.

Three of the men he took under his wing were Father McCormick, engineer Pietro Galeazzi, and most important, Monsignor Egidio Vagnozzi.

Father McCormick once served as the Rector of the Gregorian, an international seminary in Rome. He was then in Rome as an important member of the Jesuit headquarters, focusing in American relations. He also served as Pope Pius XII's English language specialist.

Pietro Galeazzi was the architect of the Vatican as well as the chief operating officer of Vatican City, and one of the pontiff's best friends.

Quigley's other middlemen in Rome who did not know of his OSS ties were Dr. Thomas Kiernan, the Irish Ambassador, and a second diplomat, Michael MacWhite, the Irish envoy to the Italian government.

Egidio Vagnozzi, one of the top members of the Church hierarchy, spoke English, had lived in the United States for ten years, and was on good terms with the ecclesiastical advisor to the Japanese Ambassador, Rev. Benedict Tomizawa, a fact duly noted by Quigley. It was Monsignor Vagnozzi whom Quigley would contact as his intermediary with the Japanese.

When Quigley called Monsignor Vagnozzi, the prelate knew who he was. They had met before, and the American asked if he could arrange a meeting as early as possible. Quigley came to Monsignor Vagnozzi's residence, and over drinks, presented his case. He began by saying that with the European war now over, it was only a matter of time before Japan would be defeated. He told the priest of his Catholic background, and the fact that his family knew William Donovan, a name Vagnozzi knew all too well. He then told the monsignor of his OSS ties.

He described his instructions from Donovan: to see if he could open up a channel of communications with the Japanese for possible peace initiatives. He went on to say that the Vatican would be the most logical place to begin negotiations. Quigley then made his pitch. Would he, Monsignor Vagnozzi, be the intermediary with the Japanese? He then went on to ask if the Monsignor would see his friend, Benedict Tomizawa, who lived in the same building. Vagnozzi was reluctant to get involved in international politics, saying that he would try, but promising nothing. Quigley said that if the prelate agreed, he would be the communications tie between the U.S. and Japan.

Monsignor Vagnozzi met with Father Tomizawa and in cautious language relayed what his unnamed American visitor told him. The Japanese priest seemed stunned but agreed to pass along Monsignor Vagnozzi's offers. What neither Quigley nor Vagnozzi was aware of was that the Emperor of Japan had given Ambassador Harada instructions to listen to any peace feelers that might come his way.

Father Tomizawa had a hurried meeting with Ambassador Harada at which time they debated Quigley's offers. A third person was called into the discussion, the Secretary for the Mission, a man named Kamayama, (also a Catholic). They drew up a list of the pros and cons regarding the peace feelers before making a decision on whether to recommend to Tokyo that any further actions be taken.

In the end, Ambassador Harada rejected Quigley's offer, saying in part, "At the present time I believe that Japan does not seek to hasten the coming of peace. Furthermore, it goes without saying that we cannot discuss such questions with a person whose official position and identity are unknown to us."

Martin Quigley's long-shot peace proposal failed to end the war. It would take the dropping of two atomic bombs on Japan to finally end the bloodshed in the Pacific Theater.

While the pope was working in tandem with the anti-Hitler generals, he laid down certain ground rules when dealing with the plots. When Josef Muller wanted to meet with the pope, he had certain rules to follow. He knew from experience in dealing with the Vatican that in order to see the pope, he had to go through Father Leiber. Father Leiber told Muller that he could not meet directly with the pope because German spies lurking inside St. Peter's Square might see him entering the Holy Father's chambers. Whenever Muller wanted to discuss his anti-Hitler business he had to use Father Leiber as in intermediary. That was the rule that was demanded by Pius XII and it was followed to the letter. The pope insisted that he alone would have a channel between the British and the German plotters. He also made it clear to all involved in the plots that he, not the Catholic Church, was the one who was dealing with the conspirators.

He did not want the Church in any way implicated in what he was doing in order to clear the Church if anything went wrong and his role in the plots were uncovered. When speaking about this, Father Leiber said, "By the order of the pope, that he requested that, when discussing the authority to convene the peace talks, they [the military conspirators] should cite the pope and not the Vatican. Because he himself [Pius] had made a point of drawing a clear distinction between the pope who, in a certain sense, was entitled and obligated to do everything for peace, and the Vatican, which had a more political status."

The main participants in the Vatican intrigues, Muller, Father Leiber, and the pope himself, had code names which they used when dealing with each other. Muller went by the code name "Herr X," Father Leiber was "Gregor" because he taught at the Gregorian University, and Pius was known as "Chief." When Father Leiber was asked if the pope knew what his code name was, the diminutive priest said, "The Holy Father had only smiled, and had even seemed pleased. The code name 'Chief' showed the thought that the pope returned the trust the plotters placed in him."[19]

Through their sources, the German High Command knew about Father Leiber and Josef Muller and what they were up to vis-a-vis the Vatican connection. This was made public to those in Hitler's inner circle when a 27-page typewritten report on the July 20, 1944 attempt to kill Hitler written by SS General Ernst Kaltenbrunner was published. The report was based on interrogations by the SD of those who took part in the plot. The report regarding Muller and Father Leiber reads as follows:

> Canaris and Oster established a connection to the Pope
> with the help of the former Munich Lawyer Dr. Joseph
> Mueller, who was "built into" the Abwehr solely for this
> purpose.. Muller got, during the War, namely in the fall
> of 1939, into contact with the Jesuit Father Leiber, the

---

[19] Riebling, Mark, *Church of Spies*, Page 73-74.

personal secretary of the Pope. From Leiber he received a lot of information on the position of the Pope and the enemy powers. He discussed possibilities of a peace and learned by Leiber that the condition for a peace agreement with Germany would be a change of the regime.[20]

Whether Father Leiber knew that the Germans had their spies tracking him we do not know. What we do know is that they did nothing to stop him and even if they tried, it would have been a huge task on their part to physically infiltrate the gates of the Vatican and take any action against him. The history books haven't yet written the complete story of how Pope Pius XII conspired with Canaris, Beck, Oster and the other conspirators. Only now is the name of Father Robert Leiber being studied as part of the covert dealings in this huge conspiracy. The work of one, lone man, who was close to the pope, helped significantly in the covert dealings during that tumultuous time.

As for Josef Muller, he returned to Munich after the war and was still on the list as a U.S. intelligence asset, code named "Robot." While working secretly for the U.S., he cofounded the Bavarian wing of the Christian Democratic Party and was active in post-war German politics. Muller led the prosecution of Nazi war criminals who were not sentenced at the Nuremburg War Crimes trials.

One of the mysteries concerning Josef Muller was how he was spared at the last moment from execution at the Flossenburg Concentration Camp on April 8, 1945. This question was looked into by the London Station of the U.S. Strategic Services after the war ended. They wrote, "Everyone else taking part in the July 20 conspiracy was killed and Mueller, while admittedly having good connections, wasn't any more important or presumably better protected than Oster, Canaris, and various others..Was he just plain lucky or did he at one time or another talk?"

James Angleton and his staff took two months to review the material concerning Muller's miraculous escape from Flossenburg   and said that Muller's story was "well corroborated from outside checks."

The CIA got its final report on the Muller story on October 30,

[20] Hesemann, Michael, *High Treason: Pius XII, Stauffenberg and the Conspiracy against Hitler.*

1955 in the person of Hans Rattenhuber, who was captured by the Soviets and put in a prison camp. Rattenhuber said that he was the one who intervened in saving Muller's life. Rattenhuber was Hitler's bodyguard and a friend of Muller's.

Walter Huppenkothen, an SS officer, said that Muller was spared because of Muller's confession on February 9, 1934, while he was in Gestapo custody, that he "sought to have Himmler put up against the wall and shot." Joey Ox, as he was called, was indeed lucky.[21]

By 1942, reports were coming in regarding the murder of thousands of European Jews by Hitler's regime. In the Vatican, Pope Pius XII was getting his information on the slaughter of the Jews from various sources, including the British Ambassador to the Vatican, Francis D'Arcy Osborne, and the new American representative to the Vatican, Harold Tittman. On March 18, 1942, the Vatican began receiving information from its representatives in Bern, telling of the anti-Semitic measures then being taken in Slovakia, Croatia, Hungary, and unoccupied France. The pope did not mention anything related to these reports and Ambassadors Tittman and Osborne began sending letters to their respective governments regarding the Pope's lack of interest in the subject. News reports were also coming in to the Vatican saying that thousands of Jews were being forcibly taken out of their homes in Poland and taken away to certain death.

As 1942 progressed, the world's newsmedia, including the *New York Times, The Daily Telegraph* and the BBC, began reporting on the exodus of thousands upon thousands of Polish Jews to the concentration camps. *The Daily Telegraph* wrote in one edition, "More than 700,000 Polish Jews have been slaughtered by the Germans in the greatest massacres in the world's history." Another headline said, "More than 1,000,000 Jews killed in Europe." Ambassador Osborne gave these reports to the Pope so he would know what was going on in Europe."

Ambassador Osborne then wrote a long letter to the pope, describing the murder of the Polish Jews and asking that he

[21] Ibid, Page 249-50.

publically speak out against the atrocities. There was some disagreement among those in the know whether the pope did, in fact, get Osborne's letter. Osborne is emphatic that the pope did get his note and that he got no response from him.

Throughout 1942, reliable reports were coming in from France and Holland saying that thousands of Jews were being sent to the Auschwitz concentration camp. Church records show that the Nuncio of France apprised the Vatican of the deportation of French Jews and the passive role being played in their deportation by Marshal Petain (the ruler of Vichy France). An attendee of a meeting with Cardinal Emanuel Suhard in 1943 regarding matters between France and the Vatican said, "Pacelli [Pius] warmly praised the work of Petain and took a keen interest in government actions that are a sign of the fortunate renewal of religious life in France."

In an unprecedented step, the ambassadors from the United States, France, Poland, Great Britain, and Brazil, wrote to the pope in September 1943, appealing to the Pontiff to speak out publically against Hitler's Final Solution. Just why the pope refused to speak out at that time is still a matter of conjecture. Maybe he didn't want to attack the Germans because of his prior attachment to that nation when he was a young man, or because he wanted to keep the Vatican out of the firing line as to what was happening in Europe.

The United States now got into the business of making the pope more aware of the Final Solution, when, in September 1942, FDR sent his personal representative to Vatican City. The man the president sent was Myron Taylor. Taylor left New York on February 25, 1940, on board the *S.S. Rex*. Traveling with Myron Taylor was Sumner Wells, who was President Roosevelt's Secretary of State. Taylor was the former chief financial officer of United States Steel, and was also the director of the American Telephone and Telegraph Company, the First National Bank of New York, and the New York Central Railroad.

The president sent Wells to Europe to meet with heads of state such as Mussolini and Hitler. This was a year before the United States was involved in the war and the president wanted to see if he could try to end hostilities before the situation led to an all-out war in Europe. Wells and Taylor were met in Naples, Italy by an American bishop, James Hurley who was eager to see both of them. Hurley was one of the most influential Americans in Rome and had a good working relationship with Pius XII. As for Sumner Wells, he went on by train accompanied by Count Galezzo Ciano, Mussolini's minister of foreign affairs. As time went on, both Hurley and Taylor would come to trust each other completely when it came to dealing with the Vatican. The *New York Times* wrote of their new relationship saying, "One thing has already been made clear, as Taylor arrived in Rome, and that is the important role Msgr. Joseph Hurley is going to play in this new diplomatic development." They met on September 18, and Taylor asked if Hurley could plead with the pontiff to publically speak out against the Nazi atrocities. Monsignor Domenico Tardini, wrote of a meeting he had with Taylor, "Mr. Taylor talked of the opportunity and the necessity of a word from the Pope against huge atrocities by the Germans. He said that from all sides people are calling for such a word."

The records of another meeting with Myron Taylor said, "Mr. Taylor said that there was a general impression both in America and Europe—and he could not be wrong in reporting this impression— that it is necessary for the pope to again denounce the inhuman treatment of refugees, and above all, the Jews in the occupied countries."

Sumner Wells accompanied Myron Taylor to see the Papal Secretary of State, Cardinal Luigi Maglione, on February 26, 1940 in preparation for meeting with the pope. On March 18, the men had an audience with the pope where Taylor was introduced and his credentials were handed over. Taylor was in the Vatican when the Warsaw ghetto fell to the Germans and still the Pope remained silent.

As time went on, Taylor would consider Hurley his most important American contact in the Vatican and wrote to high church officials that "Monsignor Hurley be counted on for contact with the Vatican Executive Organization and for such assistance as he has been rendering." Vatican officials agreed to Taylor's terms and soon Hurley was sitting at the right hand of Taylor when all-important issues were discussed.

Ambassador Osborne wrote in his diary concerning the pope's failing to speak publically of Hitler's mass killings saying, "His

91

Holiness is clinging at all costs to what he considers to be a policy of neutrality, even in the face of the worst outrages against God and man, because he hopes to be able to play a part in restoring peace. He does not see this silence is highly damaging to the Holy See and is entirely destructive of any prospects of his being listened to." [22]

Taylor was also kept informed on the on-going plots to oust Hitler by the dissident German generals. He was oftentimes briefed in secret by one of the middlemen in the plot, Josef Muller. Like Father Leiber, envoy Taylor was now in the undisputable position of knowing the innermost machinations of what was going on behind the scenes in the Vatican and he sent whatever he learned back to the president of the United States.

At the highest levels of the German government, a decision was made to hold the Jews of Rome hostage while they made plans for their deportation. The officer in charge of this operation was SS Major Herbert Kappler, who worked in Himmler's department. Before any deportation could take place, orders were issued for the Jews to hand over all the gold in their possession. The Germans used the excuse that they needed to raise fifty kilograms of gold in order to purchase arms for the army. The start of the gold collection took place on September 27 at Rome's synagogue. By later that day, Romans of the Catholic faith and others began chipping in to add to the money that the Jews had to pay. For whatever reason, the pope decided to offer money as a loan in order to meet the Germans' demands. The priest of the Sacred Heart said of the loan from the pope, "It is obvious, we want it back." Writing of this incident in his book called *Hitler's Pope,* author John Cornwell says, "The rumor nevertheless made the rounds, and persists to this day, that Pius XII had made a generous gesture, offering to make good the bulk of the ransom from sacred vessels hastily melted down. In the end, not an ounce of Vatican gold was donated or loaned."

Once the gold ransom had been met, events were put in motion for the deportation of Rome's Jews. The man in charge of this mission was Adolf Eichmann, chief of the Gestapo Section IVB4. Eichmann ordered an SS officer called Theodor Dannecker to do the job. He sent a large number of the Waffen's SS Death Head soldiers to Rome to begin rounding up the Jews. The pope was

[22] Cornwell, John, *Hitler's Pope: The Secret History of Pius II*. Viking Publishers, New York, 1999, Page 291.

made aware of what was going on and he made contact with the German ambassador in Vatican City to stop the deportation. He was turned down. It must be said that prior to the roundup of Rome's Jews, certain high-ranking papal authorities tried desperately to stop the deportations but were rebuffed at all levels.

On October 17, over 1,000 of Rome's Jews were rounded up and put on trains bound for Austria. Of course, the conditions in the trains were horrid and some of the people died along the way. The pope was kept abreast of the train's travel to Austria but did little. It took five days for the death train to reach the Auschwitz concentration camp and as soon as the train arrived, the killings began. A total of 1,060 of the detainees were killed and 149 men and 47 women were used as slave labor.

As time went on, many of the remaining Jews of Rome were rounded up and taken to Italian concentration camps and later, to Auschwitz. However, a number of Jews were lucky enough to escape deportation (and certain death) and were given sanctuary in Vatican—protected "extraterritorial" religious institutions in Rome. The deportation of the Jews took place right in St. Peter's Square with the full knowledge of Pope Pius XII. The head of the Roman Catholic Church must have shared the desperation of the Jews as they were taken off, right in front of his window. But the fact that he did not do more to try to stop the deportations of Rome's Jews and others during the Holocaust is a black mark on his reputation.

Pope Pius' time as head of the Catholic Church came to an end on October 9, 1958, when the pope died in his chambers at Vatican City of "circulatory phenomenon." The pope's body lay in state for three days while thousands of Romans and others came to pay their last respects. After all the ceremonies were over, the body of the pope was buried under the grotto of the Vatican, near where the remains of St. Peter were buried.

In an ironic twist of fate, the same pope who asked Monsignor Ludwig Kass to excavate the tombs under St. Peter's to search for the bones of St. Peter, would now rest for all eternity next to the saint he greatly admired.

James Jesus Angleton.

Allen Dulles.

Lt. General Karl Wolff.

Pope John Paul I.

Pope John Paul II.

Chapter 3

Operation Paperclip, Spies, the Swiss & the Ratlines

In 1972, author Frederick Forsyth wrote a novel called *The Odessa File* (which was later turned into a movie in 1974 starring John Voigt and Maximilian Schell). The book was an international best seller which gave the reader an insight into the darker side of World War II, dealing with material that most readers did not know about.

The book was about a young German reporter by the name of Peter Miller who is investigating the death of a man named Salomon Tauber, a Holocaust survivor. Mr. Tauber is found dead in his apartment, and a police friend who is investigating the case gives Miller a diary belonging to the late gentleman. The dairy concerns a secret German organization called Odessa, or "The Organization of Former Members of the SS." Miller is on the trail of Eduard Roschmann, the "Butcher of Riga" where Tauber was a prisoner. Miller is rebuffed at all levels when he asks the police to help him find Roschmann, whom Tauber saw shortly before his death. Miller's probe leads him to the home of Simon Wiesenthal, a noted Nazi hunter. In his meeting with Wiesenthal, Miller learns that there is a secret Nazi underground network called Odessa whose job it is to help high-ranking Nazis escape war-ravaged Europe to South America and other places of safety.

Miller meets up with members of the Mossad, Israel's noted security service, who ask him to infiltrate the Odessa and report back to them. Miller is successful in investigating the Odessa and in the end, finds and kills Roschmann.

Mr. Forsyth's book and the movie were, of course, fiction. But did the Odessa really exist and what role did it play in the taking of high-ranking German generals and other Nazi leaders to South America at the end of the war?

The Odessa did exist, and it is a troubling, convoluted story that involved the Vatican, the OSS, the Swiss government and its ties to the Nazis, and a sophisticated ratline that ran from various countries in Europe, spiriting Nazi war criminals to South America. It is also a story of American complicity in helping various Nazi war criminals out of Europe to the United States, giving sanctuary to some of the most wanted concentration camp directors as well as Nazi rocket scientists, and giving some of them jobs in American industry, including the space agency and other important American firms (this operation was called "Operation Paperclip"). Another alliance that arose in the aftermath of the war was between the United States government and German General Reinhard Gehlen, the German army's intelligence chief for the Eastern Front during World War II. After the war ended, Gehlen established close ties with the United States and agreed to turn over all the intelligence files he'd amassed during the war in return for an intelligence alliance with the United States in its new, Cold War against the Soviet Union.

In February 2005, the National Security Archives, a private organization dedicated to revealing the secret side of American history as well as a repository for scholars to do their research, posted the U.S. government's relationship with General Gehlen in a work called, *Forging an Intelligence Partnership: CIA and the Origins of the BND, 1945-49*. This opus comprised a two-volume history that was compiled by CIA historian Kevin Ruffner. This historical report was declassified in 2002 as a result of the work of The Nazi War Crimes and Japanese Government Records Interagency Working Group (IWG), and contained 97 documents which give the reader and the historian a much better understanding of just how closely the OSS and the postwar CIA worked with General Gehlen during and after the war ended.

"The documentation unearthed by the IWG reveals extensive relationships between former Nazi war criminals and American intelligence organizations, including the CIA. For example, current records show that at least five associates of the notorious Nazi Adolf Eichmann worked for the CIA, 23 other Nazis were approached by the CIA for recruitment, and at least 100 officers within the Gehlen organization were former SD or Gestapo officers." This material will be fully reported on in this chapter.

By 1944 it was becoming obvious to the top-ranking generals in Hitler's army that the war against the Allies was a lost cause, and that they had better make arrangements to ensure their personal safety. Among the top cadre of military officers who decided to take matters into their own hands were Martin Bormann and Heinrich Himmler. Before the war was over, these generals established a secret escape route out of Germany that led to the safety of South America, where they hoped to set the seeds of the "Fourth Reich" that would continue the war at a later date. Bormann dubbed the group "Odessa," an acronym for the Operation of Veterans of the SS." One the most important members of the Odessa, and a man who would later play an important role in the CIA-German intelligence alliance, was the number one member of the German military intelligence establishment during the war, Reinhard Gehlen.

Reinhard Gehlen was born on April 3, 1902 in Erfurt, Germany and went to school in the city of Breslau. He entered the military in 1920 and was commissioned in 1923. He attended the War Academy and became a member of the General Staff Corps. When World War II broke out, Gehlen was a battery commander and was promoted to the rank of major. In 1942, he was promoted to command a group known as the *Fremde Heere Ost (Foreign Armies East),* which was the German equivalent to the American G-2 intelligence operations on the Eastern Front. His unit was responsible for tracking and analyzing the Soviet Army order of battle on the Eastern Front. At one point, Gehlen was rebuked by Hitler himself when, during a briefing on war operations, he said that he believed that the German army was facing defeat.

In 1941-42, a large number of disaffected German military officers made secret plans to assassinate Hitler as a way of ending the war. This was the same plot that Pope Pius XII was involved in, and was described in the previous chapter. While not an active member of the putsch against Hitler, Gehlen was secretly approached by a few of the conspirators, including Colonel Henning von Treschow, Col. Claus von Stauffenberg, and General Adolf Heusinger, among others. At their meetings, their plans to remove Hitler were discussed.

As noted above, in 1942 Gehlen was given one of the top jobs in the German military when he was approached to head the Foreign Armies East and promoted to colonel. One of his main tasks was the collection of intelligence for the entire Eastern Front. Among the fascist groups Gehlen controlled as head of FHO was Stepan Bandera's "B" Faction of the Organization of Ukrainian

Nationalists, and other nationalist cartels. Bandera and his deputy, Jaroslav Stetsko, had at one time worked for German intelligence in organizing operations in the East.

The plot to assassinate Hitler came to a head when, on July 20, 1944, a bomb went off in the room where Hitler and his top officers were meeting. The bomb was set by Colonel Claus von Stauffenberg, who mistakenly believed that the bomb had indeed killed Hitler. In reality, the explosion only wounded the Fuhrer, and all of the top conspirators, including Stauffenberg, were quickly rounded up and hung. Gehlen's trivial part in the conspiracy was covered up and he escaped any punishment as Hitler's revenge took down all those intimately involved in the plot.

In the last days of the war, Gehlen and a small group of his most trusted advisors began to hide their most precious commodity, their huge trove of vital intelligence files on Eastern Europe and the Soviet Union, and buried them in a secret location in Bavaria. Gehlen wanted to have a trump card when dealing with the United States at a later date. He knew that after the war was over, the U.S. would turn its attention not to a defeated Germany, but to a new and powerful communist Russia. Gehlen would now be in a position, by virtue of his files, to barter for his freedom with the United States in its new conflict with the Soviet Union.

According to newly-released files on Gehlen from the CIA:

> When the Hitler armies collapsed in 1945, Gehlen is said to have escaped westward with most of the secret files of his department. He allegedly kept in his control many of the top secret lists of German agents planted in the Soviet Union and the eastern neighbor states which subsequently became Soviet satellites. He supposedly had the key to the espionage network built by Canaris, Himmler, and Schellenberg. The Americans reportedly took him prisoner but not for long because American intelligence chiefs reportedly became very impressed by his ideas and his documentation which he was able to put at their disposal. They are said to have set him up in an office and permitted him to pick a small staff with good anti-Abwehr officers (General Canaris's intelligence service) most of whom

were equipped with good anti-Nazi records. Within a few weeks, Gehlen was providing excellent reports on Soviet military and political activities in the eastern zone and was subsequently permitted to expand his staff and his scope of activities. As he expanded, however, many Nazis, SS men and SD men crept into his organization where they enjoy full protection.

Today, Gehlen's espionage organization is said to have agents in all parts of the world. The Americans reportedly supply the funds which amounts to (blank) a year. The former General is said to be able to multiply this sum to many times its original value through clever business deals. It is believed that he has already succeeded in piling up a substantial reserve which would enable him to carry on independently should the Americans cease to support him.[1]

What promoted Gehlen's change of heart was his realization that the war was lost, and more importantly, his dismissal in April 1945 as head of Foreign Armies East.

By war's end, the Allies were openly looking for German officers with an intelligence background and Gehlen was clearly in their sights. After a while, Gehlen turned himself in to an American unit and after some time, he and his men and his precious cargo were sent to the 12th Army Group Interrogation Center near Wiesbaden in June 1945. He was kept in what was called "The General's House," due to the large number of German general officers who were incarcerated there. Gehlen surrendered his files to the control of American Army Captain John R. Boker Jr.

As Gehlen was being interrogated by U.S. Army officials there were many officers in the military chain of command in Germany who did not like the fact that "there existed in many American quarters a terrible opposition to gathering any information concerning the Soviet Union." Two top Army officers, Col. Russell Philip, the commander of the Interrogation Center, and Brig. General Edwin Sibert, G-2 for the 12th Army Group, agreed to use Gehlen and his files against the Russians.

In time, the top Army men in Washington decided it was

[1] No author. Forging an Intelligence Partnership: CIA & the Origins of the BND: A Documentary History. www.gwu.ed/nsarchiv.

necessary to bring Gehlen and his files back to the United States. Captain Boker objected to Gehlen's transfer but his reservations were ignored. Gehlen and his staff left Germany for the United States on August 21, 1945 for further interrogation. The Army brought Gehlen and his "Org" to a secret retreat at Fort Hunt, Virginia where the new U.S.-German intelligence network was born.

The official name of the group that took over responsibility for Gehlen and his men was the BOLERO Group. It was headed by Army Captain Eric Waldman, prior to his assignment back to Germany. They mostly concentrated on preparing reports based on German records, but they also had almost unlimited access to U.S. intelligence files.

While the Army had found a resource in Reinhard Gehlen, the OSS had little to do with him and his Org. The OSS did not trust Gehlen and let the Army take the lead in running him. One reason for the OSS's reluctance to use Gehlen is, by the time he was in the United States, the OSS was about to be disbanded. The OSS had a friend in the person of President Roosevelt but upon his death in April 1945, the new president, Harry Truman, decided it best to disband the OSS and filter its parts to the various military services.

The Treaty of Fort Hunt, as it was called, between Gehlen and the United States contained the following conditions: a clandestine German spy organization would be created specifically to spy on the Soviet Union and share that information with the United States; this new spy agency would not be under the control of the U.S., but would act independently of it; the U.S. would fund the new organization until a new, independent Germany would come into existence; at that point, Gehlen's agency would revert to the new government; should world conditions make the new government's interests divergent from those of the U.S., the new society would consider German interests first.

In July 1946, Gehlen was released from his official American captivity and, along with 350 former German intelligence agents of his choosing, returned to Germany where they began to spy on Communist officials and their front organizations in Eastern Europe. Gehlen's new Org set up headquarters in Munich, Germany and began staffing itself with a number of former SS officers from the old German army. The United States turned a blind eye to Gehlen's recruitment of these former Nazi thugs, willing to let its new partner pursue his own agenda. The United States military and government would also turn a blind eye when large numbers of former SS men and top military officers of the German military and civilian leadership were allowed to leave war-torn Germany after the war ended and wound up in the safety of South America or the Middle East. Among those who escaped with either American sanction or ineptitude were Martin Bormann, Klaus Barbie, Joseph Mengele, and Adolf Eichmann.

When doing research for this book, the author came across a spy net that involved Reinhard Gehlen during the war. The material, which I had never heard of before, concerns a large-scale double agent network that spanned many countries which was headed by Prince Anton Vasilevich Turkul, he of Czar nobility. His prime asset was a German Jew named Max Klatt, who also went by the name of Richard Kauder, whose was said to have a spy ring inside the top levels of the Soviet military that sold material to the Abwehr.

According to authors Mark Aarons and John Loftus in their book *Unholy Trinity: The Vatican, The Nazis, and Soviet Intelligence:*

> The Vatican's nemesis was a member of the Czar's nobility, Prince Anton Turkul, arguably the greatest professional spy of the twentieth century. During Turkul's extraordinary career he penetrated the Imperial Russian army, the French Deuxieme Bureau, the Japanese General Staff, Mussolini's headquarters, both British Secret Services (Cold War and MI-6), Ribbentrop's personal intelligence service, Admiral Canaris's Abwehr, Wehrmacht Intelligence on the Eastern Front, headed by General Reinhard Gehlen, the SS Security Service (SD), and passed Soviet disinformation to virtually every nation in both the Axis and Allied camps.[2]

If, as authors Aarons and Loftus say, Turkul was the greatest spy of the twentieth century, than why have so few people heard of him? The masters of deception in World War II were many, including Allen Dulles, William Donovan, Admiral Canaris, Richard Sorge, Kim Philby, William Stephenson, and departments like the British

---

[2] Aaron, Mark and Loftus, John, *Unholy Trinity: The Vatican, The Nazis, And Soviet Intelligence*, St. Martin's Press, New York, 1991, Page 151.

Double Cross System and the American OSS. So, were does Anton Turkul fit in this mix?

After the war ended, Anton Turkul worked for such intelligence agencies as the West German Intelligence Service (the Gehlen Org), NATO, the U.S. Army Counter Intelligence Corps (CIC), and the secret State Department's Office of Policy Coordination. Authors Loftus and Aarons point out correctly that Anton Turkul was not exposed during his lifetime (he died in 1959), leaving it for historians and others to discover that Turkul's loyalty lay with the Soviet Military Intelligence, the GRU.

No one is really sure when Turkul was born; some say 1892 in Odessa, while another source states that he was born years earlier in Bessarabia. He served the Czar of Russia while a young man and later joined the White Russian army and rose quickly in rank. U.S. intelligence knew about Turkul during this time and there were reports coming from U.S. officials that "it was alleged that while in this position (command of the White Division), shipments received by him of British arms were actually turned over to the Red Forces."

What the White Russians, who were fighting the Bolsheviks, did not know was that a large number of its top military officers, including Anton Turkul, were double agents whose loyalty lay with Lenin and Trotsky. After the Russian Civil War was over, Turkul and other like-minded generals were taken to Paris by unsuspecting Allied officials who did not know their true identities.

Once encased safely in Paris, Turkul joined a secret group called ROWS, whose job it was to create an "Inner Line," or "Combat Organization" whose job it was to restore the Czarist monarchy which died when the Romanoff family were killed during the Russian Revolution.

Turkul's boss in the ROWS was Claudius Voss, alias Alexandrov. Voss was one of the most important leaders in the Inner Line in the 1920s and in time, he was in charge of counterintelligence for Slovakia. Voss was later to pledge his allegiance to the Bolsheviks, led by Lenin, not the British who assumed he was one of theirs.

In time, the old ROWS went out of business and was replaced by another organization called NTS, or People's Labor Alliance. As NTS grew, so did Turkul's power and he eventually took control of the new group.

By the 1930s, Anton Turkul's NTS had begun to work with British intelligence which was headed by Stewart Menzies. MI-6 officers had a positive view of Turkul and his NTS, while the United States took a different view of him and his group. The U.S. believed that NTS was Fascist, anti-Semitic, and anti-democratic in its politics. The main goal of the NTS (like that of ROWS) was the overthrow of the Bolsheviks and the restoration of imperial Russia. The British took on the NTS because they were anti-Soviet and used some of them on sabotage missions behind the lines. While ostensibly working for the British, Turkul was secretly hired by the French Intelligence Service, the Deuxieme Bureau in Paris.

If nothing else, Turkul was a master of deception and he developed a string of agents in all sorts of organizations in Europe, no matter what side they were on. For example, he used both his French and British connections to infiltrate his men into pro-Russian groups of Serbs in Yugoslavia, anti-Russian Ukrainian separatists movements, among others.

As Turkul's network operating out of Paris grew, so did interest in him on the part of Admiral Canaris of the Abwehr who opened up a file on him in 1927. The authors of *Unholy Trinity* write, "As we shall see, there can be little doubt that Turkul was the go-between for joint Anglo-German co-operation against the Communists. During the 1930s, Menzies's representative to the émigré groups in Paris was Charles Howard Ellis, Dick or Dickie to his friends, of whom he had many among the Russian exile community." Over the years, there has been speculation that Charles "Dick" Ellis might have been a double agent working for the Russians and might have gone by the nickname "Elli." The case of Dick Ellis will be told later in this chapter, as it is one of the last mysteries of the Cold War era and is worth telling in this context.

Stewart Menzies was a versatile spy catcher and his experience in the war was vital for the Allies to win the espionage war against the Germans. One of Menzies's top priorities was the breaking of the German codes, and he took an active role in the development of the Government Code and Cipher School, which was located at Bletchley Park. It was from this location that the British (and later American) cryptographers worked to break the German Enigma code that proved instrumental in the winning of the war.

In July 1940, William Donovan, representing President Roosevelt, arrived in England for talks with members of the British intelligence community. For a number of months, the United States and England made a secret agreement to share each other's intelligence pie. Donovan came to London to learn to run a world-class intelligence operations. One of the first men Donovan met was with Steward Menzies, "C."

Menzies met Donovan at his office at 52 Broadway, right across from St. James Park. The British had hundreds of years of experience in the spy business, having founded their secret service under the reign of Queen Elizabeth I in the 16th century. Menzies' SIS carried out two distinct functions; the gathering of information and counterespionage operations outside of England.

Menzies took Donovan under his wing, imparting to him all of England's most valuable secrets, including the operations at Bletchley Park and the existence of ULTRA, the means by which the British broke and read most of the German military codes. Upon his return to Washington, Donovan reported to FDR on his successful trip. A few months later, Donovan was promoted to lead the United States' first national intelligence agency, the OSS, Office of Strategic Services.

Shortly after the United States entered the war, Stewart Menzies took unprecedented actions to share Britain's most important counterintelligence with the OSS. On the advice of William Stephenson, who served as the Passport Officer in the United States, Menzies allowed Donovan's representatives to see what became known as "ISOS" Intelligence Service, Oliver Starchey. Starchey was the head of the enemy intelligence communications branch at Bletchley Park.

In another effort to aid the Americans, Menzies, with Winston Churchill's approval, allowed certain hand-picked OSS officers from their X-2 branch to see the ISOS's summaries, most of them coming from Section V, the counterespionage branch of the British SIS. These messages were sent to New York, where they were studied and filed. Menzies also provided OSS access to its highly sensitive XX Committee, the branch that ran German double agents.

At the end of 1940, Stewart Menzies addressed his attention once more to establishing clandestine contacts with his opposite number in German intelligence, Admiral Canaris. Through his network of agents inside Germany and elsewhere, Menzies knew that Canaris, as well as a number of other highly placed military men, were looking for a way out of the war. Menzies had a hand in running the double cross system and one of the men he met was a flamboyant Yugoslav playboy named Dusan "Dukso" Popov. Popov was sent by Canaris to set up an espionage unit in England, but he change of heart and reported his situation to an MI6 officer in Belgrade. Popov offered to work for the British, and he was accepted into the fold.

According to the popular accounts, Menzies met with Popov in December 1940, at which time Menzies asked him if he could get information on Canaris, as well as his senior officers. Writing later of his conference with Menzies, Popov related what happened. Menzies told Popov, "You have the makings of a very good spy, except that you don't obey orders. You have to learn better or you will be a very dead spy."

Popov wrote, "Menzies was contemplating a dialogue with Canaris or those close to him with a view of ousting Hitler. All information you pick up is to come directly to me with no intermediary." (Remember that, as shown in the last chapter, Canaris was one of the leading members of the anti-Hitler German underground who sought to oust him with the help of the Vatican.)

In 1942, Canaris wanted to arrange a meeting with Menzies. He sent feelers to Menzies asking if Portugal would be a good spot for a rendezvous. Menzies asked permission of Britain's Foreign Secretary, Anthony Eden, but his request was shot down. Eden said that if Stalin ever found out that the British were covertly meeting with Canaris, this would further anger the Russian leader into thinking that the British were trying to arrange a separate peace with Germany at the expense of Russia.

The historical record is rife with tidbits of information leading up to a possible covert encounter between the two spy chiefs. Canaris was in Spain during the beginning of the war and "indicated a willingness to meet with us; he would even welcome a meeting with his opposite number, C—Menzies." One possible answer as to why Eden refused to allow Menzies to meet with Canaris is the fact that Kim Philby, a double agent working for the Russians and a top member of MI6, objected to any such get-together.

So, with Stewart Menzies' intelligence portfolio at the top of his game, it was not so unlikely that he would make an arrangement with Anton Turkul to play his game.

Charles "Dick" Ellis, who was the representative to the émigré groups working for Anton Turkul, was one of the most controversial members of British intelligence during the World War II and during the Cold War. He was part of one of the most significant intelligence stories coming out of the war that involved such intelligence luminaries such as William Stephenson, Kim Philby, and a man who was involved in one of the last unsolved case of the Cold War era, Igor Gouzenko. From the investigation of Igor Gouzenko would come the allegation that during the war, Charles Ellis was either a spy for the Germans or the Russians and that he might have been the mole in British intelligence, called "Elli."

Charles (Dick) Ellis was born on February 13, 1895 in Annandale, Sydney, Australia. He was a talented young man who worked for a time for a bookseller and later played music for the Royal Melbourne Philharmonic Society. He soon moved to England and as soon as World War I broke out, he tried to enlist in the army but was rejected for being too short. As conditions changed on the battlefield, he was accepted into the service and was promoted to corporal in the 100th Provisional Battalion in July 1915. During his military career, Ellis served in the Russian Civil War, India, and Turkestan.

After the war ended, Ellis took lessons in Russian at St. Edmund Hall, Oxford and in 1922-1923, he was a captain of the Territorial Army Reserve based in Constantinople, possibly doing some sort of intelligence work. On April 12, 1923, he married a Russian woman named Elizabeth Zelensky. The marriage did not last long (they had one son) and he then worked as the British vice-consul in Berlin. It is believed that while he was working in Turkey, Ellis was reporting to both the British Special Intelligence Service as well as MI6.

He used the cover of a reporter for the *Morning Post* while he was working for British intelligence and was posted to such places as Vienna, Australia, Geneva, and New Zealand. It was during the 1930s that Ellis came into contact with William Stephenson, "the Man Called Intrepid," who would oversee the British Security Coordination operation in New York City during the Second World

War and who would play such a pivotal role in British intelligence during the war years. It was at this particular time in his intelligence career that Ellis would make covert contact with Admiral Canaris and was probably on Canaris's payroll. Authors Loftus and Aarons say, "Even after Hitler came to power, he was a paid Nazi agent and later admitted selling the rosters of British intelligence agents."

When Bill Stephenson was posted to New York to head up the BSC, he took Charles Ellis with him as his assistant director. They had total discretion as to whom to hire for their clandestine work and some of the men they took on were later to become famous in the intelligence community and for other endeavors. Some of the men they hired were Ronald Dahl, H. Montgomery Hyde, Ian Fleming, Ivor Bruce, Noel Coward, and Gilbert Highet. While Stephenson ran the BSC in New York, in 1941 Ellis was transferred to Washington where he ran the BSC's office. Ellis was now in the crosshairs of the powerful director of the FBI, J. Edgar Hoover, who did not take lightly anyone (especially agents of a foreign power) interfering on his turf. While Hoover had little respect for William Donovan, he had a better relationship with Stephenson, albeit, on his own terms.

Hoover, for all intents and purposes, had Stephenson's BSC over a barrel and he knew how to play the political game like a pro. To be frank, Hoover, if he wanted to play hardball, had the BSC in a very tight noose. Stephenson's BSC was technically working illegally in the United States, in direct violation of the U.S. Neutrality Act. The Congress did not know of its existence and if Hoover felt he was the potential victim of British blackmail, all he had to do was to call a press conference and tell the world that British intelligence was working covertly in the United States.

The BSC-FBI relationship was so close, in fact, that Hoover suggested the cover name for Stephenson's organization. In the fall of 1940, the British SIS welcomed two of the Bureau's top agents to a strategy session in London where they were trained in covert activities. A top FBI officer traveled to South America where he met with the SIS chiefs in that region and discussed how the Bureau was going to operate south of the border. Cooperation went so far as to have certain BSC agents work with their FBI counterparts in the highly technical field of clandestinely opening up mail without the recipient knowing about it. Hoover also shared with the British some high-grade intelligence provided by him to the other U.S. intelligence services, namely the Army's G-2 and the Office of Naval Intelligence. Thus, Hoover was able to raise his stock with his counterparts, making him the man to see when it came to counterespionage and other intelligence sharing.

As the Hoover-Stephenson arrangement grew in scope, so did their covert activities. The range of their actions now included the guaranteeing by whatever means necessary of suppling aid in order for Britain to survive the Nazi onslaught, as well as to counter German espionage operations in the Western Hemisphere. The FBI was already ahead of the game as it was primarily responsible for intelligence gathering activities in South America.

In 1942, Ellis was sent to the Middle East where he worked with Richard Casey who was then based in Cairo. Ellis went back to the BSC in 1942 and ultimately returned to London in August 1944.

When the war ended, Ellis worked in the SIS's Singapore office in charge of Southeast Asia and the Far East. He held this job until he retired from the intelligence service in 1953. He later returned to Australia where he helped in the creation of the Australian Secret Service. He also did some work as a reporter for the journal *Hemisphere,* which covered Asian-Australian affairs.

As mentioned above, there were hints over the years of a possible Soviet-German mole somewhere inside of the British intelligence service. One of these suspected moles was Charles "Dick" Ellis and the hint came from a Soviet defector by the name of Igor Gouzenko. The Gouzenko accusations against Ellis would haunt the highest levels of British intelligence for years and the man who tried to clear Ellis's name was none other than William Stephenson.

The man at the center of the Ellis story was a Russian named Igor Gouzenko whose defection after World Wart II really started the Cold War and brought the espionage war between the United States and the Soviet Union out in the open. Igor Gouzenko was born in Russia and his father was associated with the Czarist forces, or the White Russians, who were fighting the Bolsheviks in the Russian Revolution. After his schooling was completed he joined the NKVD (later, the KGB) as a cipher and code clerk. During World War II, he was an intelligence officer and also saw action on the front lines. By now, he was promoted to lieutenant in the GRU, and in 1943, was sent to Ottawa, Canada where he served in the Russian Embassy and his primary job was to spy on his Canadian friends.

After a short time in Canada, Gouzenko grew tired of the Communist ideology that he was supposed to support and made a decision that would change the rest of his life and the upcoming Cold War that would start between the West and the East after the war ended.

He decided to contact Canadian authorities, but his first action was to make a connection with a Canadian newspaper which was based in Ottawa. He entered the bustling office with secret files that he'd taken from the embassy and showed the editors the material he had with him. After looking at the secret papers, the editors told him that they were not interested in what he had and sent him on his way. He then made contact with certain Canadian officials, showed them his papers, and was rebuffed once again.

In a stroke of luck, one of Gouzenko's neighbors in his building was a sergeant named Main of the Royal Canadian Air Force. Gouzenko knocked on his door, told him what he had done, and pleaded with him for help. Sgt. Main told Gouzenko that his family could spend the night with him and promised that he'd contact his superiors the next day. The local police were notified and they staked out Gouzenko's apartment. As the police were watching, men from the Russian Embassy broke into the Gouzenko home and ransacked the place, apparently looking for Gouzenko and his family. The Russians were detained by the police, showed them their diplomatic papers and were released.

Officials from the Russian Embassy told the Ottawa police that Gouzenko had stolen papers from the Embassy and wanted him arrested, calling him a "capital criminal."

By this time, Gouzenko had met with the RCMP, the Royal Canadian Mounted Police, who were responsible for actions against the country. He showed them the material he'd taken from the embassy and after reading the materials, the RCMP took a different attitude toward Gouzenko from their counterparts in government. After studying the papers that Gouzenko provided, they immediately knew that they had the genuine article on their watch and proceeded to deal with Gouzenko directly. "The papers were described as detailing the largest and most dangerous spy-plot known in the Dominion in peace or war."

By now, Gouzenko had defected to Canada and he and his family were put under protective custody. He told the Canadians that the Soviets had a mole inside their intelligence service. He also named numerous officials who were working for the Soviet Union, passing national secrets. Among them were Alger Hiss, Harry Dexter White (the second highest-level person in the U.S. Treasury Department), Lauchlin Currie (one of FDR's confidants), and the atomic espionage ring led by Julius Rosenberg.

William Stephenson, a Canadian by birth, was given access to the materials that Gouzenko had handed over and after quickly reviewing, them, said that in his opinion, they were the genuine article and asked the government to take Gouzenko seriously. After all, he had given the Canadians over 300 pages of information relating to spies right in the middle of the Canadian government, a fact that could not be disregarded. As Canadian intelligence began looking over the material that Gouzenko handed over, they dubbed the investigation the "Corby Case."

The man responsible for running the Corby Case was Slim Harvison, chief of the I-Branch intelligence department within the RCMP. When Harvison met with Gouzenko for the first time, the Russian told Harvison just how the Soviet spy ring was operating in Canada. He told him that the Russians had moles inside the Canadian Department of External Affairs and that the man who was running the operation was Colonel Zabotin, who was aided by Lt. Colonel Motinov, Major Sokolov, staff of the Commercial Counsellor in Ottawa and other lesser-known people who worked in the Soviet military.

Gouzenko was now taken to a secure facility by the government called Camp X, right on the U.S.-Canadian border. This was done more for security purposes than anything else, for the Canadian authorities did not want anyone who did not need to know about what Gouzenko was up to, to accidently trip up and spill the beans about what he was telling the government.

The story of Camp X was right out of a James Bond novel, with spies running amok, underwater training facilities, miniature submarines operating in a deep lake, parachutists infiltrating Europe, trainees learning silent kill techniques, and countless other lethal skills. While the historical record is correct in that some or all of these activities took place at Camp X, the reality is much different from what was reported.

Camp X was formed when it seemed the Nazis were about to conquer Europe. With Great Britain on the ropes, it was decided by the top members of British intelligence that a safe, yet highly secret training camp had to be established out of harm's way, with the facilities to train large numbers of men for future missions inside Europe. They wanted the place to be near the United States for its communications capabilities. They chose a desolate spot about an hour from Niagara Falls, New York, the town of Whitby.

British Security Coordination used the site to operate Special Training School No. 103. ST 103 trained Allied agents in the techniques of secret warfare for the Special Operations Executive, SOE, branch of the British Intelligence Service. Hydra was another operation, a network that communicated vital messages between Canada, the United States, and Britain.

Camp X was run under the direct supervision of Stephenson's BSC in New York. Charles Vining and Tommy Drew-Brook were direct emissaries of Bill Stephenson. Drew-Brook was the head of the Canadian British Security Coordination team, and Vining was the first head of the department.

One important section of Camp X was not physically on site. It was a secret group called "Station M," based in Toronto. The men of "Station M" forged papers and documents for use by the men who trained at Camp X, and went into Nazi occupied Europe.

As the camp began its deadly business, agents were sent there from all over the world. Men from the FBI came to learn new skills and reported back to J. Edgar Hoover, who kept an eye on things from his post in Washington. On numerous occasions, William Stephenson came to Camp X to see how his recruits were doing, and Bill Donovan, the head of the OSS, paid a visit to see how the American contingent were doing. Another visitor to Camp X was Ian Fleming. It was rumored that Fleming took part in various training courses, but his prowess left much to be desired.

Another Russian whom Gouzenko spilled the beans on was Vitalii Pavlov who was the NKVD resident (or top spy) who was operating out of the Russian Embassy in Ottawa. It was noted before that the Canadian police were waiting outside of Gouzenko's apartment after he contacted Sgt. Main, and one of the men they took into custody was Vitalii Pavlov who was caught ransacking the apartment.

The outcome of the Gouzenko defection did not play well for Vitalli Pavlov. The news of Gouzenko's defection sent Moscow into a tizzy of activity (most of it bad), and the Soviets now had to deal with the fallout of their number one code clerk defecting to the West. Under pressure from the Canadians, Pavlov and his colleagues left Canada by way of New York and took a boat back to Leningrad. Those who accompanied Pavlov were GRU Colonel Boris Sokolov, and A.N. Farafovtov, who took part in the raid on Gouzenko's apartment. During the later years of the Cold War, Pavlov worked for the KGB in their "illegals" department and was their main man in Poland.

Two years after Gouzenko's defection, his case was one of the top priorities in Western intelligence circles. The services of the United States and Britain had been studying the material that Gouzenko passed along and it was filled with bombshells. "They compiled a list of more than twenty probable spies, including Canadian civil servants and scientists, four possible Soviet agents in America (one of whom was thought to be Alger Hiss), and the British atomic scientist Dr. Alan Nunn May. Gouzenko also mentioned hearing of a spy in Britain code-named "Elli," but his description was considered too vague to follow up at the time."[3]

The RCMP began a detailed investigation of Gouzenko's revelations regarding the widespread Russian espionage ring in Canada, and in February 1946, the investigation was further expanded when the Canadian Royal Commission began to look into the matter. By July 1946, they had compiled a report that ran 733-pages and had accumulated more than six thousand pages of witness testimony and exhibits. The Commission published six hundred exhibits of information, of which thirty came from Gouzenko's testimony. One of the most interesting parts of the RCMP report was Gouzenko's reference to a mole inside British intelligence who went by the code name "Elli." The investigation

[3] Knight, Amy, *How The Cold War Began: The Igor Gouzenko Affair and the Hunt for Soviet Spies.*, Carroll & Graf, New York, 2005, Page 8.

sent the RCMP and British intelligence through the "looking glass" to see who might fit the bill.

The first mention of Elli came in November 1945 in the RCMP's report on Gouzenko. At that time, the charges alleged by Gouzenko about who Elli was went unnoticed and it would take twenty years before a large-scale British investigation on just who this person was would really get underway.

Gouzenko's tale about the secretive Elli was told to Roger Hollis, who would later be investigated as being Elli, and possibly a traitor inside British intelligence. According to a report on the case mounted by the British Security Coordination headed by William Stephenson, Gouzenko said that by 1942 or 1943, he had heard from his sources about a Soviet agent in England who worked for one of the British intelligence services. This person had some connection with Russia, either working for them, or being of Russian decent. This information was so explosive that even Russian Premier Joseph Stalin was made aware of the news.

Roger Hollis, whom Gouzenko called "A Gentlemen from England," came to visit Gouzenko and it is alleged that Hollis did not take Gouzenko's allegations seriously. It is not known just why Hollis didn't think Gouzenko's story credible and even went so far as to say that in his opinion, Elli did not really exist. However, Hollis relayed this information to MI5 and MI6 for further investigation.

In October 1945, Gouzenko had an interview with the RCMP in which he elaborated on his thoughts regarding Elli:

> Gouzenko said it was possible he or she is identical with the agent with a Russian background who Kulakoff [Kulakoff was Gouzenko's replacement] who had recently come from Moscow spoke of—there could be 2 agents concerned in this matter. Corby [Gouzenko] handled telegrams submitted by Elli. Elli could not give the name of the British agent in Moscow because of security reasons. Elli was already working as an agent when Corby took up his duties in Moscow in May 1942 and was still working when Kulakoff arrived in Canada in May 1945. Kulakoff said agent with Russian connection held a high position. Corby from decoding messages said Elli had access to

exclusive info.[4]

Gouzenko was right that there was indeed a Russian mole working inside British intelligence at that time. His name was Kim Philby. It is not known if both men knew each other but when Gouzenko defected, Philby was none too happy. Philby began to wonder if Gouzenko was referring to Philby as Elli but as events were to prove, that was not the case. First of all, Philby was not of Russian descent and he did not work for MI5 or MI6. He worked the NKVD, not the GRU where Gouzenko was employed.

The Gouzenko case was then handed over to Philby in his capacity as head of Section IX (Soviet Affairs). From the outset it would seem that if somehow Gouzenko knew that Philby was a double agent, then he could have caused him irreparable harm. But that did not happen and Philby could breathe a sigh of relief. Philby later said of his time with the Gouzenko case, "The first information about Gouzenko and Elli came from Stephenson. Menzies called me in and asked me my opinion about it. I said Gouzenko's defection was obviously very important and we treated it as such. But it was a disaster for the KGB and there was no way I could help."

It so happened that there was indeed one person who was arrested in the Canadian spy ring described by Gouzenko who went by the cover name of Elli. She was Kathleen Willsher, who had been working for the Soviet Union inside the British High Commissioner's Office in Ottawa. Miss Willsher was investigated by the Commission and she was eventually given a three-year prison sentence. Most historians who have delved into this case don't believe that Kathleen Willsher was the notorious Elli described by Gouzenko. This person had a high position inside British intelligence that did not fit Kathleen Willsher.

According to author Chapman Pincher, who wrote a book on British wartime intelligence and the Elli case called *Too Secret, Too Long,* Gouzenko had told the RCMP investigation that there were two Elli's, one being Kathleen Willsher and another person living in England. Pincher wrote about the Gouzenko-Hollis meeting described above and quoted Gouzenko as saying, "I was surprised that this man, who seemed almost afraid to talk with me, asked me very little when I told him that the G.R.U. had a spy inside MI5 in

[4] Ibid, Page 238-39.

England, known by the code name "Elli." He behaved as though he wanted to get away from me as quickly as possible." Chapman Pincher has doubts about the veracity of Roger Hollis in his relations with Gouzenko and writes that Hollis might have believed that Elli worked inside the British Double Cross Section that ran captured German agents who were caught in England. But who was Elli? The two most likely candidates are Dick Ellis and Roger Hollis.

Roger Hollis was a veteran member of the British intelligence establishment, during and after World War II. Roger Hollis was born on December 2, 1905; his father was George Arthur Hollis, the Bishop of Taunton. Hollis attended the Leeds Grammar School and later attended Worcester College. He later completed his schooling at Oxford University, one of the most prestigious schools in England.

After graduation, Hollis got a job at Barclay's Bank and later became a journalist for a Hong Kong newspaper called the *Shanghai Post*. After a stint as a journalist, Hollis got a job with the British American Tobacco Company and remained in China for the next eight years. While he was living in China, he met Agnes Smedley, an American left-wing journalist who was reported to be a Russian agent, promoting revolution around the world. One of the men who he met while in China was Richard Sorge, one of the most famous spies of the war.

While in China, Hollis came down with tuberculosis and had to leave the country. On the way back to England, he stopped in Switzerland and Russia and arrived home in 1936. On July 10, 1937, Hollis married Evelyn Swayne, the daughter of a lawyer from Glastonbury. He then applied for employment with the *Times of London* but his application was denied.

He then applied for work at MI5, Britain's domestic security service but was rejected. He applied for work with the Secret Service but again was turned down. At a chance meeting, Hollis met Jane Sissmore who was MI5's first woman officer. They became friends and in the end, Sissmore persuaded Hollis to join her at MI5 as her personal assistant.

Jane Sissmore's husband, John Archer, a Wing Commander, interviewed a Russian defector named Walter Krivitsky, a former NKVD officer who had defected to the United States. Walter Krivitsky had an important position in Russian intelligence, serving as the director of operations in Europe. He told his British interrogators that he received information via a White Russian family who was based in Paris. The source told him that there was possibly a high-ranking mole in British intelligence who had connections to the White Russian community. (Note: Charles Ellis gained family connections to the White Russian community when he married Elizabeth Zelensky.) Krivitsky told John Archer that the Soviets used sleeper agents in the West. "The idea was to up agents from the inside. This method had a great disadvantage in that results might not be obtained for a number of years, but it was regularly used by Soviet Intelligence Services abroad." Krivitsky mentioned that the Fourth Department was prepared in some instances to wait for ten or fifteen years for results. He also hinted that the mole was educated at Eton and Oxford (Hollis) and an idealist who worked for the Russians without payment.

The case of Walter Krivitsky is one of the most mysterious stories of the Cold War era. He was killed in Washington, D.C. in 1941 under mysterious circumstances. He was shot in the head with a soft-nosed bullet shortly after he had met with both FBI and SIS agents while he was still in London. He left a suicide note but authorities believed that it was a fake. Dick Ellis believed that Walter Krivitsky was murdered, possibly because of his anti-Stalin political leanings.

In 1953, Hollis was appointed Deputy Director General of MI5 and three years later, he replaced Director Sir Dick White as Director General. Despite his new position, many people in British intelligence still believed, rightly or wrongly, that Hollis was a secret Russian spy and had been so for many years.

Roger Hollis died in 1973, but that did not stop the British government from investigating whether he was a Soviet spy. In March, 1981, Prime Minister Margaret Thatcher reported to the British parliament on two investigations into the activities of Roger Hollis who had served as head of MI5 from 1956 to 1965. After reviewing the findings, Thatcher said there was no concrete proof that Hollis was a Russian spy. Historians are still mulling over the facts surrounding the Hollis case but many writers of the story believed that Hollis was not a spy, rather, someone who took his duties too lightly and passed over recommendations from higher ups to investigate matters such as the John Profumo-Christine Keeler sex case that turned out to be a huge political scandal for the British government. Christine Keeler, the woman at the heart of the Profumo scandal said that she believed that Roger Hollis, whom she had known from 1959 to 1963, was indeed a Russian spy.[5]

But, if Roger Hollis was not a spy, could Charles "Dick" Ellis, the man who was working for Anton Turkul's spy ring, be the real Elli?

Charles Ellis returned to England in 1954 after his stint in Australia, and as the decade of the 1960s emerged, was soon embroiled in the defection of Kim Philby, whom he had known during his time in British intelligence. Between 1953 and 1965, Ellis worked in MI-6 archives, taking out files that were deemed no longer relevant to the British government and espionage services. If indeed Ellis was "Elli," his position in destroying incriminating material that was held in the archives was his to own. No one would be the wiser if Ellis found material that might have compromised him to Philby or support the allegations that he might have been either a Russian or German spy. If he found such material, he only had to shred it.

In 1966, the British government set up what was called the FLUENCY Committee, which was a joint MI6-MI5 investigation of a possible Soviet mole inside the British SIS. One of its inquiries was whether or not Dick Ellis was a Russian mole and it concluded, "Ellis had been a paid agent of the Germans up to 1940, and that he might have served the Soviets from as early as 1920."

During the FLUENCY Committee's investigation, they called Ellis in for questioning and he told them quite a story. He said he did not spy for either the Germans or the Russians but did say that he helped the Germans in an important espionage operation in 1939 called The Venlo Incident where two British agents were arrested and lured into a trap by high-ranking German military officers posing as anti-Hitler agents who wanted to talk to Britain about a separate peace deal. He also said that he did not know Kim Philby (which was not true) and denied having any personal or business relations with him.

The FLUENCY Committee concluded that Ellis had been a

5 Trahair, Richard, *Encyclopedia of Cold War Espionage, Spies, And Secret Operations,* Greenwood Press, Westport, CT., 2004, Page 122.

"Soviet agent for about 30 years—GRU and later KGB—and that he had spied for Germany. A later investigation by the CIA suggested that there is circumstantial evidence for the FLUENCY committee's findings."[6]

We now return to Anton Turkul, whom Charles Ellis interviewed at the request of the British government. Turkul now expanded his NTS network to the Japanese. Declassified reports of the time say, "Anton Turkul is listed as an agent who worked for the Japanese in Russia, head of the Russian fascist party in Japan, speaks fluent Japanese." The files say that the Japanese paid Turkul via a bank account in New York right up until the Japanese attack on Pearl Harbor on December 7, 1941. Turkul later claimed that his NTS was backed by the Japanese General Staff who wanted Turkul to spy on the Soviets.

Once Turkul was safely ensconced in Japan, he met up with one of the most successful spies of World War II, Richard Sorge, who was a German journalist who had infiltrated the Japanese Army for the Soviet GRU.

Richard Sorge was one of the memorable spymasters to emerge from World War II. He worked for the Russian NKVD in both China and Japan and was instrumental in providing the Russians vital information on both Germany and Japan's wartime policies. Reports from Sorge enabled Stalin to shift front-line troops from the plains of Siberia to Moscow as a defense against a German invasion.

Sorge was taken on by the NKVD, the Soviet intelligence service, in 1920 and sent to Moscow for training. Over the next 10 years, Sorge would travel to the United States, Germany, England, and the Scandinavian countries under cover as a teacher or journalist to gather intelligence.

Working as a journalist for a German newspaper called the *Frankfurter Zeitung,* Sorge was sent to Shanghai, China with instructions to set up a large Russian spy network. Using the alias William Johnson, an American, Sorge established an espionage network across China. His main purpose was to secure information on the nationalist Chinese leader, Chaing Kai-shek, and a young communist newcomer named Mao Tse-tung.

One of Sorge's most trusted spies was a beautiful American woman named Agnes Smedley. Smedley worked as the American

[6] Ibid, Page 70-71.

correspondent for the same newspaper that Sorge worked for and the two soon became lovers. Another person recruited by Sorge was a Japanese newspaper writer named Hotsumi Ozaki, who worked for the *Ashi Shimbun*. Ozaki would later have an important position in the office of the Japanese premier. Ozaki would provide Sorge with an abundance of political intelligence concerning Japanese foreign policy.

After a brief trip to Germany, he received a German passport and arrived in Japan on September 6, 1933. Once in Japan, Sorge used the services of two GRU officers to aid him in his spying: Max Klausen, a German who would serve as his radio operator, and Branko de Voukelich, a Yugoslavian and intelligence expert. He also renewed his contact with Ozaki, who had returned to Japan from China.

From Yokohama, Sorge arrived in Tokyo and, using his new persona as an ardent Nazi (his father had German citizenship), cultivated the military attaché at the German Embassy, Eugene Ott. Soon, Sorge began beguiling Ott with his expertise on Japanese culture and history and, more importantly, gave him bits and pieces of information of interest to his country.

Sorge learned that the Germans were going to attack Russia and sent this information to Moscow, which decided not to take it seriously. Ozaki gave Sorge the vital information that Japan was about to attack the Dutch East Indies and French Indochina in later 1941. Stalin took this information in earnest, and, rethinking his earlier decision, ordered a Siberian army base transferred to the capital to defend the city during the German siege of Moscow. Sorge was also to learn from Ozaki that the Japanese were planning to send its fleet into the Pacific in the fall of 1941, coming close to the U.S. naval base in Hawaii.

The Japanese espionage service, Kempi Tai, got wind of transmissions coming from Tokyo but did not know who the senders were. The Kempi Tai sent its agents to trail Ozaki because of his communist reputation and was able, through him, to track Sorge as the man responsible for the transmissions to Moscow. Sorge, hiding his clandestine activities, used a sailboat to relay his messages, going from one port to another.

The beginning of the end of the Sorge spy ring came when

the Kempi Tai interrogated a Japanese communist named Yotoku Miyagi, who was associated with Sorge. Under intense questioning, Miyagi broke down and gave away Sorge's name and location. Ozaki was arrested on October 14, 1941.

On the night of October 16, 1941, after dining with German friends, Sorge was arrested as he entered his home. He was tried in a secret court, found guilty and spent three years undergoing intense questioning. He ultimately confessed to being a spy for the Russians, and when his usefulness to the Japanese ended, he was hanged on November 7, 1944. For his gallant actions, Richard Sorge was posthumously awarded the Hero of the Soviet Union medal in 1964.

It is no wonder that Anton Turkul would affiliate himself and his NTS network in Japan with a man like Richard Sorge. They were one and the same when it came to running a successful espionage network (except for the fact that Sorge was unmasked and died a horrible death).

In 1938, Turkul decided to give his Japanese espionage net to the Germans. The man he used as an intermediary was a German Jew, code named "Max Klatt," whose real name was Richard Kauder. Klatt said that he had a spy ring inside the highest reaches of the Soviet military that was willing to sell its information to Admiral Canaris's Abwehr. However, it seems that Max Klatt-Richard Kauder was not whom he seemed to be. The historian Ladislav Farago wrote of Klatt that:

> The inscrutable man (whose real name and true identity were never established) was the Secret Agent Extraordinary of the Abwehr against the Soviet Union. Who he was, how he looked, and what made him work for the Abwehr aside from purely mercenary considerations, I do not know... suddenly he blossomed out as a secret agent on a massive scale.

Klatt arrived in Vienna, Austria in August 1938 and was soon in meetings through a friend in German intelligence with Abwehr officials. He told the Abwehr a lot about the workings of the Soviet Air Force, and said that he had good connections with people in the Soviet legation in Sofia, Bulgaria, and that most of the information he received on the Soviets came via short wave radio. Farago writes more about Klatt:

> When the deal was done, the new master spy returned to Sofia to become the top secret agent—and virtually the only direct action spy—the Abwehr had working full-time in this important sector of the secret war. This phenomenal spy never disappointed his employers. And he never ceased to intrigue them. All over the years to disclose anything at all about Klatt personally, and about his sources, proved in vain.[7]

Loftus and Aarons write that Klatt-Turkul not only worked for Canaris and the Abwehr but also for Colonel Kurt Jahnke, chief of Ribbentropp's personal intelligence service. In one of Walter Schellenberg's writings about the war, he said, "Jahnke had developed excellent connections with Japan through unusual channels, involving a former Czarist officer and a German Jew." The "Czarist officer" was certainly Turkul and the "German Jew" was Klatt. The Klatt-Turkul Japanese connections was further bolstered when Walter Schellenberg said that one of Jahnke's contacts in Japan was Richard Sorge. "American intelligence files state that Sorge passed information to Berlin through Turkul's assistant, Klatt."

Klatt was so important to the German High Command that Walter Schellenberg protected him from the Gestapo who were probably looking for him; he was their most important informant on what was going on in Japan. Schellenberg referred to Klatt, "As the chief of a world-wide information network which went through various countries and penetrated every stratum of society. He furnished quick and exact reports from the senior staffs of the Russian Army."

Things were developing quickly on the military/political front and soon Turkul's spy ring, including Max Klatt, were transferred from the Abwehr on orders from Admiral Canaris to the group belonging to General Reinhard Gehlen. Turkul and Klatt would now be Gehlen's top spies on developments on Russian operations.

But historians have held different views regarding just who Klatt was working for during the war. Heizn Hohne, who wrote a

[7] Aaron and Loftus, *Unholy Trinity*, Page 159.

book called *Canaris,* wrote about Klatt:

> The most sensational information on the Red Army, however, came from a mysterious figure... a Jewish trader named Klatt, whose code-name was Max. His information was so accurate that the skeptics of FHO often wondered whether Max was not a double agent feeding fake Russian material back to the Germans. No one in FHO knew the truth, which was that via Isono Kiyosho, a journalist living in Sofia, Max had tapped the Japanese Secret Service, which was better informed than any other about the Soviet Union.[8]

Hohne was right about Max Klatt. While he was working for Gehlen, he was secretly giving the same information to the Kremlin who couldn't wait for his next batch of information to show up. The Germans weren't the only ones to be deceived by Klatt. It seems that the Klatt-Turkul organization were providing fake information to Benito Mussolini.

However, there were suggestions among some people in the American military establishment that Max Klatt was nothing but a con man who was neither a top-notch spy nor ran any significant espionage network.

After the war ended, the U.S. Army took over a site that was run by the Germans that had once been an interrogation center. The place was in the city of Oberursel, about twenty kilometers outside of Frankfurt-am-Main and was known as the 7707, the European Command Intelligence Center, also called Camp King. During the war, the site was used by the Germans as an interrogation center for captured American and RAF fliers. When the U.S. Army took over, it was manned by graduates of the Military Intelligence Center from Camp Ritchie, Maryland. These men interrogated captured enemy soldiers and most of them spoke several languages.

One of the members of the Military Intelligence Center was a soldier named Arnold Silver who arrived at Camp King in September 1945. Years later, he wrote about his interrogation of Max Klatt while he was stationed there and the story he told was nothing like the one that has previously been written.

In the spring of 1946, the Army's CIC in Salzburg, Austria

[8] Ibid, Page 169.

stopped a kidnap attempt by the Soviets on Richard Kauder, alias Max Klatt. Also in attendance at Camp King were General Anton Turkul and another Russian named Ira Longin, alias Lang. It was Arnold Silver's job to interrogate all three men and he came away less impressed by the men as time went on. In an article he wrote about the Klatt-Turkul case, he penned, "To put the basic fact concisely, his entire network for the Abwehr was a Soviet-controlled military deception operation from beginning to end."

Silver was part of the SSU (Strategic Services Unit), the successor to the OSS in Frankfurt, when he received his orders from his superiors to investigate Klatt and Turkul. He said of Anton Turkul, "Turkul was in fact a useless oaf who had lent his name to the Klatt network as the man who allegedly recruited sources in the USSR. He never recruited even one source, although Klatt managed to convince the Abwehr that Turkul was one of his principal agents." [9]

Klatt arrived in Oberursel along with his Hungarian mistress and they were put up in a nice residence with all the amenities available to them. Klatt arrived at the SSU camp and basically sold his story to the SSU unit in Salzburg with the ulterior motive of working for the Americans.

One of Silver's informants on Klatt and Turkul was a Colonel Wagner, aka "Delius," a former Abwehr officer who was in charge of the office in Sofia, who had been arrested by the French intelligence service for a time.

After hours of interrogation by Silver, a mysterious pattern of behavior on Klatt's part made Silver believe that the information that Klatt had been giving the American was nothing but nonsense. His conclusions on Klatt are as follows: "The entire Klatt operation had been Soviet controlled. Klatt himself had not been under direct Soviet control but had suspected that his operation was, he had not dared breathe a word of his suspicion to anybody for fear that the Abwehr would withdraw its protection of him vis-a-vis the Gestapo, he intended to resist admitting his suspicion to me for fear that this would negate his chances of employment by U.S. intelligence, a prospect held out to him in 1945-46 by SSU in Salzburg."[10]

---

9 Silver, Arnold, "Questions, Questions, Questions: Memories of Oberusrel," *Intelligence and National Security*, Vol. 8, No. 2, April 1993.
[10] Ibid.

So, was the Turkul-Klatt connection one of the most important espionage networks of World War II, or did they play a con game on the various warring nations? The verdict is still out.

One of the lingering mysteries of World War II espionage was the identity of a spy whose code name was "Werther," who supplied the Soviet Lucy ring in Switzerland with German military plans. The authors of *Unholy Trinity* postulate that Anton Turkul was "Werther."

One of the best-kept secrets in the intelligence world during the war was the "Lucy Ring," run by a group of anti-Nazis who were working for the Soviet Union in Switzerland. The man who ran the Lucy Ring was Rudolf Roessler. One of Roessler's best agents was a man who went by the code name "Werther." Werther was Roessler's key agent who operated from his position inside the OKW, the supreme headquarters from which Hitler and his two generals, Wilhelm Keitel and Alfred Jodl, planned strategy. It was Werther who supplied Lucy with crucial battlefield intelligence during the war, keeping Stalin's troops one step ahead of the rapidly advancing German armies.

Throughout the war, the identity of Werther was kept secret; Roessler did not reveal the name of his agents to Moscow. Now, decades later, the identity of Werther may finally be known. But was it Anton Turkul or someone else?

Werther worked in the OKW's headquarters located at Zossen in southeastern Berlin. Werther was privy to German military tactics and the locations of its Panzer Corps, as well as the dispositions of ground troops. The information supplied to Moscow allowed Stalin to counter the German thrusts, effectively giving valuable time for Russian forces to regroup.

Werther sent his information to his contact, Rachel Dubendorfer, then on to Lucy, who directed the news via another man known as "Taylor." While most of the material sent to Moscow was high-grade intelligence, Stalin did not trust Lucy and failed to comprehend the information being sent to him. If Stalin had any reason not to trust Lucy, it stemmed from one disastrous cable from Werther which ended in the German advance on Stalingrad, costing almost 100,000 Russian casualties.

If Werther was deadly wrong about the Stalingrad incident, he had made up for it concerning the German invasion of Russia called Operation Barbarossa. From his position at OKW HQ, Werther sent a cable to Lucy stating that 100 German infantry divisions were poised along the German-Russian border. He offered information that the Germans were going to break their non-aggression pact with Russia and launch an invasion on June 22, 1941. Moscow Center did not believe Werther's warning, calling it an "Abwehr trap." When Hitler's blitzkrieg stormed into Russia, Stalin could only wish he had listened beforehand.

So then, who was Werther? Was he Anton Turkul as postulated by the authors of *Unholy Trinity,* or was he someone else? The author of a book titled *Hitler's Traitor: Martin Bormann and the Third Reich,* written by Pulitzer Prize winner Louis Kilzer, offers an answer. According to Kilzer's research, Werther was in fact Hitler's right-hand man, Martin Bormann!

Why Bormann? Kilzer writes that Bormann worked in the German High Command from 1941 to 1944. He was cognizant of the debate going on behind the scenes in the OKW, especially as it related to troop movements and the policy behind such actions. A code clerk would not have such access, writes Kilzer. He eliminates the other potential candidates for Werther, such as Hans Bernd Gisevius, Carl Goerdeler, and General Boelitz, all of whom were part of the Lucy Ring. These men did not have Bormann's entrée to the OKW center.

Unknown to Hitler, Bormann had been receiving the minutes of all staff meetings from the stenographers who transcribed notes. Bormann fit the bill as Werther for obvious reasons. No one would ever suspect him. He was Hitler's confidant, only after Speer, Goebbels, and Himmler. After the war, Albert Speer told the Americans that he had met with Herman Goering to plan ways of keeping Bormann from becoming Hitler's number-one gatekeeper, excluding anyone else.

As far as Bormann's motive, Kilzer writes that he was a socialist at heart, had great respect for Stalin, and fumed when Hitler made a speech decrying state socialism. He knew about the Lucy Ring, made covert contact with them, and became Werther.

127

One of the most controversial aspects of World War II was a secret operation by the United States called Operation Paperclip which took shape after the fighting stopped in the spring of 1945. The purpose of Operation Paperclip was to bring Nazi war criminals to the United States, providing them a safe haven where they could continue their research into all different fields, especially those of rocketry and other highly advanced areas of science. A secondary purpose of Operation Paperclip was to prevent these German scientists from falling into the hands of the Russians who were eager to get whatever information they had that would advance their scientific and technological programs. It involved the clandestine delivery of Nazi and Austrian scientists, many of them accused of war crimes, with the full knowledge and cooperation of the United States into this country in order to work on our rocket and missile systems. If this action was not bad enough, the military knowingly altered the files of many of these scientists to expunge their participation in atrocities on concentration camp inmates.

In the immediate days after the end of the war in Europe, U.S. and Russian troops began a systematic hunt for all manner of pillaged loot that had been stolen by the Nazis from their concentration camp victims. They were also looking for information on German progress on rockets and any weapons that they could get their hands on. But their most important finds were the large number of German scientists who had been caught up in the aftermath of the war and were now stateless persons. U.S. military intelligence knew the importance of gaining access to these scientists before they could be plucked off by pursuing Russians and taken to labor camps in Siberia where they would never be heard from again.

U.S. authorities combed the POW camps in Europe and, little by little, rounded up the cream of the crop of German scientists and secretly brought them back to the United States. Once safely inside the U.S., these former Nazi scientists were put to work developing the next generation of rockets and missiles that the U.S. would use against the Russians in the new Cold War. There was only one major problem with this secret deal: many of these same German scientists were formally accused of crimes against the Jews and other inmates of the concentration camps of Europe. The reputations of these people were well known inside the OSS and the infant CIA. However, it was deemed more important to the national security of the country to ignore these wartime atrocities in the new fight against Russian Communism. Many of these scientists had worked on German V-1 and V-2 rockets that were used in attacking such cities as London, , causing large civilian casualties. Many of these German scientists were brought into the United States without the consent of the U.S. State Department which was not told of the disgraceful backgrounds of some of these people. About 500 of these people were relocated to the U.S. and sent to such places as the White Sands Proving Grounds in New Mexico, Fort Bliss, Texas, and Huntsville, Alabama to work on guided missile and ballistic missile development. The long term aftermath of this secret project was the creation of NASA, which led the way to U.S. manned space flight and the landing of an American on the moon in 1969.

Even before the advent of Operation Paperclip, the Roosevelt administration knew of scientific work that these men were doing for Hitler and their possible use after the war for the United States. Shortly before his death, FDR had turned down OSS Chief William Donovan's request that that some of these German scientists be allowed to come to the U.S., including "permission for entry into the United States after the war, the placing of their earnings on deposit in an American bank and the like." FDR flatly turned down Donovan's request, by saying:

> I do not believe that we should offer any guarantees of protection in the post-hostilities period to Germans who are working for your organization. I think that the carrying out of any such guarantees would be difficult and probably be misunderstood both in this country and abroad. We may expect that the number of Germans who are anxious to save their skins and property will rapidly increase. Among them may be some who should be properly be tried for war crimes or at least arrested for active participation in Nazi activities. Even with the necessary controls you mentioned I am not prepared to authorize the giving of guarantees.

FDR was adamant in his statement that we should have no

business with any Nazi scientists who were associated in any way with death camp atrocities, but he did not live long enough to put those orders into practice.

The American team that began looking for German scientists who had any knowledge of fledgling atomic progress was called "Alsos." These agents combed Europe looking for any German scientists who had worked on the atomic bomb project. The leader of the Alsos team was Colonel Boris Pash. Aiding Pash was a scientist named Samuel Goudsmit. When they arrived in Strasbourg, France, after pouring over captured German atomic bomb records, they realized that the United States was at least two years ahead of their German counterparts. There were only two German scientists, Carl von Weizsacker and Werner Heisenberg, who had any real knowledge of the German atomic bomb project. The OSS tasked Moe Berg, a former major league baseball player turned spy, to find out if Heisenberg knew enough to successfully build an atomic bomb for Germany. If so, Berg was to kill Heisenberg. Berg decided that Heisenberg did not have that kind of knowledge and did not have to eliminate him.

The Alsos team also investigated German scientists who were involved in biological and chemical warfare experiments, often carried out on innocent inmates of the Nazi concentration camps.

Project Paperclip officially opened shop in September 1946 on the instructions of President Truman to develop "a program to bring selected German scientists to work on America's behalf during the Cold War." The President's order had one important caveat, which excluded anyone found "to have been a member of the Nazi party and more than a nominal participation in its activities, or an active supporter of Nazism or militarism."

If anyone at the top levels of the CIA read the President's directive, they did not heed his orders. Instead, they deliberately flouted his instructions and proceeded to bring into this country the butchers from such concentration camps such as Auschwitz, Dachau, Mittelwerk-Dora and other places.

One of the first Nazi scientists to come to the United States was Herbert Wagner, who arrived by military plane on May 19, 1945. He had been the chief missile designer for the Henschel Aircraft Company, and was the designer of the German HS-293, the first

German guided missile used in combat in World War II. Wagner was smuggled into the United States by a covert U.S. Navy team who hid him from the prying eyes of the general public. Wagner was a member of the brown-shirted troopers, as well as four other Nazi organizations.

During that same month, members of the U.S. Army, Navy, and Army Air Force scoured Europe looking for German scientists. At an I.G. Farben plant near the town of Gendorf, Allied soldiers hit the jackpot, finding a slew of major German scientists, including Walter Rappe, an I.G. Farben director and pharmaceutical researcher, and Otto Ambros, also an I.G. Farben chemist. Ambros, it would later be ascertained, oversaw slave labor in the Auschwitz camp. In 1951, John J. McCloy, the High Commissioner of Germany, ordered the release of Ambros, even though he was a convicted Nazi war criminal. He was later hired by companies such as J. Peter Grace and Dow Chemical Company as a consultant in the United States.

The job of investigating the backgrounds of these German scientists was given to the Joint Intelligence Objectives Agency (JIOA) under the direction of Bosquet Wev. Beginning in 1947, Wev handed over to the State Department the first background dossiers on the original Nazi scientists he wanted to bring to the United States. When the noted writer Drew Pearson penned an unfavorable article regarding some of these men, Wev rejected their past as "a picayune detail," and said that discussing their work for the Nazis was "simply beating a dead horse." He further remarked that if these men had remained in Germany they would "present a far greater security threat to this country than any former Nazi affiliation they may have had or even any Nazi sympathies which they still might have." Unknown too many people at JOIA, its Deputy Director would turn out to be a traitor to the United States.

In 1959, William Whalen was promoted to the rank of Lt. Colonel in the Army and was given the job of deputy to the director of the JOIA, which made him privy to the most sensitive materials coming out of Operation Paperclip. He had an office in the E Ring of the Pentagon and he had ready access to the top military officers in the building. In his one year as deputy head of the JOIA, Whalen was passing classified information to the Russians via his Soviet contact, Colonel Sergei Edemski, a GRU officer who was posing as a military attaché in the Soviet Embassy in Washington.

The FBI began its investigation of William Whalen in 1963 after they got news that Whalen was passing information to the Russians. The FBI learned that Whalen had destroyed or given away thousands of pages of information to the Russians on various topics relevant to American national security.

While he was working as a spy for the Russians, a government fitness report on Whalen was conducted. It was said of this investigation, "Although the investigation reported that he occasionally drank to excess and that between 1952 and 1959 he had recurrent financial problems, it did not uncover evidence that he was a spy."

In February 1960, Colonel Edemski was transferred to London and was replaced by Mikhail Shumaev. Whalen continued to meet with his new handler, giving as much information as he could. In return, Shumaev paid him $3,000.

The FBI unmasked Whalen's activities when they conducted an investigation of Colonel Stig Wennerstrom, a Swedish Defense Ministry official who was convicted of espionage in 1964 for giving away material concerning the Swedish air defense system. FBI agent Donald Gruentzel interviewed Whalen while doing his research in 1963. Not liking what he heard from Whalen, the FBI agent following Whalen's activities, subpoenaed his bank records and found that he had accumulated a huge amount of cash from undisclosed sources. Under questing at FBI headquarters, Whalen finally confessed to being a Russian mole. On July 12, 1966 a federal grand jury indicted Whalen on charges that he acted as an agent of the USSR. Although the national press got wind of the Whalen case, his participation in Operation Paperclip was never mentioned. On December 17, 1966, Whalen was sentenced to fifteen years in jail.

When the CIA was created via the National Security Act of 1947, they immediately took an interest in Operation Paperclip, especially as it involved the various German scientists who were still being held in American detention facilities in Europe. By 1948, half of the one thousand German scientists who were allowed to come to the U.S. had arrived. The rest were still in Germany awaiting visas which would give them legal entry into the country. The problem was that the five hundred who were already in the States did not have visas and technically, were here illegally. This problem was taken care of when on May 11, 1948, military intelligence chief General Stephen Chamberlain met with FBI Director J. Edgar Hoover to see if he could help expedite the visa process. Whatever Hoover did worked, and as time went along, seven scientists had legal entry visas.

The procedure to get Nazi scientists into the United States took a lot of ingenuity. Accompanied by U.S. soldiers, these men were taken to Mexico and had the proper documents given to them by the State Department. The writing on the papers said that the holder "was a person whose admission is highly desirable in the national interest." Once the border guard saw this paper, the men were allowed into the country. The same procedure took place at the northern border same men were allowed entry via Niagara Falls, New York.

The main facility in Europe that the CIA and the JIOA used to vet the Nazi scientists was Camp King, the same place where Max Klatt and Anton Turkul were kept. Camp King got its name from Colonel Charles King, who was an intelligence officer who was raised to take the surrender of a number of Nazis on Utah Beach during the Normandy invasion of France on June 6, 1944. Unfortunately for Col. King, he was double crossed by the enemy and was subsequently killed.

Camp King was one of the most secure and important intelligence gathering facilities that the Americans ran in the postwar period. In her book *Operation Paperclip: The Secret Intelligence Program that Brought Nazi Scientists to America,* author Annie Jacobsen writes, "The interrogation facility had become one of the most clandestine U.S. intelligence centers in Western Europe, and for more than a decade it would function as a Cold War black site long before black sites were known as such. Camp King was a joint interrogation center and the intelligence agencies that shared access to prisoners here included Army Intelligence, Air Force intelligence, Naval Intelligence, and the CIA. By 1948, most of its prisoners were Soviet bloc spies."

One of the interrogation programs carried out at Camp King involved the so-called behavior modification techniques that were used on unwitting prisoners. This program was called Operation Bluebird and Artichoke. Other techniques that were utilized

133

there were harsh interrogation sessions, hypnosis, electric shock treatments, and the use of drugs.

The American officer who was in charge of Camp King was Colonel William Philip, and he shared the facility with William Donovan, the wartime director of the OSS. Part of Donovan's work at Camp King was to have captured German officers write reports on such topics as the German order of battle and the Nazi High Command. Donovan had a room at Camp King until the OSS was disbanded in September 1945.

Camp King, before it closed, held Soviet defectors and a number of Russian spies. Col. Philip used the Nazi officers who were kept at Camp King to write reports on these men and their product soon became voluminous. As time went on, Colonel Philip worked closely with some of these German officers, moving some of them off-site to a location called Haus Blue, "where they oversaw counterintelligence against the Soviets under the code name Project Keystone." Soon, some of these same Nazis were put on the U.S. government payroll.[11]

A milestone in the history of Camp King and Paperclip came in the summer of 1946, when none other than Reinhard Gehlen arrived. As mentioned before, General Gehlen had been in the United States for interrogation since 1945, but now the government decided it was time for him to depart and Camp King was the logical place for him to take up residence. The Army now decided to make Gehlen the head of its entire anti-communist intelligence organization, called Operation Rusty. As time went on, Gehlen would use the services of many German intelligence officers, some of whom were, at best, of questionable character.

Over time, the Army transferred the ever growing list of Nazi intelligence officers to a new facility in the village of Pullach, on the estate once owned by Martin Bormann. The Gehlen organization now had available almost 600 intelligence officers, most of them former Nazis, in the Soviet Zone of occupied Germany.

Recently declassified documents on the Gehlen-U.S. connection said in part, "The Gehlen organization was a murderous bunch, free-wheeling, and out of control. As one CIA affiliate observed,

---

[11] Jacobsen, Annie, *Operation Paperclip: The Secret Intelligence Program that Brought Nazi Scientists to America,* Little Brown & Co., New York, 2014, Page 319.

American intelligence is a rich blind man using the Abwehr as a seeing-eye dog. The only trouble is—the leash is much too long."

Since the end of World War II, many of the CIA's records on its relationship with the Gehlen Org were still wrapped up in secrecy, with the American public not knowing the full extent of what transpired during that time. However, in February 2005, the National Security Archive, a repository of research that concerns various topics of history and is open to researchers, published on the Internet a declassified report on the relationship between the Gehlen Org and the CIA.

The title of the report was *Forging an Intelligence Partnership: CIA and the Origins of the BND, 1945-49.* The report consisted of a two-volume set called Secret Reiger which was compiled by CIA historian Kevin Ruffner and was presented to the German intelligence service, the BND, by CIA Deputy Director for Operations Jack Downing.

Despite the release of this important material, several of those who worked on the report publically criticized some of their findings regarding the relationship between the CIA and the Gehlen Org. Congresswoman Elizabeth Holtzman said, "I think that the CIA had defied the law, and in so doing has also trivialized the Holocaust and also all the Americans who gave their lives in the effort to defeat the Nazis in World War II."

Another member of the panel, Richard Ben-Veniste said, "I can only say that the posture the CIA has taken differs from all the other agencies that have been involved, and that's not a position we can accept."

According to documents from the report, there was a long-term relationship between former Nazi criminals and American intelligence organizations, including the CIA. Some of the declassified records show "that at least five associates of the notorious Nazi Adolf Eichmann worked for the CIA, 23 other Nazis were approached by the CIA for recruitment, and at least 100 officers within the Gehlen organization were former SD or Gestapo officers."

A number of scholars were tasked to work on the narrative and they released their own interpretation of the report called U.S. *Intelligence and the Nazis.* The introduction to their study reads as follows:

> The notion that the CIA, Army Counterintelligence Corp, Gehlen employed only a few bad apples will not stand up to the new documentation. Some American intelligence officers could not or did not want to see how many German intelligence officers, SS officers, police, or non-German collaborators with the Nazis were compromised or incriminated by their past service. Hindsight allows us to see that American use of actual or alleged war criminals was a blunder in several respects.. there was no compelling reason to begin the postwar era with the assistance of some of those associated with the worst crimes of the war.

Presidential historian Timothy Naftali who was a consultant to the project said of this time period, "Reinhard Gehlen was able to use U.S. funds to create a large intelligence bureaucracy that not only undermined the Western critique of the Soviet Union by protecting and promoting war criminals but also was arguably the least effective and secure in the North Atlantic Treaty Organization. As many in the U.S. intelligence in the late 1940s had feared would happen, the Gehlen Organization proved to be the back door by which the Soviets penetrated the Western alliance."

The early contact between the Gehlen Org and the U.S. Army was called the German Documents Center Project. The German contingent consisted of many top-level officers and about 400 German POW's. The intelligence nucleus consisted chiefly of officers who had been taken from a German armored train, captured in late May 1945, which had belonged to the German General Staff and which had ended the war in Austria. Members of this train had been taken to a POW camp near Bad Telz, where they were kept for several months, and they were later sent to Oberursel after U.S. Army representatives from Oberursel had visited Bad Telz to look them over.

In October 1945, many of the Germans at the Oberursel location were transferred back to the United States where some of these German officers wrote a history of the German Army experiences on the Eastern Front. Also sent to the United States were many documents that were in the possession of General Gehlen.

In April 1946, an American Army officer named Lt. Colonel Gerald Dunn, who had early contacts with the Gehlen group in Germany, went back to Germany with many of the Germans who had originally came to the United States after the war ended. These German military officers were beginning to become a political hot potato for the Army and in June 1946, the State Department said that all Germans who were then in the country were to be returned to Germany. Some in the U.S. intelligence establishment took exception to the order but were overruled. The fued between the U.S. and the Gehlen Org was finally put to an end when, on July 1, 1949, the Germans and the CIA agreed that the CIA would officially take control of the Gehlen Org.

Operation Paperclip included a so-called "Rogues Gallery" of Nazis who came to the United States under questionable circumstances to work alongside the American military in various scientific endeavors. Among them were:

Kurt Blome. Blome's crimes against humanity took the form of performing medical experiments on concentration camp victims using plague vaccines. He also performed euthanasia and other unnamed tests on camp prisoners. He used sarin nerve gas on prisoners at Auschwitz. Blome was arrested by the U.S. Army Military Intelligence Service at Darmstadt, where he had been working for the army as a doctor. He was now officially off the Paperclip list, and instead, was placed on a list of defendants who would face prosecution at the so-called "Doctor's Trial" at Nuremberg. In an act of audacity on the part of the American Army, Blome worked as the post doctor at Camp King. While at Camp King, Blome worked on "Army 1952, Project 1975,"a top-secret project which was never declassified.

Blome was an ardent Nazi and in his capacity as the deputy surgeon general of the Reich, he admitted to killing thousands of Jews in the concentration camps which involved "mass sterilization, and the gassing of Jews." It seems that Blome had a change of heart after his admissions to his Army interrogators and he later stopped talking, taking the same line that other Nazi officers took—he had only limited knowledge of what was going on as far as crimes against humanity were concerned.

He was tried at the Nuremberg War Crimes tribunal and was found not guilty. U.S. Army authorities expunged his record pertaining to the concentration camp crimes, not allowing the court access to this vital material. He came to the U.S. and went to work outside of Washington, D.C., and was paid a salary of $6,000.

Arthur Rudolph. Arthur Rudolph was one of the most notorious Nazi scientists to work for the United States under Operation Paperclip and he is best remembered for his work as a Nazi rocket scientist who helped develop the V-2 rocket for the Germans during the war. After the war was over, he was brought to the United States and worked for the newly created U.S. space command, NASA, and was responsible for developing the Pershing missile and the Saturn V moon rocket. In 1984, the U.S. government began an internal investigation into Arthur Rudolph's Nazi past, including any crimes he might have been responsible for during the war. After the investigation was over, Rudolph's U.S. citizenship was renounced. In 1987, after an investigation was begun by Harold Dunn, the Attorney General of Hamburg, Germany, it was determined that there was no basis for his prosecution and he was given German citizenship.

In the late 1930s Rudolph began his work for the Germans on their rocket program and he was assigned to work at the Peenemunde facility where the construction of various rockets and missiles was underway. After beginning their work on the V-2s at Peenemunde, the scientists were moved to a new facility near Nordhausen called Mittelwerk. He met for the first time a fellow scientist who would help shape the German (and later the American rocket) program, Wernher von Braun. Rudolph worked under von Braun and as time went on, they were able to successfully launch two A-2 rockets from the island of Borkum. At the new facility, the top German brass wanted to have Rudolph and his team produce 50 V-2 rockets but they were only able to produce four rockets which were later returned to Peenemude as not operational.

The British government soon learned of Operation Paperclip and they asked the United States if they could take possession of a number of these scientists for their own rocket project called Operation Backfire. Some of the men the U.S. shipped off to

England were Wernher von Braun, Walter Dornberger, and Arthur Rudolph. Tests were made on behalf of Operation Backfire when a V-2 was shot from an area on Germany's north coast, at a former Krupp naval gun range at Cuxhaven. The British wanted to analyze the technical data of the V-2s and four rockets were fired at a target in the North Sea.

It seems the British had pulled one over on the United States when they refused to return Walter Dornberger. Major General Walter Dornberger was the man who was in charge of the German rocket project for the army's weapons department. In that capacity, he was on the shortlist of persons whom the United States wanted to capture after the war was over. So it was no wonder that the British were in no hurry to return him to the States once they'd gotten what they wanted out of him. The British told their American cousins that Dornberger was on "loan" to them and they took him and Wernher von Braun back to London where they were interrogated for a week and were placed in Wimbledon Stadium for over a month. After all was said and done, Von Braun was returned to the United States while Dornberger remained in England classified as a POW. He was then sent to a British prison in South Wales where it seems he was not very well liked, even by his fellow German prisoners.

According to U.S. military records, Rudolph was a "100% Nazi, dangerous type, security threat. Suggest internment." Rudolph, the former director of the Mittelwerk factory at the infamous Dora/ Nordhausen concentration camp, supervised the deaths of at least 20,000 people during his brutal reign of terror. The JIOA (Joint Intelligence Objectives Agency) which ran the Nazi scientist program ignored his sordid past, and when it came time for him to apply for a U.S. entry visa, they wrote that there was "nothing in his records that he was a war criminal, an ardent Nazi, or otherwise objectionable." Rudolph became a naturalized American citizen (before it was taken away), was stationed at Fort Bliss, and later joined NASA, the national space agency, working on U.S. rocket development.

Wernher von Braun. Von Braun was, perhaps, the most important Nazi scientist brought over by American authorities under Paperclip. He was mainly responsible for the super-secret

German rocket project at Peenemunde from 1937 to 1945. It was from Peenemunde that German V-2 rockets were launched against civilian targets in London, wreaking considerable havoc and destruction on the city.

Von Braun also worked at the Dora concentration camp, and had the deaths of countless thousands of prisoners on his hands. His dossier was expunged of this incriminating material upon his entry to the United States. Von Braun, as time went on, was the man who was most responsible for the development of the American ICBM project before becoming the head of NASA, where he served as director. He is generally said to have been the father of our space program and the man most responsible for our successfully landing a man on the moon in July 1969. How a man with von Braun's criminal past was allowed into the United States is one of the most disturbing parts of Operation Paperclip. It seemed that it was more important for the United States to have von Braun work for us on our rocket development project than to see him for what he really was: an ardent Nazi whose rockets were responsible for vast destruction via his V-2 missiles that rained down on England during the war.

Van Braun was noted as the "Nazi rocketeer" and worked alongside Walter Dornberger in the development of German rockets. When the Germans began the development of their nascent rocket program, they chose the village of Peenemunde on the Baltic Sea as their prime base. Dornberger became the military commander while von Braun was his technical director. At Peenemunde, they developed the liquid-fuel rocket for aircraft and for the newly created jet planes that were then under development. They also developed the V-2 rocket that was used against cities in England.

Von Braun joined the SS horseback riding school in 1933, then the Nazi party on May 1, 1937, becoming an officer before war's end. Von Braun later said of his decision to join the Nazi party, "I was officially demanded to join the National Socialist Party. At this time (1937) I was already technical director of the Army Rocket Center at Peenemunde. My refusal to join the party would have meant that I would have to abandon the work of my life. Therefore, I decided to join." By the time the war was over, he rose to the rank of Major in the Wehrmacht and was promoted three times by Heinrich Himmler, the last time being in June 1943.

While working on the V-2 rocket program, von Braun was under surveillance by the SD for his supposed defeatist attitude as to how the war was going. Himmler began making false charges against him as being a communist sympathizer and for sabotaging the rocket program. Von Braun was arrested in March 1944 and sent to a cell run by the Gestapo in Poland where he was jailed for two weeks without being charged. It seems that the Abwehr learned of his arrest and through high-ranking channels, he was freed.

By the spring of 1945, it was obvious that the war was coming to an end and the top Nazi military leaders and the scientists who were working on the V-2 program decided to take matters into their own hands and seek American help in surrendering before it was too late. In an audacious move, von Braun and 500 others, using false papers, managed to steal a train and fled through Germany toward the American lines. The SS, fearing that the rocket scientists would make some untoward move on their own, had told them to destroy their records. However, that did not happen as the scientists buried their precious documents in a mineshaft.

After his capture, von Braun and 500 other scientists were placed under arrest and sent to a U.S. Army base in Garmisch-Partenkirchen, in the Bavarian Alps. Another top Nazi scientist who was in that facility was General Walter Dornberger. Many of these Nazis played a cat and mouse game with their Army interrogators, sometimes giving up important information, while at other times stonewalling.

By September 1945, Operation Overcast, the plan to bring certain Nazi scientists to the U.S., including Wernher von Braun, was put into motion. Von Braun and others left Germany and headed to France for the final leg of their journey to the United States. Years later, when von Braun was safely ensconced in the United States and working for the government, he told Daniel Lang, then a writer for the *New Yorker,* "We were interested solely in exploring outer space. It was simply a question with us of how the golden cow could be milked most successfully."[12]

After a re-fueling stop in the Azores, the plane stopped briefly in Newfoundland, Canada before arriving in the United States, at Wilmington, Delaware on September 20, 1945. In a story that could only be written in a spy novel, the men were flown to a naval base

[12] Anne Jacobsen, *Operation Paperclip,* Page 178.

at Quincy, Massachusetts. They were taken by boat to sea where they were put aboard a small ship in Boston Harbor. They were then taken to an abandoned Army base where they stayed for a short while until they were properly processed.

On October 6, 1945, von Braun and the other Peenemunde scientists were put on a train bound for St. Louis along with an escort, Major James Hamill, an intelligence officer with the Army Ordinance Corps. Their final destination was Fort Bliss, Texas (El Paso).

After being allowed to go back to Germany to get married, von Braun and his wife were sent to Huntsville, Alabama where they lived for the next twenty years. From 1950 to 1970, he headed the Army's rocket development team at Redstone Arsenal, which resulted in the development of the Redstone rocket.

As the years passed, he began writing about manned space flight and even worked with Walt Disney studios as a technical advisor on three television shows about outer space. He also was responsible for the creation of the Jupiter-C rocket which successfully launched the West's first satellite, Explorer 1, on January 31, 1958.

While most of the American government knew and approved of Operation Paperclip, there was one man in authority who had a different view of what was going on. His name was Samuel Klaus and he represented the State Department for the JIOA Committee. His job on the JIOA was to approve the visas for the Germans who were scheduled to come into the United States and he had a rather different view than the rest of the military who worked to get the scientists into the country. Basically, Klaus was opposed to the running of Operation Paperclip and that caused munch consternation between him and his colleagues.

Samuel Klaus was very much involved in the case against the Nazis in his capacity as the director of the Safehaven Operation, whose responsibility was to retrieve captured Nazi loot and assets, including gold that had been stolen by the Nazis during the war. Klaus believed that the German scientists who were being sent to the United States were men of lesser talent, out to save their own skins. He wanted to have only 12 Nazi scientists given entry to the United States, but as time went on, he was duly overridden.

The State Department now began to pull its weight and Secretary of State James Byrnes soft peddled his opposition to Operation Overcast and lessened the tough rules that allowed the scientists and their families into the United States under military supervision. Agreeing with Sec. Byrnes was Secretary of War Robert Patterson who believed that if the Nazi scientists remained in Germany for too long, they might be plucked up by the Russians.

On March 4, 1946, a new U.S. policy toward the German scientists still in Germany was implemented. In a program that was in "the national interest," a list was compiled of one thousand top Nazis and their families who were to be brought to the United States so the Russians couldn't get them.

By February 1947, there were 344 scientists in the United States, none of them having valid entry visas. Klaus's boss, Colonel Thomas Ford, told him to expedite the visas but Klaus balked, saying he would not do so until he saw the whole list of those coming into the country. In the end, Samuel Klaus was outnumbered by the military and civilian establishment who were responsible for Paperclip and Overcast. He left the State Department to pursue other areas of work, the one lone holdout in the terrible saga that was unfolding right before his eyes.

The most logical and simplistic explanation as to why von Braun and the other Nazi scientists were allowed into the United States after the war was over was to prevent them from falling into the hands of the Russians who were, our new Cold War enemy. It didn't seem to matter just how bad these men were, they served our purpose to advance our missile and rocket programs and stay one step ahead of the Soviets in the new space race. Project Paperclip was surely the CIA's blackest eye.

———————

How is this for a World War II spy novel? Hitler's Germany, facing bankruptcy from its war debt, makes a secret deal with "neutral" Switzerland to act as its secret banker in laundering looted gold from the central banks of the countries it has overrun. Most of the money was confiscated from the vaults of these countries and used by Germany to buy much-needed arms and equipment to carry out the war.

143

But let's take the plot one step further. Let's say that a good portion of the gold came from the victims of the holocaust, from the very people whom the Germans were murdering in the concentration camps by the hundreds of thousands? And if the writer has a good imagination, let's also postulate that the Swiss willingly went along in this grand scheme and got rich in the process. Is this just the vivid imagination of a good novelist? No! It is history, a blemished side of the secret history of World War II that has only recently come to light, 75 years after the fall of Berlin, at the dawn of a new century.

In May of 1997, the U.S. Commerce Department, under the supervision of Under Secretary of Commerce for International Trade, Stewart Eizenstat, the Special Envoy of the Department of State on Property Restitution in Central and Eastern Europe, published a 250 page report on what had become known in the popular press as the "Nazi Gold Affair," under the imposing title *U.S. and Allied Efforts to Recover and Restore Gold and Other Assets Stolen or Hidden by Germany During World War II*. The report, which was prepared by William Slany, the historian of the Department of State, with the participation of other federal agencies like the CIA, the Department of Justice, State, Commerce, Defense, Treasury, and the FBI, among others, gives the most detailed account of how far-ranging the covert relationship was between Switzerland and Hitler's Germany during the war.

The first reports of the secret deals between the Nazis and Switzerland came out at the time in various articles in leading news magazines (*Time, Newsweek* and *U.S. News and World Report*) on investigations by members of the World Jewish Congress (and its president, the heir to the Seagram Distillery fortune, Edgar Bronfman), who had been in secret communication over the years with various Swiss bank officials. They cajoled and pleaded with the Swiss bankers to release the amounts of heirless assets that the Swiss had been keeping safe in their vaults since before the war began, and refusing to release to the heirs of the Holocaust. Bronfman took his case to former first lady Hillary Rodham Clinton, who met with him and later asked her husband, President Bill Clinton, to get on the bandwagon. President Clinton ordered the various U.S. agencies to initiate a search of the pertinent materials in the U.S. National Archives, and in other departments, to find out the truth behind the Swiss-Nazi connection. The Eizenstat report was the result of that investigation. Like Operation Paperclip, the U.S.-Gehlen connection, and the links between Pope Pius XII and the Germans during the war, it is not a pretty picture.

The outcome of the report was a scathing indictment of Switzerland's relationship with the Nazis during the war, a less than honorable mention of actions by the Allies, the U.S. and Great Britain, and the breaking of the myth of "Swiss neutrality" during the war. A second phase of the Nazi gold investigation was the beginning of the so-called Safehaven program by the U.S. and other nations to block the Germans from transferring assets to Switzerland and other neutral countries. There were several major conclusions in the report, and while space limits the writer to describe all of them, here is the main story.

First, the massive and systematic plundering of gold and other assets from conquered nations and Nazi victims was no rouge operation. It was essential to the financing of the German war machine. The Reichsbank itself—the central bank of the German state—was a knowing and integral participant. It was the Reichsbank that incorporated into its gold reserves looted monetary gold from the governments of countries occupied by the Nazis. Judging by Germany's reserves at the beginning of the war, the majority of the gold was looted from central banks. It is also evident from the documents we have uncovered and reviewed that some amount was confiscated from individual civilians, including victims of Nazi atrocities and incorporated into Reichsbank gold stocks. It was the Reichsbank that assisted in converting victim gold coins, jewelry, and gold fillings into assets for the SS "Melmer" account. The Reichsbank organized the gold ingots—with their origins often disguised and therefore indistinguishable by appearance from that looted from central banks.

Second, in the unique circumstances of World War II, neutrality collided with morality; too often being neutral provided a pretext for avoiding moral considerations. Historically a well-established principle in international law, neutrality served through centuries of European wars as a legitimate means by which smaller nations preserved their sovereignty and economic viability. But it is painfully clear that Argentina, Portugal, Spain, Sweden, Switzerland, Turkey and other neutral nations were slow to recognize that this was not just another war. Most never did. Nazi Germany was a moral threat to Western civilization itself, and had it been victorious, to the survival of even the neutral countries.

Third, of all the neutral nations, Switzerland was the one with the most complex roles in World War II, together with the deepest and most crucial economic relationship with Nazi Germany: Switzerland's role was very mixed. It ended World War II as one of the wealthiest nations in Europe. It conducted trade with the Allies as well as with the Axis powers. The Swiss National Bank kept gold accounts for and received gold not only from Nazi Germany, but from the United States, Canada, and Great Britain as well. Switzerland served as a key base for U.S. intelligence gathering. It was also a protecting power for the Allies, most critically for our POWs.

But as the Swiss government acknowledged as early as 1952, there were shortcomings in Switzerland's refugee politics. Switzerland persuaded the Nazis to establish the "J" stamp which prevented tens of thousands of Jews from entering Switzerland or other potential sanctuaries. Like Canada and the U.S., Switzerland tightened its immigration policies, and during the war it virtually closed its borders to Jews fleeing deportation from France and Belgium. These agencies (War Department, Treasury) noted that in addition to its critical banking role for the Nazis, Switzerland's industries engaged in direct production for the Axis and helped Axis investments. Swiss shipping lines also furnished Germany with a large number of boats for the transport of goods.

As late in the war as the beginning of 1945, Switzerland violated an agreement it had just reached with the United States to freeze German assets and to restrict purchases of gold from Germany. The amount of Germany's gold reserves before the war was well known. Clearly, the evidence presented in this report is incontrovertible: the Swiss national bank and private Swiss bankers knew, as the war progressed, that the Reichsbank's own coffers had been depleted, and that the Swiss were handling vast sums of looted gold. The Swiss were aware of the Nazi gold heists from France and Belgium as well from other countries. Switzerland's "business as usual" attitude persisted in the postwar negotiations, and it is this period which is most inexplicable.

Fourth, the United States lent its military material and moral might to lead the world's fight against Nazi tyranny and led the magnanimous effort to rebuild Europe through the landmark Marshall Plan. Nonetheless, the report raises serious questions about the U.S. role. American leadership at that time, while greater than that of our allies, was limited. There was a demonstrable lack of senior-level support for a negotiating position with the neutrals.

Fifth, the report deals with the hotly debated issue of whether some victim gold was sent to Switzerland and other neutral countries, and whether it was also included in the TGC Gold Pool. This was the pool into which "looted central bank gold" was placed for redistribution by the TGC to the governments from which it was stolen during the war. The study concludes that both occurred.

The Reichsbank or its agents smelted gold taken from concentration camp internees and other civilians, and turned it into ingots. There is clear evidence that these ingots were incorporated into Germany's official gold reserves, along with gold confiscated from central banks of the countries the Third Reich occupied. It is also clear that some victim gold "tainted" the Gold Pool. As a result, gold taken by the Nazis from civilians in occupied countries and from individuals, victims of the Nazis in concentration camps and elsewhere was swept up into the Gold Pool. In addition, the United States and Great Britain agreed that gold bars suspected to be from the Nazis Terezin concentration camp in Czechoslovakia should also be included in the Gold Pool."

Switzerland, the nation of majestic lakes and mountains, became a hotbed of espionage during the war, rivaling Lisbon and Istanbul, where spies of all shapes and sizes vied for the top of the intelligence pyramid between the warring nations. Espionage agents from all the countries involved (and some that weren't), including England, France, Germany, the United States, and Poland, used Swiss territory to spy on each other without any penalties from their host government. One of the most important intelligence operations of the war took place in Switzerland and concerned a spy who reported vital German military war plans to the Russians.

The main character in the drama was Alexander Foote, who, unknown to the Soviets, was really a British double agent. Before the war, Foote had served in the International Brigade in Spain during the Spanish Civil War. He was recruited into the GRU, Soviet military intelligence, in 1938 and was sent to Switzerland as their top spy. Working with Foote in Switzerland were three vital Soviet intelligence rings whose job was to collect information. The man who ran the largest of these groups was Sandor Rado, code named Dora. The other two groups were operated by Otto Puenter, Pakno, and Rachel Deubendorfer, Sissy.

In the close-knit family of spies working in Switzerland, British intelligence, also working there, learned the identities of Foote and his partners. Foote distrusted the Nazis under Hitler and agreed to be a double agent for His Majesty's Government.

It was the job of the British to keep Russia in the war and do so they had to share their most vital intelligence secrets with Stalin, who never really trusted either Roosevelt or Churchill. Unknown to Stalin, the British had been reading every German military and diplomatic message with the use of the ULTRA intelligence program, the most vital secret in British intelligence. But how to get the ULTRA information to Stalin without him becoming suspicious? The answer to that vital question was solved by a man named Rudolf Roessler, code named Lucy.

Roessler worked for a Swiss intelligence called Bureau Ha. In a cleverly conceived game, Foote, the British double agent, got his intelligence via ULTRA, passed it along to Roessler who in turn gave Stalin the German military plans concerning its upcoming maneuvers on the Eastern Front. In reality, the plans sent to the Soviets by Lucy were controlled by the British.

By 1944, when the end of the war was in sight, the Swiss government closed down the three groups led by Foote and his fellow agents. Foote was arrested and served a short prison term. Roessler was also arrested after the war and subsequently released. He died in 1953. Foote continued working for the GRU (who still did not know of his links to British intelligence) and finally defected to London.

The Lucy spy ring was not the only high-level organization working secretly in Switzerland during the war. It seems that the most high-ranking Swiss official was secretly meeting with one of Hitler's top generals to achieve their own agenda.

The two main characters in this behind-the-scenes drama were Colonel Roger Masson, the wartime head of the Swiss military intelligence service, and German SS General Walter Schellenberg who has been mentioned in the previous chapter for his participation against Hitler. The two men met three times between September 1942 and March 1943 in Switzerland and the proceedings lasted for a few days, all with the knowledge and approval of the Federal Council of Switzerland (so much for Swiss neutrality).

During their third meeting, Roger Masson brought along with him the Swiss Army Chief, General Guisan, who, when pressed by General Schellenberg, said that if troops from any other nation attacked Switzerland (meaning the Allies) they would be met by force.

Their first meeting took place on September 8, 1942, in the town of Waldshut in Germany, near the Swiss border. Colonel Masson was escorted to the meeting by Hans Eggen, Schellenberg's aide whose company had business ties in Switzerland. Eggen had made many previous trips to Switzerland and he reported back to his boss what tidbits of information he picked up on his trips. Eggen had two principle Swiss contacts he relied on, Paul Meyer-Schwertenbach and Paul Holzach, who were working for Swiss intelligence.

Both men had their own, separate reasons for their meetings, but Schellenberg in particular had one idea in mind that he wanted to pitch to Roger Masson, the idea of a separate peace treaty between the Nazis and Britain and the United States in order to fight against Russia. This was not a new idea as the days of the war were coming to an end. The thought of a separate peace was not accepted in Washington and London as the Roosevelt administration wanted Germany to pay dearly for the war and decided that no bargain with the devil would be made.

For his part, Masson wanted one thing in particular from Schellenberg: "two boxes of files belonging to the French General Staff. The containers, which had been captured by the Germans in June 1940, contained secret documents on plans for Swiss-French military cooperation, if the Nazis decided to attack France by advancing underneath the Maginot line that stretched from the Swiss to the Belgian border." He wanted these papers back as they proved that if push came to shove, the Swiss would be ready to fight.

However, Masson decided not to press for the release of the boxes at that first meeting. He asked Schellenberg to release a member of the Swiss consulate in Stuttgart, who had been arrested and sentenced to death for spying. Schellenberg agreed to let the man go and in addition, Masson asked him to shut down a press agency in Vienna which was run by two Swiss pro-Nazis that was constantly attacking Switzerland. The General agreed to Masson's proposal.

The second meeting took place on October 16, 1942 in Switzerland in which Schellenberg and Eggen participated. The setting was the home of Meyer-Schwertenbach at his property on Lake Constance. It is not known exactly what the two men talked about but in the world of smoke and mirrors that was international espionage, all sorts of themes could be discussed. At this time, Switzerland was a nest of spies with both the Germans and the Americans having a large network of agents in the country, keeping track of each others' movements. Masson's intelligence people kept an eye on Schellenberg's spies in country and they, on him. Switzerland did not have an extensive spy organization because as a neutral nation, they did not have to cast such a wide net as the other warring powers did.

They did however have one organization that served their intelligence purposes. That organization was called the Viking Line that operated in Germany. The official Swiss intelligence organization was so hard up for money that they had to ask another, of-the-books organization called Bureau Ha to lend them cash. Bureau Ha was run by Captain Hans Hausmann, who was anti-Nazi and more than happy to lend Roger Masson a hand. Both Hausmann and Masson ran their own spies in Switzerland as well as other neutral countries to keep an eye on what the other side was doing. But they could not rival the networks that were spying on them, no matter how hard they tried.[13]

One matter that must have come up when Masson and General Schellenberg met was whether or not Germany would invade Switzerland. While that event never happened, it was a hot topic in both countries as well as on the Allied side. On the face of it, Switzerland supplied the Germans with all the raw materials they

---

[13] LeBor, Adam, *Hitler's Secret Bankers,* Carol Publishing Group, New York, 1997, Page 167-68.

needed to finance the war, as well as being a repository for the looted Nazi gold from the concentration camp victims. If Germany did decide to attack Switzerland, they would have to cross the Alps, not a very strategic way to fight a war. The country was rugged in part and not fit for the Panzer divisions that would have to cross the nation in order to be successful. In reality, Germany needed Switzerland more than they needed it and so it was not militarily feasible for a German invasion.

The topic of a German invasion of Switzerland was discussed in a meeting held on March 3, 1943 between Col. Masson, General Guisan and General Schellenberg. It seems that the Viking Line had passed information to Roger Masson telling him that from their sources, they learned that the Germans were discussing an attack on Switzerland at a meeting attended by Herman Goering, Himmler, and Alfred Rosenberg at Hitler's headquarters in October 1942. The Swiss really didn't have to worry about an attack by Germany, but at the meeting, General Guisan told Schellenberg that if his nation was attacked by anyone, they'd resist.

In the end, high members of the Swiss Federal Council found out about the Masson-Schellenberg-Guisan secret meetings and in the aftermath they fired General Guisan for not reporting the three meetings.

Roger Masson did not fare well either. The Federal Council began an official investigation of Masson and his secret dealings, calling them "unauthorized." For his part, Masson, in October 1945, sent a letter to Federal Councilor Karl Kobelt, defending his actions during the war. He said that the Federal Council had known all along what was going on and had given him their tacit approval. In his letter Masson wrote, "I had only relations with Walter Schellenberg, and not with the other chiefs of the SS. It is a monstrosity that you portray me as a friend of the Nazis, because I am not. I disapproved of the German attitudes, especially those of Hitler, and I said to Schellenberg that he shouldn't be surprised by the hostile attitudes of the Swiss, especially from the moment that the Germans found this term 'Herrenvolk', master race."

After Schellenberg was captured by the Allies, he had much to say about his relationship with Col. Masson. "I knew Colonel Masson personally. I do not think I was wrong in thinking that there was a certain mutual sympathy on both sides, which had gradually developed through our political discussions." Writing in his book *Hitler's Secret Bankers,* Adam LeBor says:

> Schellenberg said that his aim in his discussions with Masson was to open a regular channel for the exchange of information with him—in other words—make the head of Swiss military intelligence some kind of Nazi agent. By regularly meeting with Schellenberg, Masson had allowed himself to become, if not an agent, at least a de facto agent of the RSHA's Department VI, and while detailed records of their discussions are not available, there must have been some trading in information and intelligence taking place. There is no such thing as a free fact, especially in the shadow world in which the two spymasters moved.

Under interrogation by the Allies, Schellenberg told them that the rationale for his meetings with Colonel Masson was monetary. His department was charged with gaining foreign currency and Switzerland was the natural place from which to gain so much needed money to finance the war. A report dated December 13, 1946, in relation to one of his interrogation sessions with the Americans, said, "When Swiss-German relations grew worse, Schellenberg undertook trips to the Swiss border. Subject claims he could not afford to lose Switzerland as a market for foreign currency and as a base for his secret service operations."

Beside meeting with General Schellenberg, Roger Masson often times met with the United States' top spy in Bern, Allan Dulles. Dulles headed the OSS's spy network in Switzerland having been sent by President Roosevelt himself to represent U.S. interests in that country. According to published accounts of this time, Masson wrote a letter to Karl Kobelt, the head of the Swiss military department: "Finally, I had on a number of occasions to talk with Dulles, who was representing President Roosevelt in Bern about Schellenberg. He had a good opinion about these conversations."

Author Adam Lebor in his book on the Swiss in World War II, *Hitler's Secret Bankers,* writes about Dulles' time in Switzerland: "Dulles was power-mad, writes historian Marc Masurovsky, running intelligence operations that were so complicated it was sometimes difficult to see what lay behind them. He was an egomaniac; he wanted to run the war out of Bern. He was a very successful lawyer, and he had a tremendous amount of friends in the German business and legal community. He was not pro-Nazi, but he was pro-German. He thought very highly of himself. He was devious and condescending, and as far as he was concerned anything that was good for international business was good for him and vice versa."

While serving as OSS chief in Bern, Dulles made friends with Roger Masson and cultivated him as a source of information on all things German. Dulles also had an ongoing relationship with Captain Hausmann's Bureau Ha. Both men got their information from their Viking Line and passed some of it along to Dulles.

There were any number of anti-Hitler plots emanating from Swiss soil, but the most famous was called Black Orchestra. Dulles had a source inside the Black Orchestra named Gero von Gaevernitz. Von Gaevernitz in turn, gave Dulles the name of another anti-Hitler plotter named Hans Bernd Gisevius, a German diplomat who worked in the consulate in Zurich. Gisevius was well connected to the anti-Hitler plots and worked in tandem with Claus von Stauffenberg in the assassination plots against Hitler in July 1944. Gisevius became one of Dulles' most important links to the anti-Hitler plotters while he was stationed in Bern. The German opposition leaders all told Dulles that they wanted to make a separate peace treaty with the Allies but nothing came of that offer. Our Russian allies would not go for it and both Churchill and Roosevelt made sure that didn't happen.

The one important factor that Dulles and the OSS took from their position in Bern was the laying of the groundwork for an elaborate Allied spy network that was set up after the war was over. The target of this new operation was the Soviet Union in the new Cold War that was gripping Europe after the surrender of Germany. The United States used a number of these Nazis (as mentioned in Paperclip) to work for Allied intelligence in the new, secret war against the Soviet Union, many of them unscrupulous people.

The conclusions of the U.S. government's report on Swiss activities during the war were damming enough. But there is more to the story of the Swiss-Nazi connection. Switzerland, the beautiful land of mountains and clear lakes, was also Hitler's willing and able partner in the Nazi conduct of the war. The majority of the bankers and high government officials in Switzerland were supportive of the Nazi war effort and hostile to the Jews who were systematically being murdered in the concentration camps. The chief of police was an ardent Nazi supporter and aided in sending back to Germany, and certain death in the camps, hundreds of Jews who wanted to seek asylum in Switzerland. A large number of Swiss citizens worked covertly for the German secret service, providing information on Jews trying to get into the country. The Swiss government allowed German troop trains containing large quantities of guns, ammunition, and military supplies to use Swiss rail lines to carry vital war material back into Germany and Italy to fight the Allies.

The Swiss, with the knowledge of the bankers, deposited millions of dollars in gold and currency that were looted from the conquered nations of Austria, Czechoslovakia, Poland, Denmark, and Holland, into the banking system of Switzerland. Among this looted money were personal items made of gold—rings, teeth, coins, watches, etc.—that were taken from the victims of the concentration camps. This gold was resmelted and put into the gold pool for sale and deposit in Bern, Zurich and Basel. In late 1944, as the end was near for Germany, a number of Swiss bankers allowed top Nazi military and civilian leaders to set up secret bank accounts for use after the war.

To combat the Germans using Switzerland as their money laundering headquarters, the Roosevelt administration began a program to block Germans from transferring assets to Switzerland and other neutral countries called the Safehaven Program. The Safehaven project was launched at the United Nations Monetary and Financial Conference at Bretton Woods in July 1944. The main purpose of the conference was the creation of the World Bank and the International Monetary Fund. From the beginning, interagency infighting broke out, with the State Department trying to water down the program, while the Justice and Treasury Departments and the fledgling intelligence services, OSS and the FBI, wanted to make Switzerland pay a high price for dealing with the enemy.

As noted previously, a detachment of soldiers, while in the Merkers salt mine, found 18 bags of silver and gold bars and

189 parcels, boxes, and suitcases containing jewelry, watches, and dental crowns, all from the Reichsbank, Germany's central bank. Also captured at Merkers was Albert Thoms, head of the Reichsbank's Precious Metals Department. This looted money, according to Thoms, was put into a special SS account called the "Melmer" account, named after Captain Bruno Melmer. According to Reichsbank Vice President Emil Pulil, sometime in the summer of 1942, Reichsbank President and Reichsbank Ministry of Economy Walter Funk informed him of an agreement between Reich Leader of SS and Heinrich Himmler and Reich Finance Minister Lutz von Krosighk whereby the Reichsbank "was to receive shipments of confiscated jewelry and securities from the SS, which would use the cash proceeds from the conversion of these shipments to finance its industrial enterprise." Captain Melmer's first shipment of this loot was delivered on August 26, 1942. The tenth delivery, which was shipped in November 1942, contained large amounts of dental gold from concentration camp victims.

The OSS worked closely with the Safehaven Project giving vital information on German clandestine activities in Switzerland. The Safehaven Project worked under the direction of the Secret Intelligence Branch (SI) that was responsible for intelligence gathering in neutral countries, as well as German occupied Europe. Working along with SI was the OSS counter-intelligence branch, X-2, of which James Angleton was a part. "Safehaven thus emerged as a joint SI/X2 operation shortly after its inception, especially in the key outposts of Switzerland, Spain, and Portugal, with X-2 playing a dominant role."

Before the war ended, many top Nazi military leaders, including Adolf Hitler, were planning for a new, Fourth Reich to be born in the flames of defeat. One of Safehaven Project's most important finds was the so-called "Red House" document that was discovered by U.S. military officials. This entailed a secret Nazi-Swiss economic collaboration which was dated November 27, 1944, and marked "Secret." It was compiled by the Economic Section of U.S. G-2 (military intelligence) and was compiled by Lt. Colonel John Easton at SHAEF, The Supreme Headquarters Allied Expeditionary Force. The subject was "Plans of German industrialists to engage in underground activity after Germany's defeat; flow of capital to neutral countries." The person who gave the Red House document to U.S. intelligence was an unnamed spy who worked for the French intelligence service, the Deuxieme Bureau. The report said of this man, "This agent is regarded as reliable and had worked for the French on German problems since 1916. He was in close contact with the Germans, particularly industrialists, during the occupation of France, and he visited Germany as late as August 1944."[14]

The Red House document referred to a hotel in Strasbourg where, on August 10, 1944, a number of highly placed German industrialists and other military officials met to plan a Fourth Reich. They discussed how to finance their new nation and they turned to Switzerland as their secret benefactor. Their supposed new headquarters would be located in Bern with the full cooperation of the Swiss banks who would launder their money and provide secrecy at all times.

The meeting was presided over by a Dr. Scheid who was once a German military officer. It is said that some of the participants in the meeting were representatives from such important German industries as Krupp, the arms manufacturer, Messerschmitt, snd Volkswagen, among others. Dr. Scheid implored his fellow industrialists to make contact with other large companies who would be willing to give them money in secret, in order to provide financing for their new, Fourth Reich. Also in attendance at the meeting were representatives from the German Navy and the Ministry of Armaments.

In order to help finance their new nation, they looked toward American firms who had connections to Germany. Some of those companies were the Zeiss Company that produced lenses for cameras, and the Hamburg-American shipping line that plied the waters between the United States and Germany.

Part of the Red House report spells out how the new Fourth Reich would be funded: "German industrialists must, it was said, through their exports increase the strength of Germany. They must prepare themselves to finance the Nazi Party which would be forced to go underground as Maquis (resistance). From now on the government would allocate large sums to industrialists so that each could establish a secure postwar foundation in foreign countries. Existing financial reserves in foreign countries must be placed at the

[14] LeBor, Adam, *Hitler's Secret Bankers: The Myth of Swiss Neutrality During the Holocaust,* Carol Publishers, New York, 1997, Page 58.

disposal of the part so that a strong German empire can be created after the defeat."[15]

The two main banks that would be the repositories for this money were the Basler Handelsbank and Credit Suisse, both based in Switzerland.

British intelligence also got wind of what was going on and they too wrote up a report on what they learned. A British document dated February 1945 says, "The German underground movement disposes of considerable funds in Switzerland. The assets consists chiefly of foreign currency, mostly in Swiss banknotes and of diamonds, probably also of other precious stones. From the beginning of its activity in Switzerland the underground movement avoided opening bank accounts with Swiss banks, and not even bank safes were used. The assets at the disposal of the movement are deposited in the safes of private individuals."

The World Jewish Congress, who followed the flow of looted money from Swiss banks for decades, had one of their representatives speak on behalf of that organization in regard to the Red House report. This person said, "I almost feel proprietary about them. The Red House report is scary, like something out of a Robert Ludlum or Graham Greene novel."

In the United States, one man who took an avid interest in combating the Swiss-Nazi bank connection was Treasury Secretary Henry Morgenthau, a close confidant of President Roosevelt. Morgenthau served as secretary of the treasury in the Roosevelt and Truman administrations from January 1, 1934 until July 22, 1945. He was born into a well-to-do Jewish family in New York and his father, Henry Morgenthau Sr., was an ambassador to the Ottoman Empire. During World War I, Henry worked for President Herbert Hoover in the U.S. Farm Administration of the United States Department of Agriculture. He then went into the publishing industry and published a magazine called *American Agriculturist.* He was a friend of Franklin Roosevelt who was then the governor of New York. Roosevelt appointed Morgenthau to the post of state commissioner of conservation. After FDR's election as president, he was appointed secretary of the Treasury. Morgenthau helped the U.S. finance FDR's New Deal administration and when World War II started, he helped in the war effort by selling war bonds to the

[15] Ibid, Page 60-61.

American people.

As the war began, and accounts started coming in of the extinction of the Jews in the concentration camps, Morgenthau, then the only Jew in the cabinet, asked the president to take immediate steps to allow large numbers of Jews into the country. One proposal he made was to have the U.S. acquire British and French Guiana in order to allow the European Jews a safehaven in which to live. That proposal was turned down.

As news reports kept coming out of Europe, Morgenthau had three of his associates at Treasury, John Pehle, Randolph Paul, and Josiah Du Bois write up an18-page memo entitled "Report to the Secretary on the Acquiescence of This Government in the Murder of Jews." They soon met with the president at the White House and asked him to do something to rescue the Jews who were being killed in the camps. In light of the meeting, the president issued an executive order establishing the War Refugee Board on January 22, 1944.

Morgenthau was very aggressive in his thinking as to what Germany would look like after the war was over. He wanted that country to be dismantled as far as its armaments industry was concerned in order to keep Germany from being able to conduct another war in Europe. He wanted Germany to be divided up into two different states, and to cut back how much industrial production it could put out. But some of the top members of the Roosevelt administration including Secretary of State Cordell Hull and Secretary of War Henry Stimson opposed his plan. The U.S. government did however put in place a number of regulations to stop Germany from becoming a new threat to the world including reducing that country's living standard. Production of oil, rubber, merchant shipping, and aircraft production were stopped.

Secretary Morgenthau was very concerned that the Safehaven Project look into any possible German links to U.S. banks and he took dramatic steps in that direction. On June 2, 1942, Morgenthau received a note from a Treasury Department employee named Mr. Foley who asked him to put Treasury agents inside branches of Swiss banks in the United States, including the Swiss-American Corporation and Credit Suisse in order to see their bank records and find out if they were in collaboration with Berlin. Morgenthau agreed and for a time, U.S. Treasury agents were placed inside these banks and were able to monitor what the banks were doing.

A report by the Treasury Department on Swiss-Nazi collaboration says the following: "It would be difficult to avoid the conclusion that these Swiss banks were fronts for Nazi economic interests in the United States, actively aiding the Third Reich under the pretense of neutrality."

Using his influence during the Safehaven Project, Secretary Morgenthau took an interest in the family of Raoul Wallenberg, who, while risking his own life, saved thousands of Jews from certain death during the war. Raoul Wallenberg came from a very wealthy Swedish banking family that was founded by his uncle, Marcus Wallenberg. Marcus owned the prosperous Enshilda Bank that was the largest bank in that country. Another uncle, Jacob Wallenberg, was also part of the bank that had trading rights with most of the other well-connected depositories in Europe, especially with those in Germany.

Raoul received his education in the U.S., studying architecture at the University of Michigan, returning to Sweden after graduation. In 1938, he decided to join his family's banking firm but soon he was to have a change of heart that would forever alter his life. In that year he was sent to Palestine to open a branch and was instantly met with a flood of Jewish refugees who were fleeing the beginning of Hitler's bloodbath in Europe. Caught by the enormity of these tales, Wallenberg returned to Stockholm.

Upon his return, he met a new partner of the firm who happened to be a Hungarian Jew who told him horror stories concerning the fate of his fellow Jews. This man could not get back to Hungary so Wallenberg went in his place. After seeing the horror in Budapest, Raoul decided that his life's work would be to help the Jews of Europe escape death by any means he could.

Meanwhile, the family's Enshilda Bank began a covert relationship with the Soviet intelligence services in order to broker a peace deal between Russia and Finland. Wallenberg also had a clandestine relationship with the British Secret Service and he aided the struggling British in gaining access to Swedish raw materials without the Soviets finding out about it. But his most notable success was the saving of over 20,000 Hungarian Jews from the

Nazis, using Swedish papers, and hiding thousands of them in safe houses in Budapest.

Unknown to Raoul Wallenberg, the Russians had been tracking his every move, including his secret meetings with German army officers who were known to be pro-Soviet in their political leanings.

Morgenthau learned from his Safehaven agents that both Jacob and Marcus Wallenberg had made deals during the war with the Allies as well as the Axis powers. "In 1942, Boris Rybkin, the NKVD (forerunner of the KGB) resident in Stockholm, arranged a deal to supply the Soviet Union with high-grade Swedish steel for the aviation industry."

Like Switzerland, Sweden profited from its covert dealings with the Germans. For example, they handled German gold in payment for millions of tons of iron ore that was made into materials for German Panzer tanks. In 1944, Sweden finally stopped accepting German gold as payment for the iron.

Morgenthau's Treasury Department made a strong case that Jacob and Marcus Wallenberg were sympathetic to the Nazi cause. In a report dated February 7, 1945, he laid out some of his points against them. "While Marcus Wallenberg was apparently sympathetic with the Allied cause, Jacob Wallenberg, his brother, and partner in the Enshilda Bank, was known to be sympathetic to and working with the Germans. Jacob Wallenberg was the author of the Swedish-German trading agreement, and Marcus Wallenberg came to the United States in 1940 and attempted to purchase on behalf of German interest an American-held block of German securities. Enshilda Bank has been repeatedly connected with large black market operations in foreign currencies, including dollars reported to have been dumped by the Germans."

The mystery of how Raoul Wallenberg died is still being debated today, and while we need not go into a lot of detail surrounding the fate of Raoul Wallenberg, the reader should be apprised of the story.

On January 7, 1945, as Wallenberg was about to go to a conference with a high-ranking Soviet military officer in Budapest to discuss the distribution of food to the Jews of the city, he disappeared. Not since that fateful meeting has the fate of Raoul Wallenberg been known. Some reports have it that he was seen alive in Russia well into the 1970s and 1980s. Another report stated that he died shortly after his meeting in 1945. Many years ago the magazine *U.S News and World Report* wrote of new information concerning Wallenberg's links to U.S. wartime intelligence agency, the OSS. The new information obtained by the magazine was gleaned from declassified materials from the CIA on the Wallenberg case (see the *U.S News and World Report* May 13, 1996 edition).

The files show that Wallenberg was appointed with the approval of President Roosevelt to be an intelligence asset to the U.S. His wartime job was to provide the OSS with information on the anti-Hitler resistance and to help in the release of Jews in Europe. According to the magazine, "It is a reasonable conclusion that Raoul Wallenberg was of benefit to American intelligence." Donald Jameson, a former senior CIA official, calls this statement "a virtual admission that Wallenberg was used by us. It is a minimum statement the CIA can make and still be plausible."

According to the declassified files, Wallenberg was to be used by the OSS as a penetration agent to make reconnaissance missions into Hungary where Bill Donovan's secret soldiers had no direct "in." In today's spy parlance, Wallenberg was a "contract agent," not really on the OSS payroll but subject to its laws. The files also report reliable sources seeing Wallenberg alive in Russia decades after his "official" death.

In recent years, a new twist to the Wallenberg story has come to light. It involves the publication of Russian KGB General Ivan Serov's diaries that saw the light via his grandchild, Vera Serov. The name of her book was *Notes from a Suitcase: Secret Diaries of the First KGB Chairman, Found Over 25 Years After His Death.* According to the book, General Serov said that "Wallenberg was killed in a Soviet prison and Serov quotes his predecessor, Viktor Abakumov, as saying the order to kill Wallenberg came from the top: Joseph Stalin and then foreign minister Vyacheslav Molotov."

The main theory has been that Wallenberg died in a Russian prison in 1947. In 1957, the Soviets said that he died in prison after suffering a heart attack and there the matter rested until 1991, when a joint Swedish-Russian investigation was established to make further inquiries. In 2000, the commission came to the conclusion that they could not make a definite conclusion because all the relevant documents had gone missing.

Serov died in 1990 at age 84, but in his diaries he said that that Wallenberg's body was cremated after his death, substantiated by a document that was signed by two officials in the Lubyanka Prison in 1947.

Viktor Abakumov was arrested in 1951 and executed for treason in 1954. It was reported that while under questioning, he said that Serov said that Stalin and Molotov had ordered Wallenberg to be put to death. With the ending of the Cold War and the breakup of the old Soviet Union, the "true" events concerning the mystery of Raoul Wallenberg may finally come to light.[16]

Some of the Nazi gold stolen from the concentration camp victims wound up in a most unlikely place, Argentina. During the war, Argentina was ruled by its powerful leader, Juan Domingo Peron and his lovely wife Evita. After being neutral for most of the war, Argentina went over to the Allied side on March 27, 1945, two months before the war in Europe ended. Why Peron waited so long is still being debated years later but what is undisputed is that many fleeing Nazis wound up in Argentina after the war with money and art looted from the concentration camp victims (there is also circumstantial evidence that Adolf Hitler wound up in Argentina).

By 1947, thousands of Germans had found safety in Argentina under the watchful eye of the Peron government. A writer named Enrique Krauze wrote a piece on this topic for *New Republic* magazine, detailing what he learned about Peron and his alliance with these former Nazis after the war. He wrote that many of these people found sanctuary in Argentina with millions of dollars in stolen money and other valuables. He wrote that in 1945, just as the Nazi regime was in its final collapse, "Two German submarines docked [in Argentina] and unloaded their cargo. It included tens of millions in various currencies, 2,511 kilograms of gold, 4,638 karats of diamonds, piles of jewels, and works of art formerly deposited in the Reichsbank in Berlin."

Mr. Krauze further stated that Peron and his wife took personal charge of the loot and, furthermore, provided the German military attaché at the embassy in Buenos Aires with 8,000 Argentine passports and 1,100 identity cards to be given to the newly arrived Nazis. When the Peron government was overthrown in 1955, he

[16] Aderet, Ofer, "Is the Mystery of Raoul Wallenberg's Death Finally Solved?" www.haaretz.com/Israel-news August 7, 2016

found refuge in Egypt, along with a secret Swiss bank account.[17]

Another powerful Swiss institution that Henry Morgenthau looked into was the powerful Bank of International Settlements (BIS) which had official ties to some of the most important banking institutions in the world, including the Bank of England which handed over to 5.6 million pounds worth of gold to the Hitler regime. The BIS was the second most powerful banking institution that was used for the channeling of stolen Nazi gold, after the Swiss National Bank. After the war was over, the BIS had to refund $4 million to the Allies, as well as to some of its lenders including the Bank of England.

The BIS was involved up to its neck in the transferring of large amounts of Czech gold that was located in the Bank of London to the German Reichsbank. The gold was held on deposit in the Bank of England in the name of the BIS, which had its headquarters in Basel. When the Germans took over Czechoslovakia, they went directly to the offices of the National Bank and forced the Czech directors to transfer two large payments to the BIS. The first transfer was 23.1 metric tons from the Czech BIS account, which was held in the Bank of England to the Reichsbank BIS account. The second was the transfer from the Bank of England of almost 27 metric tons of gold held in the National Bank of Czechoslovakia to the BIS's gold account at the Bank of England.

While the first transfer went through, the second did not. After a great hue and cry from a leading member of the British parliament, George Strauss, a Labour MP, the British government ordered John Simon, the Chancellor of the Exchequer, to order all banks to block all Czech assets.[18]

The BIS was founded in 1930 and its wartime president was an American named Thomas McKittrick. The other members of the bank were Roger Auboin, of France, and the assistant general manager Paul Hechler, a German, who was a Nazi party member. "The BIS's wartime directors included two war-criminals-to-be, Reichsbank vice-president Emil Pohl and his boss, Walter Funk, as well as bankers from London,. Brussels, Rome, and Japan. And,

---

[17] Lebor, Adam, *Hitler's Secret Bankers*, Page 212-213.
[18] Lebor, Adam, "Never Mind the Czech gold the Nazis stole: The Ban for International Settlements actually financed Hitler's war machine," www.telegraph.co.uk.

conveniently for Berlin, the BIS even shared a wartime chairman with the Swiss National Bank-the main channel for looted gold-in the person of Ernst Weber."

The founding purpose of the BIS came out of the Young Plan as a conduit for German payments owed to the Allies after World War I. The owners of the bank were a number of powerful central banks around the world such as the Bank of England, the Reichsbank, the Bank of Italy, the Bank of France, and the First National Bank of New York. The charter of the bank made it immune from seizure in times of war or peace. In a description of the bank's work, Roger Auboin, said of the perks the bank received, "The most important of these, was that the bank, its property and assets, and all deposits and other funds entrusted to it are immune in time of peace and war and from any measure such as expropriation, seizure, confiscation, prohibition, or restriction of gold or currency export or import, and other similar measures."

The BIS was not your ordinary bank, as events during the war would tell. In effect, the monies collected by the BIS were interconnected with the daily upkeep of the German economy and without the money taken in on a daily basis, the Third Reich would not have survived. The BIS carried out monetary dealings with the Reichsbank and took in looted Nazi gold.

Thomas McKittrick was the president of the BIS and as far as Washington, and in particular, Henry Morgenthau, was concerned, his public relationship with Hitler's Germany was a black mark on the United States. One of McKittrick's friends was none other than Allen Dulles who passed on to him information coming from the bank. McKittrick was an asset of Dulles and he even had his own code name "644."[19]

Declassified wartime documents released in recent years point to a secret role that McKittrick played that was called the "Harvard Plan." The Harvard Plan was a psychological and propaganda warfare operation to cripple the morale of the German people and front line troops. Such techniques were not new, but those who participated in its various, subtle techniques, literally wrote the book for future practitioners.

The department that was responsible for "psy ops" was the MO or Moral Operations Branch. The MO Branch conducted two types

[19] Ibid.

164

of psychological warfare: "Black" and "White." White propaganda is content or information that comes from an open source and is attributable to the government it represents. "Black" propaganda, however, must disguise its source and its consequences. It is non-attributable to any national entity.

The Harvard Plan was run by the MO out of its Washington office and it was aimed for German businessmen, convincing them that the top members of the German government would be detrimental to the war effort and their own well-being. It also promised local businessmen that American industry would help rebuild factories destroyed in the war.

The vehicle for this propaganda onslaught was a newspaper edited in Washington by OSS officers called *Handel and Wandel.* This newspaper reported that the top brass in Berlin had special assault teams in every major German company, whose job it was to destroy industry, thereby removing it from enemy hands. It urged business owners to set up "counter groups" to protect their factories.

The declassified Harvard Project papers reveal that Thomas McKittrick was in close touch with many Nazi industrialists and had "close cooperation between the Allied and German business world. Thus while Allied soldiers were fighting through Europe, McKittrick was cutting deals to keep the German economy strong. This was happening with what the U.S. documents describe as the full assistance of the State Department."

Thomas McKittrick was born in St. Louis in 1889 and graduated from Harvard University in 1911. He joined the U.S. Army in 1918, and when the war was over, he was transferred to Liverpool, England. He worked in tandem with the British intelligence services to make sure that there were no spies along the docks at that vital seaport. After the armistice that ended World War I, he was sent to France to work with Allied occupation forces. After completing his military service he returned to New York where he worked for an investment company called Lee, Higginson & Company.

In 1921, he was sent to London where he worked in the company's London branch and soon became a well-known figure in Europe's banking community. He first got involved with the BIS in 1931 when he joined the German Credits Arbitration Committee, which settled disputes involving German banks. One other member of this committee was Marcus Wallenberg who owned the Swedish Enshilda Bank. Marcus Wallenberg taught McKittrick the fundamentals of international banking. When McKittrick took over the BIS in May 1939, he counted on Marcus Wallenberg's expert assistance for years to come.

While working at the BIS, McKittrick worked hand-in-glove with two of the most important German officials, Reichsbank vice president Emil Puhl and his boss Walter Funk, both of whom would be convicted of war crimes.

From his vantage point in Washington, D.C., Henry Morgenthau and his friend and colleague in the Treasury Department, Harry Dexter White, lobbied hard for the closure of the BIS at the Bretton Woods Conference in July 1944 in which the Allies planned for the postwar financial system. Harry Dexter White, who, unbeknownst to the Roosevelt administration, was a Russian spy and good friend of Morgenthau's, said of the BIS, "There is an American president doing business with the Germans while our boys are fighting the Germans."

The influence of the BIS and its powerful supporters was enough to spare the BIS from being shut down after the war ended. In the decades after the war, the top ranking members of the bank were responsible for the establishment of the euro and the creation of the European Monetary Institute, also called the European Central Bank.

The role of Switzerland during World War II is a tragic story for the simple fact that they were the bankers to the Third Reich, a depository for their looted gold from concentration camp victims, and not as neutral as they appeared to be.

On May 25, 1946, Switzerland and the Allies signed the Washington Agreement whereby the Swiss agreed to pay $58.1 million in gold to a commission set up by the Allies after the war. The money was to be put into a fund to rebuild Europe. In return, the Allies dropped any further claims to the gold that Switzerland got from the Nazis during the war. In 1997, the United States government mounted an inquiry into the Swiss-Nazi money connection called the "Eizenstat Report" in which it was estimated that Switzerland held $305-409 million in looted Nazi gold.

In December 1962, after efforts by Jewish agencies worldwide and in Israel, the Swiss Bankers Association asked Swiss banks to investigate bank accounts that may have belonged to Holocaust victims. A total of 9.5 million Swiss francs were turned over to those interested parties. In February 1996, the Swiss Bankers Association said that after an internal investigation about $32 million was found in 775 dormant accounts (mostly held by Jews).

In April 1996, then U.S. Republican Senator Alfonse D'Amato (N.Y.) began hearings on the role the Swiss played in the Holocaust before the Senate Banking Committee, and the Housing and Urban Affairs Committee. This investigation led President Bill Clinton to approve an official U.S. investigation of the role the Swiss played in the Nazi gold affair, resulted in the Eizenstat Report in May 1997 (the report is available on line).[20]

But the Swiss were just one conduit for the top Nazis who wanted to save their own skins (and their money). Soon after the war was over, a large number of these Nazi war criminals, as well as top-ranking German military officers, formed a secret alliance with the Vatican and other interested parties in Europe to take them out of Germany to a new safe haven in South America and other places where they would be welcome. This was the so-called Ratline that would ferry these men to a new home where they could plan for a Fourth Reich.

———

When Frederick Forsyth wrote his book called *The Odessa File,* he really didn't know how much of a firestorm he'd created. As mentioned in the start of this chapter, his book concentrated on a spider-group of fleeing ex-Nazis who decided to depart the end of the Third Reich and make a new home in other parts of the world, e.g., South America and to a lesser extent, the Middle East. After the time that Mr. Forsyth's book came out, other writers of fiction and filmmakers pounced on his theme of fleeing ex-Nazis and captivated the American public. Adding to this genre was a book by the noted thriller writer Helen Macginnes who wrote a novel called *The Salzburg Connection,* in which a treasure once held by the Nazis is placed in a lake for future Nazi purposes (the book wouldone day be made into a movie starring Barry Newman).

[20] A Chronology Of Events: Frontline/PBS.

Another on this theme was a movie called *The Boys from Brazil* in which young children (twins) were cloned to make future, perfect Nazis for a Fourth Reich.

In 1996, Mr. Forsyth gave an interview to *The Independent* out of the United Kingdom that offered new light on the material in wrote about in his book. The materials written about by *The Independent,* were based on Project Safehaven which has been described in this chapter. "Mr. Forsyth confirmed that his novel was based on reports of a meeting in France in August 1944. This meeting detailed in U.S. documents seen by *The Independent* which were collected by a top-secret intelligence operation called Project Safehaven at the end of the war." He told interviewers that the information he got for his book came from "friends in low places."[21]

The Odessa that Mr. Forsyth was writing about was a real-life organization that worked in the effort of sending ex-Nazi military leaders (some at the top of the Nazi government) to safe havens outside of crumbling Nazi Germany. Many of these Nazis were helped via the Vatican Ratline that used looted gold and money taken from the concentration camp victims to expedite their passage to freedom.

The man who ultimately found out and exposed the Odessa Ratline was Simon Wiesenthal, a Nazi concentration camp survivor who made it his life work to track down and expose the Nazi leaders who fled after the war.

Wiesenthal said that he first learned about the Odessa from a conversation he had with a former member of German counterespionage whom he had met at the start of the Nuremburg trials after the war ended. This person told him that Odessa was first started in 1946 after many of the fleeing Nazis had been captured by U.S. Army officials. The original scope of the Odessa was to give aid and comfort to those Germans who were being kept in POW camps throughout Europe. It soon morphed into an elaborate escape and evasion route out of Europe.

An intricate network was soon established among the Odessa community to aid these men in escaping war-torn Europe. Escape routes were established with maps of transit points made out in

---

[21] Jeffrey's Daniel, "Fourth Reich plot revealed: Jewish group uncovers secret papers that prove conspiracy by Odessa File Nazis," The Independent, September 6, 1996.

detail for them to follow. Some of these were Nazi bigwigs who subsequently began working secretly for the United States and its allies,; they were given new identities and allowed safe passage out of Germany and on toward their final destination. The name given to this secret network was "Die Spinne" (The Spider), which supplied false papers, false passports, safe houses, and contacts who would smuggle fugitives across the Swiss borders. Once they safely arrived in Switzerland, they went on what was called the Monastery Route. "Roman Catholic priests, especially Franciscans, helped Odessa move fugitives from one monastery to the next until they reached Rome. According to Wiesenthal, one Franciscan monastery, Via Sicilia in Rome, was virtually a transit station for Nazis, an arrangement made possible by a bishop from Graz named Alois Hudal. Wiesenthal speculates that the motive for most of the priests was what he viewed as a misguided notion of Christian charity. Once in Italy, the fugitives were out of danger, and many then dispersed around the globe."[22]

Before his death in 2005 at age 96, Simon Wiesenthal dedicated his life to tracking down Nazi criminals who served the Third Reich during World War II. He was an architectural engineer by trade but after his liberation from the concentration camps at the end of the war, he made it his life work to find the man responsible for the Holocaust. He worked out of an office in Vienna called the Jewish Documentation Center where he and his team of dogged researchers collected and catalogued a large number of tips regarding the whereabouts of Nazi fugitives. He later wrote a book called *The Murderers Among Us* (1967), and a second volume called *Justice, Not Vengeance* (1990).

In postwar politics, Mr. Wiesenthal became embroiled in Austrian politics and had frequent run-ins with Austrian Chancellor Bruno Kreisky. His critics disapproved of his friendly relationship with United Nations Secretary General Kurt Waldheim, the Austrian president who concealed the fact that while he was in the German army during the war, his intelligence unit was implicated in atrocities in the Balkans.

His search for Nazis was plagued by criticism that he overestimated his role when it came to tracking these men down.

[22] "The SS: Organization of Former SS Members (Odessa)," Jewish-virtuallibrary.org.

He was challenged regarding his role in the capture in Argentina of Adolf Eichmann in 1960 by Israeli agents who tracked him down and forcibly removed him from the country (more about Eichmann later in this chapter). His actions regarding the whereabouts of Josef Mengele, the Auschwitz death camp doctor who fled to South America, were criticized when his reported sightings of Mengele in South America proved fruitless. He was also taken to task by the husband and wife team of Nazi hunters Serge and Beate Klarsfeld (he, a Paris based lawyer) who were instrumental in tracking down the Nazi Gestapo leader Klaus Barbie in Bolivia. The Klarsfelds "faulted him for not supporting their anti-Nazi demonstrations in South America and Europe."

Mr. Wiesenthal however, did his due diligence when it came to the capture of two of the most notorious criminals to come out of the war: Franz Stangl, the former commandant of the Treblinka and Sobibor death camps in Poland, who was extradited to West Germany in 1967 and died three years later while serving a life sentence; and Gustav Franz Wagner, the former deputy commandant of Sobibor, who died during extradition proceedings in 1980. He was also involved in the capture and extradition from Argentina of Josef Schwammberger, an SS officer convicted in the killings of prisoners and slave laborers in concentration camps in Poland. He was also responsible for the capture of Karl Silberbauer, who was a police officer in Vienna, Austria who had been the Gestapo aide who arrested Anne Frank and her family when they took refuge in an apartment in Amsterdam.

Mr. Wiesenthal also had run-ins with postwar German politicians including Chancellor Bruno Kreisky, who was also Jewish, whom he accused of having a political relationship with certain ex-Nazis who were active in government circles. In return, Chancellor Kreisky accused Wiesenthal of having collaborated with members of the Gestapo, which amounted to nothing.

He also took exception when the Jewish Congress, in 1986, investigated Kurt Waldheim, who would serve as the Secretary General of the United Nations, for his service in the Second World War. The Jewish Congress said that Mr. Waldheim was active in the war, when, as a lieutenant in the German Army, his intelligence unit carried out deportations and atrocities in the Balkans. In his book called *Justice, Not Vengeance,* Wiesenthal said, "I was not prepared to attack Kurt Waldheim as a Nazi or a war criminal because from all I knew about him and from all that emerged from the documents, he had been neither a Nazi, nor a war criminal."

The feud between Mr. Wiesenthal and the World Jewish Congress grew when Eli Rosenbaum, the former counsel of the World Jewish Congress and later director of the Justice Department Office of Special Investigations, which was a Nazi hunting task force, linked Mr. Wiesenthal to a Waldheim cover-up. In a book that Mr. Rosenbaum wrote with his co-author William Hoffer, he wrote that Mr. Wiesenthal, acting on an Israeli request, had found Mr. Waldheim's secret file in French-held archives dating back to 1979 but did not reveal this information for political reasons. The book accuses Mr. Wiesenthal of covering up his alleged knowledge of Kurt Waldheim's links to the Nazi regime in order to secure his own reputation.

After his release from a Nazi concentration camp in May 1945, he regained his health and began a tedious study of Nazi war criminals and gave his information to members of the United States Army's War Crimes Services, as well as the Office of Strategic Services. He served in the Army's Counterintelligence Corps, and headed the Jewish Central Committee of the United States occupation zone in partitioned Austria.

In 1946, he gave evidence regarding these Nazis to U.S. authorities in the American zone of Austria and with help from friends, founded the Jewish Historical Documentation Center in Linz, Austria, whose purpose was to collect as much historical documentation on these ex-Nazis for later evidence when they came to trial. However, his information went for naught when, as the Cold War against the Soviet Union started, many of these men came to the United States under Operation Paperclip.

Simon Wiesenthal went on to write a number of books, including, *Concentration Camp Mauthausen* (1946), *I Hunted Eichmann* (1961), and *The Secret Mission of Christopher Columbus* (1973), in which he postulated that the Columbus' voyage of discovery in 1492 was in part an effort to find a homeland for Europe's persecuted Jews.[23]

---

23   Blumenthal, Ralph, "Simon Wiesenthal, Nazi Hunter, Dies at [96,] *New York Times*, September 21, 2005.

In my book called *The Secret History of the United States: Conspiracies, Cobwebs and Lies,* there is a chapter called "Was Columbus Jewish" in which I give the reasons behind the most recent speculation that Columbus came from a family of baptized Jews, that Columbus had many contacts with Jews of that time, and sometimes wrote in Hebrew.

Another man who took an active interest in the Nazi Ratline coming out of Rome, Italy but whose exploits were not as well known as those of Simon Wiesenthal, was an American Army agent named William Gowen. As William Gowen began to investigate this Vatican-Nazi connection, he discovered a shadowy network called Intermarium that had its roots right in the middle of St. Peter's Square.

William Gowen was a member of the U.S. Army Counterintelligence Corps and he and his team made large strides in finding proof of a connection between the Vatican and the escape of large number of Nazis to South America:

> The American officers, concluded that the Vatican was the largest single organization involved in the illegal movement of emigrants in and through Italy, and that the Holy See's justification for its participation in this illegal traffic is simply the propagation of the Faith. For it was the Vatican's desire to assist any person regardless of nationality or political beliefs, as long as that person can prove himself to be a Catholic.[24]

Vincent La Vista, a U.S. State Department intelligence officer, wrote in a report regarding this topic, "The Vatican brought pressure to bear on Catholic countries in South America, especially Argentina but also Mexico, Cuba and others. This resulted in the foreign missions of those countries taking an attitude almost favoring the entry into their countries of former Nazi, and former Fascists or other political groups, so long as they are anti-Communist."

The Gowen family was right in the middle of the Vatican-Nazi connection as his father, Franklin Gowen was a senior State Department official who served in 1940 as the assistant to Myron Taylor who was FDR's personal representative to Pope Pius XII.

[24] *Unholy Trinity*, Page 48.

Going through all of his intelligence records while employed with the Counter Intelligence Corps, William Gowen was able to piece together the roots behind the Intermarium, saying that they were part of an organized network of Central and Eastern European Nazi emigres which were operating at the fringes of the Vatican and with its full cooperation. The Intermarium began in the 1920s in Paris in the wake of the takeover of power by the Bolsheviks in Russia. These people began calling themselves "whites" as opposed to the "reds" who were now in power in Moscow. This group wanted to remake Europe in their own brand and restore order to what they viewed as a reign of terror then being inflicted on the peoples of Europe.

William Gowen centered his search for information on the Intermarium in the person of a Hungarian named Ferenc Vajta who was linked to an important and well financed Nazi-smuggling network. He thought that Vajta would be able to reveal the connection between the Vatican and the large number of fleeing Nazis. In 1947, Gowen tracked Vajta down in Rome where he was in hiding. Gowen told Vajta that if he provided him with information that he wanted on the ratline, he'd help Vajta in getting back his papers and passport that had been taken from him by the Italian police. In their discussions, he told Gowen that he worked for two years with both the French and British intelligence services, organizing "two clandestine movements against the Russians." He said that the Vatican had supported these operations, "informally working with the French and the British to revive Imperium after World War II."

Vajta said that he was the Hungarian Consul General in Vienna when the war ended and that he was responsible for the evacuation of Hungarian industry and to establish secure routes for refugees. He said that the French used him to secure money to run espionage operations after the war which also aided in the reestablishment of the Intermarium after the war ended.

Gowen established that Vajta was employed by the French High Command in Austria in 1945-46 and worked for the Deuxieme Bureau and was on very good terms with Charles de Gaulle who was the head of the Free French forces during the war and later became president of France. Working with the French intelligence services, Vajta was able to organize clandestine espionage cells in such places as Innsbruck, Freiburg, and Paris. He revealed that De Gaulle had established a close relationship with the Vatican hierarchy for their mutual interests. In time, Vajta was to become one of the leading members of the Intermarium. Gowen said of Vajta, "His reputation as a conceited adventurer true only to money did much to drive the Hungarians away from Intermarium." By 1945, the French had passed Vajta over to the British secret service and he did the same kind of work for them as he did with the French.

One of the men who would play a large part in both the operations of Intermarium and the ratline was a Croatian priest named Father Krunoslav Draganovic, the Secretary of the Confraternity of San Girolamo in Rome. Father Draganovic was to be the Croat representative to Intermarium in "quasi-official capacity."

Aarons and Loftus write about Father Draganovic in their book *Unholy Trinity:* "After the war, Father Draganovic skillfully used the benevolence with which the Vatican viewed San Girolamo, to build a thoroughly professional Nazi-smuggling system. With the help of other fanatic Croatian nationalist clerics, the Institute became the headquarters of the Ratlines."

Draganovic was born in Bosnia in 1903 and was headed for the priesthood at a young age. He took his vows in 1928 and was soon employed in Rome working in the Vatican Archives. He was then employed as the secretary to Bishop Ivan Saric of Sarajevo. Working in Rome in August 1943, representing the Ustashi and the Croatian Red Cross, allowed him to build up his escape routes for Nazi war criminals. As a result, he could move in the highest circles, meeting regularly with Secretary of State Maglione, and even Pope Pius XII. He also had close contacts with Axis diplomats at the Vatican, which would later prove invaluable."[25]

The authors of *Unholy Trinity* write that Father Draganovic had close connections with Assistant Secretary of State Montini who helped him gain access to the Pope's Refugee Assistance Commission. They write that by 1944 his ratline was fully established and that Father Draganovic began supplying identity papers to both legal and illegal refugees.

While Father Draganovic was gearing up his new ratline, it seems that Vajta had his own agenda. He had talks with the Spanish Foreign Affairs department which subsequently allowed the entry of

[25] *Unholy Trinity,* Page 57.

"Eastern Europeans to Spain." The U.S. government found out what he was doing and turned a blind eye. In order to curry favor with the United States, Vajta provided the United States with information on the Soviet "Tangiers network."

It now seemed that Vajta's luck had turned for the worse. In 1947, upon his return to Rome, he was arrested by the Italian government, probably on the request of the Hungarian government. William Gowen found out that Vajta had been released even though Vajta was a noted war criminal and a man of dubious character.

Over time, it seems, that William Gowen had a change of heart regarding his prime-time source (Vajta) and he took steps to rein him in. In 1946, the Hungarian government asked for his transfer but both the British and French intelligence services refused to give him up. Right after the war ended, the OSS took further steps to corral Vajta and they placed him on a "Black List" of wanted Nazis, making him a target for arrest. He was then taken as a POW to the Dachau prison camp, where to his surprise, he met a fellow POW, the Crown Prince of Siam who got in touch with the British and Vajta was released. Gowen learned that Vajta had worked for the Hungarian Secret Service before World War II began, and had contacts with various western intelligence services.

Says *Unholy Trinity*: "He had also been a senior Nazi propagandist for German-sponsored newspapers which spewed out an incessant pro-Nazi and anti-Semitic barrage that poisoned Hungarian public opinion and prepared the ground for the anti-Jewish measures adopted during the German occupation in 1944."

When the U.S. government did an investigation of Vajta they concluded that he had been a member of the pro-Nazi party and had "allegedly denounced numerous anti-Nazis. Reputation generally unsavory."

As Gowen and the CIC made further investigation of both Vajta and Intermarium, they came up with a lot of disturbing information. Gowen and his men came to the conclusion that during the war, Intermarium "was believed to have been an instrument of the German intelligence [the Abwehr]. They also discovered that the Abwehr used Intermarium members "as agents of influence abroad as well as reasonably reliable sources of information on émigré communities of Europe."

Like many other questionable Nazi leaders, Vajta came to the United States in December 16, 1947 and the U.S. government took notice. A U.S. government report on Vajta dated March 10, 1952 said that, "Immediately after his entry, public denunciation of him said that he was a dangerous 'Hungarian Nazi' whose name appeared on the list of war criminals" and who had been "the right hand man" of Hungary's Nazi leader, Ferenc Szalasi. It was further alleged that he had escaped from American custody while awaiting trial on war criminal charges. Investigation among the Hungarian element in the United States indicated that these charges had substance. An immigration warrant of arrest was issued on January 9, 1948, and Vajta was immediately taken into custody under the warrant."

When Vajta was interrogated by the Army after his capture, the report says that Vajta urged the Hungarian government to rush deported Jews from Budapest, and gave assurance that he, Vajta, would be able to distribute them among the various concentration camps in Germany and Austria. Martin Himler (Himler was a U.S. official who testified at Vajta's deportation hearing) said that "Vajta definitely came within the war criminal classification established by the United Nations War Crimes Commission."

Vajta then escaped from American custody and entered the French zone of Austria. He told the French the location of 6,000 kilograms of buried gold which the French took possession of. Vajta was employed as an informer by the French security forces.[26]

Once out of U.S. custody, it seems that Vajta's fortunes soon turned for the better. In 1947, the United States turned its attention to the new Cold War that was beginning take effect with the Soviet Union. The U.S. and its allies needed to know more about what was going on in Eastern Europe and who better to given them that information than Ferenc Vajta. In that same year, the Hungarian government asked for Vajta's extradition but it seems that the wily Vajta had fled to Italy and was said to have taken refuge at Castelgandolfo that was the residence of the various pope's when they left Vatican City. He stayed there until September 1947 when he returned to Rome and was given sanctuary by his many Vatican contacts. While in Rome, he was given false identity papers by the French that enabled him to travel around Europe without being noticed.

[26] Letter to Senator McCarran, dated March 10, 1952.

Vajta traveled to Spain under the watchful eye of both William Gowen and the United States government. In Spain, he started a new anti-communist group called the Continental Union on behalf of the United States.

If one part of the American government looked at Vajta in a favorable light, another took the opposite approach. In February 1948, the Army's Intelligence Division contacted the U.S. European High Command because of derogatory information they'd learned concerning Vajta and Gowen. Vajta had been given a visa to travel to the United States marked "Diplomatic." It seems that Gowen pulled strings to get his friend into the States despite the fact that the U.S. knew of Vajta's Nazi connections.

The reason for his trip to the United States was to gain support for his fledgling Continental Union but it seems that two of the nation's top reporters of the time, Drew Pearson and Walter Winchell, found out that he was in the country. Vajta was arrested on February 3, 1948 when he arrived at Ellis Island in New York. A congressional investigation regarding Vajta was held but the results of that inquiry were never released to the public. William Gowen later said that he had full knowledge of Vajta's escape, plus his "close personal knowledge of the Vatican's role in hiding and assisting known Nazi fugitives.

The presence of Vajta in the United States was soon too much to bear and he was picked up by the Immigration and Naturalization Service and thrown out of the country in February 1950. He wound up in Colombia after Italy and Spain refused to take him in. He spent the rest of his life in Bogota and worked as an economics professor.

The recruitment of both Anton Turkul and Ferenc Vajta were symptomatic of the United States' need for reliable intelligence operatives during the war. It didn't matter that they were unscrupulous characters or were charged with being on the side of the Nazis. If they could provide information on our enemies, so much the better. The war needed to be won and these people, good or bad, were part of the mix.

What is not in dispute is that many Nazi leaders fled Europe at the end of the war for safety. But how did they do it? One way was the above described Nazi Ratline that led to Central and South America that facilitated the escape of Nazi war criminals as well as leaders of the Third Reich out of the country. It has been estimated that over nine thousand Nazi war criminals fled to South America after World War II ended. Many of these people were Croatians, Ukrainians, Russians and other people who had help via certain members of the Vatican hierarchy to flee war-torn Europe. About 5,000 went to Argentina where they were protected by the Nazi-leaning Juan Peron and his wife Evita, while an estimated 1,500 to 2,000 went to Brazil, and up to 500 to 1,000 to Paraguay and Uruguay.

One of the main facilitators of the ratline was a German Bishop named Alois Hudal who was a highly placed priest to the German Catholic community in the Vatican. One of Bishop Hudal's associates was Martin Bormann, one of Hitler's most trusted advisors. Bishop Hudal was a staunch anti-communist, and a Jesuit trained priest. In 1944, he took control of the Austrian division of the Papal Commission of the Episcopate for German-speaking Catholics in Italy. That same year he took command over the Austrian division of the Papal Commission of Assistance (PCA) that was set up to aid displaced persons. Bishop Hudal's PCA would form the backbone of the Nazi ratlines used to aid escaping Nazi leaders. Among those whom Bishop Hudal helped escape Europe were SS lieutenant Franz Stangl, the commanding officer at the Treblinka concentration camp, and Gustav Wagner, the commanding officer at the Sobibor camp. When Stangl reached Rome, Hudal found a safe house for him to stay while he made plans for him to leave the country. He arranged for Stangl to receive a Red Cross passport, along with a Syrian visa.

Among the other high-level Nazi officials whom Bishop Hudal helped flee Europe were Joseph Mengele, a doctor who performed experiments on concentration camp victims, as well as Martin Bormann's aide, Alois Brunner. Brunner was responsible for the running of the Drancy internment camp near Paris. In 1947, Hudal's activities were unearthed by a German language newspaper called *Passauer Neue Presse,* which accused him of running his ratline organization. Despite his being exposed in aiding escaped Nazi war criminals, the bishop continued his work, and in August 1948, he contacted President Peron in Argentina asking for 5,000 Argentine visas for German and Austrian soldiers who requested asylum in other countries.

The destination of the ratline was South America, particularly Argentina, Paraguay, Brazil, Uruguay, and Chile. Other endpoints were the United States, Canada, and the Middle East. There were two main routes out of Europe, the first from Germany to Spain, then on to Argentina, the second from Germany to Rome to Genoa, then South America. As noted, ccording to authors Loftus and Aarons, the major Roman ratline was run by a "small but influential network of Croatian priests, members of the Franciscan order, led by Father Krunoslav Draganovic. He organized a highly sophisticated chain with headquarters at the San Girolamo Seminary College in Rome, but with links from Austria to the final port of Genoa."

Genoa was the hotbed of activity from which many Nazis began their trip to safety. The Archbishop of Genoa, Cardinal Siri helped Hudal and Father Draganovic to supply these Nazis with all the necessary papers to aid them on their way. The organization founded for this operation was called the Vatican Relief Commission. In a book called *History vs. Apologetics: The Holocaust, the Third Reich and the Catholic Church,* author David Cymet says that Archbishop Siri set up an organization called "The National Committee for Emigration to Argentina" which was the country that took in a large number of fleeing Nazis.

Another organization that took an active role in smuggling Nazis out of Europe was the Red Cross whose primary job was to provide help to the thousands of displaced people then residing in POW camps across Europe. Red Cross officials did not have the manpower to check the identities of those who were seeking asylum in other parts of the world and they gave immigration papers and other travel documents to people who were wanted by the Allies. Some of these men were war criminals; others were not. But in the chaos of the end of the war, that distinction was left unchecked. Bishop Hudal and his fellow priests often times wrote letters of recommendation or forged papers for these lucky persons and sent them on their way to their new homes.

Some historians believe that the funding for this massive ratline program came from the Vatican Bank. The bank was the conduit for all money coming in and going out of the Vatican and in the decades to come, it would be embroiled in a scandal that would rock the pope of Rome and the Vatican in particular (more on the Vatican Bank scandal in an upcoming chapter). It has been written that most of the money to fund the Rome ratlines came from Catholic organizations in the United States, including the National Catholic Welfare Conference whose bishops arranged the funds. The American who was most responsible for aiding the NCWC was New York's Cardinal Francis Spellman, one of the most powerful and influential prelates in the United States. Cardinal Spellman had powerful friends in the Vatican. At one time, Francis Spellman had worked in Rome in the Papal Secretariat with the future pope, Eugenio Pacelli, and a bond between the two men was forged. Spellman was once called "by far the greatest business head the Church has ever had in America, a bishop who had turned his see, financially into a flourishing enterprise. Spellman directed the flow of money from the United States into the Vatican coffers. Montini, head of the PCA, would, after becoming pope, always remember that most of the funds for his relief organization came from the U.S. Catholic Church."[27]

Father Hudal found a friend in the person of Adolf Hitler. Hudal was as anti-Sematic as Hitler and the men found a common ally in each other. In 1937, Hudal wrote a book in favor of German National Socialism which must have pleased Hitler immensely. Hudal's ratline was ongoing and an article in the German Agency Nord Press which was published on December 6, 1949 said that by the end of 1949, Hudal was receiving from 60 to 100 Germans each day in Rome who wanted his help in getting them false papers to travel abroad.

Father Draganovic set up his own ratline based in Rome, the Pontifical College of San Girolamo degli Illirici which provided papers and other travel documents mainly for the many Croatian war criminals who desperately wanted to flee Europe. One of the major war criminals who used Draganovic's ratline was Ante Pavelic, who ran the Nazi puppet state in Croatia during the war he wound up in Argentina. A U.S. intelligence report on Pavelic said, "Pavelic's contacts are so high and his present position so compromising to the

[27] Madigan, Kevin, "How the Catholic Church Sheltered Nazi War Criminals," *Commentary Magazine* 12-1-20II.

Vatican that any extradition of Subject will deal a staggering blow to the Roman Catholic Church."

In 2006, records declassified at the U.S. National Archives regarding these Nazi war criminals showed that the United States was aware of the location of Adolf Eichmann, the mastermind of the "Final Solution," more than two years before his capture by Israeli agents in Argentina where he had been living for years. According to the documents, in 1958 the West German intelligence service told the CIA that Eichmann was living in Argentina under the alias Ricardo Klement, despite years-long denials from the Argentine government that Eichmann was living in that country. One of the reasons that West Germany did not want to see Eichmann arrested was because they were concerned what he would say about a man named Hans Globke, who was Chancellor Konrad Adenauer's national security advisor. Globke had served in the Jewish Affairs Department of the Nazi regime in World War II and was involved in writing laws designed to remove Jews from German society.

The records say, "The CIA, which worked closely with Globke, assisted the West Germans in protecting him from Eichmann. In 1960, in an elaborate undercover operation inside Argentina, Eichmann was captured by Israeli agents and smuggled back to Israel on an El Al flight."

In the 1970s, the U.S. government created an organization called the Office of Special Investigations in the Justice Department to look into the role of Nazi fugitives and their relationship with the American government. Over time, the CIA released 1,365 pages of materials relating to Adolf Eichmann. "They include published materials, declassified documents, interrogations, confidential reports from agents or informants, and CIA analytical reports."

In the late 1950s, American CIA agents spoke to two of Eichmann's colleagues, Kurt Becher, an SS officer, and Wilhelm Hoetti, a con man to the core. Both men said that the last time they saw Eichmann was in Bad Aussee in Austria during the latter stages of the war. The CIA files on Eichmann also show that the agency was surprised that Eichmann had been captured by the Israelis in May 1960 and cables from the time show that Allen Dulles, the CIA director, demanded that officers find out more about his capture.[28]

[28] Adolf Eichmann CIA Files: www.paperlessarchives.com/adolf-eichmann-ciafiles.

At the end of the war, Eichmann knew he was one of the top men the Allies were after and his fears were confirmed when the lawyers at the Nuremberg War Crimes Trial made him the number one target on their list. Eichmann fled war-torn Berlin and made his way to safety. He worked under an assumed name as a lumberjack in Germany and through an intermediary named Richard Kops, he was able to find his way to Argentina.

Simon Wiesenthal believed that Bishop Hudal helped Eichmann flee Europe, giving him a new identity as a Croatian refugee named Richard Klement and sent him to Genoa. There, Wiesenthal believed, Archbishop Siri hid Eichmann in a monastery before sending him on to Argentina. An historian who worked for the Vatican by the name of Father Robert Graham said, "Hudal might have helped a handful, a mere handful of Nazi war criminals to escape." Hudal said regarding his knowledge of Eichmann fleeing to South America, "I don't know. I helped a lot of people and Eichmann may have been among them."

Bishop Hudal was well connected in the hierarchy of the Vatican beginning around 1930, as a worker in the Holy Office, "working in the most rigorous secrecy," as U.S. intelligence reported. The intelligence report goes on to say, "As Hudal's views grew more stridently and publicly pro-Nazi, nothing was done either to discipline or remove him from his powerful post. Instead the Vatican promoted him in June 1933 from priest to titular bishop, an extremely rare honor for a relatively lowly rector of a teaching college."

When he arrived in Argentina, Eichmann hid in plain sight, working in a factory near Buenos Aires. By now he had his family with him and they tried to resume their normal lives. However, he was spotted in Argentina by informers and word got back to the Israelis who sent an elite Mossad team who successfully spirited him back to Israel for trail.

Back in Israel, Eichmann was put on trial for crimes against the Jewish people as well as being a war criminal subject to the Nuremberg court. He was put on trial in 1961 and that lasted for eight months. One hundred eleven survivors of the death camps testified against him and he was convicted on all counts and sentenced to death. Eichmann was hanged on June 1, 1962. He was prosecuted under the provisions of the Nazi and Nazi Collaborators Punishment Law which was established by the government of Israeli Prime Minister David Ben-Gurion. The lasting outcome of Eichmann's trial was that a worldwide audience now heard the real truth of the Holocaust and the role that Adolf Eichmann played.

Among the files released by the CIA were those concerning Dr. Josef Mengele, the notorious death camp doctor who oversaw the deaths of hundreds of thousands Jews in the concentration camps. Mengele escaped Europe and wound up in Paraguay; he lived there as well as other South American nations from 1951 on, obtaining his Paraguayan citizenship in 1959 under his own name. It seems that his identity was confirmed in Paraguay and Mengele fled to Brazil using the alias "Wolfgang Gearhart." In 1979, Mengele suffered a fatal stroke while swimming at a Sao Paolo, Brazil beach. In 1985, a Brazilian German couple named Bossert (who had befriended Mengele) told authorities that Mengele died in 1979 and gave the location of his grave in the town of Embu outside of Sao Paolo. When the discovery of Mengele's grave was revealed, a forensic investigation of his remains was conducted by people from the U.S., West Germany, and Israel. The final report from these investigators said that the remains they worked on from the cemetery were in fact those of Josef Mengele and that he had died in Sao Paolo in 1979.

The CIA files make mention of the Odessa in relation to Josef Mengele. On July 18, 1965, the CIA sent a response to the Justice Department request for a trace on a Dr. Theodor Binder for information regarding Mengele. Binder was the head of the Albert Schweitzer Hospital in Pucallpa, Peru. The CIA's file on Binder contained a document from the State Department to the U.S. Secret Service regarding the circulation of counterfeit U.S. currency in Peru. It is alleged that a number of former officers were allegedly involved, including some who worked for an organization of former SS officers (Odessa) in South America.

The CIA files say that the agency had no knowledge of the whereabouts of Dr. Mengele after his escape from Europe. The CIA began it search for him in 1972 and concluded that he had escaped to Paraguay, where he lived under the protection of the Paraguayan government, vanishing in 1960. The files say that Mengele might have gone to Brazil at some point and it wasn't until 1985 that the

CIA devoted a large-scale investigation into the postwar activities of Dr. Mengele.

A July 1972 CIA report on Dr. Mengele reads as follows:

> Josef Mengele arrived in Paraguay for the first time around 1951 and lived alternately Paraguay, Brazil, Argentina and Uruguay. He worked for some time as a salesman for German farm machinery firm in Paraguay and Argentina. During time he was in Paraguay, Mengele never tried to hide his identity or use a false name, even during frequent trips to Argentina and Brazil. On 27 Nov. 59 was naturalized as Paraguayan citizen under the name Josef Mengele.

More information on Mengele's time in South America came via a CIA "Memorandum for the Files" dated December 7, 1984 from John Leonard, otherwise unknown. In his memo, he tells of a meeting he had on December 3, 1984 with a man named Robert Posner, a New York lawyer visiting Paraguay for research on a book he was doing on Josef Mengele. He said that he had met a man named Col. Alejandro von Eckstein, a Russian émigré who had lived in Paraguay for 50 years, and further said that he was in charge of intelligence matters for President Stroessner of Paraguay. Von Eckstein told Mr. Posner that he had information relating to Josef Mengele and that he'd provide it to him.

Von Eckstein told Mr. Posner that Mengele first came to Paraguay in 1954 or '55 when he was still living in Buenos Aires. When Mengele was in Asuncion, he would stay with a man named Werner Jung who was a representative of the Mengele firm in Germany that manufactured farm equipment.

Von Eckstein said that he was introduced to Mengele by Colonel Hans Rudel, the famous German pilot in World War II. Other persons who were close to Mengele during that time period were Alban Krugg, at whose heavily fortified farmhouse near Encarnacion Mengele stayed, and Otto Biss, a Hungarian Nazi.

Von Eckstein said that he vouched for Mengele when the latter applied for and received Paraguayan citizenship in 1959. He said, "Since he knew Mengele was coming to Paraguay regularly since

1954 or 55, he didn't feel that he was stretching the truth when he supported the latter's claim of having resided here for 5 years, in order to gain his citizenship."[29]

Another person who used Bishop Hudal's ratline out of Europe was the so-called "Butcher of Lyon," the notorious Klaus Barbie. Klaus Barbie was wanted for war crimes, and like other men of the time, was used by the United States after the war in its early fight against Russian communism.

August 14, 1947 was a hot day in Memmingen, Germany. People were outside doing their shopping or just taking in a beautiful summer day. In a café, three men met for the first time, taking stock of each other. By the time the meeting was over, the United States would put on their intelligence book, one of the most wanted members of the Gestapo and a noted war criminal to boot. His name was Klaus Barbie and he would come to haunt the CIA and the American military years after the war ended.

The three men who met that August day were Kurt Merk, a former officer in the Nazi German military intelligence agency, the Abwehr, headed by Wilhelm Canaris, whose name has come up quite often in this narrative. At the time of this meeting, Merk had been on the payroll of the United States intelligence services for some time. The second man in attendance was Robert Taylor, an officer in the Army's Counter Intelligence Corps (CIC). The third man, and the center of attention in the meeting, was a Nazi war criminal who was wanted for the killing early in the war a large number of Jews and Slavs. He personally ordered the deportation of 44 Jewish children at Auschwitz in 1944.

In November 1942, he was assigned to Lyon, France as section chief. One of his jobs at Lyon was to build torture chambers for captured members of the French Resistance. One of his victims was a noted French Resistance leader named Jean Moulin. Sources at the time alleged that Barbie tortured Moulin to death. Due to the atrocities that Barbie committed, he was given the moniker as "the Butcher of Lyon." The meeting that August day was not to remember old times but to talk about the future. More importantly, the meeting was to cement a deal with the United States military and Klaus Barbie to make him an American intelligence operative, despite

---

[29] Memorandum for the Record, December 7, 1984, From POL-John F. Leonard. www.paperlessarvhives..com/josef-mengele-cia-files.html.

his sordid past. Before the meeting ended, Robert Taylor, who was part of the 66th Counterintelligence Corps under the European Command stationed in Munich, Germany, would officially recruit Klaus Barbie into the American fold.

It seems that CIC agent Taylor did not inform his superiors the he offered Klaus Barbie an undercover post with the CIC. He did however, check in with his superior officer, Lt. Col. Dave Garvey, the Commanding officer of Region IV on April 14-15, 1947 and the decision was made to use Barbie as an informant, provided that he break off any connections he may have had with illegal SS elements.

Taylor met with Barbie once again around April 18, 1947 and a deal was agreed to. Barbie told CIC agent Taylor that he was willing to break off his former SS ties because his connection with SS elements was necessary only to retain his own personal freedom. While Taylor did not tell his superiors about taking on Barbie, he did have a number of things to say about his new recruit. He wrote that Barbie was "an honest man both intellectually and personally, absolutely without fear. He is strongly anti-communist and a Nazi idealist who believes that he and his beliefs were betrayed by the Nazis in power." Three decades later, Taylor said of Barbie, "I have regrets today." He insists that he was unaware that Barbie was a member of the Gestapo.

There were other Americans who knew of Barbie's background during the time he was in our custody, among them, Col. David Erskine who approved Barbie's recruitment and was instrumental in helping him evade the French who were banging down the door for his extradition to France. On May 3, 1950, the Army's European Command sent Col. Erskine a memo regarding news reports concerning Barbie: "French newspapers are making a large splash stating that Barbie is guilty of war crimes. Request any information regarding Barbie." Erskine called a meeting of his top aides and as the Barbie files show, "It was decided that Barbie should not be placed in the hands of the French."

Col. Dale Garvey was one of the men who approved of recruiting Barbie "provided that he break off any connections he may have had with illegal SS elements." The fact remains that Barbie did no such thing. Col. Garvey later said, "I made the decision that I made on the basis of the best information I had at the time."

One CIC officer, Captain Eugene Kolb, even went so far as to say that he didn't believe that Barbie was guilty of any war crimes. Kolb was the regional CIC operations officer who was responsible for Barbie while he was in American hands. He said that he didn't know that his prisoner was accused of any misdeeds and further said, "Some of the allegations may have been exaggerated." He also said that it was his opinion that the U.S. was right when they made the decision not to turn him over to the French.

Another man who had dealings with Barbie was Major Erhard Dabringhaus, who in 1948 learned from another German informant of Barbie's background but was told by his superiors not to reveal what he knew. French intelligence officers queried Dabringhaus regarding his knowledge of Barbie's whereabouts but he told them nothing. He did have the foresight to report what he knew to his commanders and for this action he was transferred to another posting. Many years later, Dabringhaus saw a show on television regarding the Barbie affair and wrote a letter to NBC news about what he knew regarding Barbie. He later assisted the U.S. Justice Department on its investigation of Barbie's wartime activities. He made this telling comment regarding what his old wartime buddies told him. "They told me I should have kept my mouth shut."[30]

Kurt Merk had worked for Taylor since June 4, 1946 and was well liked and respected by Robert Taylor. Some months earlier, on April 10, 1946, Kurt Merk told Robert Taylor about his friend, Klaus Barbie and suggested that they meet. That recommendation culminated in the August meeting between the three men.

Kurt Merk had a story to tell. He was captured by Allied forces at the end of the war and was let go in 1946. He went by the alias "Peterson" and led a team of German spies hired by the 66th CIC Detachment stationed near the Kempten-Memmingen area, but was engaged in intelligence collection operations throughout Europe. Merk worked and collaborated with Barbie in the Dijon area of France in 1942 and was no stranger to what Barbie was doing at the time. When he learned that the CIA had reservations about hiring Barbie, he became a character witness for him and said that Barbie was an expert on French Communists and that Barbie's information on them would be critical in the next phase of the Cold War.

[30] Anderson, Jack, "Those Who Helped Klaus Barbie," *The Washington Post,* October 21, 1984.

The CIC was desperate for competent men who would be able to aid them in their new fight against communism, no matter what their backgrounds were. Barbie admitted to the CIC that during the war, he and a few of his SD colleagues, who had no money, posed as plainclothes policemen and invaded the home and "confiscated" the jewelry of a Jewish woman of a wealthy "Aryan" baron. Despite that confession, Barbie was offered a job on Merk's team in April 1947 and was eventually made its deputy chief because of his ability to recruit informants.

The reason the CIC was so interested in Klaus Barbie was the fact that he worked for the British intelligence service for the past year. The CIC wanted detailed information on British interrogation techniques that Barbie could provide. They were also interested in finding out the identities of former SS officers that the British were interested in locating.

The background story of how the CIC recruited Barbie and others like him reads like a spy novel. By the late 1940s, the U.S. Army's intelligence unit, the Counter Intelligence Corps, had established many agent networks within the European occupation zones, and extended into Eastern Europe. Many of the men they employed were veterans of the war and were thought to be an official asset for the U.S. In order to monitor these groups, the CIC infiltrated one of their own agents posing as a Swiss Nazi to report on what he learned. Barbie helped the CIC run a counterintelligence net named "Buro Petersen" which monitored French intelligence. In 1948, Barbie helped the CIC locate former Gestapo informants. In 1949-50, he penetrated German Communist Party activities for the CIC in the Augsburg area. It seems that the leaders of the CIC were not initially aware that Barbie had been hired and were at a quandary about keeping him on. By March 1950, the French were pressing the Americans to hand over Barbie to them for war crimes charges. By the time his service with the United Sates was over, the U.S. was complicit in enabling Barbie to flee to South America where he stayed hidden for almost 30 years.[31]

Eugene Kolb, an Army intelligence officer who worked with Barbie wrote of his relationship with him saying, "Due to his long association with CIC, subject (Barbie) knows the identity of most

[31] Klaus Barbie CIA Files. www.paperlessarchives.com/klaus-barbie-cia-files.

KPD (German Communist Party) penetration sources used by this office, due to the fact that he either handled these sources or because he recruited such sources."

Barbie was one of the leading figures in one of the Eastern European networks operating in the Marburg area and called himself "Becker." Checking their vast records, the CIC's file on Barbie said that he was the head of the Gestapo in Lyon, France. The CIC's note on him said, "Barbie was listed as long a member of the SD a dangerous conspirator who was last heard of in November and December 1944 in a hospital in Baden-Baden, Germany, near the French border."

The CIC report on Barbie revealed that:

> One of the leaders was thought to be Barbie, whose group was believed responsible for the procurement of supplies for the organization and the establishment of an intelligence network throughout the British and American zones. Specifically, members of Barbie's group were believed to be people who have been connected in the past with one or more of the German Intelligence organizations, such as the Amts and RSHS. CIC believed that the group led by SS Captain Barbie has concentrated on the establishment of an intelligence network throughout the United States and British Zones, and possibly further.

Just what where the charges brought against Klaus Barbie that ultimately led the French government to ask for his extradition from American control (which never happened)? The Free French government led by General Charles de Gaulle, knew about Barbie's dubious past, well before the war ended. During the period of 1942-44 they knew that Barbie was the ringleader of atrocities committed against French Resistance leaders and a number of Jews, located at Dijon and in the Lyons region of St. Genis-Laval, Montluc, and in Lyons itself. "Most damming, he had signed the notorious April 1944 deportation order removing Jewish children from their refuge in an Izieu orphanage to Drancy concentration camp, and thence to the Auschwitz gas chambers." In 1952 and 1954, a military court in Lyons found Barbie guilty of torture, executions, deportations, and looting and was sentenced to death in absentia.

By August 1945, the French Ministry of Interior, while conducting an investigation relating to crimes perpetrated by French collaborators, came across Barbie's name. This came to light during a trial of Rene Hardy, a French Resistance hero charged with having betrayed some of his friends under torture by Barbie. The French then asked that Barbie be sent to France to be a witness at Hardy's trial. French authorities deposed Barbie a total of four times by January 1950 in the American Zone with permission from the CIC. Subsequently, an arrest warrant was made and was circulated to the personnel in the American Zone. The CIC was of course notified of the Barbie extradition notice but they kept him on, nevertheless.

The French Ministry of Interior pressed the Office of Military Government, and forcefully asked that Barbie be sent back. "Resorting to the rationalization that Barbie knew too much about the network of German spies CIC had planted in various European Communist organizations—but presumably as much to avoid the embarrassment of having recruited him—in 1951 the CIC sponsored his escape to South America via a ratline operating through Italy."[32]

The American government's report on the Barbie case says something very interesting and disturbing regarding his subsequent escape to South America and the reason the U.S. did nothing to stop him:

To have exposed BARBIE to interrogation and public trial would not have been in consonance with accepted clandestine intelligence operational doctrine. He was knowledgeable of high-level operational procedures, which would have been compromised. Through procedures at that time, Barbie was therefore assisted in 1951 in leaving Europe for resettlement. U.S. Army Intelligence has had no further contact with Barbie subsequent to his departure from Europe.

The United States now turned to the ratline operated by Father Draganovic to get Barbie to Bolivia. Using Vatican as well as Red Cross resources, Barbie was clandestinely taken to his new home

[32] Analysis of the IRR File of Klaus Barbie, www.archives/gov/iwg/research-papers/Barbie.

190

in Bolivia where he was given a new name, "Klaus Altman," and returned to his old lifestyle, taking up with the repressive regime of President Rene Otuno who aided the government in "matters of internal security." In 1957 Klaus Altman/Klaus Barbie had become a citizen of Bolivia and he began working with the Otuno regime in various illegal and unethical operations.

The CIA worked actively to beef up the government of President Ortuno and Barbie was at the center of activities. Barbie and a fellow ex-Nazi named Frederich Schwend, who was a forger during the war, established a business called the Estrella Company which sold assault rifles and other goods to all comers. Barbie's Estrella branched out into selling guns as well as drugs. Barbie's supplier of guns was a German company called Merx. Barbie and his associates sold these weapons to right-wing regimes throughout South America, including Bolivia where he was then living.

Barbie and the CIA began working together when the agency found out that Che Guevara, one of Fidel Castro's most important colleagues and fellow Cuban revolutionary, was formenting trouble in Bolivia by inciting the native Indian population to demand better living conditions. The Agency asked Barbie for any information he had on the whereabouts of Che in Bolivia as well as asking him to keep them informed on military matters then going on in that country.

When the repressive regime of Hugo Banzer Suarez came to power in 1971, the new dictator made Barbie an honorary colonel as well as a paid consultant for the Ministry of the Interior and the notorious Department 7, the counterinsurgency department of the Bolivian Army, both of which were funded by the CIA.[33]

Barbie was paid $2,000 a month by the Bolivian government but that was just chicken feed compared to what he and his partners got from selling arms. While the French government was still actively looking for Barbie and the United States government remained silent as to his location, it seems that Barbie was free to travel at will. He toured South America and other places getting new clients for his arms business.

Back in Bolivia, Barbie turned to the cultivation of coca paste which was the main ingredient in a number of illegal drugs. Working

[33] "The Butcher of Lyon," *Dailykos.com,* March 8, 2014.

with the Suarez regime, Barbie sold his drugs to the Medellin cartel. The cartel business made him wealthy and he gave some of the profits to President Suarez.

By the early 1980s, Barbie's luck had finally changed for the worse. A new government was in power and the French government now pressed hard for his return to France to face his wartime crimes. In February 1983 he was sent back to France to stand trial and was subsequently found guilty of war crimes and died in prison on September 25, 1991.

The secret European ratlines set up by Bishop Hudal as well as Father Draganovic were responsible for shepherding of hundreds of ex-Nazis of all persuasions and ranks to South America and other places around globe. Adolf Eichmann, Klaus Barbie, and Josef Mengele were part of the ratline which was known about by both the Vatican and the United States government. The story of the ratlines reveals one of the most despicable and corrupt sides of World War II, one whose story should disturb all thinking people.

By August 1945, World War II was finally over. The western Allies had defeated both Japan and Germany after six, bloody years of warfare that left countless millions on all sides dead. In order to ensure a long-lasting peace, the Allies created a new world body called the United Nations which, it was hoped, would develop the atmosphere for a new, peaceful world order. However, the advent of the "Cold War" against the Soviet Union, once the ally of the United States, changed the worldwide political dynamic and pitted the Russians as the new enemy.

In order to plan for any eventual attack from the Soviet Union against the West, members of British intelligence and the newly created American CIA, began a series of clandestine steps in Europe to protect it in case of an invasion from the east. What these intelligence planners created was a super-secret "Stay Behind Network" composed of thousands of troops with enough supplies to thwart any Soviet advance if the need arose. Another, unspoken task of these networks was to fight off any internal subversion by communist forces in the western governments who planned the armed takeover of these freely elected governments.

The existence of these Stay Behind Networks was one of the most closely guarded secrets of the Cold War era, and its existence has only come to light in the last few decades, as researchers have pried away the layers of secrecy from archives of these respective countries.

The genesis of these covert networks was the idea of Allen Dulles, who has played such a large role in this narrative. Dulles' original plan was to create a secret, anti-communist force across Europe during the war. Dulles was aided in this scheme by Sir Stewart Menzies, "C," the head of British intelligence during the war, and by Paul Henri Spaak, the Premier of Belgium. Their original meeting took place sometime between 1949 and 1952, under the sponsorship of a body called the Clandestine Coordinating Committee, which had major input from the American Joint Chiefs of Staff. The original funding and staffing came from the CIA. Later, many of the day-to-day operations of the groups were taken over by NATO (the North Atlantic Treaty Organization). This network was soon manned by large numbers of intelligence officers from the member countries. As time went on, funding was provided by donations from wealthy, anti-communist, anti-fascist persons and groups.

The British and Americans shared most of the responsibility for running the web and they divided the European continent into two distinct regions of operations. For example, the British were responsible for running the groups in France, Belgium, Holland, Portugal, and Norway. The United States would have sovereignty in such nations as Sweden, Finland, and other parts of Europe.

During the early 1950s, other European countries such as Italy, Germany, and Greece joined the club. Each nation that participated in the Stay Behind Networks had cover names for their units. For example, Italy was called "Gladio," France "Glaive," (named after a gladiatorial sword), Austria, was known as "Schwert" (also sword), while in Turkey, the name was "Red Sheepskin." Switzerland was known as "P-2," while in Britain, the title was simply, "Stay Behind."

In an article written by David Guyatt in 1997 called *"Operation Gladio,"* he reports that a senior member of the British military told the *Guardian* newspaper that the Stay Behind Networks were first developed in England shortly after the fall of France in 1940. Secret arms caches were stored in various locations in England by a regiment of the Scots Guards under the leadership of Brigadier "Mad Mike" Calvert. Once the war was over, this system was expanded to other European countries.

The first major operation for a Stay Behind Network was not a Soviet invasion, but the thwarting of a possible communist coup in Italy, called 'Operation Gladio." The Gladio system was run with the full cooperation of the Italian Secret Service, headed by General Giovanni de Lorenzo, and also with the full cooperation of the "boys in Via Veneto"—the name for the CIA agents working in the Rome embassy.

Remember that James Angleton was stationed in Rome during the war and it is not inconceivable that he might have had a hand in running the Gladio operation on the sidelines. A staff of over 1,000 men, trained in the arts of guerilla warfare and espionage, were put on the Gladio payroll. These men were trained in Sardinia and, according to the declassified records, "139 weapons and ammunition dumps were hidden in Northern Italy." It is reported by high-level people involved in the Italian operation that the Gladio action was not reported to the leaders of the Italian government.

In an article in *The Independent* (dated II/16/90), "Gladio was set up to engage in clandestine, non-conventional resistance in the event of invasion. 622 people were recruited and trained by American and British intelligence at the Capo Marrargui base on the northern tip of Sardinia. They were organized in 40 independent cells. Six were responsible for intelligence gathering, 10 for sabotage, 6 for code and radio communications, 6 for running escape routes and 12 for guerilla warfare."

Documents on Gladio reveal that its most important task was "internal subversion." It was to "play a determining role not only on the general policy level of warfare, but also on the politics of emergency." Its second responsibility was dealing with "invading military forces" and both were arranged in close cooperation between the Italian and American secret services.

In a rather revealing mission statement, the Gladio papers document a dual role for its forces. "The first is objective and concerns defense of Italian territory and population." The second is defined cryptically as "subjective" and is "concerned with the legitimate authority of the state, and with the eventuality of any serious offenses against its integrity."

Conspiracy theorists have had a field day regarding Gladio and certain events in Italy concerning the secret organization called "Propaganda Due" or P-2, the sinister brain behind Gladio.

P-2 was headed in the 1970s by Licio Gelli, a wartime member of Mussolini's "Black Shirts," who worked for Hermann Goering's SS. In the middle of the 1970s, some of the most important political, business, and military leaders of Italy were members of P-2.

In David Guyatt's "Operation Gladio" article, he writes that in 1974, Gelli had a secret meeting with General Alexander Haig, the former NATO commander, and Nixon White House Chief of Staff. It was agreed that the U.S. would continue funding Gladio's Italian operations, and called for plans to develop "internal subversion" in Italy.

Gelli used the services of Roberto Calvi, the chairman of the powerful Banco Ambrosiano, a leading bank in Italy (Calvi was also a member of P-2) to launder millions of dollars, using the Vatican Bank as a cover. Soon, Calvi's bank would be ruined in the scandal that was to come. Gelli was called the "Puppet Master," a man who had control of the files on the other members of P-2, supplied to him by the Italian secret service. P-2 was even accused of the murder of the Italian Prime Minister, Aldo Moro. in 1978.

Soon, Calvi's role in the Vatican Bank scandal became headline news, and on June 17, 1982, his body was found hanging underneath London's Blackfriars Bridge. Calvi's hands were tied behind his back and a brick was stuffed in his coat pocket. Some people believed that Calvi's killing was a Masonic ritual murder, and that he might have been killed because he tried to launder mafia drug money.

With the demise of the Soviet Union, any reason for the Stay Behind Networks to remain in operation died. They were a relic of the days of the Cold War, steeped in conspiracy and the hidden hand of powerful men who did everything in their power to protect the state from communist and fascist beliefs.

In the postwar decades, a new breed of church leaders would take their place at the head of the Vatican, leading the church in new directions. No longer did they have to deal with a global war in which they had a role to play. Now, a new, Cold War was taking shape around the world, with new rules and new players. But some things still remained the same. In the 1980s, a new pope would be at the center of the storm between the East and the West, and he would almost pay for it with his life.

Reinhard Gellen, as an SS officer and when older.

William J. Donovan in uniform.

Martin Bormann.

Arthur Rudolf at NASA.

Kurt Blome.

Werner von Braun.

Klaus Barbie as an SS officer and later in South America.

Chapter 4

The Plot to Kill the Pope

On May 13, 1981, as Pope John Paul II was riding in his official car around St. Peter's Square in the Vatican, he was shot by a would be assassin, a 23 year old Turk named Mehmet Ali Agca, a man with a sordid past who was a member of a terrorist organization at that time called the Grey Wolves, an extreme right wing, anti-communist group. The pope would survive his wounds and became one of the leading figures in the Catholic Church during his papacy. Pope John Paul II reigned during one of the most difficult and tumultuous times in the history of the church, as well as during the heyday of the cold war between the United States and the Soviet Union. The pope was of Polish origin, a fact that was not taken too kindly in the halls of the Kremlin. During his papacy, the new pope fought openly for the liberation of those countries that were under the yoke of Soviet domination, and the men in the Kremlin did not take kindly to his open remarks that must have driven them crazy.

But were the Soviet's behind the assassination attempt on the pope, as many people around the world believed, or was there another, sinister connection to the events surrounding the wounding of the pope? The more the pope spoke out against the Soviet Union, the more the people under their sway began to make their voices known. Demonstrations and riots erupted in such Soviet satellites as Poland (the home of the pope), as well as in Lithuania. As time went on, reporters began looking into possible Bulgarian connection behind the assassination and whether or not Mehmet Ali Agca had any connection with them. Bulgaria was an ardent Soviet state backer and it would not be out of the realm of possibility that Agca was put on the Soviet payroll in order to kill the pope. If so, and if it could have been officially proven that the Soviet Union was behind the attack on the pope, who knows what the international consequences would have been.

The Vatican Conspiracy

In the months to come, intelligence officials in Italy and other interested countries began looking into Agca's connection with the Turkish Mafia and what possible role they might have played in the assassination attempt on the pope.

The attack on the pope quickly caught the attention of the CIA and they immediately began a series of investigations to try to find out as much as they could regarding the events in St. Peter's Square as well as anything they could find regarding the background of Ali Agca.

At Langley headquarters, CIA Director William Casey, a veteran of the OSS during World War II and President Ronald Reagan's campaign manager, soon took a keen interest in the assassination attempt on the pope. For Casey's part, the CIA had been working secretly with a high-ranking member of the Polish General Staff, a man named Colonel Wladyslaw Kudlinski, the CIA number one mole inside the Polish intelligence service. Among the bits of information supplied by Colonel Kudlinski to the CIA were the operational plans for martial law crackdown on the newly created Solidarity movement that had been sweeping Poland with the support of the pope in Rome. Casey relayed this information to the White House who read it with interest.

Colonel Kudlinski was now fearing for his life and telling the CIA that he was about to be exposed. He urgently asked for an exfiltration plan for him and his family and Langley went into action. In the end, they were able to safely remove the Colonel, as well as his family out of Poland and relocate them to the United States.

Shortly after their relocation to the United States, Polish police units began a nation-wide campaign to arrest over 5,000 members of the Solidarity Movement, thus, effectively ending what was being described at the time as the "Polish Spring."[1]

Both Ronald Reagan and William Casey were anti-communists in their political views and when Reagan was elected president in 1980 he began calling the Soviet Union the "evil empire."

When Ronald Reagan was elected president of the United States, one of his first appointments was that of his old friend, and campaign manager, William Casey to be head of the CIA. This was

[1] Woodward, Bob, *Veil: The Secret Wars of the CIA 1981-1987,* Simon and Schuster, New York, 1987, Page 177-78.

a political appointment to be sure, but what the critics did not know, or chose to forget, was that William Casey's roots went back to his participation in the early days of the OSS under William Donovan.

Bill Casey was born and bred in New York City, living in the borough of Queens with his family. He attended Fordham University, soon married, and began his career as a lawyer. One of young Bill Casey's hobbies was to read spy novels and he kept that interest throughout his life. He was an avid collector of books and magazines and after his death his wife found literally thousands of books and magazines stuffed all around his home. His family's politics were that of the New Deal of FDR but soon Bill gravitated to the Republican Party. He campaigned for Wendell Wilkie, then running against Franklin Roosevelt.

As the war spread in Europe, it was obvious that eventually the United States would have to enter the conflict. Casey was offered a job by his friend Leo Cherne in a think tank called the Research Institute of America. The RIA's work was to debate and write about the pressing international problems facing the world. Casey helped write a book that came out of this work called *The Business of Defense Coordinator.*

On February 22, 1941, Bill married Sophia Kurz and spent their honeymoon in Cuba and the Caribbean. But soon, Bill Casey and the rest of the country would be caught up in the whirlwind of war. To that effect, on June 5, 1943, two years after the U.S. entered the war, Casey was commissioned as a lieutenant J.G. in the U.S. Navy. His first assignment was with the Office of Naval Procurement in Washington. As the war progressed, Casey, who had poor eyesight and was not allowed into a combat role, made a call to a man whom he knew as somehow involved in secret work, Jerry Doran. Doran's former law partner was Otto Doering, then working in Bill Donovan's newly created OSS. Doran got Casey an interview with Doering and Doering sent Casey to meet a man named Colonel Vanderblue. The secretive Vanderblue was a recruiter for the OSS. The two men spent hours talking and the Colonel said he'd get back to Casey. Two weeks later, Casey met Otto Doering again and got good news; he was accepted into the OSS. His first posting was London in November 1943. It was there that his first daughter, Bernadette, was born.

Casey and a few other men worked in a section that read and handled cables that came in during the previous night from OSS agents and outposts across the globe. It was their job to filter each piece of intelligence that was sent to Donovan's desk. While working with Donovan in those early years in London, Casey said this regarding his new boss, "I was just a boy from Long Island. Sure, I had worked with high-level government officials, generals, and admirals. But never had I been in personal contact with a man of Donovan's candlepower. He was bigger than life. I reveled in my association with that man. We all glowed in his presence."

In late 1944, with allied victory in sight, Donovan ordered his London station to draft a report on how the United States could develop a permanent intelligence organization. Bill Casey's job was to serve as the secretary to this committee, and when the report was completed, he went to Washington to deliver its recommendations directly to Bill Donovan.

Once back in Europe, Casey was promoted to chief of intelligence in the London OSS station, and traveled to Paris to oversee the liberation of the city from Nazi rule. He wrote an important policy paper Vis a VI the agency's German operations called, "An OSS Program Against Germany." Its most basic task was the scope and detail of OSS covert operations against the German army in the field. One of his jobs, as the war neared its end, was the recruitment of agents among all categories of people; communists, POW's, etc. Casey obtained their services, oversaw their training, and was on hand when they were sent behind the lines.

The end of the war saw the dismemberment of the OSS and the (temporary) end of the road as a spy for Bill Casey. He returned to civilian life, and went into the legal publishing business. When someone asked him of his time as an OSS agent he replied, "It was the greatest experience of my life." Little did Casey know that twenty–five years later he would get a second chance in the intelligence business, this time, as head of the CIA, the successor to the OSS, into another covert battle against the enemies of the United States?

In the intervening years between the ending of the OSS and his ascendency as DCI, William Casey lost an election for Congress from Long Island, was appointed by President Nixon as head of the Securities and Exchange Commission, and was president of the Import-Export Bank.

With the election of Ronald Reagan over President Jimmy Carter in the 1980 election, Casey had met his ideological soul mate. Reagan won the election determined to restore America's role as the number one super-power. The United States had been humiliated in the 444 day Iran-hostage incident, and its covert action arm failed to get the hostages freed in a bungled rescue operation. The new president was determined to restore the vigor to the CIA and he tasked that very important job to Bill Casey who was now to serve as DCI.

At age sixty-seven, Casey was the oldest man to head the CIA. He did not keep a good personal appearance, wearing old, un-pressed suits, his with hair asunder, sometimes slurring his words. It was these personal qualities that kept him from becoming either Secretary of State or Secretary of Defense. However, he was rewarded with cabinet rank as head of the CIA. As DCI, Casey reverted to the old style business at CIA headquarters where secrecy was paramount and the ever inquisitive press would not be able to pry into the agency's affairs.

Casey was not long at CIA when he was the object of an investigation in the so-called "Debategate" affair. As far as scandals went, this one had no legs. Casey was accused by James Baker the White House Chief of Staff of providing him with a copy of Jimmy Carter's briefing papers before a debate between the president and Ronald Reagan. Despite his denials of any wrongdoing, the FBI, under the direction of William Webster, initiated an investigation. Casey was interviewed by the bureau, and he was eventually cleared of any wrongdoing.

Later on in his tenure as DCI, Casey would be embroiled in the Iran-Contra scandal that almost took down the Reagan administration as well as the sending of arms and equipment to the Nicaraguan Contras who were fighting the Sandinista regime in Managua. He would later become embroiled in the sending of arms and supplies to the Afghan resistance who were fighting the Russians after their invasion of Afghanistan.

But that was all in the future. For now, the Reagan administration had to deal with the aftermath of the shooting of the pope.

Six weeks earlier, President Reagan had been shot by a would-be assassin in Washington D.C. as he was going to an event. Now, another assassination attempt on a world leader had taken place and the CIA went into overdrive to see if there were any connections.

The next day, May 14, Casey gathered together the members of the Foreign Intelligence Board on F. Street in Washington to discuss the recent events. The subject was what role in worldwide terrorism was sponsored by the Soviet Union and their possible role in the attack on the pope.

The main terrorists groups at the time were non-state actors, such as the PLO (Palestine Liberation Organization) led by Yasir Arafat, the Red Brigades in Italy, The Red Army Faction in Japan, The Baader-Meinhof group in Germany, and of course, the number one terrorist at the time, "Carlos the Jackal."

Casey had previously asked Lincoln Gordon, the former president of Johns Hopkins University who was one of a few people whom the CIA asked to give their opinion on ways to combat terrorism to make a study of the topic and report back to him. Lincoln Gordon got his information from various U.S. intelligence sources including the NSA, including raw intercepts of information as well as codes that the NSA had broken. The name of the report that Lincoln Gordon wrote and presented to Casey was called "Soviet Support for International Terrorism" and it had more questions than answers. If Casey and the CIA had wanted a clear message from the report about Soviet sponsored state terrorism they were wrong. "Overall, however, Gordon said, "the Soviets were not using terrorism as a primary tool to destabilize the Third World and the Western nations."

Even before the attempt on the pope's life, there was a heated debate among certain members of the Reagan administrations on whether or not the Soviets were involved in international terrorism. General Alexander Haig was one proponent of the Soviet-as-worldwide-terrorist doctrine and he gave Casey his reasoning for such an assertion. Bill Casey was enthralled by an article he had read by the noted terrorism author, Claire Sterling who wrote an article in the *New York Times* called *"Terrorism: Tracing the International Network"* which was adapted from her book called *The Terror Network,* which claimed that the Russians were behind the worldwide spike in terrorism incidents. If, as Sterling theorized—regarding

Russian terrorism—could they have been behind the shooting in St. Peter's Square? Sterling quoted from her writings that, "There is massive proof that the Soviet Union and its surrogates, over the last decade, have provided the weapons, training, and sanctuary for a worldwide terror network aimed at the destabilization of Western democratic society. A Guerilla International as Cubans, KGB instructors, Palestinians and Red Brigades intertwined in their conspiracies, holding conventions and meetings at various terrorist training camps."

Casey asked his staff to look into Sterling's thesis regarding Soviet terrorism charges, resulting in the report sent by Lincoln Gordon who disagreed with Sterling's thesis. So, who to believe?

Another person who disagreed with Lincoln Gordon's findings was DIA Chief General Eugene Tighe who pressed Casey to disregard Lincoln Gordon's findings and made his case for Soviet involvement in international terrorism, one that Casey himself believed to be correct. So, in the wake of the Pontiff's shooting, no one in the CIA or the DIA was able to come up with a definitive conclusion regarding the role of the Soviet's in international terrorism.

The CIA's debate over whether or not the Soviets were behind the shooting of the pope was seen in the testimony of Robert Gates in October 1991 when he testified before Congress as the CIA director-designate. The Senators wanted to know about a report that the CIA made in a 1985 intelligence report titled, "Agca's Attempt to kill the Pope: The Case for Soviet Involvement." The Senators wanted to know whether Gates supervised the production of the contradictory paper to please the anti-Soviet wishes of his boss, Bill Casey who had previously died. Gates said that he did not rewrite a summary of the key judgments of the "assessment and dropped a "scope note," defining the purpose and limits of the paper-that had said the assessment was one-sided. The authors of the report backed up Gate's claims." Gates also told the Senators that he was remise in writing a cover note to then Vice President George Bush in April 1985 calling the assassination study, "the most comprehensive" the agency had done. He later said that, 'I think in retrospect, the covering note probably should have indicated what in fact, was the primary deficiency of the paper and that was that it did not thoroughly examine all the alternatives that were available."[2]

In 1991, new documents that were not made public before regarding the Gates testimony were released and shed new light on his testimony and what the CIA's report on the papal shooting revealed. The notes say that there was infighting going on inside the CIA on what conclusion that'd come up with on whether or not the Soviet Union was responsible for the assassination attempt. The documents assumed that the Soviet Union was responsible for the pope's attack and wanted to slant that view, whether or not there was ample evidence to assume such a finding. The Senate Intelligence report was responsible for putting forth this new information and it consisted of internal memorandums, letters, intelligence assessments and handwritten notes, when reviewing Robert Gates' testimony.

One person who gave critical testimony before the committee was Melvin Goodman, a former intelligence analyst at the CIA. He testified in 1985 that Mr. Casey instructed Mr. Gates to prepare a new report on the assassination attempt. Mr. Goodman revealed that at Gate's instructions, no effort was made to examine evidence suggesting that the Soviets were not involved and the research project was assigned to analysts who had limited knowledge in Soviet foreign policy at the CIA.

"Mr. Goodman charged that Mr. Gates personally rewrote part of the report and dropped a "scope note," a written explanation attached to the report that acknowledged that the paper had made no attempt to analyze arguments against Soviet involvement in the assassination attempt."

In July 1985, a CIA task force sent a detailed letter to Robert Gates concluding that there were "serious shortcomings" in the agency's overall performance in analyzing the papal assassination attempt in the years since the shooting occurred. This group was made up of three senior analysts and they found that "the efforts to assess the assassination attempt were undercut by jurisdictional fights, turnover in personnel, scares resources, lack of coordination and constantly shifting priorities."

The Committee reported that many of their analysts "believed that Mr. Casey had a strong gut feeling that the Soviets were involved, but believed that John McMahon, the agency's No. 2

[2] Babcock, Charles, "Gates Admits Deficiencies in Note On Pope Shooting," *The Washington Post,* October 4, 1991.

official, was persuaded that the tradecraft exhibited did not bear the marks of a Soviet operation."[3]

Besides the investigation of the Gates report by members of the congress, the CIA did an extensive look into one of the most controversial aspects of the papal shooting, the possible Bulgarian-Soviet connections to the event. The CIA had been following developments from its spies in Italy and other parts of Western Europe and they were filling in the blanks that Washington did or did not want to hear. The case of whether or not the Soviets or their Bulgarian allies were part of the papal plot had ramifications way beyond the borders of the United States and if it could be proven, would shake the world political order to its core.

According to sources who were familiar with the CIA's findings, the agency "concluded-with what officials said to be 99% certainty-that officials of the Bulgarian government had advanced knowledge of the assassination attempt against Pope John Paul II by Turkish terrorist Mehmet Ali Agca, with whom Bulgarian intelligence agents were working in Rome." However, they would not commit in writing that neither the Bulgarians nor Soviet Union instigated the attack.

Some of the conclusions of the CIA were revealed at the time in an article in the January 20, 1983 issue of the *Los Angeles Times* by reporter Robert Toth, called, "Bulgaria Knew of Plot on Pope, CIA Concludes." The reporter said, "no smoking gun, or absolute proof of Bulgarian complicity has been found by U.S. intelligence officials. Nonetheless, the Times has learned, CIA specialists believe that Bulgarian intelligence agents knew Agca was bent on killing the pope but regarded him as an unstable person who probably would be captured." Bulgaria, at the time was a hot-bed of heroin and gun-smuggling operations, linked to various, private companies who traded illegally with different factions as well as nations around the world and there was circumstantial evidence that Agca might have been involved with certain people who ran these organizations.

"The CIA conclusion makes the Bulgarians-and by extension the Soviets, who control the Bulgarians-accessories before the fact, a source said. It dilutes their guilt, but not very much."

[3] Johnston, David, *"The Gates Hearings: Documents Show CIA Feud on Papal Shooting," New York Times*, October 2, 1991.

One reporter who was also chasing down the Bulgarian connection was Marvin Kalb who worked for NBC, and who was part of a TV special looking into the papal plot. The show, entitled "The Man Who Shot the Pope—a Study in Terrorism," had a large audience at the time and it revealed a lot of information that the public did not know about. One of the themes of the show was that the pope was a target of the Kremlin-Bulgaria connection because of his recognition of the Polish Solidarity trade movement that was growing in Europe at that time. One significant part of the show was the allegation, which was denied by the Vatican, that Pope John Paul II sent a letter to Russian Premier Leonid Brezhnev in 1980, saying that he would leave the papacy and lead any resistance if Russian troops invaded Poland. In his NBC report, Kalb said that he learned that certain CIA officials in Rome "have actively discouraged reporters from pursuing the issue" (the events surrounding the papal attack).

According to the article by Robert Toth in the *LA Times,* the basic conclusions of the CIA report were as follows:

•There is a 99% certainty that the Bulgarians—and by inference the Soviet KGB, which has controlling ties to the Bulgarian intelligence agency—knew that Agca intended to shoot the pope but apparently chose not to stop him. Agca's public threat to kill the pope-during John Paul's visit to Turkey a year earlier was already a convicted assassin who had broken out of prison.

•Three Bulgarians were implicated in the plot to kill the pope, among them, important members of the Bulgarian Mafia who played a large part in drug and arms smuggling. Among those arrested or implicated were Sergei Antonov who worked as the deputy director for BalkanAir, the Bulgarian state airline, Omer Bagic, who worked as a butcher in Olten, Switzerland, Musa Cerdar Celebi, head of the Grey Wolves Federation in West Germany, Bekir Celenk, co-Godfather of the Turkish Mafia in Sofia, and Oral Celik, the Grey Wolf who lived in Malatya, the home town of Al Agca. The arrest of Sergi Antonov was big news in Italy and the newspaper *Corriere della Sera* made it a large part of their daily stories. They wrote the following regarding the arrest of Antonov, "Anatonov's arrest was sensational confirmation of an international plot to assassinate the Polish Pope, John Paul II. Personages tied ideologically to the extreme right, Ali Agca and his Turkish Gray Wolves, were used to mislead investigators. The plot was conceived and executed by the Bulgarian secret service." The findings of Toth's article continued by saying that Bekir Celenk allegedly offered Agca $1.2 million to kill the pope.

•Agca was "a known crazy," according to one U.S. official, and too unstable to be included in an assassination plot, let alone trusted to do the shooting, and almost certain to be caught. Agca was operating in cooperation with the Bulgarians but they were not his employer.

In order to discredit the Bulgarian connection, the Soviet press began a disinformation campaign against two well-known journalists who were doing investigative work on the pope's shooting, author Claire Sterling who published a detailed report in *Readers Digest,* and someone who had become a thorn in the side of both the Soviet's and certain members of the CIA who were trying to downplay any Soviet-Bulgarian connection, as well as Michael Ledeen, a former State Department specialist in anti-terrorism subjects. While Sterling and Ledeen were picked out by the Russians, they did not mention Marvin Kalb, whose report by NBC-TV was viewed by a large audience. Kalb reported that, "a great deal of evidence, although some is circumstantial, links the attempted killing of the pope to the political and diplomatic needs of Red Square. A Soviet connection is strongly suggested, but it cannot be proved."

While the CIA was trying to disprove the Bulgarian connection, another reporter had just received information regarding Agca's testimony to the Italian Judge, Martella, and he had some rather interesting things to say. The journalist who reported on this story was a Turk named Orsan Oymen who wrote for the journal, *Milliyet.* His story began in the edition dated July 11 and ran to four installments. Orsan Oymen got his scoop from Agca himself who began telling his story to Judge Martella beginning from May 1-7, 1982. His confession consisted of one hundred typewritten pages and thus was reported in *Milliyet.*

According to Agca's story, he was hired by the Turkish Mafia whose primary source of income at the time was the smuggling of arms and cigarettes to Turkey and the Middle East via Bulgaria and also had links with "an international Mafia extending from Turkey to Bulgaria to Switzerland and London." The Turkish Mafia used the Grey Wolves to help in the papal plot. Agca said that the two co-Godfathers who hired him were Abuzer Ugurlu and Bekir Celenk whom he had both met in Sofia, Bulgaria. He further stated that both men were not directly linked to the Bulgarian Secret Service but "both Celenk and Abuzer were smuggling to Turkey with the knowledge of the Bulgarian authorities."

Both Celenk and Ugurlu were connected to a secretive company known as Kintex that was run through the Bulgarian government. Kintex, an import-export company was supposed to have exported terrorism and smuggling weapons to various terrorist groups across the globe. Kintex, it was alleged, was part of the Bulgarian Secret Service. Kintex exported drugs throughout the world, including the United States, in order to take in hard currency for its weapons exports and used Turkish smugglers as their employees. It was also reported that by mid-1972, numerous Soviet advisors held positions in Kintex at all levels, including senior posts.

While he was on the run, Agca was helped on numerous occasions by Ugurlu who got him into Iran, and finally to Bulgaria. Ugurlu also arranged for Agca's counterfeit Indian passport in the name of Yoginder Singh, and another one in the name of Frank Ozgun. Another prominent person who aided him on his journey was Abdullah Catli. Catli was instrumental in getting Agca's passport cleared through customs at the Turkish-Bulgarian border. Catli picked up the bogus Frank Ozgun passport from Omer Ay. Catli then had it stamped for the purchase of 540 Deutschmarks in what was called "tourist currency at the Taksim branch of the Osmanli Bank in Istanbul, on August 27. He then took the passport to the Turkish border point at Kapikule-Ugurlu's "private estate. In Kapikule, Catli obtained an exit stamp marked Edrine dated August 30, 1980, paying a bribe of 5,000 Turkish lira.[4]

Agca stated that both Catli and Oral Celik played a large part in getting him freed from the military prison at Kartal-Maltepe and further, said that it was Celik who got him the Browning pistol from

[4] Sterling, Claire, *The Time of the Assassins*, Page 11-12.

a man named Horst Grillmayer, who was a gun dealer in Vienna. Right after the pope was shot, Horst Grillmayer decided to flee the scene and he was never heard from again. Agca told investigators that Horst Grillmayer made frequent trips to the Soviet Union, Bulgaria, and Belgium. What Mr. Grillmayer was doing in these countries is not known but it probably was nothing legal. Agca also noted that Oral Celik paid Grillmayer and another arms dealer named Otto Tinter, 60,000 Austrian shillings ($2,800 at that time) for four Browning semi-automatic pistols, magazines capable of holding 14 cartridges and about 10 packages of bullets. The police traced the guns to a cache of 21 pistols from a Belgian arms factory that passed illegally via Zurich into Austria, whom Agca said had obtained it from the Bulgarian secret service. Before taking possession of the pistols, Agca said that they were kept for him by several Turkish friends who lived in Vienna, including Celik, Abdullah Catli, and Maehmet Sener. When Judge Santiapich asked Agca why he needed the pistols he replied, "We wanted to resume our terrorist activities." He also opined that, "My terrorist activity never provoked an innocent death." It seems a bit dubious that four, lonely pistols would do much damage to western civilization.

While the worldwide press was painting Agca as the number one terrorist in the world, he was drawing a very different picture to the Italian judges. When questioned about his so-called terrorist past, Agca said that, "he was more an ideologue than a militant terrorist." And he said that he helped to organize the killing of editor Ipekci whom he was accused of murdering. He said he took the blame for killing Mr. Ipekci, in order to protect others involved like Yalcin Ozbey, a Turk who was then jailed in West Germany. He ended his statement on whether or not he was a terrorist by saying, "I made plans, drew up projects against the system. I never killed anyone. I had the reputation, let's say, of an ideologue." While Agca was vacationing in Palma de Majorca from April 25 to May 9, 1981, "he was finally told what the ring behind him had hired him for." According to Agca's report to the Italian Magistrate, "He was offered 3 million Deutschmarks-around $1,350,000-to kill the pope, he declared. The proposition came through Bekir Celenk, via a middleman whom Agca refused to name."

While many in the CIA and the American government tried

to downplay the so-called Bulgarian connection, there were some members of the agency who took a different view. When looking into the evidence compiled by Antonio Albano, the Italian prosecutor who alleged that there were Bulgarian ties to Agca, one CIA official said of the matter, "It looks substantial. There is too much evidence to be coincidence." Another CIA source said, "There's something to it." Part of the evidence that these CIA sources were referring to were information gleaned from the Italian probe, including intercepted phone calls regarding certain Bulgarians over a period of time. One source said of the Italian probe, "They have done things we wouldn't be able to do." One person in the know said regarding the Bulgarian connection, "It's fair to say there is a good deal of smoke, but there's no smoking gun. I think the Italians can make a persuasive case that there was a Bulgarian connection. Whether that was for the purpose of using Agca to kill the pope, we don't know. Maybe they were keeping him paid for some other purpose. He came out of shady circles."

Others in U.S. law enforcement such as the DEA, Drug Enforcement Administration, had a different view concerning Agca. One DEA official said that Agca was possibly "an enforcer for the drug trade." The DEA at the time was headed by John Lawn, who told a House panel that the DEA had information that indicated that "the government of Bulgaria has established a policy of encouraging and facilitating the trafficking of narcotics through the corporate veil of KINTEX, the state trading company." The DEA at that time was looking into the activities of two of Agca's friends and handlers, Bekir Celenk and Omer Mersen on drug smuggling charges. In an interesting coincidence, in May 1984, the DEA said regarding Bulgaria and their drug trade, that the Hotel Vitosha in Sofia, Bulgaria, where Agca stayed, was a meeting place for their illicit drug trade. However, the files of the DEA stated that they had no concrete information that Agca was in the drug trade.[5]

As Claire Sterling writes in her book on Agca and the plot to kill the pope, *The Time of the Assassins,* "The plot as I reconstructed it was necessarily complex; there could be no such thing as a *simple* plot to assassinate the head of the Roman Catholic Church. I maintained that the Turkish Mafia, operating out of Sofia under tight

---

[5] Babcock, Charles and Woodward, Bob, "Aides Agree on Bulgarian Role In Turk's Shooting of the Pope," *Washington Post,* July 13, 1984.

Bulgarian control, had picked the suitable hit man and provided the suitable cover. The hit man had a ready-made image as a right-wing terrorist killer, an image polished until it shone as he was passed across Europe from one neo-Nazi Grey Wolf to another."

"In reality, the Grey Wolves were involved here were working for the Turkish Mafia, which was controlled by the Bulgarian secret service, DS, which was working for the Soviet KGB."

While the CIA was conflicted about what role, if any the Bulgarian's played in the assassination attempt, the pope himself had things to say regarding Agca and the government in Sofia. In a talk with his long-time friend, Cardinal Andrzej Maria Deskur of whom he partook in many confidential and personal conversations, said that he didn't believe the Bulgarians played a part in the attempt on his life. Cardinal Deskur recalled a meeting with his friend, the pope whereby he Pontiff told him, "I was always convinced from the beginning that the Bulgarians were completely innocent, they had nothing to do with it. Cardinal Deskur said that the pope never elaborated any further just why he made that statement but he took the pope's word for it. Cardinal Deskur further asked the pope, "Why aren't you following the trials (of Agca and his alleged conspirators). And the pope said, "It doesn't interest me because it was the devil who did this thing. And the devil can conspire in a thousand ways, none of which interests me."

Another top Italian official who talked with Pope John Paul II about the shooting was Giulio Andreotti, the leader of the Italian Christian Democratic Party and later, the premier of Italy. Andreotti met with the pope and told him that in his opinion, there was nothing to the Bulgarian connection or that they were working in tandem with the Soviet's to kill him. "I told him," said Andreotti, "the evidence I had was such to exclude a Bulgarian connection and therefore we had to search for the truth somewhere else." The premier told the pope that he wouldn't pass along his evidence and the pope responded by saying, "we must be very cautious and wait for some evidence."

In a gesture of good will on the pope's part, he met with the vice president of Bulgaria to mark the feast of St. Cyril, a Bulgarian patron saint, a few days before the trial of Ali Agca was to begin.

Like the analysts in the CIA and other western intelligence

sources, many men in high places inside the Vatican were of two minds regarding the evens in St. Peter's Square. Among these prelates who believed in a possible Soviet connection was Secretary of State Casaroli who postulated that the Soviet's had ordered the plot on the pope in order to ruin the power of the Solidarity movement in Poland. With Solidarity gone, the belief went, the power of the pope would be destroyed and Poland would once again fall into the Soviet orbit. In January 1995, Secretary of State Casaroli stated, "Surely, the assassination was not an isolated attack."

A second person who had doubts in this regard was Cardinal Achille Silvestrini, who was Casaroli's deputy at the time. He said, "It was clear to us that it was not a random accident, not simply the act of a madman. It was something aimed at a goal, there was something behind the killer. We have to keep in mind the situation in Poland and Eastern Europe at the time. If the assassination attempt had succeeded, it would have been the gravestone for Poland and for those who were challenging the control of the Soviet system."[6]

It seemed that the CIA wrote a report on the Papal shooting that was conducted by one of its employees Ross Cowey that was dubbed the "Case for Report. Some of the people who did the study wanted to call it "The Case for Soviet Involvement," and said that the evidence "stacked the deck" in favor of this argument and ran the risk of appearing biased."

The "Case for" report had been ordered by Gates, four years after the May 1981 attempt on the pope's life. It seems at that time that the CIA's operations directorate had received information from spies on the ground in certain countries that was described as being secondhand or third hand, not your usual noteworthy intelligence collection. One part of the Cowey report said, "Many participants in the process thought that without the qualifiers, particularly on source reliability, the key judgments give readers the impression that the agency is saying-more definitively than the paper intends or the evidence warrants-that the Soviets were responsible." The Cowey report also concluded that, "In their view, the paper was deliberately skewed to make the case for Soviet complicity look more solid than it is; they thought the authors had been manipulated."

New, blockbuster information on the CIA's investigation into the murder attempt against Pope John Paul II in May 1981 is revealed

[6] *His Holiness,* Page 296-298.

216

in a new book that has recently been published called *A Pope and a President: John Paul II, Ronald Reagan, and the Extraordinary Untold Story of the 20th Century* by author Paul Kengor, a political science professor at Grove City College. The author delves into what he calls a "super-secret investigation" surrounding the shooting of the pope by American authorities. In his book, Mr. Kengor details the role played by the Soviet GRU (military intelligence) and its infamous leader, Yuri Andropov.

In his book, the author states that Director Casey organized a secret investigation into the shooting which was headed by two women agency employees (whom he didn't name). In an interview with the *Daily Signal*, Mr. Kengor writes that, "Their suspicions ran completely contrary to the establishmentarians in the institutional CIA, at the State Department, and among the White House pragmatists. That being the reality, Casey, I learned, actually ordered a truly super-secret investigation into the shooting, researched by two impressive women in their 30s and 40s, known only to a handful of people." He goes on to say that Casey's report was never released to the public and remains filed away in the records of the CIA. A source told Mr. Kengor that "the report was the most secretive thing I've ever seen. We had to practically remove the eyeballs of those who read it, the source told him. That report was the blockbuster of the 20th century."

In his talk with the *Daily Signal,* the author went further into the subject by saying, "I did get the results of the investigation, the background, the thinking of Reagan and Casey. I even pinpointed the date/time that I believe Casey briefed Reagan on the conclusions; May 16, 1985, II:02-II-17 a.m. I have the president's daily schedule from that day. The pope was concerned about starting World War III and shrewdly figured that people would rightly blame Moscow anyway. Reagan was asked several times about a possible Soviet role in the shooting, but was very careful not to say what was truly on his mind."[7]

He further states that the Soviet Union saw both President Reagan and Pope John Paul II as a threat to their way of life. The leaders of the Kremlin were diametrically opposed to any lessening

[7] Mooney, Kevin, "CIA Confirmed Russian's Role in Shooting of Pope John Paul II, Reagan Biographer Writes," stream.org/cia-confirmed-Russian-role-shooting-pope John-paul-II, May 7, 2017.

217

of tensions between the East and the West and were horrified to see any of their satellite states, i.e., Poland, move toward democracy. He writes in the book that, "The pope implored his people to choose God's side over what the Protestant Reagan and the Roman Catholic Church both called "godless Communism." The Soviet's called President Reagan "The Crusader" and felt the pope was "a grave threat to their existence" and that they wanted him dead.

When speaking about the Casey inspired secret report on the assassination attempt, the author writes in his book, "The 1980s intensified fears of World War III between the two nuclear-armed superpowers. Now imagine if news broke that the U.S. government had discovered a Soviet-orchestrated assassination attempt on the leader of the world's largest religion, who was a voice for those suffering under Soviet communism."

In doing research for his book, Paul Kengor wrote that he had a conversation with one of his sources and he told this person that another source told him that Bill Casey went to his grave agreeing with Claire Sterling's findings that the Soviets were behind the attack. "My source on the report was struck by this, not expecting that I had the confirmation on Casey. He said simply, Hmm, with a slight grin and a nod that I took as a tacit acknowledgment. He could not and would not say anything else." In speaking about his secret report that blames the GRU for the attack, one of Kengor's sources said jokingly about it, "This was so classified that they nearly shot the secretary who typed it."

If Professor Kengor is right about Yuri Andropov and the GRU as the responsible party in the pope's shooting, then who was he and what was in role in Soviet espionage throughout the years? Yuri Andropov was head of the Soviet KGB from 1967 to 1982 and then became Secretary General of the Communist Party, the highest official in the country. As head of the KGB he was in the loop of all major decisions that went on in Russia, including over -seeing all intelligence operations that Russia conducted in the cold war years.

He served in World War II and after the war ended he was named ambassador to Hungary in 1954 and played a leading role in the stamping out of the ill-fated Hungarian revolution in 1956. He was appointed head of the KGB in 1957 as well as being promoted to the Politburo of the Soviet Union that made all the crucial decisions of the country. As he did in Hungary in 1956, Andropov also was instrumental in the crushing of the nascent revolt in Czechoslovakia headed by the government led by Alexander Dubcek in 1968. He warned his superiors in Moscow that a large-scale revolt against communist rule was in the making and the Russian sent tanks to quell the uprising.

By the early 1980s, Andropov's star had risen in the Politburo and when Russian Premier Leonid Brezhnev died in 1982, Andropov was named as his successor.

When he became Secretary General, many of the western press who had little knowledge of his prior life as a KGB mastermind, began to praise him. Some admired him as "a relatively open minded man, a strange description for a longtime Czechist." Some diplomats and others praised him for learning English when dealing with other politicians.

Andropov did not last long as Secretary General of the Soviet Union. Three months later he became very ill due to his diabetic condition and he died on February 9, 1984.

With Yuri Andropov's vast KGB and intelligence background, it would not be out of question to expect him to be aware of just how much of a threat Pope John Paul II was and to take drastic steps to contain him, even going to such lengths as to assassinate him. Going back to the Stalin years, the Soviet's had no compunction to eliminate (kill) their political opponents of any stripe if they thought these people were a threat to the nation, If Stalin and his henchmen could send thousands of people to their death, then would they be reluctant to kill one man, no matter how powerful he was?

The Soviet Union, throughout the decades has had no compunction when it came to eliminating their foes, by any means necessary. What began in the time of Lenin and Stalin, and continuing into our present day with the brutal and corrupt regime of Vladimir Putin, assassination of one's foes in present-day Russia continues on a ruthless pace. (As of this writing, there is an ongoing investigation in the United States that the Russian government, under the direction of Vladimir Putin, interfered in the 2016 election for president).

One of the earliest persons to feel the terrible wrath of Soviet vengeance was Leon Trotsky, one of the most famous revolutionary figures in Russian history. After falling out of favor with the men in the Kremlin, Trotsky fled to Mexico City where he continued to rail against the Soviet state and continued his work without the prying eyes of the state looking over his every move. In 1940, the Russians sent a killer by the name of Ramon Mercador, alias Jacques Mornard, alias Frank Jacson, to kill Trotsky. Mercador burst into Trotsky's home and killed him with a hatchet.

John Barron, one of the leading specialists on Russian intelligence history, wrote the following when it came to the Russians eliminating their foes, "The Soviet Union decided in late 1962 or 1963 to entrust future assassinations not to Soviet personnel, but to hire foreign criminals and other nationalities, who could not easily be linked to the Soviet Union." Was Ali Agca one of these hired assassins on the Russian payroll?

Another person who was killed by the KGB was the late president of Afghanistan, Hafizullah Amin, who was shot and killed in his Presidential Palace on December 27, 1989. The orders to kill President Amin came directly from the corridors of the Kremlin and soon after, the Soviet Union invaded Afghanistan, creating a series of events that would give rise to the Taliban and culminate in the attacks on the United States on September II, 2001.

The Russians were not content with killing Leon Trotsky and Hafizullah Amin. There would be others who would share the same fate. One of these victims was a Russian named Alexander Litvinenko who was murdered by a Soviet hit squad using a deadly form of polonium-210, on two separate occasions, October 16 and November 1, 2006. The hit on Mr. Litvinenko took place in England and after years of investigating the incident, British authorities were able to identify two Russians who they say were the ones who killed him, Andrey Lugovoy, a former KGB bodyguard, and a former soldier named Dmitry Kovtun. Both men entered England with supplies of polonium-210 and supposedly poisoned Mr. Litvinenko while eating dinner with him in a London hotel called The Millennium on November 1, 2006. The Royal Courts of Justice in London who did the investigation of the murder of Mr. Litvinenko said that there was another attempt on his life when the same two men met with Litvinenko on October 16 of the same year.

He was poisoned when the two men put the deadly cocktail into

Mr. Litvinenko's tea while at dinner. The two assassins arrived in London and stayed at the Best Western Hotel on Shaftesbury Avenue where they had two separate rooms. They kept the polonium in a safe place where no one from the hotel staff would notice it.

After they poisoned him, the two men fled the country with Mr. Kovtun going to Germany. He met a man only known as D3 and told him, "Mr. Litvinenko was a traitor with blood on his hands who did deals with Chechnya."

The news of the death of Mr. Litvinenko was of worldwide interest at the time and showed just how ruthless the enemies of Russia would be. However, this was not to be the last time Mother Russia took care of its enemies.[8]

Another Russian execution on foreign soil could have been the plot for a cold war novel. In September 1978, a Russian writer named Georgi Markov was walking on London's Waterloo Bridge when a passerby pricked him with the tip of an umbrella that was laced with poison. Mr. Markov once worked for the BBC and had lived in exile in London since the late 1960s. He was married to Annabel Markova, a novelist who writes under the pen name Annabel Dike. At the time of Markov's death at age 49, they had one daughter, Alexandra, who was only two years old.

Years after Mr. Markov's death, new information on the case has been unearthed which shed more light on the events at Waterloo Bridge that day. The case of Mr. Markov's death has a stunning connection to Ali Agca (if not in fact than in its coincidences). The man whom police said did the killing was a Bulgarian named Francesco Gullino, a Danish national of Italian origin, who worked for the then Communist regime who owned an antique shop as a cover for his spying for Bulgarian Secret Service. Mr. Gullino went by the code name of "Agent Piccadilly" and worked for the old Bulgarian intelligence service DS from around 1978 to about 1990. New files regarding Mr. Gullino reveal that he received around 30,000 pounds from the DS for his services. It is said that Mr. Gullino was ordered to move to Copenhagen, Denmark in 1978-the same year that Mr. Markov was killed. Documents uncovered in the case say that Mr. Gullino, whose identity was revealed by a Bulgarian journalist, said

---

[8] Rayner, Gordon, and Whitehead, Tom, "Alexander Litvinenko was poisoned twice with polonium-210 inquiry hears," www.telegraph. co.uk, January 27, 2015.

that Gullino entered Britain, driving an Austrian-registered car, and was ordered to go to London to "neutralize" Markov. His orders came directly from the country's leader, Todor Zhikov.

In 1993, he was detained in Denmark after Danish authorities got a tip from MI6 and was held for questioning but was let go for lack of evidence. The information on the Markov case came from a journalist named Klaus Dexel who said, "Gullino received 30,000 pounds from the DS between 1978 and 1990 and was frequently invited to security service events in Bulgaria. I think that means he had an important role in this murder but there is no evidence he was trained to be a killer. He is, however, a very well trained liar and able to cover his trail." Mr. Dexel also wrote that another agent called "Woodpecker" joined Gullino in London one day before Mr. Markov was killed:

> This Woodpecker could have been the murderer, or been used to carry the murder weapon in, or indeed Gullino may have played that role," Mr. Dexel said. Mr. Gullino was finally traced to his home in Austria and had denied all charges against him in the Markov case. A friend of Markov's, Dimitar Botchev, said at that time that," There is plenty of evidence that he was involved in some way in the murder of Markov. But not a finger has been raised against him.[9]

In the 1960s and the years prior, the KGB, under its various leaders, had a formal assassination unit called Department 13 which had an official sanction to conduct political assassinations. In the United States, after the Kennedy assassination, the CIA looked into any possible involvement that the Russians may have played a part in the events of November 22, 1963 and one of its most prominent men, James Angleton, whose story has been told in chapter 2 of this book as it relates to the Vatican intrigues during world War II, was right in the middle of trying to find out what, if anything Department 13 was up to.

Angleton was obsessed with the notion that the KGB's

[9] Holdsworth, Nick, and Menkick, Robert, "Prime Suspect in Georgi Markov's umbrella poison murder tracked down to Austria," www.telegraph.co.uk. March 23, 2013.

Department 13, which specializes in political assassinations, mostly on foreign soil, had a hand in Kennedy's demise. In some cases the KGB and Department 13 would use agents of other nations whom they were friendly with to carry out assassinations on the host country's soil. In other cases, they did the deed alone. Angleton believed that the Cuban's would not act alone in such an important matter as the murder of an American president, and as Oswald's connection grew in size, he regarded a Soviet-Cuban alliance in the president's death to be a certainty.

Right after the assassination, Angleton said that, he "discounted 1 million percent that the event was a domestically carried out plot. And why did he come to this conclusion? Because the Soviet's said the event was planned by certain right wing elements within the United States. Well, if the right wing, who truly hated President Kennedy carried out the assassination, than that automatically put the blame not on any domestic conspiracy, but rather, directly upon the Soviet Union.

Documents released under the JFK Records Act, and obtained by the writer, provide additional information on Department 13 and the CIA's interest in any possible Soviet involvement in the Kennedy assassination (or the shooting of the pope by Agca who might have been a sleeper agent working for the Russians as a member of Department 13).

The formally "Top Secret" document on Department 13 begins as follows:

> In 1936, Soviets wanted to assassinate opposition outside the USSR (e.g., Trotskyites and Czarists emigres). In Word War II, 13th Department sabotaged German army in Ukraine, and murdered collaborators even after the war. In the late 1950s, it de-emphasized assassinations but since then has continued to use assassinations against Soviet defectors and intelligence agents.
>
> In the event war is likely, it is to use sabotage to weaken enemy's will to fight. It targets civilian facilities such as broadcast, communication and power facilities. In a war, Soviet military intelligence probably would have responsibility for sabotage of enemy military installations.

223

The Central Committee must approve any assassination. The KGB is tightly controlled by Central Committee. An attempt on Kennedy would have to have been approved by Khrushchev.

Normally, personnel are permanently assigned to Department 13 throughout their KGB career. Anytime KGB communicates information on its agent operations, it classifies information TOP SECRET and puts it in pouch rather than risk interception and decoding of an electronic signal.

In some cases, special trained KGB personnel have actually performed killings. In one case, the KGB recruited a Russian to do the killing but he was not technically KGB. In other cases, KGB recruited foreigners.

Basically, anyone who will kill. It often uses "hoods" or "thugs." It looks for someone who is pro-Soviet or someone who will kill for money. One common thread is that it looks for people who have a grudge against their country.[10]

Does anything referred in the above mention paragraphs on Department 13 and the use of "hoods" or "thugs," or "someone who was not a member of the KGB fit Ali Agca? It is something to think about while studying the plot to kill the pope.

While there is no definitive proof that Andropov directed the shooting of the pope, it is not out of bounds to see him as part of a Soviet led conspiracy to kill him. As we have seen by the above mentioned attacks on Russian dissidents over the years, assassinations of ones enemies by the Soviet Union was not out of the question, and unfortunately, has become routine when the interests of the state are in jeopardy.

Right after the pope was shot, the Soviet Union tried to put the blame directly on the shoulders of the United States and the CIA. Didn't the U.S. and the pope have common ties, and political beliefs, all rooted against the Soviet Union? After the shooting, various Soviet newspapers, such as Pravda, started writing anti-CIA and U.S. articles pinning the blame on the attack of the pope directly at Washington's doorstep.

[10] CIA Briefing Book on (Alleged) Soviet/Cuban Assassination. Date 1/15/76. Record No. 157-10011-10029.

They could find no obvious Turkish connection-Ali Agca was a Turk—so why not divert attention to the real culprit, the United States?

Over the decades since the pope was shot, many authors began writing books and articles on the event and came up with different version of what happened. In 2011, an author named Marco Insaldo, a journalist with the Italian paper *La Repubblica,* co-wrote a book with a Turkish writer named Yasemin Taskin called *Kill the Pope: The Truth about the Assassination Attempt on Pope John Paul II.* Their theory was that the CIA concocted a story of a Communist conspiracy after Secretary of State Alexander Haig asked the U.S. intelligence community to provide him information on material to be used against the Communists in the Papal shooting. Mr. Insaldo wrote that, "Alexander Haig, then secretary of state, had asked the CIA to find anything that could be used against the communists. The CIA knew the Grey Wolves had connections with Bulgaria through organized crime and that Agca had visited so when he tried to kill the pope they were very smart and exploited the connection."

After his arrest, Italian authorities found out that Agca was a member of the Grey Wolves, an extreme right wing, anti-communist organization. However, there was no reason why the Grey Wolves would make an attempt on the pope and even if there was proof that Agca was affiliated with them, why would he implicate that organization in the first place? (More about Agca and the Grey Wolves later in this chapter).

The two authors postulate that the so-called Bulgarian connection to the plot against the pope, which had gained widespread notice in the world's press, was a false flag operation in which the Bulgarians and the Russians took part in the assassination attempt was incorrect.

In their book the authors say that, "The Bulgarian connection is the creation of the CIA. Agca, who belonged to an outlawed ultra-nationalist and pro-Islam Turkish group called the Grey Wolves, tried to kill the pope purely because of his and the groups fanatical anti-Western ideology." They postulated that Agca's visits to Bulgaria "were due to flourishing links between the Grey Wolves and Bulgarian organized crime, and that the CIA was aware of this."

Mr. Insaldo also claimed that the Italian secret services were in bed with the CIA that forced Agca to confess to a Bulgarian connection, a confession that he later retracted.

The authors of the book made a startling claim regarding the so-called Bulgarian connection by saying that during one of their meetings with Agca, the man said, "the attempt wasn't complicated," in which he meant that the Bulgarians were not involved.

However, Judge Ferdinando Imposimato, who led an investigation into the assassination attempt, called the book "rubbish." The judge further told news media outlets at the time that he believed the Russians were so worried about the Polish pope's anti-communists pronouncements that the people of Poland might revolt and undermine Soviet domination over Poland.[11]

Two years after the shooting of the pope, then Senator Alfonse D'Amato of New York railed against the CIA saying that the agency was not doing enough to find out the circumstances surrounding the event. He told the press that in his opinion, there was a deliberate cover up by both the State Department and the CIA over their probe of the events in St. Peter's Square. Senator D'Amato made his own trip to Italy to meet with investigators to get details that only they knew regarding the actions of the shooter, Ali Agca and to learn what he could about the alleged Bulgarian connection that had been growing in the press for some time.

The Senator said that he believed that top-ranking CIA officials, including the Director William Casey were behind the efforts to downplay the immensity of the shooting. He charged the CIA of not putting enough effort into searching for answers behind the pope's shooting for reasons he couldn't explain.

"I am deeply disturbed by the conduct and attitude of the CIA," he said. "So are we and so should every American." The Senator said he believed the reason for the foot dragging by the Reagan administration at that time was not to offend the Soviet Union. But didn't President Reagan call the Soviet Union "an evil empire?" At that time, President Reagan was about to meet with Soviet leader Andropov, the same man who it is alleged by some to have been responsible for the attack on the pope's life.

Another CIA link to the assassination attempt was put forward in 1983 by a Soviet journalist named Yona Andronov, who wrote an article published by the *Bulgarian Literatuern Front* of Sofia and

---

[11] Day, Matthew, "CIA tried to frame Bulgaria for John Paul II assassination attempt," www.telegraph.co.uk.news, April 21, 2011.

the *Soviet Literary Gazette*. The basis of the article is that the CIA was behind the attempt on the pope and that the agency "guided" Ali Agca in the shooting. Yona Andronov said she traveled to various places in Europe and Turkey in the investigation.

After his conviction, Ali Agca said that the Bulgarian secret service and the Soviet KGB planned the assassination. He also told Italian authorities that a man named Sergi Antonov, a Bulgarian Airlines employee in Rome, and two Bulgarian Embassy officials were his accomplices. *The Literatuern Front* charged that, "the present inhabitants of the White House are obsessed by the delirious and maniacal idea of a crusade against communism. Agca is only an instrument of foreign will and, according to the CIA rules, may possibly not know who are the real perpetrators of the killings."

A leftist magazine in Rome wrote what it said were telegrams showing the U.S. Embassy in Rome worked out a plan to link Bulgaria to the shooting of the pope. In reaction to these allegations, the U.S. Embassy said the telegrams were "fabrications." In Washington, the U.S. State Department said the KGB apparently forged the cable that was published in the periodical. The State Department further said regarding this matter that, "They fit a pattern of KGB forgeries and similar fabrications which the Soviets have been circulating in Europe. We are not able to prove it was the KGB, but we are pointing out who has the obvious benefits."[12]

In the Vatican itself, the pope startled his Swiss guards by saying that, "Let's pray that the Lord will keep violence and fanaticism far from the Vatican's walls." The pope made this startling revelation because he had previously been given information from the French secret service, the SDECE, that an attempt would be made on his life. The information was provided by a Bulgarian defector. The information the French gave to the pope was presented by the legendary SDECE leader, Count Alexandre de Marenche, who said a colonel and general had been sent to the Vatican on April 20, 1981 to warn the pope of the impending attack.[13]

The defectors name was Iordan Mantarov, the deputy commercial attaché at the Bulgarian Embassy in Paris who told the French

---

[12] United Press International article dated July 14, 1983 Sanitized copy released by CIA.

[13] Sterling, Claire, *The Time Of The Assassins: Anatomy of an Investigation,* Hold, Reinhardt and Winston, New York, 1983, Page 236.

about the plot on the pope's life. He further stated that he heard that the Bulgarian secret service on the orders of the Soviet KGB were part of the plot. Mr. Mantarov stated that he had heard of the plot from man named Dimiter Savov, a high-ranking official in the counterintelligence division of the Bulgarian intelligence service.

In 1979, according to the story played out by Mantarov, Savov told him that the Kremlin was so worried about the new Polish pope, Karol Wojtyla's efforts to help his native Poles get out of the Soviet sphere of influence that they would take active measures to stop him once and for all. "Eastern European intelligence services began discussions with the KGB-or one of the Eastern European services-began discussions with the Bulgarian intelligence service about a way to eliminate John Paul II." Mantarov quoted Serov as saying that Agca was selected as the assassin because he was known as a "rightest" for his role in killing the liberal Turkish newspaper editor and had no links to any Communist country.[14]

Further information concerning Soviet involvement in the papal shooting came from a document dated November 15, 1979 when the full secretariat of the Central Committee of the Soviet Communist Party approved a project called "Decision to work against the Policies of the Vatican in Relation with Socialist States." The men behind this new policy were Yuri Andropov and Viktor Chebrikov, then the deputy chairman of the KGB. "The document instructed all Soviet departments and political organizations, from the KGB to the state organs of propaganda, to undertake specific assignments in an anti-Wojtyla campaign, mostly in the area of propaganda." The specifics of the plan were then sent to the Communist leadership of all the Warsaw Pact nations then aligned with Moscow.[15]

The Soviets were so willing to put the blame on the CIA's shoulders that they accused a former, discredited agency employee named Frank Terpil as being part of the plot. The gist of the story is that Frank Terpil was supposed to have been Agca's trainer in Libya under the brutal regime in the eccentric Muammar Qaddafi. During the 1980s, Libya was one of the hot beds of international terrorism and was a base for various terrorist groups who used Libya as a staging area to plan attacks against western targets. While there was

[14] Bernstein, Carl and Politi, Marco, *His Holiness: John Paul II and the Hidden History of Our Time,* Doubleday, New York, 1996, Page 307.
[15] Ibid. Page 308.

no concrete proof that Frank Terpil had any connection to Agca, his story is worth telling, as he teamed up with one of the most infamous CIA agents of the day, Edwin Wilson.

Frank Terpil, an ex-CIA agent and international fugitive wanted in the United States for gunrunning and other illegal activities, could have been a character from one of Robert Ludlum's spy novels. But Frank Terpil's life has been far from the world of fiction although he combined aspects of both into a dangerous reality.

Terpil was born in Brooklyn, New York on November 2, 1939, just one of thousands of neighborhood kids surviving to make it in the mean streets of the Big Apple. While other kids were playing baseball on the street or trading cards, Frank made his first illegal gun sale at age 15, a machine gun. The event led him to jail but he soon was let go. The event sent a message through the young man who immediately knew that his life was destined to be spent traveling the back alleys of foreign nations, meeting shady characters and making high-risk deals.

At age 18, Frank left the old neighborhood and joined the Army. He served for four years, including a posting to the Far East. After his military commitment was over he joined the CIA in 1965. He started working in the agency's Technical Services Division but made no effort to rise to the top of his game. His CIA career was nothing but undistinguished, and he quickly got a reputation as a liar, a conman, not the type of qualities that would distinguish himself to his superiors. During his overseas postings, he was caught red handed stealing government items from the places he worked. In order to make extra money, Terpil would often times engage in black market activities, including illegal currency trading, the buying and selling of illegal liquor, jewels, and other articles.

When he wasn't making bogus deals with criminal types, Terpil gained entry to the dark world of international gun smuggling and made his own, unique contacts with some of the most important arms merchants in the world.

During his posting to New Delhi, India, Terpil branched out in various illegal activities, all under the noses of the CIA. He began smuggling illegal whiskey, and was told that if he continued his nefarious dealings, his career would be over. All the while, he prospered in the trading of foreign currencies that he converted into

Indian rupees. It was on one of these illegal sojourns that Terpil found himself in the rugged hills of Afghanistan just when the war between India and Pakistan began in 1971. Not being able to return to India, he was summarily fired by the CIA, for being AWOL.

Now that he was not bound by the CIA's rules, Terpil began his second career as an arms middleman, brokering shipments of military supplies to various countries in the Middle East and Central America. He soon had a large network of contacts in the burgeoning 1980s arms trade when it seemed that every two-bit nation both wanted as many arms as possible to ferment their "wars of national liberation."

Among the many influential people whom Frank Terpil came in contact with during his stay at the CIA was his fellow agent, Edwin Wilson. It was through his close association with Edwin Wilson that he began an illicit partnership that would pit the two ex-government spies against the institution they both worked for.

In time, both Terpil and Wilson decided to pool their talent and went into the arms procurement business together. In Edwin Wilson, Terpil found his soul mate, whose hatred against the CIA, matched his own. Terpil soon began making contacts with people and groups with well-known terrorist links, traveling to such militant countries as Libya, Syria, and Lebanon.

With their newfound business venture on track, Terpil opened his headquarters in Tripoli, Libya, while Wilson worked out of London. The third member of their organization was a former CIA officer named Kevin Mulcahy who would act as their intermediary in Washington. He had a drinking problem that caused the break-up of his marriage. To be honest, Wilson was not forthright in telling Mulcahy just what kind of business he was running. To Mulcahy, who was paid $1,000 a month, the firm called "Consultants International" was simply an import-export business, not an agency that procured arms for international terrorists organizations. Acting on his own, Mulcahy contacted the BTAF (Bureau of Alcohol, Tobacco and Firearms), regarding the shady goings on at Consultants International but his concerns weren't taken with much credibility by the Feds.

After a while, it seems that Kevin Mulcahy got religion and went to the Feds to tell what he knew about the shady dealings of both

Wilson and Terpil. When a grand jury began looking into Wilson and Terpil's dealings, Mulcahy was a witness and the grand jury issued an indictment against both men.

In October 1982, under what was then called mysterious circumstances, the body of Kevin Mulcahy was found in a cabin in Virginia. Local authorities could find no evidence of foul play in the death of Mr. Mulcahy and the case was closed. Kevin Mulcahy's father, who also was a former CIA officer, said the police found his son deceased in a cabin in the Shenandoah County at 8 in the morning, about 90 miles from Washington. The body had apparently been there for many hours before the police arrived. When the police searched the room that Mulcahy was staying in they found a number of papers and documents that related to the CIA but what they contained was not revealed.

One of the most notable international terrorists whom Frank Terpil got in touch with was the infamous "Carlos the Jackal," whose real name was Carlos Ramirez Sanchez. Carlos had been responsible for numerous assassinations in various parts of the world. Besides his association with Carlos, Terpil established himself as a highly paid advisor to the Palestine Liberation Organization headed by Yasir Arafat. He also was in touch with over a dozen foreign government spy networks allied to both the U.S. and the old Soviet Union.

In 1976, Terpil made covert contact with the cousin of Libya's leader, Muammar Qaddafi, Sayed Quaddafadam. Both men met in London where Sayed was working out of the Libyan embassy in London where his mandate was to procurer weapons that were under an arms embargo by the west. Quaddafadam wanted weapons ranging from assassination devices, to explosives, to aircraft, and all assorted high-tech implements. Terpil was the intermediary in this highly illegal arms deal, and he went so far as to develop a cover story whereby the explosive ordinance being supplied to Quaddafadam was to be used in oil drilling activities in that oil rich nation (Libya). In reality, the arms were to be used by experts in "training selected students in covert sabotage operations, employing the latest techniques of clandestine explosive ordinance." As part of the deal, Terpil would travel to Libya where he would train the men who would carry out later operations. It didn't matter to Terpil that

231

Libya was one of America's bitter enemies. Business was business.

Another part of Terpil's duties in Wilson's worldwide gun running enterprise, was his assignment to purchase silent guns that were also "sterile" (untraceable), many of them built in Switzerland and not easily detected. All their troubles paled in comparison when, in December 1979, Terpil and a friend named Gary Korkula were arrested for selling 10,000 British made guns to an undercover New York cop. They were supposed to sell the guns to a fake revolutionary group for $2 million, collect the money, and take off for parts unknown.

Meeting with so-called intermediaries in a New York hotel on December 22, 1979, both men were arrested in a perfect sting operation.

Terpil was put under arrest but to the dismay of the Federal prosecutors was allowed free on a $10,000 bond. Eluding his ever-watchful undercover federal agents, Terpil slipped out of the country via Canada, and headed for Lebanon. For years he lived under the good graces of Yasir Arafat's PLO, left Beirut when the Israeli army attacked that country looking for the PLO, and wound up in Uganda where he worked for the late dictator, Idi Amin. Terpil slipped from sight, with the intelligence services of a number of nations hot on his tail.

After his stint in Lebanon, Terpil fled to Cuba where he was taken in by the government of Fidel Castro. By now, he had been sentenced to 53 years in jail by the United States government in absentia for illegally selling weapons to Libya. He started a relationship with the Cuban intelligence service and they even gave him a code name of "the guinea pig." They used him to try and recruit a CIA agent in Czechoslovakia. Frank Terpil died in Cuba in 2015.

Still, many unanswered questions remain regarding the activities of Frank Terpil and his covert activities, including the most tantalizing one of all-did the CIA condone or help Terpil in any of his clandestine ventures?

———————

In the early days of the Reagan administration, a little known event took place, out of the prying eyes of the press who were constantly camped out in St. Peter's Square, looking for any information they could find on the dealings of the new pope. A man passed through the portals of the Swiss Guard whose job it was to protect the pope and one of them escorted the guest to the papal office. There, seated behind his desk, Pope Paul II met William Casey, the Director of the CIA. The reason for Casey's visit to Vatican City was to brief the pope on behalf of President Reagan on the hotspots around the world. Like the members of the OSS in World War II who visited Pope Pius regarding the fight against Nazi Germany, the new enemy was the Soviet Union whom both President Reagan and the pope considered their number one enemy on the world stage. Casey was a Catholic and so he felt comfortable in the presence of the Holy Father, someone whom he admired and respected. Casey then took out of his briefcase a photo that had been taken from a spy satellite in orbit in space. The photo showed the pope in Victory Square in Poland when he made a trip to his homeland in 1979.

That first meeting between the pope and the CIA Director was the beginning of a secret relationship that would be forged between the Reagan administration and the Vatican that would last for years. They would meet at least six more times in secret, with Casey giving the pope some of the most guarded secrets coming out of the CIA and other U.S. intelligence agencies. A lot of the information supplied by Casey was related to the on-going crisis in Poland and that nation's efforts to break away from the Soviet Union.

From the outset of his administration, President Reagan saw the pope as his comrade-in arms against their ruthless nemesis, the Soviet Union. If the pope didn't have an army, he certainly did have the power to sway his flock of Catholics across the globe away from the Soviet Union and into the realm of freedom. They were kindred spirits, Reagan and the pope, natural allies in the cold war, eager to use each other for their common purpose. In their discussions, Casey told the pope that the CIA was secretly giving money to the Solidarity movement in Poland and that it was the policy of the Reagan administration to wean Poland away from the Soviet orbit.

One of the things that Casey and the pope talked about was the Solidarity movement in Poland and the Soviet's efforts to destabilize it. The pope told Casey that when Lech Walesa, the leader of Solidarity met with him, he told him about a man named

Luigi Scricciolo of the Italian Labor Confederation. It seems that Scricciolo had traveled to Poland in 1980 to meet with Lech Walesa on matters relating to the movement. Prior to his arrival at the Holy See Casey had been informed by the U.S. Embassy in Rome that Scricciolo had been secretly working for the Bulgarian's for some time. If this was true, then the most secret information relating to Solidarity would wind up in the coffers of Moscow and would be a detriment to the movement.

Poland

Besides William Casey, another man in the Reagan administration who played a pivotal part in the back channel communications with the Vatican was William Clark who was Secretary of State's Alexander Haig's deputy whose title was counselor to the secretary. Unknown to most people in the government, by the spring of 1981, both Casey and Clark were making secret trips in Washington to meet with the pope's apostolic delegate, Archbishop Pio Laghi. When Archbishop Laghi came to the White House, he was escorted through the "back door" at the southwest entrance to the building to avoid the prying eyes of the waiting press. Most of their conversations centered on the events going on in Poland and both Clark and Casey shared what they'd been told with their honored guest.

The president now turned to another man who was high in the American Catholic hierarchy, Cardinal John Krol of Philadelphia. Cardinal Krol was well informed about what was going on with the Solidarity movement and he reported all he knew to the administration. Krol also served as an intermediary between the Reagan administration, the Vatican, and Poland.

In years past, Cardinal Krol had worked in the Vatican and made a friendship with Karol Wojtyla before he became pope. Once Karol Wojtyla was elected as Pope John II, it was Cardinal Krol who helped cement the close, personal relationship that developed between the White House and the Vatican.

In February 1983, the U.S. Senate Permanent Select Committee on Intelligence, headed by Arizona Senator Barry Goldwater and its vice-chairman, Democrat from New York, Daniel Patrick Moynihan, conducted hearings on the possible Russian-Bulgarian connection to the papal shooting in the wake of Director Casey's CIA investigation of the papal plot. Many members of the committee, including Senators Goldwater and Moynihan, were troubled about the way the CIA conducted its investigation and wanted answers from Casey and his surrogates at Langley headquarters.

After the meeting concluded, there were mixed signals coming from certain members of the committee. For example, Senator Goldwater said that in regards to the CIA probe, "I don't think they've been dragging their tail." Senator Moynihan agreed with his colleague.

The CIA's handling of the papal investigation was attacked when NBC TV did a show on national television on the assassination attempt and said that the CIA was not doing enough to investigate the case and furthermore, tried to discourage American journalists and the Italian government from doing due-diligence in reporting on the case. The Reagan administration got into the act by sending Secretary of State George Schultz to clear up the matter. In an address to the Conservative Political Action Conference, he told the audience that the U.S. did not try to suppress a thorough investigation into the shooting. The Secretary of State mentioned Bulgaria by saying, "The Government could not have a fruitful relationship with Bulgaria as long as it supported terrorism."

Other committee members at the time who did not want to go public said, "The agency has not used its resources to trace Agca's background and examine his connections with Bulgaria. The CIA could do that without interfering with the Italians."

As we can see from the evidence at the time, there were various, conflicting reactions among many members of the CIA, as well as certain lawmakers in regard to the U.S.'s probe of the papal attack.

After the arrest of Agca, he told Italian authorities that he acted alone in the shooting of the pope and was sentenced on July 22, 1981 to life in jail. In May 1982, after beginning his sentence, Agca further embellished his story by saying that he had been aided by three members of the Bulgarian embassy staff in Rome and four Turks as his co-conspirators. He further astonished the Italian police by saying that there was going to be an assassination attempt on the life of Lech Walesa when he came to Rome to visit the pope in January 1981. The plan was to detonate a car bomb near the hotel where Walesa was staying but it never took place because of tight security.

While all this was going on, Scricciolo had been arrested by

Italian authorities on charges of espionage on behalf of Bulgaria, and he added more information to the alleged plot to kill Walesa. His lawyer told the Italians, "I can tell you for sure that there was also a Bulgarian connection to the murder plot against the pope, although my client was not involved. Scricciolo and Agca each identified the same three Bulgarians indicted for the attempt on the pope's life as participants in the plot to kill Walesa."[16]

At the time that Agca was telling his story about a Bulgarian connection, the American NSA—National Security Agency— whose job it was to monitor all secret communications worldwide, began picking up an increase in cable traffic between Bulgaria and Italy within two weeks of the attempt on the life of the pope. The NSA began a sweep of all communications between the embassies of Communist countries and their home countries in the months surrounding the attempt on the pope's life. In March and April 1981, the NSA saw a high-level of cable messages between the Bulgarian Embassy in Rome and the headquarters of the Bulgarian Secret Service increase. In the two weeks before the assassination attempt these communications lessened.

While in custody, Agca told a startling story about how he was to have escaped after shooting the pope. He said that he was to be driven from Italy to Yugoslavia in a truck that had diplomatic plates. It does seem that after his arrest a truck did leave the Bulgarian Embassy without Agca by unknown persons. He also said that he traveled to Sofia, Bulgaria in July 1980 where a member of the Turkish underworld and another person, hired him to kill the pope for the amount of $400,000. Agca claimed that these two men were connected in some way to the Bulgarian secret service.

During the investigation by Italian authorities, it was ascertained by using hotel records that Agca and these two alleged accomplices did in fact stay at lavish hotels in Sofia, Bulgaria in July 1980. In what now turned out to be a month of travel for Agca in Europe, the assassin-to-be stayed in fancy hotels in Vienna, Zurich, and Palma de Mallorca. He said he had a total of $50,000 on him when he made his way across Europe but where did a poor Ali Agca who had no job, no income, get the money for his lavish lifestyle? Someone had to bankroll him. But who? He also was in Milan where he supposedly received the Browning 9mm pistol he used to shoot the

[16] Ibid. Page 302-303.

pope from members of the Grey Wolves.

On the day of the assassination attempt, according to Agca, he and two Bulgarians and the man from Turkey entered St. Peter's Square to stake out the crowd and see what kind of police presence was there. One of the men whom Agca said was with him in the square was a Turk named Oral Celik.

Another person who met with the pope and relayed American intelligence secrets was Vernon Walters a diplomat who served in various American administrations including that of Franklin Roosevelt, Harry Truman and, Dwight Eisenhower as a translator. He also accompanied Vice President Nixon on his trip to Venezuela in 1958 that saw massive anti-U.S. riots during Nixon's visit. Upon being elected president in 1968, Nixon named Vernon Walters to the post of deputy director of the CIA.

When Ronald Reagan became president, he nominated Walters to become his ambassador-at-large and gave him some of the most sensitive missions around the world. One of these trips was to see the pope in the Vatican and share with the pope, some of the U.S.'s most secret information. One particular piece of information he gave to the pope was a satellite photo of large amounts of Russian military equipment in Poland and the fact that thousands of members of Warsaw Pact troops were being sent to the borders of Poland. These units comprised troops from Russia, East Germany, and Czechoslovakia. He also showed the pope satellite pictures of Russian missiles in their silos, aimed at the west. He further told the pope that the United States would do all it could covertly to aid the Solidarity movement with money and other types of help as best it could.

Between 1981 and 1988, General Walters met with the pope at approximately six-month intervals giving him a wide-ranging overview of what the American intelligence community was hearing. These intelligence sessions were drawn from all facets of the intelligence community including information coming out of the White House, the CIA, and the State Department. Among the items discussed with the pope were Central America where the rebel Sandinista guerillas were trying to overthrow the government of Nicaragua, U.S. negotiations in the Middle East, Soviet nuclear capability, Chinese military power, and much more. Richard Allen who was Reagan's first national security advisor gave a glowing report on the close relationship between the president and the pope "as one of the greatest secret alliances of all time." He also told the president as the secret relationship was brewing that, "An ideal intelligence agency would be set up the way the Vatican is. It's intelligence is first rate."

In the National Archives in Washington, the CIA has made public the information it has on the shooting of the pope. These consist of 218 pages (which are available for purchase) which contain information on the events in St. Peter's Square on the day the pope was shot, information on the Vatican and it's relationship with Poland during that time period, and material on the Soviet Union. Also in the collection are allegations of the Bulgarian connection in the papal shooting.

A part of the released files from the CIA discusses Moscow's possible role in the attempt on the pope's life including the following information:

Moscow's recent public statement denying involvement in the assassination attempt on the pope and the strong protest over U.S. press coverage delivered by the Soviet chargé d'affaires in Washington on Monday indicate the Soviets have decided to play a more active role (rest in blank. Comment: Moscow until recently has avoided direct involvement in the controversy, and its activism suggests new concern that the case is damaging the USSR's interests because of the Western press implications that General Secretary Andropov, during his tenure as head of the KGB, might have played a role in the attempt. The Soviet Ambassador presumably hoped to persuade the Italian Government to play down the issue. The Soviets are likely to continue to defend Bulgaria against its accusers.

The secret back channel between William Casey and Vernon Walters covertly cemented an on-going relationship between the Reagan administration and the Vatican that was one of the most guarded secrets of the cold war. The pope and the president had common bonds, shared many political beliefs and were ant-communist to the core. No wonder they got on so well.

What circumstances drove the young Mehmet Ali Agca to St. Peters Square to try to assassinate the pope? Did his background have anything to do with events that were about to occur? How did a poor, relatively uneducated person from a small town in Turkey with no obvious monetary support system, travel in luxury on his way to attempt to kill the pope? The more one looks into the murky world of Mehmet Ali Agca, the more there are questions than answers.

Mehmet Ali Agca was born in 1958 in Malatya, a town with much history attached to it. As a young man he did not have a police record, although while in high school he wrote a letter against the Armenians, and was the subject of a brief police investigation. He was not active in any political or radical organization that one can think of, just a rebellious young man, like many others in the area. Ali Agca had a sister named Fatma, an ordinary young woman who liked history and literature and lived with her mother at the time her brother tried to kill the pope. The family told a visiting reporter that Ali Agca had a mild form of epilepsy as a youngster but over time had grown out of it. In order to help the family with the bills, a young Agca did many jobs including selling water at the railroad station, working on construction sites, carrying sand, among other menial jobs. His mother said that as a young man he liked to read as much as possible, his favorite subjects being Turkish history and historical novels. She also said that from age 10 or 11, he liked to write poetry and even wrote a novel at age 13. In questioning his family, it was learned that Ali Agca attended the University of Ankara for two years before transferring to Istanbul. It would seem that this fact was not known to the investigators who plied into his background after his capture.

In 1975-76, Agca took an educational exam while in high school to see what kind of college education he wanted to do. He qualified for the History and Geography Faculty at the University of Ankara, which he entered in the fall of 1976. He told is family that he wanted to be a teacher and with that kind of a job, he'd be able to help support the family. He later took another exam and wound up at the

University of Istanbul.

Paul Henze, an author and former diplomat who wrote a book called *The Plot to Kill the Pope,* had a different theory about what happened to Agca when he was in Ankara, besides studying. He wrote that when Agca was in Ankara he could have been recruited by various East European intelligences services that knew of his background as a radical student. "From Ankara," Mr. Henze wrote, "he could have been sent for training to a PLO camp." He further speculates that Agca might have gone to Lebanon as early as the summer of 1976, but could not be certain. When he was arrested in Rome, Agca said that he had been to a PLO training camp but later, like many of his other statements, rejected that account. Agca told investigators that while he was in the employ of the PLO, he worked for the group lead by George Habash.

Claire Sterling, in doing research for her book, met in Israel with her Mossad contact and she asked that person questions about Agca possibly being in a PLO training camp. Without divulging that person's identity, her contact told her that, "They all used false names in the camps, and it happened five years ago, if it happened. We simply don't know either way, I was told in Tel Aviv."

In an interview with the late author and writer, Claire Sterling, Agca's mother told her that her son had no trouble at home until he left for college in Ankara and Istanbul. "Those villains got him," she said. While living at home, Agca made friends with people of various political persuasions including leftists and rightists. Agca later wrote of this time by saying, "In 1977, I decided to go to Palestine on the recommendation of a schoolmate from Malatya, Sedat Sirri Kadem. There I met Teslim Tore, who went with me to Beirut. After a 40-day course at a training camp, Teslim Tore helped me get back into Turkey." It seems that Sedat Serri was arrested in 1981 as a member of Turkey's dangerous left-wing organizations called Dev-Sol and said he knew Agca who came from the same town. Teslim Tore was chief of the THKO (Turkish People's Liberation Army, a rabid communist group. At that time, police in Ankara said that Tore was an instructor at a Palestine training camp in Lebanon. With radical friends like Tore and Sedat Sirri Kedma, it is not out of the question to believe that at some point, Agca became radicalized by these (or other men whom he came in contact with), which set him on his course that led up to the shooting of the pope.

When Agca was arrested, among the huge claims he made was that the Bulgarians were behind his assassination plot against the pope. One of the witnesses, a man named Yaclin Ozbey, based his testimony on two other Turks, Oral Celik and Sedat Sirri Kadem, who knew Agca. "Celik and Kadem told me," said Ozbey, "that the Bulgarians simply knew about it (the conspiracy) but did nothing to support them." Agca said that both Celik and Kadem were his accomplices in St. Peter's Square at the time of the shooting.

When Agca's initial trial began in the winter of 1983, there was not much of an effort to find out the complete truth of what happened the day the pope was shot. If they wanted to find out all about a possible widespread conspiracy of those behind the assassin, they did not do a good job. However, the court, in its wisdom, did compile what was called "A Statement of Motivation," which was buried in the mass of documents and legal briefs that accompanied the Agca trial proceedings. This Statement of Motivation was were largely unpublished in the press, account for a vital trove of information culled from various intelligence and police sources in Europe and beyond. These include" dozens of Italian police and secret-service reports; telexed exchanges with their opposite numbers in West Germany, Switzerland, Austria, Turkey, Tunisia; communications to and from Interpol; texts of Agca's earliest interrogations; and a first hand-written confession." The information gleaned from the Statement of Motivation would be crucial in sorting out the mystery of Ali Agca and his road to Rome.

In the months and years before his attack on the pope, Ali Agca was a man on the run, aided and abetted by persons unknown. On February 1, 1979, Turkey's most important newspaper editor, Abdi Ipekci was killed. The man whom the authorities arrested for his murder was Ali Agca who was said to have shot five bullets into his torso, thus making the meek Agca, Europe's number one terrorist. It took the police another five months to arrest Agca and he was placed in the Kartal-Maltepe military prison where he stayed for a short time before making a daring escape. It is not known if he had any help in his escape, but a short time after breaking out, he sent a letter to the late Abdi Ipekci's paper, *Milliyet,* saying,"

"Western imperialists, fearful that Turkey and her sister Islamic nations might become a political, military, and economic power in the Middle East, are sending to Turkey in this delicate movement the Commander of the Crusades, John Paul, disguised as a religious chief. If this visit is not cancelled, I will without doubt kill the Pope-Chief. This is the sole motive for my escape from prison. Furthermore, the responsibility for the attack on Mecca (the armed seizure of Islam's holiest Mosque in 1979), of American and Israeli origin, will not go unpunished. Signed Mehmet Ali Agca."

This "confession" by Agca that he was targeting the pope years before he fired the almost fatal shots, was a prime motive for the attempt on the pontiff's life in 1981.

Even though Agca admitted to killing Mr. Ipekci, there were others who looked into his murder that case doubt on whether or not Agca had anything to do with the killing. One of these men was the former Interior Minister of Turkey, Hasan Gunes, a man with quite a shady background. It seems that his family had been investigated for various crimes with his brother, the mayor of a town near Istanbul, having been arrested for allegedly heading his local underground Communist Party in that area. His two sons were also arrested for a jewel robbery linked to finance Teslim Tore's group.

Gunes at one time served in the cabinet of Turkey's Prime Minister's Ecevit's Socialist cabinet in 1979. He was in charge of the investigation of Agca and some people accused him of creating stories about Agca at that time. One person, a former informant for the secret service (MIT), swore that he was in the room when Gunes paid Agca to take the blame for Ipekci's murder and link it to the Grey Wolves whom Agca was associated with. When a reporter asked Gunes if this allegation was true, he replied, "If everything he said about me was true, I'd be hanged by now." When asked about Agca's guilt, or innocence he said, "Agca was helped by German and Italian extremists. He's tough, He won't talk."

He also elaborated that while he thought that Agca was responsible for the editors killing, there were other people involved and that Agca may not have been the one to target Mr. Ipekci in the first place. When Minister Gunes asked Agca under questioning why he killed Ipekci he replied," Because he was not a Moslem." Gunes said that while he was questioning Agca, it seemed that the young man was constantly acting, as if he were on stage and wanted everyone to see what he was about.

When reporter Claire Sterling interviewed Minister Gunes for her book, as it related to Agca' shooting of the pope, he had a lot to say. "I'm not sure of Agca's motives," he said. "And I cannot fully put the emphasis on either the right or the Communists for trying to kill the pope. I see no advantage for either side, in Turkey." He said he believed that Agca worked for either the West or the East and that the East might have done it to "get the Poles under control." If the West did it, said Minister Gunes, it was to "provoke a Polish revolt and pull Poland out of the Warsaw Pact."

Sterling then asked Gunes an important question that she wanted an answer for; Did Agca have any connection to the Bulgarian Turkish Mafia run by Abuzer Ugurlu? Gunes said that Abuzer Ugurlu was the "the Godfather" of the Turkish Mafia. He's famous, the biggest." Gunes replied that when he was a minister in the cabinet he mounted the first large-scale police investigation of the Ugurlu clan, beginning in 1979. In time, Abuzer Ugurlu was arrested but did not spend much time in jail. Soon, he was out again, operating his gunrunning operation, free of police interference.

The so-called Bulgarian Mafia connection to Ali Agca was one of the most talked and written about topics among those journalists and writers who cared enough to look into the case after many of the mainstream media of the time decided not to pursue the story any further. Ali Agca said that he got a certain amount of cash for the attack on the pope from Musa Serdar Celebi—a leader of the Turkish Grey Wolves who said he was only acting as a middleman for Bekir Celenk, a Turkish Mafia boss. Agca also said that he had met with Abuzer Ugurlu, who, while on trial in Turkey admitted to having met Agca in Bulgaria and given him money. Both Celenk and Ugurlu were Sofia-based Mafia bosses. This also explains Agca's Grey Wolves connection. The Grey Wolves were being run by a huge contraband ring, the Turkish Mafia—unique in the world in that it was really working for a Communist state of Bulgaria. In fact, both Celenk and Ugurlu had been working directly for the Bulgarian Secret Service, Celenk since the mid-60s and Ugurlu since 1974. But Ugurlu wasn't the only one admitting to have known Agca. Following his extradition from West Germany to Italy, Celebi—the middleman working for Celenk also admitted meeting Agca and giving him money. Celebi was known as a Turkish businessman.[17]

After his escape from jail, Agca was on the run and was aided and abetted by persons-unknown in Europe and elsewhere. In December 1989, Turkish police said that Agca was responsible for the murder of Haydar Serangah, who had ratted him out. A death sentence was placed on Agca's head for the murder, but while the legal proceedings were going on, Ali Agca was on the run, winding up in such places as Iran with a false Indian passport and a large sum of money (around $17,000) "supplied by persons I do not intend to name who are supporting me," he said.

He stayed in Iran for three months (in 1980) and it is not known what or whom he was doing or seeing on that trip, nor do we know who supplied him with the funds to live during that time. Then, in early July, he was in Bulgaria and stayed for fifty days.

It is in Sofia, Bulgaria, where things begin to get very interesting for Agca where he will meet with various, important people who will take him on his journey to St. Peter's Square, a year later.

In Bulgaria he bought the 9-mm pistol that he was to use in the shooting of the pope. He claimed that a Syrian student named "Ahmed" supplied the gun. While staying in the posh Hotel Vitosha, he met a fellow Turk named Omer Mersan. Mersan told Agca that he'd get him a fake passport—in the name of Frank Ozgun—which was found on his person after his arrest. It seems that Omer Mersan was arrested by local authorities and he told them that he had known Ali Agca as "Metin" but refused to tell just what kind of a relationship he had with Agca.

In a rather unexplainable foray, Agca then left Bulgaria on a long trip that would take him to Yugoslavia, France, Great Britain, Belgium, Switzerland, Denmark, Austria, Italy, Spain, and again to Italy. The Italian court said of this time that his journeys were "the incessant pilgrimage of a nomad anxious to cover his tracks" But from whom?

He also spent a considerable amount of time in West Germany where he denied ever being, and was recognized by many of his fellow Turks as being in one city or another. He was carrying false documents on his person and met with a number of Turkish citizens who were wanted by police in Ankara for various crimes. While on

[17] Novick, Peter, "Blue Print of an Assassination: The Soviet Union Vs the Vatican," *Back Channels*, Vol. 2, No. 3, Spring 1993, Page 7.

the run, Agca was thinking about two other assassinations that he was looking into; the murder of Queen Elizabeth of England and taking out the Council of Europe's president in Strasbourg, Simone Weil.

Agca then told quite a story that involved a man named Mustafaeff whom he had previously met while in Bulgaria. It seems that they met again in a hotel in Tunis where, on November 29, 1980, he asked Agca if he would consider killing the president of Tunisia, Bourguiba, and Maltese Premier Dom Mintoff, who was supposed to make a trip to Tunis. Agca turned down this offer because he said there would be too much security. Whether this is true or not, is not known or just another story conjured up by Agca for his own purposes.

The Statement of Motivation, as referenced above, asked many relevant questions about Agca and his various international ties. Among them were:

•Was it true that Agca had worked clandestinely in Turkey with underground groups of both the extreme right and left?

•Had he actually been put on a secret payroll at the age of 19?

•Who got him out of prison in Istanbul, took care of his hideouts and false passports, and piled him with "conspicuous funds-around $50,000, police thought—for his European travels?

•Who guided him through safely through the vast enemy territory of Western Europe—Agca's most notorious terrorist fugitive, confessed and convicted murderer of Abdi Ipekci?

•Who taught him to use the Browning 9-mm weapon, the professional assassin's perfect weapon, to aim it in regulation style, with both hands, over the heads of the crowd, at a moving target whose vital organs he missed by a hair?

•If he was not "a terrorist who came from nowhere, where did he come from? What "hidden minds" sent him?

All these were relevant questions at the time but it seems that some in the press and many in the governments of the world, including the CIA and the United States, did not really want to delve into such a mystery.

After his arrest, Agca told the court that he was Jesus Christ, giving his detractors ammunition that implied that he was mentally ill, while no evidence of that existed. He then went on a brief hunger strike in December 1981, but it did not last long. One year later, Agca had a change of heart and he decided to cooperate with Italian judges and began spilling his story (as mentioned about in this chapter).

While in custody, another event took place that went relatively non-covered by the foreign press but was covered locally. It seems that a 15-year old girl named Emanuela Orlandi, a Vatican resident, and whose father was a Papal messenger, went missing. She was taken on June 22, 1983 at approximately 7 p.m. in front of a bus stop near her music school in Rome. Her family put out posters around Rome and even the pope himself asked for her release during one of his messages to those assembled in St. Peter's Square. On July 5, her family received a call from her kidnappers saying that she had been kidnapped and asked for the release of Ali Agca in return for her safety. It is not certain that the kidnappers really wanted the release of Agca in exchange for the girl but at the time it just made the case of the papal assassination attempt more bizarre.

While the events surrounding the kidnapping of Emanuela Orlandi was going on, Agca was being transferred in an armored car for questioning regarding an exchange for the girl. He told the Italians that he wanted no part of the deal, did not want to be traded and put up quite a fuss about the matter. When he had a chance to respond to reporters shouted questions he said that, "I am with the innocent girl. I am with Italy. I am with the Vatican. I am doing very well in Italian jails. I thank the Italian justice and the Italian state. I am repentant for the attack on the pope. I admire the pope and I thank the Italian justice."

Before Agca was taken away by the police, a reporter shouted a question to him and asked, "Was it the Bulgarians who sent you to Italy?" He responded by saying, "Yes, the Bulgarians. I have been several times to Bulgaria and in Syria—and in the attack against the pope even the KGB took part. Yes, the KGB."

For a man who was born to say the most outrageous things, Agca had by accident or not, put the blame on the Soviet's via the KGB in the assault on the pope. He couldn't stop there, and before he was pulled away by the police he said, "I have been trained in

Bulgaria. I have been in Bulgaria. I stayed several times. I have been trained by special experts in international terrorism."

He said he was trained in Syria and Bulgaria and had "stayed several times." The record in ripe in the fact that he was in Bulgaria but we still are not sure if he was in Syria and he claimed.

The Italian press had a field day with the story, trying to find out who was really responsible for Emanuela Orlandi's kidnapping. They even went so far as to try and implicate such figures as the American archbishop Paul Marcinkus, the former president of the Vatican Bank that was involved in one of the most spectacular scandals in Vatican history (the story of the Vatican scandal will be told later in this book). Upon hearing of the allegations against the late Archbishop Marcinkus, a Vatican spokesman scolded the media saying the information came from "a source whose value is highly dubious." The source was supposed to have been Sabrina Minardi, who was a girlfriend of Enrico De Pedis, a mobster who was killed in Rome in 1990.

Other possible kidnappers were laid at the feet of unknown Bulgarian agents, the Sicilian Mafia, the KGB, and even Roberto Calvi, known as "God's Banker" for his part in the Vatican Bank case.

In a twist that could only have come in pulp spy novel, investigators turned their attention to a murdered mobster named Enrico de Pedis, a member of the Magliana crime family who was killed in Rome and whose remains were buried in a crypt under the basilica of St. Apollinare, in Rome. In 2005, an anonymous phone call came into a television station that added more intrigue to the story. The caller said that authorities should begin looking in the crypt of St. Apollinare to examine the bones that were located there. Just why Mr. De Pedis's remains were buried in consecrated ground is not known, but that's what the caller said. The caller also said that the girl had been kidnapped on the orders of Cardinal Ugo Poletti, who died in 1983 and was the vicar general of Rome.

In 2015, in an unusual move on its part, the Vatican agreed to have Mr. De Pedis' grave opened so investigators could see what was inside. Pietro Orlandi, the brother of Emanuela Orlandi said at the time the crypt was opened, "It's very positive. Especially because his hadn't been the case in the past. The Vatican's silence for 29 years remains inexplicable for me. I never expected her to be buried there, but it was important to clear up a doubt." He reflected that he thought the truth behind her sister's disappearance "is known to many people."

A writer who did a book on the case, Roberta Hidalgo, said that, "the reopening of the tomb is to throw people off the track." When the police opened the crypt they found the remains of Mr. De Pedis using fingerprint analysis. Whether or not the kidnapping of the young woman had anything to do with Agca or was just a horrible coincidence, is just one more mystery to the already twisted story of Agca and the attempt on the pope's life.[18]

As the investigation went forward, Agca made so many conflicting statements to the Italian court, some backed by facts, others highly improbable that the Italian judicial system began its own probe of the events a few years later. In March 2006, the Associated Press broke the news of what the panel found and it placed the blame on the shoulders of the Soviet Union. They concluded that the Kremlin was to be liable for the pope's shooting due to the fact that he was seen as a threat to their control over Poland due to the ever-growing Solidarity movement. The Italian report said that Soviet military intelligence—not the KGB—was responsible. After the report was issued, a Russian spokesman named Boris Labusov called the charge "absurd" (what else were they going to say?). Mr. Labusov also replied that, "All assertions of any kind of participation in the attempt on the pope's life by Soviet special services, including foreign intelligence, are completely absurd." The report said that Moscow was alarmed because, "Poland was the main military base of the Warsaw Pact, its main supply lines and troop concentrations were there. "This commission believes, beyond any reasonable doubt, that the leaders of the Soviet Union took the initiative to eliminate the pope Karol Wojtyla.'"

At the time the report was released, it had no official bearing on Agca's trial but nonetheless, it was an important statement for the

[18] Povolendo, Elisabetta, and Pianigiani, Gaia, "Crime Boss's Tomb is Exhumed for Clues in Missing Girl's Case," www.nytimes.com 2/05/2012.

world to see and hear regarding what might have happened before the pope was shot. They also concluded that a picture of Sergi Antonov, the Bulgarian who worked for Balkan Air at the time of the shooting—and who was ultimately acquitted of involvement in the shooting of the pope—was in St. Peter's Square when the pontiff was shot by Agca. While it was widely known among intelligence services at the time that the Bulgarian secret service worked hand-in-glove with the KGB, the court said that they had insufficient evidence to link Bulgaria in the plot, despite a large number of shady Bulgarians who had links to Agca as he made his way to Rome in 1981. Antonov's lawyer said at the time that his client was not in St. Peter's Square and it was a case of "mistaken identity." Senator Guzzanti, the commission's president, replied that the photo of Antonov was not used at trial because the technology of the time couldn't determine if it was actually Antonov, but "recent computer comparisons with other shots of the Bulgarian show that there is a 100 percent compatibility."

Agca told the court so many conflicting stories about who was behind the plot that the court was never clear who he was working for. He said that the Russians were behind the plot and in 1991 then Soviet Premier Mikhail Gorbachev hotly denied there was any Soviet involvement.

The ostensible reason for the commission's birth was to establish any KGB penetration of Italy during the cold war era.

The commission's president, Senator Paolo Guzzanti, said he made the decision to open an investigation at the national level after he read the pope's book called. *Memory and Identify: Conversations Between Millenniums,* that "someone else planned it, someone else commissioned it."[19]

In an interesting twist, the Italian commission, as part of it work, received information on the case from a French antiterrorism judge, Jean-Louis Bruguiere in relation to information he received on the case of the notorious international terrorist of the time, Ilich Ramirez Sanchez, a.k.a., "Carlos the Jackal" who was captured in the Sudan in 1994. Just what kind of information the judge received regarding Carlos the Jackal was not mentioned but it adds another twist to the intelligence gathering process that came out of the trial.

[19] Simpson, Victor, "Italian Parliamentary Panel: Soviets Behind Shooting Of Pope John Paul II," www.nysun.com , March 2, 2006.

The Vatican Conspiracy

Carlos the Jackal was one of the most wanted terrorists of the 1970s. For those readers who don't know much about him, here is his story:

A Venezuelan by birth, he left the prosperous home of his father to seek his own future among the militant, pro-revolutionary groups fighting for justice as they saw it.

It was into this dangerous world of spies and assassins that Ilich Ramirez Sanchez would fashion his own indomitable future.

In September 1968, Ilich and his brother Lenin arrived at Patrice Lumumba University in Moscow where their father had sent them to study. Less than one year after arriving in Russia, Ilich began to show disfavor with his classes, and the indoctrination he was forced to listen to, along with the cold, hard Soviet winter. He began to rebel, drank too much and made the authorities take more than a passing glance at him.

For a brief while in 1969, he left Moscow and returned to London to visit his family. He then mysteriously disappeared, probably heading for the Middle East. Much has been speculated about Carlos' disappearance during this time. It has been postulated that he was under the control of the Soviet KGB (possibly like Ali Agca) who was running him as an agent. He had now taken on a new identity—CARLOS.

Carlos then went to Jordan, where he was introduced to Dr. Waddieh Haddad, the leader of the PFLP. It was under Haddad's direction that Carlos was transformed from an inexperienced street tough to a first class terrorist.

Under the hot desert sun, Carlos studied and trained in the fine arts of guerrilla warfare, learning how to use automatic weapons, codes, and other deadly weapons. Joining Carlos in Jordan and later in Lebanon, were members of other terrorist groups such as the German Baader-Meinhof gang, the IRA, the Japanese Red Army and the E.T.A., a Bosque terrorist group seeking independence from Spain. It was from this deadly group that Carlos would make his worldwide contacts and plan future missions.

Dr. Habash decided that Carlos was now ready to go operational and in July 1971, he was sent to Europe to head a clandestine cell of the Mohammed Boudia organization. Carlos roamed Paris and London, organizing a series of informers, safe houses and possible

250

targets for assassination.

His first mission was to hijack a train carrying Soviet Jews en route from Czechoslovakia to Austria bound for Israel. With the train successfully stopped in Austria, the terrorists demanded and received assurances from Prime Minister Bruno Kreisky to close down the Schonau transit camp where the Jewish refugees were being held.

His next mission was Joseph Sieff, the president of Marks and Spencer stores in London. Sieff, a prominent British Jew was in his home on the night of December 7, 1973 when Carlos barged his way past Sieff's butler and shot Sieff in the head at close range. Somehow, Sieff survived and Carlos managed to slip away.

Now acting on his own, Carlos traveled to Paris where he sent a grenade spinning into a crowd at a Latin Quarter drugstore, killing two and wounding thirty-four.

By now the Israeli Mossad had begun to track Carlos. Acting with precision they killed Mouhammed Boudia in France along with Dr. Basilal-Kubaisi, also a PFLP member.

Working closely with the French DST, a double agent called Michel Mukobal, (who was also a Mossad spy) led French police to the house where Carlos was staying in Paris. As the police entered Carlos' flat, he killed three DST men, including Murkobal. He then escaped.

In December 1975, Carlos would be given the most dangerous assignment of his short but bloody career.

During the Christmas season Carlos and six of his cell members joined the thousands of holiday travelers converging on Europe. Using different routes and false papers, (just like Agca did) they met in Vienna where the ministers of the OPEC (Organization of Petroleum Exporting Companies) were meeting. The group entered the nearby rooms of the hotel where the meeting was taking place and spoke to several members of the press about the progress of the gathering. Security was minimal, with only two Austrian policemen on duty. Without warning, Carlos and his gang stormed into the OPEC conference room, taking 70 hostages and killing two people; an Austrian policeman and the Iraqi oil minister.

Within minutes Carlos had the OPEC ministers separated into groups, issuing orders and letting the world know what he had done.

Austria's Special-Command, took up places outside, surrounding the building.

Carlos began negotiating with the Austrian's and secured a promise from Prime Minister Kreisky for safe passage out of the country. Leaving Vienna with a seriously wounded team member, Carlos and the OPEC ministers took off for Algiers where he let a few of the hostages go free.

Still in his hands were 15 hostages, including the Saudi Minister, Sheikh Ahmed Zaki Yamani. While in Algiers, Carlos spoke with Haddad by phone and was assured by him that the ransom payment that they demanded was on the way. Carlos released his final hostages and with a million dollars in his hands, fled without harm, back to the protective embrace of his revolutionary brothers.

In the late 1970s, Carlos established a covert relationship with Edwin Wilson, an ex-CIA agent turned international arms dealer who was supplying Libyan leader Muammar Qaddafi with illegal plastique explosives.

Wilson introduced Carlos to his partners including Frank Terpil and Rafael Quintero, an ex-Bay of Pigs soldier and CIA contract agent. Wilson asked Quintero if he would kill someone who was wanted by various intelligence services. Quintero agreed, thinking the hit would be made on Carlos. Later, Quintero found out that the target was Umar Muhayah, a Libyan political leader in Egypt.

Years ago in a Public Broadcasting interview on the old *McNeil-Lehrer News Hour,* former KGB General Oleg Kalugin, once Chief of the KGB Counterintelligence unit, said that when Carlos was in the Soviet Union he was always under surveillance by Domestic Counterintelligence staff. He also said that Carlos was never employed by the KGB and might have been working for the Libyans.

It took almost twenty-five years before the world's intelligence agencies were finally able to track Carlos down. By 1994, with Carlos now in residence in Sudan, his luck finally ran out. He was no longer considered a major threat and was turned over to the French. Carlos's exploits hit the big screen with the 1973 movie *The Day of the Jackal,* based on the novel by Frederick Forsythe.

As the Italian commission's investigation proceeded, they began to find that out that other countries intelligence services as well as their politicians were reluctant to aid them in their investigation. Nonetheless, Senator Paolo Guzzanti and Magistrate Martella carried on as best they could. In order to find out more information regarding Agca and the plot against the pope, Martella arrived in the United States in October 1982 to view two recent U.S. media reports on the pope's shooting which suggested that the Soviet Bloc were somehow involved in the event. (The two media reports were the NBC report by Marvin Kalb and Claire Sterling's article in *Readers Digest*).

Before leaving for the States, Martella told Italian journalists that in his opinion, there was no hard evidence to prove East Bloc involvement. However he did tell one reporter in a telephone interview that he could not rule out the possibility. Martella said that he found other countries reluctant to cooperate with his probe (for reasons unknown), and one U.S. intelligence source said there had not been much "visible" evidence of international coordination in providing information on the case because it would expose them to "criticism over their handling of terrorism or could cause diplomatic strains with the Soviets." (Particularly, Bulgaria.)

When talking to correspondent Sari Gilbert in Rome, Martella said of the case he was building, "You have to finish the foundation before you can start thinking about the roof." One of the men whom he was looking into very closely was Abuzer Ugurlu, the Turkish crime boss who has been mentioned in this chapter. Martella said that he did not have enough solid information at that time to link Agca, Ugurlu and the Bulgarians and the Soviet's but would comment further if he found information to change his mind. He also commented about a report that suggested that an associate of Ugurlu sent a courier to see Agca on the island of Majorca to offer him 3 million German marks and sanctuary in Bulgaria for shooting the pope. Martella commented that there had been no solid evidence that Agca was ever in Majorca. Speaking about the large number of news reports about the case he said, "Journalists can afford to make what they see as logical deductions. I can work only on the basis of facts."

Magistrate Martella did however find one country that would aid him in his investigation, Switzerland. At his request, he contacted police in the city of Olten in northern Switzerland because they arrested a man named Omer Bagci and charged him with supplying Agca with the gun used in the attack on the pope. The Swiss charged that Bagci was a member of the Grey Wolves, a Turkish terrorist organization. The Swiss said that Bagic gave the Browning 9-mn automatic to Agca on May 9, 1981, four days before he shot the pope. Also related to the Bagci case is an intercept of a telephone call by the Italians from Agca in Milan to Bagci in Olten asking for the gun to be delivered. It is not known just why the Italians found it necessary to record the call but it probably had something to do concerning something nefarious that Bagci and or Agca were up to. After Rome's Court of Assizes convicted Agca of shooting the pope and two American tourists in St. Peter's Square, the jury asked Italian magistrates to try and find those who helped Agca, saying his act was "the result of a complex plot orchestrated by hidden minds interested in destabilization."[20]

The CIA, as mentioned in this chapter, took an active interest in the Agca case and they wrote a lengthy report on the findings of Judge Martella's and Senator Guzzanti's internal probe. The narrative, which was written on April 1, 1987 from the Directorate of Intelligence was called "The Papal Assassination Conspiracy Trial: Inconclusive Results." The account was extensive and it is worth taking a close look at just what their findings were.

Part of the Summary reads as follows:

> Despite rigorous efforts to uncover the truth, its results were inconclusive. While the trial yielded little evidence to substantiate allegations of Bulgarian complicity in the attack against the pope, it also failed to exonerate the Bulgarians— and the Turkish defendants—and so has left lingering doubts about their guilt or innocence.

In a page titled "The Papal Assassination Conspiracy Trial; Inconclusive Results" they wrote the following:

> *The event that had been touted as the "trial of the century" produced more questions than it did answers. In so doing it affirmed the view of many that the truth surrounding

---

[20] MaCartney, Robert, "Papa Shooting Probe," *The Washington Post,* October 6, 1982.

the attack against the pope may never be known.

*It provided circumstantial evidence highly suggestive of some kind of conspiracy, but failed to prove one.

*It raised questions as to whether Agca was a shrewd calculating actor, or merely crazy.

*It failed to clarify the circumstances surrounding the February 1979 murder of Turkish newspaper editor Abdi Ipekci, to which Agca confessed: Agca's escape from a Turkish prison some months later; his written threat against the Pontiff if he visited Turkey in late November 1979, as scheduled; and the relationship of these events, if any, to his eventual attack on the pope.

*It failed to uncover the nature of the relationships between and among Agca, the Turkish rightwing extremist organization called the Grey Wolves, the smuggling network known as the "Turkish Mafia," and the Bulgarian authorities.

*It failed to determine Agca's real reasons for trying to kill the pope, as well as his motives for undermining the trial. It was, after all, Agca's lack of credibility that delivered the fatal blow to the trial proceedings.

The CIA document faulted Agca for not telling the truth to his Italian prosecutors and took exception to the Bulgarian airline official Sergi Antonov who was absent for half of the trial. They also wrote that the inability to question the alleged coconspirators in the case, Oral Celik and Bekir Celenk was a major blow to the proceedings. Celenk who was reported to have been Agca's alleged paymaster in the plot, died three months following his departure from Bulgaria where he had been under house arrest since 1982.

The narrative then went on to look at Agca's many claims about the case and his part in it:

*The would-be assassin's most critical assertion, however—that he had been in direct contact with Bulgarian officials for the express purpose of conspiring against the pope—has remained unproven.

*In early December 1985, Italian customs officials testified that they had received a considerable sum of money in exchange for not sealing the Bulgarian TIR truck Agca claims was to have spirited him and his accomplices out of Italy following the shooting. This testimony adds credibility to Agca's pretrial statements that Sofia had agreed to help Agca leave Italy following the assassination attempt.

*Omar Bagci's testimony confirmed many of Agca's pretrial statements regarding his acquisition of the weapon used in the shooting. Bagci affirmed that he had traveled from Dulliken, Switzerland, to Milan, Italy to deliver to Agca four days before the shooting the Browning pistol he used against the Pontiff.

*The trial was unsuccessful, however, in is efforts to resolve a number of fundamental questions concerning a conspiracy in the Papal shooting. It is highly questionable, moreover, whether these will ever be answered satisfactorily.

The narrative spoke about the many relationships that Agca had with Turkish rightwing groups and the fact that a new team of magistrates had to be taken on in order to pursue the Turkish connection to the Papal attack. The report also questioned how many and who might have been with Agca when he shot the pope in St. Peter's Square on May 13, 1981.

They further studied the movements of the Bulgarian defendant Antonov on the day of the shooting. Prosecutor Antonio Marini accused Antonov of having lied when he told Italian investigators that he was not present when the pope was shot; the Prosecutor also charged Bulgaria with having destroyed documents needed to substantiate Antonov's version of events:

*The personal details Agca provided about Bulgarian defendants who claim they never met Agca. The court has not resolved how Agca was able to provide such information.

*The disposition of the funds allegedly paid to the Turkish gunman and his accomplices. No trace of the money was ever found by the court or pretrial investigators.

*The numerous meetings Agca said had taken place between him and the Bulgarian defendants. No independent corroboration of such contacts surfaced in the courtroom.

*The Justification of Sentence. An Italian court document made public in November 1986, contends that the three Bulgarian defendants provided suspicious alibis that failed to refute evidence that Agca had dealings with them before the Papal shooting, according to press accounts. The document, required under Italian law, is a "justification of sentence" that explains how the court assesses evidence during a trial and reaches a verdict. This particular document, signed by Presiding Magistrate Santiapichi, concluded that while no firm evidence emerged to link he alleged coconspirators to an assassination plot, there were solid indications that Agca had not acted alone. The document maintains that Agca willfully destroyed his credibility as a witness, seemed intent on protecting his accomplices, and might have had reason to believe that he would be helped to escape from prison if he was successful in sabotaging the prosecution's case. The document concluded by attributing some credibility to the hypothesis that Turkish alleged coconspirators were "commissioned" by "another group" that wished to "disguise the political "motivation of the act.

The fact that the CIA went to such pains to make a detailed report like the one described showed how important they felt it was to investigate all aspects of the attack on the pope in the years following the incident.

After a wave of gang related attacks in Turkey that rocked that nation to its core in the late 1990s, that led up to an attack on a television studio in Istanbul by 50 armed men on May 2, 1997 in support of Turkey's Deputy Prime Minister Tansu Ciller, the government in Ankara undertook a parliamentary commission to investigate these attacks as well as the right wing Grey Wolves who had been a thorn in the side of the government for over a decade. The commission wanted to find out if Turkey, then and now a vital NATO (North Atlantic Treaty Organization) country was allowed to now

"operate death squads and to smuggle drugs with impunity." What the commission found was not only a link to the papal assassination plot but a large-scale arms-for-drugs operation that ran from Turkey to the Middle East and beyond.

The incident that triggered the Turkish commission was a simple car crash that they police were investigating. However, by the time they figured out the circumstances beyond the crash, it would lead to a scandal going to the highest reaches of the government.

The incident took place on November 3, 1996, in the village of Susurluk in Turkey. In the aftermath of the crash, three people lost their lives when their car hit a tractor and overturned. Just another car accident, you say? The crash killed Husseyin Kocadag, a top police officer who commanded the Turkish counterinsurgency units. The other persons who were killed were Abdullah Catli, a convicted criminal was wanted for drug smuggling and murder, and his girlfriend Gonca Us, a Turkish beauty contestant. Catli was also linked to Ali Agca, the man who shot the pope. The lone survivor in the crash was Sedat Bucak, a militia leader that had been armed and financed by the Turkish government to fight Kurdish separatists. When questioned by the press regarding the circumstances of the crash, the police responded by saying that they were carrying two captured criminals.

As the investigation proceeded, a different story emerged. It seems that Catli, a wanted criminal and drug smuggler by trade, was carrying diplomatic credentials given to him by the Turkish government. He was also carrying on his person a government issued weapons permit as well as six ID cars, each with a different person's name. Catli was also carrying many handguns, silencers, and quantity of narcotics. Why would Catli, a dangerous criminal wanted by the police, be in possession of these items and did the police have any role in giving him these items?

In the wake of the now brewing scandal the Turkish Interior Minister resigned. Also, several high-ranking law enforcement officers, among them Istanbul's police chief, were suspended from duty.

Catli was once a leading figure in the Grey Wolves whose name has been mentioned in this chapter in its association with Ali Agca. In 1978, Catli was charged with the murder of seven trade union officials and he went deep underground to avoid capture.

When Catli testified in September 1985 as a witness at the trial of three Bulgarians and four Turks who were charged with complicity in the attack on Pope John Paul II he said that he gave Agca the gun he used to shoot the pope. Catli had also helped Agca escape from his jail cell where he was serving time for the killing of Editor Abdi Ipekci. Catli was also responsible for aiding Agca in his travels prior to shooting the pope when Agca made his way through several European countries such as West Germany, Switzerland, and Austria.

Working hand in glove with Abuzer Ugurlu, Catli's Turkish Mafia thugs went across the so-called smugglers route through Bulgaria. "These routes were the ones favored by smugglers who reportedly carried NATO military equipment to the Middle East and returned with loads of heroin. Judge Carlo Palermo, an Italian magistrate based in Trento, discovered these smuggling operations while investigating arms and drug trafficking from Eastern Europe to Sicily." Another part of Magistrate's Palermo's investigation was the fact that large quantities of NATO supplies including tanks, Cobra assault helicopters were smuggled from Western Europe to nations in the Middle East during the 1970s and early 1980s. Palermo discovered that the military equipment was exchanged for shipments of heroin with the help of the Grey Wolves into Bulgaria and northern Italy.[21]

From these locations, the drugs were taken in by Mafia dealers and sent to North America (mostly the United States) where the morphine paste was sold in what was then called the Sicilian run "Pizza Connection" on the streets of the major cities in the United States.

The so-called "Pizza Connection" had its heyday in the late 1970s and early 1980s when a large number of pizza parlors in New York, New Jersey, Long Island and the Midwest were used to distribute heroin—not cocaine—brought into the United States by Sicilian gangsters.

A dramatic sequel to the original Pizza connection of the 1970s came in September 1994 when 79 persons were arrested in New York by FBI agents in one of the largest drug interception cases in history. Operating out of the famous Original Ray's Pizza on Third

[21] Lee, Martin, *On The Trail of Turkey's Terrorist Grey Wolves,* 1997.

Avenue near 43rd Street, the feds busted a drug smuggling ring that was operating out of the back of the store. The pizza parlor imported cocaine from Columbia to serve New York's drug appetite. The establishment also used New York as a transit point to deliver drugs to three longtime organized crime groups in Italy, where cocaine was sold at the time for three times what it cost in New York.

The men who ran the pizza-drug smuggling operation were three brothers, Aniello, Francesco, and Roberto Ambrosios and were also rounded up by the FBI. The FBI at the time said that Ambrosios brothers also arranged for some of the coke to go directly from Columbia to Italy, collecting a commission from the Columbians for setting up the sale. One of these shipments was intercepted at the Bogota, Columbia airport where 168 pounds of cocaine was smuggled in crates of flowers that were en route to Italy.

The arms for military equipment scheme had at its roots a small import-export company located in Milan called Stibam International Transport. Stibam was run by a Syrian businessman named Henri Arsan who, it was learned later, was on the payroll of the U.S. Drug Enforcement Agency. Sitbam also had covert links to the well-known, criminal bank directly tied to the Vatican called Banco Ambrosiano, headed by Roberto Calvi who died under mysterious circumstances in London in June 1982. Using its many business outlets in such cities as London, Zurich, New York, and Sofia, Bulgaria (there we go again with the Bulgarian connection), Stibam officials recycled their profits through Calvi's bank. In the mid to late 1970s, Banco Ambrosiano handled most of Stibam's foreign currency exchanges and was tied in closely with Calvi and his Vatican led international crime organization

Sitbam was also closely linked to Kintex (mentioned in this chapter), which was a Sofia based, state-controlled import-export firm that worked under the direction of the Bulgarian government and was the home of many undercover spies who worked for both Bulgaria and the Soviet Union.

There were many people who looked into the Bulgarian connection to the pope's shooting and tried to knock that theory down. When Catli testified in Rome in September 1985, he said that he had "been approached by the West German BND spy organization, which allegedly promised him a large sum of money if he implicated the Bulgarian secret service and the KGB in the attempt on the pope's life."

After spending several years in jail in France and Switzerland for heroin trafficking, Catli was back in action after escaping from a Swiss jail and once again linked up with the Grey Wolves and other neo-fascists groups. He was now employed as a death squad leader for the Turkish government in its war against the Kurds who longed to separate from both Turkey and Iraq.

The outcome of the investigation into Abdullah Catli's death opened up the fact that the Turkish government at the time was protecting a large network of drug smugglers and other nefarious people for its own political ends. Was there any other connection that we don't know regarding Catli's secret relationship with Ali Agca? If there is, the story remains silent.

Was Ali Agca a spy in the employ of the Bulgarian secret service? While on the surface it might seem to be a fanciful claim, but if one looked deeper into the possibility that it might not sound as far-fetched as it seemed.

At the center of this controversy was Luigi Scricciolo, who served as a socialist trade union leader and also worked as the foreign affairs director of his labor federation, UIL. It seems that Mr. Scricciolo had been arrested in February 1982 and had astonished his jailers by telling them that he worked for a Bulgarian spy ring since 1976. He was charged of establishing contact between the Red Brigades, a terrorist group whose spectacular success had been the kidnapping of U.S. General James Dozier and the Bulgarians. He also was charged as being close to the Solidarity Trade Union in Poland whom Pope John Paul II supported and was said to have provided information to them on what the trade union was up to. He told authorities that he was approached by the Bulgarians to plot to kill Polish Solidarity Union chief Lech Walesa on his trip to Rome in January 1981 (he turned down the offer).

Both Luigi Scricciolo and Ali Aga told the same exact story regarding the Lech Walesa plot even though both men did not know each other. So, who was right? It was alleged by two of the leading

Italian judges who were studying the papal plot, Judges Imposimato and Martella, that both Agca and Scricciolo worked in Rome for Ivan Tomov Dontchev, who was the chief of the Bulgarian spy agency in the city. Dontchev had an arrest warrant out for him that was signed by Judge Rosario Priore (as the arrest warrant was being issued, Dontchev had returned to Bulgaria).

It seems that spying was in the family business, as Luigi's wife, Paola, had been employed by the Bulgarian's since 1979, while Luigi began his work with them in 1976. Both husband and wife were in Sofia, Bulgaria in August 1980 but did not cross paths with Agca while he was in the city. At the time they were in Sofia, Ivan Dontchev was their controller and he guided them in their undercover work.

The charges filed against Dontchev by Judge Rosario Priore were the following:

> ...serious acts of espionage; creating an information network to gather confidential information on the Italian labor movement; recruiting Italian students studying in American universities, so as to gather U.S. Scientific and technological knowledge; gathering sensitive information on the activities of Solidarity in Poland; and establishing a structure of collaboration with the Red Brigades.

In his talks with Judge Imposimato, Scricciolo told him that he knew of Dontchev's plans to kill Lech Walesa during his trip to Rome between July 15 and 19. When Judge Imposimato showed a picture of Dontchev to Agca, among others, he readily picked him out and further said that he met with Dontchev at his home where plans to kill Walesa were discussed.

This information came from Claire Sterling's book *The Time of the Assassins,* and she wrote the following regarding Agca and Dontchev:

> Evidentially, Agca was not merely hired for a special occasion: he was an all-purpose hit man at the disposal of the Bulgarian spy ring operating in Italy and reporting to the Russians. In that event, no overeager sub lantern in the

Bulgarian services could possibly hatch a plot against the pope on his own. The rings designs on Lech Walesa indicated a calculated policy, with fallback positions. Agca himself told the judges that this was one of several alternative plans that Dontchev's ring had in mind.

With all of Ali Agca's Bulgarian connections in the persons of Abuzer Ugurlu, Musa Cerdar Celebi, Oral Celik, Omer Bagci, and Abdullah Catli, it is so unbelievable that he could have been recruited by Ivan Dontchev and ordered to come to Rome in May 1981 for purposes other than the killing of Pope John Paul II? We probably will never know that side of the story but it is one aspect that should not be dismissed out of hand.

The possibility of Soviet involvement in the assassination attempt on the pope took another turn when former Secretary of State Henry Kissinger weighed in on the topic. In an interview he did in December 1982, Kissinger said he believed the Soviet's had a role in the events in St Peters Square in May 1981. Speaking to a newsman for a story that was to be aired on national television a few days later, Kissinger had many things to say on the topic. He opined that:

> ...the Soviet secret service was behind it. Here is a Turkish terrorist, who suddenly shows up in Bulgaria, which is not the normal thing for a Turk to do, lives in the best hotel in Bulgaria, emerges with $50,000 and a weapon, travels all over Europe. It cannot happen without the Bulgarian secret police.
>
> It's nonsense to say, as I read somewhere, that maybe something got away from the higher levels. That does not happen in Bulgaria. Then it had to be the Soviet's. The Bulgarians have no interest in coming after the pope. "They must have thought that they had to crush Solidarity. At that time in 1981, they must have thought that the possibility existed that the Red Army would have to go in. In that case if there were a Polish pope who did what he was alleged to have threatened, go to Poland and oppose them, which would be a formidable psychological problem.

In his remarks, Kissinger made a rather interesting comment when he said that Richard Helms, the former Director of the CIA told him that, "it had all the earmarks of a KGB operation. If you try to square the known facts, it really leads to no other conclusion."

When the reporter asked Kissinger what the ramifications would be for US-Soviet relations if it was confirmed that the Soviet's had a hand in the assassination attempt on the pope, he said, "I take it we will never know more than we know. We don't negotiate with the Soviet's because we like them. The Soviets will ruthlessly pursue their own interests. Our problem is whether in a nuclear world the Soviets pursing their own interest and we pursing our interest can ease the potential conflicts and reduce the danger of confrontation."

At the time of the attempt on the pope, the United States was introducing new weapons systems to Western Europe as well as discussing intermediate-range nuclear missile talks with the Soviets in Geneva, Switzerland. While in office, Henry Kissinger engaged in discussions with the Soviet Union in SALT-I and SALT-II treaty to limit each other's stockpile of nuclear weapons. Kissinger served as both the national security advisor and Secretary of State in the Nixon and Ford administrations. Like him or not, Kissinger was one of the most influential men in Washington for many years and his comments were not to be ignored by the men in power in the White House and Congress. For Kissinger to say that he believed the Soviets were behind the papal assassination plot just added another layer to the ever growing conclusion that the men in Moscow, i.e., Yuri Andropov, approved the hit and made the Bulgarians a scapegoat for the event.[22]

The plot against Pope John Paul II is one that a good spy novelist could dream of; international spy networks, gun and drug smuggling, the gunman as a lone assassin or someone who had links to two countries, the Soviet Union and Bulgaria, his association to many men in the so-called Turkish Mafia who helped him finance and aid him in his journey across Europe, staying in the best hotels, eating in the best restaurants, men who were able to forge passports for him as if on cue, others who had a plan to spirit him out of Rome after he shot the pope.

[22] "Kissinger Believes Soviets Behind Attempt on Pope's Life," Associated Press, December 31, 1982.

The lack of interest by many of the western intelligence agencies who would rather not look into the actions that the assassin took for their own selfish reasons, the interest the CIA took in the assassination attempt by digging deep into the act and then coming up with different views of what happened, the interest of NBC television in the United States in the form of two separate prime-time shows that that gave the American people vital insights into what happened to the pope, the close association between President Ronald Reagan and Pope John Paul II, the covert meetings between the pope and CIA Director William Casey as well as other intelligence officials who briefed the pope on the most important international matters then going on, the allegation by author Paul Kengor that the Soviet Union's foreign military intelligence agency was behind the attempt on the pope's life in the form of the GRU.

Then we have the fact that William Casey once believed that the Russians were behind the papal plot and the fact that two different factions at Langley headquarters were on complete opposite tracks as to what happened in Rome. Was the Bulgarian connection set up to take the heat off the Russians as so many people were beginning to postulate? We now know that Casey met with author Claire Sterling whose book on the shooting opened up many minds among the intelligence community. Did Sterling tell Casey something that we still don't know about?

Casey was the one who asked Sterling to meet him and they had a private meeting somewhere in New York. While there are no notes or other memorandums about what the gathering was about, we can surely postulate that they were comparing notes regarding the assassination attempt in St. Peter's Square. When the intelligence community was doing a National Intelligence Estimates regarding any connection of Russia in the plot (they said there was none), Casey snapped and said, "I paid $13.95 for Sterling's book and it told me more than you bastards whom I pay $50,000 a year."

Among the still unanswered questions are the connections between Ali Agca and so many Turkish criminals and Mafia leaders like Musa Serdar-Celebi—the leader of the Turkish Grey Wolves, Bekir Celenk, a topnotch Mafia boss, the godfather of the Turkish mob, Abuzer Ugurlu who was based out of Sofia, men like Abdullah Catli, Oral Celik, Omar Bagci, who paths crossed with Agca as he traveled across Europe, the professional link between the Soviet and Bulgarian intelligence services and what role they may have played in setting up Ali Agca before the assassination attempt.

Claire Sterling gave the last straw to the story that Abuzer Ugurlu was indeed working for the Bulgarian's as an active secret service agent. Speaking to members of the Martial Law Command in Ankara's Mamak Prison, the generals in charge of the facility told her that Ugurlu had "very probably" been recruited by the Bulgarian DS in the early seventies. Her hunch was confirmed by a source of hers in Interpol who, when she asked this person if the rumor was correct that Ugurlu had been recruited by the DS, this person said, "You have my oath on it. It's true." Was there any connection between Agca and the spymaster Ivan Dontchev and was he somehow involved with his spy ring in Rome?

Did Agca really have targeted Solidarity leader Lech Walesa? Then we have conflicting testimony on Agca's part regarding the murder of the newspaper editor Ipekci of which he was convicted of killing and spent time in prison. Also of interest to the entire story is the secretive role played by the Bulgarian-linked Kintex Company which was the conduit of weapons and drug shipments to various countries and organizations in the world. Among the employees of Kintex were former members of the Soviet KGB at all levels who played a vital role in the operation of Kintex. Also under question in the relationship between Omer Mersan a fellow Turk whom Agca met in Sofia, Bulgaria in the hotel Vitosha. Mersen was said to have offered Agca a forged passport with the name Frank Ozgun, which Agca had on him in Rome. Mersen also arranged a meeting between Agca and a man only known as Mustafaeff in Tunis while Agca was traveling across Europe. It seems that there was more to the Omer Mersen story than meets the eye. It was confirmed by the DEA that Omer Mersen was as known as a heroin-trafficker since December 1981 and was an associate of Ali Agca.

The DEA also reported that Mersen had bought 5.5 kilos of pure heroin in May 1982, which was ultimately seized in Istanbul, Turkey on November 5, 1982. Of course, the fact that Omer Mersen was an international drug dealer and had associations with Agca does not make Agca himself part of any drug ring. No evidence proves that, but it does say something that Agca was associating himself with so many unscrupulous people along his journey to Rome.

Adding to this mix was the desperate actions taken by the Soviet's to blame the CIA and the United States for the pope's shooting. Why the United States would try to kill the pope was ludicrous at best but the Russians had to blame someone (if they weren't guilty). The United States and the Vatican saw eye to eye in trying to free Poland from the Soviet orbit and the pope was their best spokesman.

When Sergi Antonov, the Bulgarian Airline official who was arrested as being part of Agca's plot, the Soviet press went into overdrive to condemn his arrest. The Russian Tass News agency, the official print arm of Moscow, wrote about the arrest of Antonov, "as a totally illegal, arbitrary and absolutely unwarranted hostile act." Tass continued by saying regarding the arrest of Antonov, "Logic proves that the charge made against the Bulgarian citizen is completely groundless. The illegally arrested Bulgarian citizen does not and could not have any connection whatsoever with this criminal act. The Soviet media was now coming to the aid of its ally, Bulgaria.

Not to be out done by TASS, the Russian government sent out a man named Yona Andronov, a former KGB officer as their main propaganda arm. Over time, he wrote books, pamphlets, and newspapers articles attacking the CIA as being responsible for the attack on the pope and linking Agca and his Grey Wolves directly at the door of the CIA. His articles often times appeared in the western press where they were soon noticed by the CIA who must have read them with interest.

Following the lead of the Russians, the Bulgarian government too went on the offensive railing against those who said their country was in league with Agca and attacking those writers who took that position. They especially attacked Claire Sterling whose expose in *Readers Digest,* accusing the Bulgarians of aiding Agca hit a nerve. They also went after Paul Henze another journalist who did reporting on the incident. The Bulgarian's even went so far as to publish a 178-page attack against Sterling called "Dossier on the Anatomy of a Culumny." Herbert Romerstein, a former communist and an authority on communist affairs, testified before congress saying that Sterling and the other writers delving into the attack on

Note - Copied Title from Professor Marjorie Bowkoris the Anatomy of a Novel. Did...

the pope were subjected to an "incredible smear campaign in the (Soviet controlled) Bulgarian press which is then replayed in other parts of the world."

The Russians once again took to the airways to attack NBC's show called "*The Man Who Shot the Pope: A Study in Terrorism*" (which later won the Peabody Award for journalism) which concluded, along with Sterling, that Agca and his cohorts had been in league with the Bulgarian secret service and the Soviet KGB. One of the major claims that came out of the Russian critique of NBC's show was the accusation of CIA involvement in the attack on the pope. This claim had never been seen before and it now added a new element to the story.

The Russians did more than just attack the United States in the press regarding any possible role they might have played against the pope. It seems that Moscow had put out an all points infiltration and espionage operation against the Vatican under the direction of Yuri Andropov. Andropov asked the Fifth Directorate of the KGB to infiltrate and monitor religious groups, including the Vatican. An author named John Koehler who wrote a book called *Spies in the Vatican,* wrote, "Besides the prime target, the pope, he (Andropov) was particularly interested in the activities of Archbishop Agostino Casaroli. Eventually, every department of the Church had been infiltrated."

While the pope was recovering from his gunshots, his attention was turned to an event that took place sixty-four years to the day of his shooting. It was something he'd been thinking about for a while and he now wondered if it had any religious meaning. The event in mention took place on May 13, 1917 in Fatima, Portugal, when the apparition of the Virgin Mary was supposed to have returned to earth and was said to have been seen by a few young girls. On his part, Pope John II deeply believed that his shooting in May 1981 had some deep religious connections to the so-called "Third Secret of Fatima."

The Secrets of Fatima took place between May 13 and October 13, 1917 in Fatima, Portugal and has started a controversy in the church that still rages today. When asked to explain what the three children had seen, the church said it was some supernatural event that could not be explained. The three children were ridiculed and called all sorts of names throughout their lifetimes, something they did not deserve. The names of the children who said they saw the Virgin Mary were Lucia dos Santos and her younger cousins Jacinta and Francisco Marto and their story begins on May 13, 1917, a Sunday. The girls had taken their sheep out to pasture after church to a place called "Cove of Irene" or "Cove of Peace" when they saw a flash of light in the sky. As the clouds passed, they saw a white figure of a lady appear before them. One of the children described the light coming from the figure as "more brilliant than the sun," radiating a "clear and intense" light. Lucia said the figure of the woman appeared to be about seventeen years old.

Lucia, then ten years old, had a conversation with the apparition and she asked it where she came from. The answer was from heaven. When she asked the apparition what she wanted, her reply was that they should come to the exact same spot on the thirteenth day of each month for six consecutive months. The apparition then said that in time, she'd tell the girls why she had come to earth.

When the Lady appeared again, she told them of three events that would take place. The first prediction was that war then raging would end but that another one, even more deadly would arrive. The second prophecy warned against the coming of the eruption of atheistic communism. "Russia would spread its errors throughout the world, raising up wars and persecutions of the Church." One of these pronouncements took place on July 13, only three months before the Bolshevik revolution in Russia that ousted the Czar and his family (who were brutally murdered by the new regime). not All -

What was the Third Secret of Fatima? It was put away in the secret vaults of the Vatican for a century until it was finally revealed. The Third Secret was the envisioned attack on the pope of Rome— something that would occur in the future.

The Lady told the girls something about their personal fates. She told the two cousins that they did not have long to live. Both Jacinta and Francisco died within three years, victims of an influenza outbreak. Lucia lived to the age of ninety-seven, long enough to see the three secrets come true. Years later, Lucia would become a sister of the church, a Carmelite nun.

On October 13, 1917, a week and a half before the outbreak of the Bolshevik Revolution, a group of seventy thousand people, including the three girls, stood in Fatima to see an extraordinary event. As the skies parted, only the three girls could communicate with the Lady and she told them, "I am the lady of the Rosary." She said the war then going on would soon end and that they'd see their loved ones again. Lucia then recalled what happened next. She explained that the rosary opened her hands and "made them reflect on the sun, and as she ascended, the reflection of her own light continued to be projected on the sun itself." The girls then saw the Lady vanish in the sky and then saw Saint Joseph with the Child Jesus aside the Lady robed in white with a blue mantle. It was the Holy Family.[23]

When questioned by reporters if he thought the Soviets or the Bulgarian were involved in the shooting, President Reagan was circumspect in public, not wanting to give his own, personal answer. He said that he'd leave it up to the Italians to investigate the crimes and see what they came up with. When pressed by a reporter some time later about what effect it would have on US-Russian relations if it was proved they had some role in the event, the president said, "Well, I think that it would certainly would have an effect, I think it would have an effect worldwide, and I'd meet that problem when we got to it."

In private, President Reagan was more candid than he was in public. In meeting with his aid, William Clark, the president, according to Clark, believed the Bulgarians were behind the attack, which put the ultimate suspicion on Moscow's doors. Clark added, "The Bulgarians had no incentive to or motive to do this on their own. And it was the typical pattern of the Soviets to always get someone else to do their dirty work."

Writing in his book *A Pope and a President,* Paul Kengor said that:

> The president and Casey were both convinced of the Soviet-KGB connection. However, we didn't want to reveal our thinking at the time because doing so would have accomplished nothing. People already suspected or assumed it. If it was proven, or if we said we were certain about it,

23 Kengor, Paul, *A Pope and A President John Paul II, Ronald Reagan, and the Extraordinary Untold Story of the 20th Century,* ISI Books, Wilmington, Delaware, 2017, Pages 14-18.

what could we do? Bomb Moscow over it? Of course not.

Casey felt he had proof. I saw the intel at the time. Ronald Reagan believed it as well. Knowing their (the Soviets) propensities and how they felt about the Holy Father and how they wanted to get him out of the way… it's almost too crude to want to believe that they would want to assassinate him, but that's how they operated.

Other high-ranking U.S. Intelligence officials besides William Casey believed that the Russians were behind the attack on the pope. Among them were the National Security Council's director for Soviet and European affairs, John Lenczowski. In an interview with author Paul Kengor for his book *A Pope and A President,* he said, "that Moscow was indeed behind the assassination attempt" since the Italian judicial investigation "did find a credible link with the Bulgarians. It was always clear that the Soviets did most of their dirty work through proxies, and that these proxies did not act independently without Moscow's permission."

A further person who worked on the NSC staff, Kenneth deGraffenried, said that, "I had already come to the conclusion of Soviet involvement early on. Put me on the list with the others. Knowing something of the awful Soviet history of assassinations, Bill Casey and Bill Clark certainly saw the Soviet hand behind this attempt." He also said that, "Casey and Clark of course had knowledge in parallel with the pope and the Church, which was unknown to almost everyone in the U.S. Government."

As mentioned earlier in this chapter about the disagreements among many of the CIA officers regarding the validity of a possible Soviet role in the assassination attempt, deGraffenried adds more to the story. He said that in several meetings he had with people like CIA deputy director, John McMahon, and Robert McFarland, that the "institutional" members of the agency were not willing to accept the idea of Soviet involvement. "The shooting of the pope," he added, "was just one of the many serious issues in which we struggled with the institutional CIA over regarding Soviet intelligence activities, and their larger strategic meaning and the shortcomings of our own counterintelligence response. These were very nasty, no-holes-barred battles."

Bill Casey's son-in-law, Owen Smith who was later to become a law professor and who ran the Casey Foundation weighed in on what Casey privately thought about the Russian connection. In 2005, he told author Paul Kengor that, "Yes, I can confirm that he did feel that way. He was convinced that the Soviets were involved." Casey's daughter, Bernadette said that her father had read Claire Sterling's book, *The Time of the Assassins,* which postulated that the Bulgarians were behind the attack and after reading her book Casey replied, "My dad thought the book was right on."

President Reagan was circumspect when it came to publically making comments on his beliefs regarding the shooting of the pope in order not to unduly antagonize the Kremlin. In a memo written by William Clark to the president dated August 5, 1983, there is relevant passage in this regard. It involved a possible face-to-face meeting between the president and Yuri Andropov. "We would want to be sure that the trial of the pope's would-be assassin in Italy is unlikely to produce persuasive evidence of a Bulgarian connection, since you will not want to sit down with a man whom the public believes—right or wrong—to have taken out a contract on the pope."

On December 27, 1983, an extraordinary event took place. On that date the pope met in person in his prison cell with his would-be-assassin. It was quite a meeting on its own and the pope forgave Agca for his act. He called him, "my brother." The pope had further things to say regarding his one-on-one with Agca. The pope wrote in 2005 that, "Ali Agca, as everybody knows, was a professional assassin. This means that the attack was not his own initiative, it was someone else's idea; someone else had commissioned him to carry it out."

The pope also recalled that, "In the course of our conversation it became clear that Ali Agca was still wondering how the attempted assassination could possibly have failed. He had planned it meticulously, attending to every tiny detail. And yet his intended victim had escaped death. How could this have happened?" Throughout his meeting with the pope, Agca never asked for forgiveness.

In 1985, CIA Director Bill Casey came to the White House and delivered the secret report that blamed the Soviet GRU for the attack on the pope to President Reagan. Sheepishly, the president asked Casey if he could see the report in person and Casey told him he could. The president however, was not the only one to read the shocking report according to Robert Gates who would serve in a few presidential administrations, including President Obama. He said the other recipients of the narrative were Vice President Bush, Secretary of State George Schultz, Secretary of Defense Casper Weinberger, Joint Chiefs of Staff Chairman George Vessey, National Security Advisor Robert McFarlane, and Anne Armstrong who was chief of the president's Foreign Intelligence Advisory Board. Gates said that the report (of which Gates' role was mentioned earlier in this chapter) "drew together all of the strands suggesting Soviet involvement." The report, according to Gates, was delivered to a number of other CIA officers who were not immediately involved in writing and researching it and it was not received very well among the "institutional" CIA. There were a lot of skeptics who did not believe the Russians were involved.

In summing up the narrative, Gates said:

> This paper on the assassination attempt against the pope published in May 1985 was the CIA's last major analytical assessment of the awful event. We never would get additional information from our sources, even after the collapse of the Soviet Union. As a result, the question of whether the Soviets were involved in or knew about the assassination attempt remains unanswered and is one of the great remaining secrets of the cold war.

Years after the attack on the pope, explosive evidence linking the Soviet/Bulgarians came to light. This news was revealed by two Italian newspapers, *Corriere della Sera* and *Il Giornale* that caused worldwide headlines and broke the case wide open. The two papers quote documents found in the files of the former East German intelligence service that confirmed that the Soviet KGB had ordered the assassination attempt and assigned it directly to Bulgarian agents, who enlisted the services of Turkish extremists, including Agca. The East German secret police, the Stasi, was tasked to coordinate the operation and cover it up. The files say that in August 1982,

Markus Wolf, who was the director of East German intelligence, started a secret program called Operation Papst (Pope) in response to requests from Bulgaria to help cover up Agca's tracks that might lead their way. The plan called for a disinformation campaign to blame the attack on the West that went into effect shortly afterward. This shocking report coincided with the conclusion of the Italian court that the Russians were behind the attack.

Markus Wolf was one of the most important cold war era spy chiefs to serve in the communist orbit and his skill and tenacity were legendary. At the height of his power, Wolf controlled over 4,000 spies inside East Germany, many of whom infiltrated into the centers of power in the west, even sending a spy by the mane of Gunther Guillaume right into the office of West German Chancellor Willi Brandt. Wolf entered the East German intelligence service in August 1951 and he rose quickly to prominence in the system. His work as a spymaster was well known in both the East and West and it is not out of the realm of possibility that he could have been the conduit between the Stasi and either the Russians or the Bulgarians in the plot to kill the pope (The role of Marcus Wolf will further be explained in the last chapter of this book as it relates to the deaths of the Swiss Guards in the Vatican).

This conclusion was also reported in the person of Ion Mihai Pacepa, the highest-ranking defector from the Soviet bloc, who also said that Bulgarian and the GRU were in the loop. Mr. Pacepa wrote a book with author Ronald Rychlak called *Disinformation,* which reported that it was, "Soviet military intelligence-the GRU-that had tried to eradicate the pope. Backing up this account came from the late Carter administration official Zbigniew Brzezinski (father of news reporter Mika Brzezinski) who said, "It takes an act of faith to believe the Bulgarians did it. I do still suspect that the KGB was behind it." He further stated that in his opinion, the leaders of the Kremlin thought the new pope was a "menace."[24]

We know that the pope himself believed the Soviets were behind the attempt on his life but he wanted to keep it to himself. In October 1989, President George H. W. Bush appointed Thomas Melady as ambassador to the Vatican. Ambassador Melady had a meeting with the pope and their discussion turned to the assassination attempt on his life. The pope told Ambassador Melady that the U.S. government

[24] Kengor, Paul, *A Pope and a President,* pages 526-529.

should not make a big deal about what Ali Agca had done. The new ambassador told the pope that the he wanted the U.S. government to investigate further but the pope told him, "No, not now." The pope told him that he wanted better relations with Mikhail Gorbachev, the new Russian leader (they would meet two months later).

Ali Agca served ten years in jail for the shooting of the pope and was freed in the summer of 2010. The pope, in an act of kindness, met with Agca and basically exonerated him for his actions.

But is there more to the story? History is still open for new information, no matter how long it takes to see the light. Maybe someday, this will come to pass.

Pope John Paul II was not the only Pontiff to be involved in events beyond his control. Another man would assume the Papacy to lead the world's Roman Catholics. He too would find fate, just as unkind.

Mehmet Ali Agca when arrested.

The Fatima children.

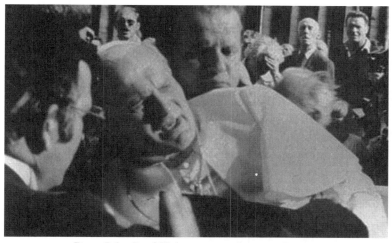

Pope John Paul II the moment he was shot.

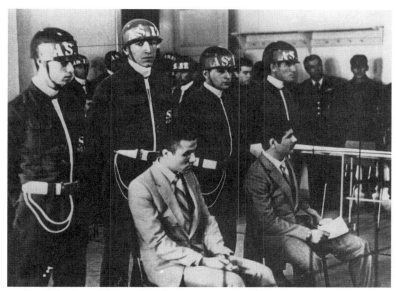

Mehmet Ali Agca on trial.

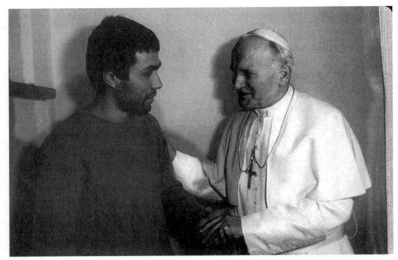

Mehmet Ali Agca meeting Pope John Paul II.

Mehmet Ali Agca in 2010.

Chapter 5

The Mysterious Death
of Pope John Paul I

Vatican City is one of the most intriguing and powerful places on earth, yet it is small in comparison to other cities in the world. It is the seat of power of the pope, who presides over this flock of millions of Christians around the world. The Vatican is comprised of 108.7 acres of land, an independent state that is recognized by most of the countries around the world. It is the size of St. James Park in London, and is one-eighth the size of New York's Central Park. Each year millions of tourists from around the world flock to the Vatican to see the historical sights and maybe, on a Sunday, hear the pope give his weekly address from his balcony. The pope is guarded by an elite group of soldiers called the Swiss Guards whose history goes back in time. One of the Papal Guards was one of the Lincoln assassination conspirators, John Surratt who lied his way into the guards and ultimately fled to Egypt where he was arrested and sent back to stand trial.

The Swiss Guards are noted for their fancy costumes of varied colors and their distinguished peaked caps. While they are not armed, inside the bowels of the Vatican lay an arsenal of modern weapons that can be used in case of an attack on the city. In the 21st Century it can reasonable be assumed that no nation is going to attack the Vatican and take the pope away. But while no overt threat is imminent, that is not to say that there are other hidden agendas at work that cannot be seen (unless, of course, the Swiss Guards are waiting for an invasion from the Freemasons and the Illuminati).

That very agenda was on the mind of Pope John Paul I when he assumed the Papacy in August 1978 after the death of his predecessor, Pope Paul VI. At 65, Albino Luciani, the former Archbishop of Venice was not among those whom the pundits in the news media in Italy and around the world would have picked as the new Pontiff. He didn't have the standing of his predecessors and was seen to be a caretaker pope until someone else of greater stature would be elected. He was immediately called the "Smiling Pope" for his genteel manner and outgoing personality. But underneath that public façade, the new pope was ready to dramatically change the way the church was run. For hundreds of years, the Popes of Rome clung to their dogged rituals of the church, never looking to change the way things had been done for generations. But unbeknownst to those in the hierarchy of the Vatican and their allies in the banking and political world, this was about to change and change fast. The old ways of doing things in the Vatican were about to become much different and those people were now standing up and taking notice.

Among those who saw the new pope as an impediment to their secret work was a high-ranking Cardinal of the Church who saw the new pope's appointments to high positions in the Vatican as something to be worried about. The pope had just begun the process of stripping many of these men of their power base in the Vatican, something unheard of before. This same Cardinal was deeply worried by the fact the Pope Paul I was looking into one of the oldest organizations in the world, one whom the Vatican had been at war with for hundreds of years, the Masons. The church did not take kindly to the Freemasons to say the least and to be one was grounds for excommunication. It seems that there were indeed over one hundred Masons encased within the Vatican comprised of priests and cardinals. Pope Paul I was also investigating an illegal Masonic Lodge called P-2 that was run by a man named Lico Gelli. This high-ranking Cardinal was also alarmed by the fact that the pope was going to have an audience in the near future with a delegation from the United States State Department to discuss, of all things, artificial birth control, a topic that was never discussed openly and which the church was opposed to. The man to whom we are referring to was the Vatican secretary of state, Cardinal Jean Villot.

The other man who was watching closely regarding the goings on in Rome, was in September 1978, living in Buenos Aires, Argentina and he too did not like what he was seeing. He was a secretive banker and conman, the chairman of one of the largest banks in Italy, Banco Ambrosiano. This man had lots to be worried about as the Bank of Italy had been secretly investigating the operations of Banco Ambrosiano and what they found was something highly illegal, to say the least. If the Bank of Italy found out that he was skimming over a billion dollars out of the Vatican's coffers, the game would finally be up. That man was Roberto Calvi.

The third man whom Paul I was scrutinizing was a banker who, in September 1978, was then in New York where he was fighting his extradition back to Italy for the crime he committed. The officials in Milan were asking the U.S. government to turn over this Sicilian banker for fraud on a massive scale, the diversion of $225 million. To his horror, a judge in New York had agreed to the government's extradition request and he was now heading back to Italy for trial. The case against him took another bizarre turn when a hit man for the Mafia, Luigi Ronsisvalle, who was a professional killer, put out a hit on a witness named Nicola Biase, who had testified against this man in court for his extradition request. The same mob then put out a contract on John Kenney, who was the chief prosecutor in the extradition proceedings. The cost of killing John Kenney was $100,000. The man whom the new pope was looking into was Michele Sindona, who was primarily responsible for the collapse of Banco Ambrosiano.

A Cardinal of the church of high standing was another person whom the pope was seeking out. He was a prominent American who ran the archdioceses in Chicago, whose finances were now under review in Rome. The Cardinal's work ethics (or lack thereof) made many priests and others petition Rome for his removal. Accusations of fraud and mismanagement were ripe in Chicago and John Paul was now considering finally getting rid of the mischievous priest. His name was John Cody.

The last person who caught the eye of the new pope was the man who was in charge of Vatican finances, the so-called Vatican bank or IOR, Institute for Religious Works. One of his favorite sayings was, "You can't run a church on Hail Mary's." Over the years, he would make a devils pact with both Roberto Calvi and Michele Sindona in a huge Ponzi scheme that would cost the church millions of dollars and would ally the Vatican with some of the most ruthless Mafia members around the globe. His name was Bishop Paul Marchinkus of Cicero, Illinois.

What all these men had in common was a hatred of the new

pope, whose very existence would put in jeopardy their financial wealth that they'd worked so hard to gain. Wouldn't it benefit them if the pope just faded away?

Well, that's exactly what happened. After serving only 33-days in office, Albino Luciani died unexpectedly in his papal bedroom. It is not known what time he died, nor the circumstances surrounding his passing. Was the pope's death by natural causes, (heart attack, sudden stroke, or some other ailment?). Or, was there a conspiracy in the pope's sudden demise, caused in part by the above-mentioned actors? Who benefits most when a person who is trying to blackmail you or investigate is found dead? That is what examinations are made for.

While this story tells the facts as we know them to be regarding the pope's death, there is a much larger back story which is just as complicated, one, which is just as important.

Albino Luciani was born on October 17, 1912 in the small village of Canale d'Agordo, in the mountains, seventy-five miles from Venice. His parents were Giovanni and Bortola, who were taking care of two other daughters from his father's first marriage. His father did not have a steady job but worked to provide for his family as a bricklayer and an electrician but had to leave his family to work these jobs in other countries such as Switzerland, Germany, Austria, and France, leaving Bortola to keep the family in check. Both parents had widely different views of the world around them. His mother was a very religious woman who taught her children the ways of the church and all it stood for. His father was just the opposite, a Socialist in his politics who really did not like Catholics very much (it seems like a very interesting marriage, to say the least). Giovanni tried to run for an elected post in the town and he had posters of himself plastered around the city. What the reaction of his wife was when she passed them on the street is anyone's guess.

At his mother's urging, Albino entered the seminary at age eleven, with the tacit approval of his father who was then living abroad. The philosophy at the seminary was as strict as could be. There were restrictions about type of books the children could read and not read and informers were ripe to tell on anyone who deviated from that principle. Even newspapers were banned and that did not suite well with young Albino who wanted to learn about the world and resented being told what to do with his ever-growing mind. As a young child, he began reading books by Jules Verne, Mark Twain, and Charles Dickens, which opened his mind even further. In school he asked so many questions that one of his teachers called him, "too lively." Albino was happy when his father made a visit to the seminary and in his spare time he continued to work for the Socialists and their cause. It is not known if the priests knew about Giovanni's politics and if they did, what was their reaction.

After finishing his classes at his first seminary, he enrolled in one of higher education at Belluno. At one point in his studies, he asked permission to join the Jesuit order but was politely turned down. At age twenty-three he was ordained as a priest on July 7, 1935, in San Pietro, Belluno. The next day was one of the proudest days in his life when he celebrated mass at his hometown of Canale. In 1932, he was appointed vice-rector of his old seminary in Belluno and turned the areas of study on its head. No longer were the strict orthodoxies of the past in play, as he urged the students to grown in ways that he was not allowed when he was young.

After working for four years at Belluno, Albino Luciani moved to Rome where he enrolled in the Gregorian University in order to get his doctorate in theology. The subject of his thesis was "The origin of the human soul according to Antonio Rosmini."

Luciani was a priest during World War II and he tried as much as possible to stay out of the limelight when it came to the politics of war. At one point in the war, the seminary where he was living was home to a number of resistance fighters who were battling the Germans. On April 4, 1950 he became, after much hard work and effort, a doctor of theology and had his thesis published. In 1947, the bishop of Belluno, Girolamo Bortignon, made Luciani pro-vicar-general of the diocese and asked him to organize the approaching synod that was to be held in Feltre and Belluno.

Lucian's star was now to get even higher in the church pecking order. Upon taking his place as the new leader of the Christian church, Pope John XXIII appointed him as the new bishop of Vittorio Veneto, and for another nine years as the Patriarch of Venice. At 46 Albino was ordained bishop by Pope John in St. Peter's Basilica, two days after Christmas in 1958. He was now in rarified air, meeting with the rest of the Bishops and met one of them who would later become pope, Karol Wojtyla of Poland. As the new Bishop of Vittorio Veneto, he became a true teacher to both his students and the various priests who were under his control. He urged them to think on their own, and made their studies more open to various teachings.

As the Bishop of Vittorio Veneto, Luciani had many interests, one of which turned out to be the Banca Cattolica del Veneto. The bank was called the" priests bank" whereby all members of the clergy from the region had personal accounts. Up until 1972, the bank had provided its depositors with low interest loans that were used for humanitarian causes throughout the region. They would now have to pay full interest on their loans that caused quite a stir among its members. The clergy now appealed to Rome to find out what was going on and to see if it could be stopped. What the majority of the clergy did not know was that Banca Cattolica de Veneto was part of the larger Vatican Bank operating in Rome with the permission of the pope. It turned out that Banca Cattolica which had been home for their financial dealings for so long had now been sold. The man responsible for the selling of the bank was the president of the powerful Vatican Bank, Paul Marchinkus. The man who bought the bank was Roberto Calvi of the Banco Ambrosiano, Milan.

The Bishops were stunned by the sale of the bank to Calvi and they pleaded with Luciani to take the case directly to Rome and speak to the pope (Paul VI) about what had transpired. Luciani began looking into the secret dealings surrounding the sale of the bank, learned as much as he could about Roberto Calvi and his partner in crime, Michele Sindona. As Luciani studied the situation at hand, he knew that he'd come upon two formidable foes, and he had to devise a strategy that would thwart them. It would not be an easy task.

The man whom Luciani turned to was Monsignor Giovanni Benelli, who was the number two man in the Secretariat of State's Office under Cardinal Villot (these were the men mentioned in the first part of this chapter who had their own reasons to see the new pope removed from office). At one point in their conversation, Luciani told Benelli, "I have not, of course seen any documentary evidence." "I have," responded Benelli. "Calvi is now the major shareholder in the Banca Cattolica del Veneto. Marchinkus sold him 37 percent on March thirty."

Benelli "told the wild-eyed Luciani that Calvi had paid 27 billion lire [approximately $45 million] to Marchinkus and that the sale was a result of a scheme hatched jointly by Calvi, Sindona, and Marchinkus. He went on to tell of a company called Pacchetti, which had been purchased by Calvi from Sindona after its price had been grossly and criminally inflated on the Milan stock exchange, and of how Marchinkus had assisted Calvi in masking the nature of this and other operations from the eyes of the Bank of Italy officials by putting the Vatican Bank facilities at the disposal of Calvi and Sindona."

When Luciani asked Benelli what it all meant, he came straight to the point. "Tax evasion, illegal movement of shares. I also believe that Marchinkus sold the shares of your Venice bank at a deliberately low price and Calvi paid the balance via a separate thirty-one billion lire deal on another bank."

He then told Luciani that the pope had appointed Paul Marchinkus as head of the Vatican Bank in order to handle the church's vast wealth and that both had been close to each other. Benelli told Luciani in passing that he'd have to wait out Marchinkus because "Marchinkus will overreach himself. His Achilles' heel is his greed for papal praise." Unfortunately for Luciani, the wait would be long.[1]

As time went on, Albino Luciani who as Bishop of Vittorio Veneto, had been receiving more disturbing news regarding that goings on in the Vatican Bank and the role Paul Marchinkus was playing. All this began with a series of newspaper articles in the major Italian press, among them *Il Mondo* which wrote an open letter to him discussing what they knew regarding secret Vatican finances. The paper's editors asked the Bishop the following question, "Is it right for the Vatican to operate in markets like a speculator? Is it right for the Vatican to have a bank whose operations help the illegal transfer of capital from Italy to other countries? Is it right for that bank to assist Italians in evading taxes?

A financial editor named Paolo Panerai attacked the Vatican in its links with Michele Sindona, Luigi Mennini (the banks managing

[1] Yallop, David, *In God's Name: An Investigation Into the Murder of Pope Paul I,* Bantam Books, New York, 1984, Page 35-39.

director) and Paul Marchinkus, head of the Vatican Bank and their "dealings with the most cynical financial dealers in the world, from Sindona to the bosses of the Continental Illinois Bank in Chicago (through which, as your Holiness's advisors can tell you), all of the Church' investments in the United States are handled."

He also lashed out at Paul Marchinkus for the fact that he had a private, profitable account in a bank in the Bahamas called the Cisalpine Overseas Bank at Nassau, "using tax free havens that is permitted by earthly law, and no lay banker can be hauled into court for taking advantage of that situation; but perhaps it is not licit under God's law, which should mark every act of the Church."

At a dinner meeting between Albino Luciani and Cardinal Villot, the latter told Luciani that the pope had instructed him to conduct a full-blown investigation of the Vatican Bank and its president, Paul Marchinkus. His orders were, "No department, no congregation, no section is to be excluded." This news was greeted happily by Luciani who now had the chance to get back at both Marchinkus and Roberto Calvi for the fiasco regarding the sudden sale of the Banca Cattolica del Vento in which many priests lost countless amounts of money. For his part, Luciani wanted to probe the finances of the Vatican Bank or as it went by its official name, Istituto per le Opere di Religione (IOR), the Institute For Religious Works. Unbeknownst to Luciani, he was now unleashing a series of events that could come back to haunt him as his career in the church reached its pinnacle of power, a few years later.

With all the secrecy and investigations now going on inside the halls of Rome, an event was to take place that would elevate Albino Luciani to the highest office in all of Chrisindom. On August 6, 1979, Pope Paul VI—Giovanni Battista Montini—died at 9:40 P.M. A new pope would now have to be elected.

After his election as Pope Paul I, Albino Luciani began to make swift changes to the way things worked inside the Vatican, ruffling many feathers that had never been ruffled before. Cardinal Villot was removed from his position as president of the pontifical council, or "Cor Unum." The man who took over that job was Cardinal Bernardian Gantin, The purpose of Cor Unum was to pass monies collected from the various churches all over the world to be distributed to the poorest nations around the globe.

One day while he was working in his office, Pope Paul I found a letter that had been signed by the Minister of Foreign Trade Rinaldo Ossola, which took aim at the Vatican Bank. The letter said that the Bank, run by Paul Marchinkus were governed as all other foreign banks would operate, in effect, the Vatican Bank would not get special treatment when it came to its business affairs.

Writing in his book *In God's Name,* David Yallop tells the story regarding Luciani and the sale of Banca Cattolica del Veneto. He writes that before Luciani became pope, he had a meeting with Pope Paul VI and told him of his displeasure that the bank had been sold and the way the sale was conducted-via Sindona and Marchinkus. The pope responded by telling Luciani, "Even you must make this sacrifice for the Church. Our finances have still not recovered from the damage caused by Sindona. But do explain your problem to Bishop Marchinkus." Luciani then went to see Bishop Marchinkus and a heated exchange then took place. Marchinkus was supposed to have told Luciani, "Your Eminence, have you nothing to do today? You do your job and I'll do mine."

While all this was going on, Pope Paul I took action on his own to investigate the goings on inside the Vatican Bank. This news must have rattled the cage of Bishop Marchinkus who saw the new pope's probe of his vast, illegal operations to be a direct threat to him and all he had been working on for so long. He was too long involved with both Roberto Calvi and Michele Sindona to stop now; things could not stand as they were.

The pope turned to two of his close advisors to help him along in his bank probe, Cardinal Benelli of Florence and Cardinal Felici. In his conversations with Cardinal Benelli he learned from him of a secret investigation then going on, on behalf of the Bank of Italy into the so-called "Pope's Bank," Banco Ambrosiano. The Bank of Italy's investigation into Banco Ambrosiano was wide spread and it now ran right into the laps of Roberto Calvi and his Vatican associates. As the investigators began their probe, they soon learned that some of what Calvi was doing was highly illegal and that if they could collect enough evidence against Calvi, criminal charges could be brought against him. If that could be proven, the links to Bishop Marchinkus would also be exposed.

In Buenos Aires where Lico Gelli was now in residence, he was being kept informed on the probe of Banco Ambrosiano by his contacts inside the Vatican.

In another development that came to the attention the new pope was an article in an Italian newspaper that listed the names of members of the so-called "Great Vatican Lodge." The Great Vatican Lodge was a list of top ranking Vatican officials who were members of the outlawed Masonic lodges. The list included 121 bishops, cardinals, and other high-ranking members of the clergy. The writer of the article was a reporter from the newspaper *L'Obsservatore Politico*, Mino Pecorelli, a former member of P-2 whose motive for writing the story was to get back at Licio Gelli with whom he had fallen out of favor with.

Among the top ranking Vatican officials whose names were listed as being Masons were the following. Cardinal Villot, whose Masonic name was Jeanni, lodge number 041/3, enrolled in a Zurich lodge on August 6, 1966, the foreign minister, Monsignor Agostino Casaroli, the Cardinal vicar of Rome, Ugo Poletti, Cardinal Baggio, Bishop Paul Marchinkus, and Monsignor Donato de Bonis of the Vatican Bank. The pope studied the information given to him regarding the Masons inside the Vatican but decided to hold off any decision on what to do for a later time.

As he decided what to do with his knowledge of the Masons, he now had to decide what to do regarding the members of Lico Gelli's P-2 which came to his attention. Lico Gelli was the head of the Masonic Lodge in Italy that was called P-2, or Propaganda 2, made up of Freemasons, people who throughout the centuries took part in revolutionary activities against existing governments. P-2 was one of Italy's most secretive organizations and was banned by the Italian Parliament when an investigation revealed that it was linked to some of highest members of the Italian parliament, the military, and the press. There were also allegations that P-2 took part in assassinations, kidnappings, and illegal arms trading across the world. Gelli was well connected in Vatican circles due to his friendship with Cardinal Paolo Bertoli, who worked in the Vatican's Diplomatic Corps. Cardinal Bertoli even introduced Gelli to Bishop Marchinkus. Once the Vatican scandal erupted in plain sight, Gelli did not fare well. After the collapse of Banco Ambrosiano, the

Italian police raided Gelli's private offices on March 17, 1981, and confiscated a number of vital information which included lists of the names of the P-2 members, which included members of parliament, the armed forces, and heads of the Italian secret services, and information on Roberto Calvi and Michele Sindona.

Gelli joined a regular Masonic Lodge in November 1963, but over time he was able to re-organize it into a secret society in Italy that catered to all sorts of influential people in all parts of the country. Gelli's plan was for his new P-2 to become one of the most influential political organizations in Italy with him at the head. His new organization was so influential at its beginning that the CIA in Italy was actively supporting him, and along the way. P-2 had offices in Argentina, Venezuela, Paraguay, Bolivia, France and the United States.

One of the most notorious members of P-2 whom Gelli came in contact with was the "Butcher of Lyon." Klaus Barbie who was then hold-up in Bolivia.

Lico Gelli's entry into the inner circles of the Vatican came in the person of an Italian lawyer by the name of Umberto Ortiolani who was also a member of P-2. He had a checkered past and served in World War II in counterespionage and operated two military intelligence units for SISMI, the nation's espionage service. After the war, his service to the nation was not forgotten and Ortiolani made friends with many of the top Vatican officials, gaining important contacts over the years. He was instrumental in a meeting at his home that ultimately ended in the election of Pope Paul VI. The pope gave him the title of "Gentleman of His Holiness" and he was responsible for getting Gelli into the secret society called the Knights of Malta and The Holy Sepulecher.

By late 1981, after the SISMI raided Gelli's home, they found a list that numbered at least two thousand members of the P-2, many of whom were high-ranking members of the Vatican. When the list was published, the Italian Senator Fabrizio Cicchitto remarked, "If you wanted to make it to the top in Italy in the 1970s the best way was Gelli and P-2."

One of P-2's tenants was a hatred of Communism in any form and Gelli tried to put the word out to his influential friends across the world to do anything possible to rid governments of that evil ideology. There were persistent rumors over the decade of the late 1960s and 1970's that P-2 had been responsible for a number of terrorist attacks around the globe but the police in these various countries never had enough evidence to convict Gelli or his P-2. According to a man named Elio Ciolini, P-2 was responsible for an attack at a Bologna train station in 1980 in which 85 people were killed, and an additional 182 injured. According to Ciolini, the attack was planned at a meeting in Monte Carlo on April 11, 1980 and that Gelli was the grand master of the meeting. These attacks, and others, were to be blamed on the work of communists in order to further inflame resentment against them.

In July 1976, an event took place that shook Italy and its politics to its core. This concerned the murder of an Italian magistrate named Vittorio Occorsio who was investigating the links between the P-2 and the neo-Fascist organization called the National Vanguard. Judge Occoriso was shot to death on July 10, 1976 by machine gun wielding attackers. A group called the New Order took credit for the killing and the death of Judge Occoriso stopped any further investigation into the actions of P-2 and its leader, Lico Gelli.

By the early 1960s, Gelli had introduced his friend and financial partner, Michele Sindona, to his P-2 and Sindona soon joined the group. The two men's illicit financial dealings soon came to the attention of both the CIA and the European police unit, INTERPOL. In November 1967, INTERPOL had begun an investigation of Sindona and their Washington office sent the following telegram to the Italian police regarding both men, "Recently we have received unverified information that the following individuals are involved in the illicit movement of depressant, stimulant, and hallucinogenic drugs between Italy, the United States, and possibly other European countries." The Italian police said they had no concrete proof that Sindona was in the drug trade but both organizations were deeply skeptical that Sindona's hands were clean when it came to drugs. We don't know if the pope was aware of any of this behind the scenes goings on but it can be said without a doubt that if he did know what "God's Banker" was up to, he would not have been too pleased.

If the pope had been aware of what the CIA knew, he again, would have been astonished. It seemed that the CIA had a large file on Sindona going back years and what it contained was shocking in its entirety. The files contained information that linked Sindona to the most notorious crime families in New York, the Gambino Mafia family, and the others, including the Colombo, Bonanno, Gambino, Lucchese, and Genovese- had an interconnecting conspiracy to sell cocaine, marijuana and heroin across the globe. The drugs were smuggled onto boats and airlines, including the Italian airline Alitalia in suitcases that were stacked with drugs and which were picked up at the end of their destination. Sindona was instrumental in funneling the profits from the drug trade to banks in Sicily that were out of reach of Italian authorities as well as from the Vatican. When Sindona was picked by Pope Paul VI to become the Vatican's chief banker his illegal-dealings were only known to a few top officials in the Vatican, something that would only come out later.

The connection between the Mafia and the Vatican Bank and its head, Bishop Paul Marchinkus, took an ominous tone in April 1973, years before Albino Luciani became pope, but one that was at the very heart of the illegal activities of what Marchinkus was up to. On April 25, 1973, Msgr. Giovanni Benelli received four important guests from the United States Department of Justice, William Lynch, the chief of the organized crime and racketeering section of the Justice Department, William Arnonwald, the assistant chief of the strike force in the Southern District of New York, and two FBI agents. Benelli left the room and the four Americans then told their story to Benelli's aides. The story involved a link between the Mafia and the Vatican "which described that a package of $14.5 million of American counterfeit bonds had been carefully and painstakingly created by a network of members of the Mafia in the United States. The package had been delivered to Rome in July 1971, and there was substantial evidence to establish that the ultimate destination of those bonds was the Vatican Bank."

William Lynch then told Benelli's associates that the final total of the illegal bond sale would be worth $950 million and shocked them even further when he told them that the person behind the scheme was Bishop Paul Marchinkus himself.

When the Italian police got wind of the scheme, they arrested a man named Mario Foligni, who called himself "The Count of San Francisco." In the course of the investigation, Italian authorities issued a search warrant for his home and when the cops raided it, they found a letter signed by Pope Paul VI, giving him his blessing. It seems that Mr. Foligni had worked with others to gain access to the Vatican, one of them being Leopold Ledi who was the initiator of the entire deal. The price for the illegal bonds was now up to $950 million with a purchase price of $635 million. A commission of $150 million went back to the Vatican, giving the Mafia a grand total of $485 million and the Vatican with bonds that had a face value of nearly $1 billion.

Marchinkus, according to Foligni, asked that a total of $1.5 million of the bonds be put into an account in a bank in Zurich. A second deposit of $2.5 million was then deposited in the Banco de Roma in September 1971. Then something happened that ruined the entire deal. Both banks then sent samples of the bonds to New York to see if they were genuine. The NY Bankers Association replied that they were false and the game was now up.

The reason the Vatican requested that the bonds be purchased went straight to the hands of Michele Sindona. The bank needed to cash the bonds in order to purchase a company called Bastogi, an Italian company who had interests in mining, and chemicals. The firm was located in Milan, right were Sindona also had his headquarters. Who were the two hidden hands behind the sale? Michele Sindona and Paul Marchinkus.

When Mario Foligni talked to William Lynch of the Justice Department he dropped another bombshell regarding Marchinkus, the head of the Vatican Bank. He said that Sindona helped Marchinkus set up secret bank accounts for himself in banks in the Bahamas for his private use.

Both Lynch and Aronwald met with three representatives of the Vatican. They listened carefully but were not yet ready to give their all -out support for their own investigation. Both men told the Vatican officials that large portion of the fake bonds were eventually going to wind up inside the coffers of the Vatican Bank and if that came to light, the Vatican would have a lot of egg on their face. At one point in the meeting, the U.S. officials took out of their bag a document that had the Vatican seal on the cover. What it contained was a Vatican order for nearly $1 billion worth of counterfeit securities. The Vatican officials were now convinced that they had been duped, not only by Sindona, but also by Paul Marchinkus.

The stage was now set for a final confrontation between the visiting American Justice Department officials and the man whom they had in their sights; Paul Marchinkus. On April 26, 1973, Aronwald, Lynch and the two FBI agents met with Marchinkus in his private office. Marchinkus had no idea how much the Justice Department men knew about his shady dealings and his association with Michele Sindona. As the meeting began, Marchinkus appeared cool, not giving anything away. They told the Bishop the story of the fake bonds and all they knew about his relationship with Sindona and what they were planning to do with the bond sale. The Bishop said that he had business interests with Sindona but they were just minor ones and that he could shed no more light on the subject. When they pressed him on whether or not he had private bank accounts in the Bahamas, the Bishop denied all charges. He said he would reluctantly testify in an American court but would only do so only if it was absolutely necessary. What he failed to mention was that he was on the Board of Directors of the Banco Ambrosiano Overseas in Nassau, Bahamas since 1971. He also did not reveal that Roberto Calvi and Michele Sindona asked him to become a member of the board. So much for having powerful friends!

As time went on, Calvi and Sindona gave the Vatican Bank and Marchinkus 2.5 percent of the Nassau bank's stock. Later it would rise to 8 percent. In the understatement of the year, Marchinkus told the Americans, "You know my position within the Vatican is unique." He then tried to impress the Americans by telling them that he reported directly to the pope who gave him his orders as to how to handle the Vatican's finances. If it was good for the pope, it was good for him.

After the probe of the securities fraud was over, a number of people were found guilty but the buck stopped at the feet of Paul Marchinkus. In an interview with author David Yallop, William Aronwald told him:

> The most that could be said is that we were satisfied that the investigation had not disclosed sufficiently credible evidence to prove or disapprove the allegations. Consequently, since we were not morally satisfied ourselves

that there was anything wrong, or that Marchinkus or anyone else in the Vatican had done anything wrong, it would have been improper of us to grab some headlines.

William Aronwald also told author Yallop, "We were not about to waste that amount of taxpayers' money unless we took the evidence very seriously indeed. At the end of the investigation the case against Marchinkus had to be filed for lack of evidence that might have convinced a jury."

When Albino Luciani became pope, he probably learned that the FBI had interviewed Bishop Marchinkus regarding the fraudulent bond sale. But what he did probably did not know was that the American FBI had taken an active interest in the activities of Roberto Calvi, Bishop Marchinkus, and Michele Sindona. Recently declassified FBI reports show that the bureau was looking seriously into the allegations of money laundering on the part of Calvi and Sindona.

In a memo dated 8/20/82, the FBI spelled out what they learned regarding the Calvi-Sindona connection. "Archbishop Marchinkus was interviewed at Vatican City on 4/28/83, by the FBI and New York Organized Crime Strike Force and DOJ attorneys regarding fraudulent financial deals. This was one of several interviews concerning Mario Foligni who was under investigation in a $959 million bond deal out of New York. The Archbishop professed no knowledge of the counterfeit bonds, which were allegedly destined for the Vatican bank, but described two unsuccessful attempts by Foligni to engage the Vatican Bank in other transactions totaling 100 and 300 million dollars. Both of these proposed transactions had been brought to Archbishop Marchinkus through other clerics in the Vatican rather than directly from Foligni. The Archbishop thought Foligni had implicated him in the counterfeit bonds movement, because he refused to enter the previous agreements. This information was corroborated in subsequent interviews at the Vatican and of Foligni. When asked about Michele Sindona, the Archbishop referred to Sindona as a good friend with whom he had few financial dealings and described him as one of the wealthiest industrialists in Italy."[2]

2 Best, Emma, "The FBI and the mysterious death of "God's Banker,'" www.muckrock.com/news/archives, March 7, 2017.

The Bureau was definitely interested in the goings on of Banco Ambrosiano and Bishop Marchinkus. One memo gets right to the point and describes just how much interest the FBI took in the matter. "For information of Bureau and WFO Instant matter involves the Italian investigation of the failure of Italy's largest bank, "Banco Ambrosiano" of Milan, Italy. This is a most important case in Italy and of interest to the Bureau as it involves several subjects Michele Sindona and blanked out. It is a most complex case involving foreign intrigue, murder, and the highest echelons of the Vatican. The case broke wide open in 1983 when the then president of Banco Ambrosiano, Roberto Calvi, was found hanging by the neck beneath Black Friars Bridge in London."

Banco Ambrosiano was not the only topic of interest the FBI was looking into; Roberto Calvi was next on their radar. In an airtel dated June of 1981 from Rome labeled "La Cosa Nostra," the FBI wrote, "He might be a key to the growing interest in international money laundering. FBI has received airtel as it pertains to Roberto Calvi. It appears he might be a key to the growing interest in international money laundering. Legat should recontact Italian authorities and determine what, if any, current information exists. If the information exists, task continental offices approximately with leads."

When Roberto Calvi was found dead in London (more about that subject in the next chapter), the FBI wrote, "On Friday, June 13, 1982, Calvi had disappeared from his Rome, Italy residence. No final determination has been made as to the cause of death. At present two theories abound; one suicide and the other murder. Autopsy reports have not as yet been received by Italian authorities."

Despite the fact that the FBI had an interest in both Sindona and Marchinkus, there were other people in the know who had a different take on what the Bishop was up to. One of these men was Tom Biamonte who once served as the FBI Agent in Charge in Rome during the Marchinkus/bonds deal. Author John Cornwell contacted Tom Biamonte at his Newark, New Jersey office for an interview concerning Bishop Marchinkus. By now, Tom Biamonte had left the FBI and was working as director of investigations into consumer fraud for the state of New Jersey. He was at first rather reluctant to speak on the record but Conwell talked him out of it. He had a story to tell regarding the affairs of Bishop Marchinkus that he wanted to get off his chest. He told Cornwell that he "believed that he (Marchinkus) got a bad deal there. The record should be set straight. I'm convinced of Marchinkus's innocence."

Tom Biamonte had served in the FBI in Italy beginning in September 1962. His duties took him to such places as Cyprus, Greece, Israel, Lebanon, and was the legal attaché at the U.S. Embassy in Rome. While in Italy he was known by all the intelligence services in Italy and the people whom he came in contact with over the years came to respect him for his professional ability. He said he first met Bishop Marchinkus in 1963 when he was just a monsignor. He said that he was the agent in Rome who investigated the above mentioned bond case and he told Cornwell they story as he saw it.

He said that Marchinkus's troubles first came to light when he made an association with Michele Sindona and Sindona's business associate, Mark Antinucci. He further elaborated that there was bad blood between Marchinkus and Cardinal Giovanni Benelli of the Secretary of State's office. Cardinal Benelli was a ruthless man, said Biamonte, who wanted to control all affairs at the Vatican and whose main ambition was to become pope. The former FBI agent said that one day while he was in his office in Rome, he was paid a visit by a stranger named Mario Foligni, the same man who had met with Justice Department Agents, Aronwald and Lynch and told him the same story he told them regarding the bogus bond sale and the role played in it by Marchinkus. Biamonte took Mario Foligni to the Italian police as well as an Interpol agent where he told them what he knew.

Biamonte said that during his investigation of the fraud case he came across an incriminating "statement under a Vatican letterhead signed by a monsignor. I checked this so-called evidence out and discovered that the letterhead is phony and the monsignor is a defrocked priest and a fraud. So I finally, in one sum-up cable, warned them in Washington not to swallow this bullshit about the Vatican connection, because it couldn't be substantiated." When Aronwald and Lynch arrived in the Vatican to meet with Bishop Marchinkus, Biamonte met them and arranged for them to see the Bishop. He believed that Marchinkus was innocent and when the Italian press got wind of the story that was the final blow for Marchinkus. He said, "The Italians love to attack the church; and the Italian magistrates when they have an opportunity to attack the Church, especially if they're Communists, they make every effort to do so."

When Cornwell asked him about the possibility of a conspiracy in the death of the pope by foul play, he said there was nothing to it. He said that from his perch in Rome for seventeen-years he had a good working knowledge about what was going on there and he said a cover-up of this magnitude was out of the question. When he was asked about a cover-up he replied, "To me, it's inconceivable that out of the thousands of priests who work in the Vatican there wasn't one who would say, "Hey, I'm not going to be part of his cover-up. No such priest has ever come forward to this day. No, it's complete crap." Biamonte told Cornwell that as an agent in Rome in 1985, it was his job to look into the leads for the Warren Commission who were investigating the Kennedy assassination. He said that he had a suspicious mind when it came to investigating cases of much importance, "and by the time I left the FBI in Rome, 1978, there was nothing in the files of the Federal Bureau of Investigation that would even create a scintilla of evidence that Archbishop Marchinkus had any connection with any wrong-doing."

He also opined on his opinion on whether or not there were any Freemasons then working in the Vatican. He categorically said no, but said he knew about the P-2 and Lico Gelli and what his group represented in Italy.

Their conversation ended with a discussion of the death of Roberto Calvi in London. He said that he believed that Calvi killed himself, despite the many investigations that took place years later involving Calvi and the Vatican Bank.[3]

Author John Cornwell who wrote a book on the death of Pope Paul I called, *A Thief in the Night,* interviewed Paul Marchinkus and asked him why he did business with Roberto Calvi. His answer was illuminating to say the least. "When Calvi was in jail I asked somebody, Hey, What's going on? And the fellow said, nah, if you're not caught, you're not worth anything."

In doing research for this book, the author came across a little known fact that linked Sindona to the Watergate break in in a tangential way. It seems that Sindona bought up a real estate

[3] Cornwell, John, *A Thief in the Night: The Mysterious Death of Pope John Paul I,* Page 168-177.

company called Societa Generale Immobiliare (SGI) that owned the Watergate complex in Washington. That in itself means nothing but it did, in some people's mind, make him an afterthought in one of the most complex conspiracies in American history. Two men who knew Sindona made cryptic comments about what role if any, Sindona had in the Watergate affair. They were Carlo Bordoni and Nino Sindona, Michele's son. Without getting into any detail, both men hinted that Michele Sindona was one of the protagonists in the Watergate affair.

When the congress starred investigating the Watergate affair, they were told by Alexander Butterfield, one of the White House Staff members that there were taping systems hidden in the president's office, they demanded that those tapes be handed over to them as part of their investigation. It came out that for some undisclosed reason, Rose Mary Woods, the president's secretary, had inadvertently or did so on purpose, erase 18 ½ minutes of a critical Watergate tape whose contents remain unknown to this day.

In 1972 when President Nixon was running for re-election, Sindona approached Maurice Stans who was in charge of the money for the Committee to Re-elect the President (CREEP). Sindona wanted to get on Nixon's good side, as he knew that at some point the American government would be coming after him for his various bank schemes. If he had a friend in the Nixon White House, Sindona thought, maybe the feds would go easy on him. They met at the New York's University Club where Sindona said he wanted to give one million dollars to the president' re-election campaign. The Italian told Stans that he wanted the money to be paid out in cash so it would not be traced back to him in Italy. Stans told Sindona that all contributions had to be made by check and that he could not accept his donation.

The first Watergate break-in took place in 1969 when jewelry and a papal medal were stolen from the home of President Nixon's long time secretary Rose Mary Woods who had an apartment in the complex (how she could afford such a high rental is not known).

If the new pope had any knowledge of what was going on behind the scenes regarding his two nemesis, Calvi and Sindona, not to mention Bishop Marchinkus, he would have been carless not to put distance between himself and all three of his opponents. As we have seen by their dark backgrounds, is it possible that all three had some role in the pope's subsequent and sudden death?

As many have speculated, the pope was considering major changes as he assumed the papacy. Some have suggested that these proposed changes to Vatican policy were considered to be so radical that the pope needed to be removed from office, one way or another. One point that the pope was considering was a monumental change in the way the church looked at artificial contraception. The fact that millions of Catholic women worldwide were on the pill was not a good thing for the Church to bear. The fact that the pope was now even talking to his advisors about changing that policy was tantamount to treason inside the Vatican walls. The pope even went so far as to have an audience with a group of people who were open to lessening the strictures on birth control sent shock waves inside the pope's palace.

No one really knew who was behind an article on the birth control question when such a story was published in the paper, *L' Osservatore Romano* in August 1978. The article was a tome that stipulated the time worn policy of the church that birth control was not to be used among the flock and did not reflect the new pope's interest in possibly changing that policy.

On the afternoon of September 28, the pope met in his office with Cardinal Jean Villot to discuss a number of pressing matters. One of the most important matters was what to do about the Vatican Bank and its president, Paul Marchinkus. The pope knew all about the Bishops secret relationship with Roberto Calvi and Michele Sindona and we don't know whether or not he discussed this knowledge with Cardinal Villot. Villot told the pope that a number of Bishops had learned about the Vatican Bank scandal and wanted to be let in on what was going on. He also told the pope that *Newsweek* magazine had somehow gotten wind of the story and was going to run it in an upcoming edition. The pope had met for forty-five minutes earlier in the month with Marchinkus and he decided that he was going to replace Marchinkus and make him the new auxiliary bishop of Chicago (Marchinkus was a native of Cicero, Illinois). How Marchinkus would have reacted to his demotion is not hard to imagine. When Marchinkus learned of these rumors about his possible replacement, he told one friend, "You will do well to remember that this pope has different ideas from the last one. There are going to be changes here. Big changes." He told Villot that he wanted Marchinkus out as Vatican Bank president the next day and that he should also take a leave of absence. Albino Luciani wanted to replace Marchinkus with Msgr. Giovanni Angelo Abbo, secretary of the Prefecture of Economic Affairs of the Holy See.

The pope now turned to another person whom he wanted out of power, Cardinal John Cody of Chicago. He had been aware for some time that Cardinal Cody was not up to doing the job in Chicago and he wanted the papal nuncio in Washington to offer him a few names to replace Cody. He told Villot, "There has been a betrayal of trust in Chicago."

Other changes he wanted to fashion were to make Cardinal Pericle Felici the new Vicar of Rome and make Cardinal Ugo Poletti the archbishop of Florence.

In his discussions with Villot, the Cardinal was frank with the pope regarding his new changes to church policy. He told the pope the following, "These decisions will please some and distress others. There are cardinals within the Roman curia who worked hard to get you elected who will feel betrayed. They will consider these changes, these appointments contrary to the late Holy Father's wishes."

What must have shocked Cardinal Villot the most was the fact that the list of names whom the new pope wanted to replace were all Masons. The Masons were the enemy of the church and had to be purged. The power they had used in the past was now going to end and who would fill the void? Men chosen by the new pope, men of good will and good conduct who would broach no more business as usual in the Vatican.

That night, the pope had dinner and spoke with Cardinal Colombo in Milan. It was a good conversation, with both men speaking about the changes the pope wanted to make. The pope also reread the notes of a speech he wanted to make to a gathering of the Jesuits on September 30. It was an ordinary night. The pope saw two of his most trusted friends walking down the hall, Father Magee and Father Lorenzi and bid them goodnight. He returned to his private quarters at 9:30 and prepared for bed. That was the last time anyone saw him alive. His lifeless body was found the next day peacefully asleep in his bed. But what happened between the time the pope went to bed and the time his body was found? Was he murdered or was it just a natural death?

If Albino Luciani had been poisoned, as many people who have investigated the death of the pope believe, was he the first to die in such a tragic way? Going back over church records there is a long list of pope's who had died unnaturally, going back hundreds of years. The first pope to be assassinated was John VIII who was poisoned in 882 by members of his own faction. It took so long for the poison to take effect that the perpetrators of the crime had to club him to death. Another pope to die was Pope Formosous who was poisoned by one of his aids. To add to this grisly scene, ten years after his death, his successor, Pope Stephen VI had the body exhumed and it was dragged through the streets of Rome for all to see. The body was then thrown into the Tiber River. Other popes found a similar fare beginning in the 10th century when John X was poisoned as he lay in jail by a woman named Marozia, his mistresses daughter (I guess they weren't as pious as they are today—but who knows?). In the eleventh century it was the fate of Sylvester II, known as the "Magician" for his alleged dealings with the devil, and then Clement II, and his successor Damascus II.

It seems that all the Popes did not get along and there were grudges among them that lead to all sorts of mayhem. Pope Celestine V was said to have been poisoned by his successor Boniface VIII, who was thrown into a dungeon after taking part in his abdication, Benedict VI was said to have died by a powered glass of figs that may have been laced with some sort of chemical, Paul II died after "eating two big melons," poisoned, again suspected. The famous Borgia Pope Alexander died in 1503 in which the poison was supposed to have been intended or someone else. After investigating the death, it was said that the pope died of arsenic poisoning which was put in his wine.

One pope did indeed survive an assassination attempt but he was not what one would call an exemplary person. Once Pope Leo X came to office he decided to get wealthy by auctioning off cardinals hats. A Florentine doctor was hired by five cardinals to whack the pope by introducing poison into his rectum. Luckily for the pope the plot was nixed in the bud and the person in charge, Cardinal Alfonso

Petrucci, was strangled with a rope of crimson silk.

There was a strange story of a pope dying in modern times but it too was not backed up by fact. The story begins with a book written by Nino Le Bello called *The Vatican Papers* which say that in 1939, there was a plot hatched to kill Pope Pius XI because he was going to make a speech attacking Fascism and the rule of Benito Mussolini. He was going to make a speech to a number of Bishops regarding the above mentioned topics when one day before the speech he was given an injection by Dr. Francesco Petacci who was the father of Mussolini's mistress, Carla Petacci. The pope was found death the next day (just like Pope John Paul I) and conspiracy theorists have pointed to Dr. Petacci as being the ringleader behind the pope's death.[4]

John Paul I had been Pontiff for just thirty-three days when his body was found the next morning lying peacefully in his bed. Immediately, conspiracy theories began to rumble throughout the Vatican, with some believing the "smiling pope" had been murdered by person—or persons—unknown. Others in the Vatican hierarchy said that it was just the will of God, who had taken Albino to his final resting place. Conspiracy theories have a mind of its own, especially if the official record in as befuddled as was the reaction of the Vatican once the pope was found dead. Here are some of the contradictions that immediately came to light.

Who found the body?

When the body was found?

The official cause of death.

The estimated time of death.

The timing and legality of the embalmment.

What the pope had in his hands at the moment of death?

The true state of his health at the time of his death.

The whereabouts of personal belongings from the papal

---

[4] Cornwell, John, *A Thief In The Night: The Mysterious Death of Pope John Paul I,* Simon and Schuster, New York, 1989. Page 47-48.

bedroom.

Whether or not the Curia ordered and performed a secret autopsy.

Whether or not the morticians were summoned before the body was officially found.

For those people in the know behind the scenes at the Vatican who were well versed regarding the changes that the new pope was going to make, there wasn't too far for some people to look to. The pope had enemies, lots of them, including Bishop Paul Marchinkus, Alberto Calvi, and Michele Sindona, along with certain other powerful leaders of the Vatican who took notice of what Luciani was planning.

One of the first theories involved a vast Masonic conspiracy inside the Vatican, of whom the pope was trying to dismiss. Lico Gelli and his P-2 organization come straight to mind and that avenue was immediately talked about.

Then there was the contradiction involving what reading material the pope had in his hands when he was found dead. The Vatican Radio reported that the pope was reading *Imitation of Christ,* a book on Catholic devotion, which was popular at the time. This material came out at 2:30 P.M. on September 28, 1978. This statement was corrected on October 2 and there was no consensus about what he was reading when he died.

Another discrepancy was published by ANSA, the Italian news agency that said that it was not Father John Magee, the papal secretary who found the pope dead but a sister Vincenza, a nun who worked in the pope's household. ANSA said the body was not found at 5:30 A.M., as the official statement said, but rather at 4:30 A.M. There were also stories that the lights in the pope's bedroom had been left on all night and no one checked it out.

Following the death of the pope, a family of morticians, the Signoracci brothers, Erenesto and Rernato, according to ANSA were called by Vatican officials at dawn and proceeded to go to the Vatican by car at 5 A.M. As John Cornwell writes in his book, the Signoracci family arrived at the Vatican before the pope's body had been found. Why would that happen? In the days following the incident, the Vatican did not repudiate that claim.

As in all good conspiracies, fact or not, the press and independent writers of all stripes began to look into the matter and begin writing about the death of the pope. In 1983, Jean-Jacques Thierry wrote a book called *La Vraie Mart de Jean Paul I,* which outlandishly theorized that Cardinal Villot, the secretary of state, substituted a double for Paul VI and planned the pope's murder when he found out about the high level Freemason's who were inside the Vatican.

In that same year, Max Morgan-Witts and Gordon Thomas wrote a book called *Pontiff.* The theme of their book was that the assassination story was a rumor started by the KGB to discredit the Vatican. This theory was the same as the one that the Russians were behind the assassination of Pope John Paul I1 by Ali Agca, substituting the KGB for the GRU. This thesis really held no water but it was a good story for those interested in a different take on the matter.

In 1983, a novel-style book was published by Roger Peyrefitte called *Soutane Rouge,* which when read, was not all off the mark. The author writes that the KGB, along with other groups like the Freemasons, the Mafia and members of the Vatican Bank, and P-2 all conspired to kill the pope. The book also told the story of shady business dealings then going on inside bank by crocked prelates. Does this all sound familiar? The characters in the book sound exactly like Michele Sindona, Roberto Calvi, and Paul Marchinkus. In Peyrefitte's work, Roberto Calvi is known as "Salvi", the head of the Banco Ambrosiano in Milan. Calvi is linked with Sindona, aka "Bindona," a corrupt lawyer from Sicily and a financer who had been arrested in the United States and Italy for fraud. Bishop Marchinkus is known as "Larvenkus" and all of them were in league with Lico Gelli and his P-2 group. The jest of the story is that Cardinal Villot aka "Hulot" conspired with Larvenkus to kill the pope by using a poison syringe (there is the use of poison again) in order to protect all these men from losing their powerful jobs in the Vatican.

If these books were entertainment based on loose facts, this cannot be said for another tome written by David Yallop called *In God's Name* that became an international best seller across the Atlantic. The protagonists in the book were all well-known actors, Michele Sindona, Roberto Calvi, Lico Gelli, Cardinal Villot, Paul

Marchinkus, and Cardinal John Cody of Chicago. Author Yallop contends that these men ordered the death of the pope using digitalis as the murder weapon. He depicts the pope as a reformer who wanted to make drastic changes to the way the church was run and made many enemies along the way.

At the time that Yallop's book was published most of the players in the saga were already off the board. Villot had died, Calvi was found dead hanging from Blackfrirers Bridge in London under mysterious circumstances, Sindona was incarcerated in a New York jail, and Gelli was somewhere hiding in South America, trying to evade the law. The only person who was still in the game was Paul Marchinkus who now saw his powerful position as head of the Vatican Bank slowly crumbling.

In David Yallop's book he describes a scene that took place in the early morning hours when the body of the pope was found in his chambers. One of the first men to be notified of the pope's death was a member of the Swiss Guard Sgt. Hans Roggan. On instructions from Cardinal Villot, Sgt. Roggan went to the pope's residence. It was now that Sgt. Roggan met Bishop Marchinkus at the courtyard near the Vatican Bank at 6:45 A.M. No one knows just what Bishop Marchinkus was doing at that early hour of the day at the Vatican as he lived in the Villa Stritch on Via della Nocetta in Rome. The Villa Stritch was a twenty-minute drive to the Vatican. When Stg. Roggan saw the Bishop he said, "The pope is dead." Marchinkus said nothing and the Sergeant said, Papa Luciani. "He's dead. They found him in his bed. A few days later, Bishop Marchinkus said of his tone deafness toward Sgt. Roggan by saying, "Sorry, I thought you had gone mad."

At 5:00 A.M. Cardinal Villot was inside the pope's bedroom where the Pontiff lay dead. He then did something that made people believe that he was somehow involved in the demise of the pope. He took a pillbox from the nightstand that contained the medicine the pope used for his low blood pressure and put it in his pocket. All who watch crime dramas on television know that medicine in the room of a deceased person is evidence in a possible crime and should not be tampered with. He then took into his possession the papers that the pope was reading at bedtime, as well as the pope's last will and testament, a paper that would normally have important significance in any case of potential murder. Someone also took the pope's glasses and slippers that were never seen again. Why did Cardinal Villot take these items? Was he up to something nefarious or is there an easy explanation for his actions? He then told his staff only what he wanted to tell them and did not say that in fact Sister Vincenza had found the body of the pope first.

Father Diego Lorenzi was a personal friend of Albino Luciani and he somehow found out that the pope had died, and he immediately called the pope's doctor, Giuseppa Da Ros who had treated him for some twenty years. Father Lorenzi said that that Dr. Da Ros was stunned to hear of his friend's sudden passing. He next called the late pope's nice Pia, who was as close a family member that the pope had. Dr. Renato Buzzonetti was allowed to enter the pope's room at 6:00 A.M. and he made an eye-to-eye examination of the body. From what he saw he said that the pope had died of an acute myocardial infraction, a heart attack. He put the time of death at 11:00 P.M. (If the pope went to bed at 9:30 P.M. the night before, he either died of natural causes or was helped on his way in that hour and a half time period).

David Yallop writes about the discrepancy regarding the book the pope was supposed to have been reading when he was found dead, *The Imitation of Christ*. Yallop says that there was no copy of the book then in residence in the Vatican at that time and that the only copy was located in Venice. The pope however got a copy of the book from another source and he returned it before he died. It was not until October 2 when the Vatican publically retracted the story regarding the book.

A story attributed to the Roman Curia had Father Magee going to the pope's residence at 10:00 P.M. supposedly telling him of a shooting of student in Rome. Some people believed that the shock of this news so unnerved the pope that he had a heart attack. This incident made up by the Curia was a total fabrication.

There had been some discussion after the death of the pope as to his medical condition before his passing. It has been ascertained that in the 33-days he was in office, not one of the many doctors who worked in the Vatican's medical department took the time to do a physical examination of the pope. He suffered from swollen ankles, a condition, which if treated early enough would have solved that problem. Two Vatican doctors, Buzzonetti and Professor Mario Fontana were never asked to examine the pope while he was still alive. Doctor Buzzonetti told John Cornwell that he didn't know the condition of the pope and so he had no cause to treat him. He told Cornwell that even if he had known about the pope's health he would not tell him because of doctor/patient confidentiality. At that time, Dr. Buzzonetti was in charge of the Health Services for the Vatican, a very important job at best. When asked if he knew what kinds of medicine the pope was taking, the doctor said no. Yet, this was the same man who signed the pope's death certificate. Wouldn't it make medical sense for the doctor who signed anyone else's death certificate, yet alone the pope to know what medicines his patient was taking? Dr. Buzzonetti said that he and Doctor Fontana made the call that the pope had died of a heart attack.

A niece of the pope's, Lina Petri told John Cornwell a lot about Albino's early health condition. She said he was not in terrible heath for a man of his age and suffered from conditions such as gallstones, had an operation for hemorrhoids, and had some respiratory conditions as a child. She said that as a young man, Albino liked to climb mountains. After a trip to Brazil in 1975, he returned home with a very bad eye infection and loss of vision. His diagnosis was that of a thrombosis of the retinal artery. She postulated that stress would not have been a cause of the pope's death as he was a man of great strength and knew how to take care of his workload, even after he became pope. Nice Petri said that her uncle did not have a doctor during the short time he was in office but needed one as a precaution.

There were so many discrepancies surrounding the events that led up to the demise of the pope and answers were few and not forthcoming. One cardinal who wished to remain anomalous said, "He, Villot, told me what had occurred was a tragic accident—that the pope had unwittingly taken an overdose of his medicine. The camerlengo pointed out that if an autopsy was performed it would obviously show his fatal overdose. No one would believe that that His Holiness had taken it accidentally. Some would allege suicide, others murder. It was agreed that there would be no autopsy."

The fact that there was no official Vatican autopsy should send shivers among those people who believed that the pope had died under mysterious circumstances. If he had died naturally, then there would have been no qualms about doing an autopsy on the pope's body. If indeed there had been foul play which many people believed, then not doing an autopsy to find out the real reason for the pope's death makes sense to those who were most likely to benefit from the act. Just why Cardinal Villot was so adamant about not ordering an autopsy and quickly agreeing that the pope had died of a heart attack, looks like a man who may have something to hide. Remember that Villot was in a rather precarious position within the Vatican and his tenure in office was hanging by a thread. Within hours of his death, all the pope's official papers were taken away and put in storage. Also, by the end of the day, most of anything related to the events of his 33-day Papacy had been carted away, as it he had never been there in the first place. Is that the way things were done in the Vatican on a regular basis? Why take such drastic measures if there was nothing to hide?

The pope's remains were then taken to Clementina Hall where the embalming process began. It took three hours to finish the job and was done by a Professor Cesare Gerin, along with Professor Marricino and Erensto and Renato Signoracci. The Signoracci brothers said that in their opinion the pope had died between 4 and 5 A.M., not the original 11 P.M. time that was mentioned before. The body of the pope was embalmed 12 hours after he was found dead, no time now for any official autopsy if one were so ordered.

The Italian press was now asking questions about why there had been no autopsy and the Vatican was getting nervous about their inquiries. Monsignor Senigaglia, Luciani's secretary in Venice for six years said that before the pope was sworn in he had a full physical and the results "had been favorable to all respects." The Vatican countered by saying (wrongly) that it was not required that an autopsy be performed, an edict that had been put into effect by Pope Paul VI in 1975. As was mentioned before, the pope received little to no medical attention in the days before his death. The then noted heart surgeon, Dr. Christian Barnard, upon hearing of the pope's death, remarked, "If this was to happen in South Africa, the doctors responsible would have been denounced to their Medical Association for malpractice."

The question of why no autopsy had been done on the pope

had been performed now, by the first week in October, began to percolate in the press. One Italian newspaper, *Corriere della Sera,* printed a headline called "Why Say No to an Autopsy?" A correspondent for the paper, Carlo Bo wrote provocative articles hinting on the possibility of foul play in the death of the pope and wrote, "The Church has nothing to fear, therefore nothing to lose. On the contrary, it would have much to gain. Let us not make out of a mystery a secret to guard for earthly reasons and let us recognize the smallness of our secrets. Let us not declare sacred what is not."

At the time of the pope's death there were fifteen doctors working in the Vatican who could have responded to a request for an autopsy to be done yet none of them went forward to request one. The matter of the pope's health was further explored when the pope's brother, Edoardo Luciani, asked his brothers' doctor, the day after the burial if his brother was in good health. The answer was, "The doctor reassured me that my brother was in excellent health and that his heart was in good condition."

The doctor then said that Albino did not have any heart problems that he knew of. If, as many people who knew the pope before his death and knew of his prior medical condition, replied that he had no symptoms of any heart trouble, then why did the Vatican rush to judgment in saying right off the bat that the pope had died of a heart attack? Did they do this to cover up some other event that might have taken place?

As controversy began to swirl around the true nature of the pope's death, certain Cardinals of the church began to offer their own opinions of what happened. In Mexico City, the bishop of Cuernavaca, Sergio Arceo published a letter asking that an autopsy be performed on the body. The outcry from Rome was so intense that the letter that bishop Arceo wrote soon disappeared as if it never happened.

One man in the church had the audacity to appeal directly to Rome in order to find out what happened to the pope. That man was Secretary Franco Antico who was in charge of an organization called Civilta Christiana. Antico's remarks caught the attention of much of the world's press and his allegations against Rome were now catching fire. He told the press that he was going to send a letter to Rome telling them that he believed the pope had been killed: "by a person or persons unknown."

He continued by saying, "If President Carter had died under such circumstances, you can be sure the American people would have demanded an explanation." The Civilta Christiana also spoke to the facts of who found the body, the circumstances in that vein, and the fact that no death certificate had been issued.

To add to the tumult, the radical priest Archbishop Marcel Lefebvre said, "God did not want him to be pope" and continued by saying, "It's difficult to believe that the death was natural considering all the creatures of the devil who inhabit the Vatican."

Archbishop Marcel Lefebvre was a noted radical in the church hierarchy who had placed himself at odds with the Vatican since the reign of Pope Paul VI. To say that there was bad blood between the followers of Lefebvre and the Vatican is an understatement. He and his followers believed that the Second Vatican Council was without merit and he asked that Mass be delivered only in Latin. This was heretical talk and the church did all it could to place him in disrepute. If anyone in the church had the opportunity of doing away with the pope it would have been the followers of Lefebvre but no evidence whatsoever pointed in his direction.

But then an event took place in Vatican City that was not seen as coming. On October 3, at around 7:00 P.M., the Swiss Guard closed the gates and posted a round-the-clock guard on what was going on inside. It seems that at that time, the Vatican had allowed a number of friends and former parishioners of the late pope to come to pay their last respects to him. Once they however, arrived in the Vatican they were told they could not enter and would be told when they could do so. What happened next was extraordinary. It seems that a number of doctors entered the area where the pope's casket was lying in state and protected from the outside by the Swiss Guards, performed some sort of medical examination of the remains.

The examination took place until 9:30 that night and it was done as soon as it took place. After the doctors did what they were looking for, the visitors who had been waiting in the Square for all those hours were allowed to view the pope for one, last time. Just why did this sudden, unexplained examination take place? No one knows for sure and the Vatican, in its wisdom, did not further elaborate. Did this examination take place because of all the fury in the press about the true nature of the pope's death? Were the conspirators getting edgy about what they had done was about to be revealed? Did something more have to be done before the body was buried?

The answer as to what took place that night came out after the burial. An official from the Vatican told the ANSA Italian news agency on and off the record meeting, "The medical examination was a normal check on the state of the preservation of the body and that it was carried out by Professor Gerin and Ernesto and Renato Signoracci, among others. It also told ANSA that several more injections of the embalming fluid were made.

After the so-called examination it came to light that a number of things that were said to be true by the Vatican were indeed not. It seems that neither Professor Gerin nor the Signoracci brothers admitted to have been present during the procedure.[5]

In a rather forthright statement on what was going on in Rome at that time, a Catholic psychologist named Rosario Mocciaro, said of the men then running the Vatican, were "A sort of Mafia-like *omerta* [silence] disguised as Christian charity and protocol."

After the public farewell to the pope in which hundreds of thousands of mourners flocked to St. Peter's Square to pay their last respects, the body of Albino Luciani was encased in three coffins made up cypress, lead, and ebony and placed near the remains of two previous pope's, John XXIII and Paul VI.

In the early part of October 1978, the Cardinals of the church met in conclave and picked a successor to Albino Luciani. He was Cardinal Karl Wojtyla of Poland, a compromise candidate who would, it was hoped, reverse some of the edicts that his predecessor was going to discharge. In an ironic twist, the new pope, John Paul I1 would be the target of an assassination plot hatched by a Bulgarian named Ali Agca with the backing of the Soviet Union. Unlike Albino Luciani, the new pope survived his assassination attempt and he played a large part in the tearing down of the communist rule in Russia and in Eastern Europe.

Pope John Paul I1 was made aware of the changes that Albino was going to make and he decided not to go along with any of them. The status quo would stay as it was and nothing out of the ordinary would take place. Cardinal Villot stayed on as Secretary of State, and Cardinal Cody remained on in Chicago. In different parts of the

[5] Yallop, David, *In God's Name*, Page 240.

world, the other protagonists in the drama, Calvi, Sindona and Gelli all heard of the new pope's decisions and must have been delighted at what they had seen. For now, at least, they were off the hook and it was time for them to continue with their illegal money making scams.

So, just how did the conspiracy to kill the pope take place, just thirty-three days after taking office? Cardinal Villot, realizing that Albino Luciani was about to make major changes to how the Vatican was run, from the firing of its top leadership, to taking a different view on birth control, decided it was time to act. Talking with his henchmen like Sindona, Calvi, and Gelli, the trio gave him the go ahead to take out the pope. The scenario can go like this. Sometime on the night of September 28 or the early morning of the 29th, he slipped into the papal bedroom and gave the pope poison from whatever means he had available to him. The reaction of the poisoning to the body of the pope would have caused vomiting and that is the reason he took away the slippers of the pope, which, if found containing the remains of the vomit, would be a sign of poisoning. He then took the pope's will, along with any other incriminating or personal material that he could find. He then ordered a series of edicts as to how the pope's body should be taken care of, offered no death certificate, had the body embalmed as quickly as possible and told the world that the late pope had a serious medical condition, despite the fact that his personal doctor told the world the opposite. In a short while, all the late pope's possessions were taken away. The deed was done and the new pope, John Paul II would run the Vatican as it had always been run for centuries.

However, there is a twist to the story regarding the whereabouts of the pope's slippers and glasses after his death. He pope's niece, Dr. Lina Petri, told author John Cornwell in an interview he conducted with her in Rome where she told him that her family took possession of both the glasses and the slippers that the pope used to wear.

During his research for his book, author John Cornwell was able to find an ex-priest who knew Albino Luciana for years and he shed new light on his state of mind in the days before his death. The man in question was Father Giovianni Gennari who was the founder of a newspaper in Italy called *Il Globo*. Father Gennari left the priesthood in 1984 and at that time was the religious-affairs correspondent for the Italian paper *Paese Sera,* a left-wing daily in Rome. He said he first met the future pope when they both attended seminaries and at bishops conferences. They began a friendship and spent considerable amount of time together over the years. Mr. Gennari said that Albino was a very lonely man during the short time he was the pope. Gennari told a story about a time when a friend of his named Father Pattaro who knew Albino said that a few days before his death, the pope asked him to come to Rome to see him. He said that the pope was in disarray, not really knowing what he was doing and seeking assistance from anyone who could help him. The pope said he was "utterly lost" and didn't know if he was capable of carrying out the duties of his papacy.

Gennari told Cornwell that he had information coming from the top-level of the Vatican of the major changes that Albino was going to take. He wanted to make new appointments, such as firing Cardinal Villot and replacing him with Cardinal Benelli. The pope talked with Cardinal Villot about these matters in the hours before he died and according to Gennari Cardinal Villot was none too happy regarding his future in the Vatican. "Villot told him that it would be a tremendous change from Paul VI's policies, and it would indicate the triumph of the Curia over the council. He said it would be the end of the openness that had been the hallmark of the Catholic Church for the previous twenty years."

After Villot left the pope called Cardinal Giovianni Colombo who answered as Cardinal Villot had. All one can do is wonder just how much the pope was worried and confused after taking the calls from both Cardinals. They were both telling him the same high-octane information that his new policies were going to cause in the Church's functions. Did he have the moral right to do all these things without realizing the ramifications of what he was doing? Gennari said that he believed that pope took an overdose of his medicine that led to a fatal heart attack.

Gennari finished up his interview with these words. "Now I heard this from good authority from the inside, and I believe it to be true. The problems started when those people who had quarreled with him the night before now found themselves having to control the news. All the lies, the half-truths, the rumors, the obscurities, started up because of blind fear and shock. They made the poor

313

man pope and he found himself on his own. He could not carry the burden of it. He tried to make a go of it, but he didn't have the psychological resources."

So, how does this conspiracy, if one believes it, organized by Roberto Calvi, Michele Sindona, Paul Marchinkus, Cardinal Cody, and Licio Gelli, stand up to other conspiracies in history? Could these four men have organized such an intricate plot and have it carried out without anyone knowing about it? Here are just some of the most important conspiracies in which one can compare to the plot against the pope.

On April 14, 1865, a conspiracy long in the making to take the life of President Abraham Lincoln took fruit. The conspiracy was hatched months before with a number of accomplices including the ringleader, the noted actor John Wilkes Booth. Working hand-in-glove with Booth were others like Dr. Samuel Mudd, Mary Surratt, her son John Jr, David Herold, Louis Weichmann, Michael O'Laughlen, Samuel Arnold, and Lewis Powell, all were participants in the plot. Booth hand a longstanding, secret relationship with Dr. Mudd and met with him at least two or three times before the president was shot. Over the years, there has been new research done that points to the hand of the Confederate government and its Secret Service to aid Booth and his pals in the plot against Lincoln. Dr. Mudd was well connected with a number of prime players in the Confederate Secret Service in the Bryantown, Maryland area, with such men as John Surrat Jr, Thomas Harbin, and Samuel Cox. In time, Surrat and Harbin would join Booth in his Lincoln kidnap plot.

At the trial of the Lincoln conspirators, information was given to the court that implicated Booth (who had been killed by Federal troops while trying to escape). John Wilkes Booth had contact with various individuals who were linked, one way or another with the Confederate Secret Service, although that fact was never introduced at the trial. Booth was an ardent Southern sympathizer who did not join the Southern cause but continued his acting career while working as a low-level courier for the South. During the war, Booth traveled to such places as Baltimore, New York, Philadelphia, and Montreal, Canada meeting with Confederate agents. Booth confided to his actor friend Samuel Chester in New York that he was planning to kidnap President Lincoln and asked if he would like to take part in the operation (he declined). He also told Chester that he had at least 50 men allied with him.

Booth arrived in Canada on October 18, 1864, and registered at the St. Lawrence Hall Hotel, a hotbed of Confederate Canadian operations. For the next ten days, Booth had various meetings with Patrick Martin and George Sanders, both Confederate agents, and it is not out of the realm of possibility that the Confederate plots to either capture or kill the president were discussed.

While in Canada, Booth was able to used money set up for him in the Ontario Bank in the amount of $455 Canadian dollars. This money was most likely supplied to Booth by the Confederate commissioners who were then living in the city. Immediately after leaving Canada, Booth came to Washington where he got a room at the National Hotel and made deposits in a bank owned by Jay Cooke.

Booth was never far removed from his association with the members of the Confederate underground, if not their leaders. One year after his Canadian trip, Booth and his accomplices devised a plan to kidnap the president when Lincoln was to attend a performance at the Campbell Military Hospital about two miles from the Capitol. The date for the abduction plan was March 17, 1865. Booth and his men waited on the road back from the hospital where their plan was to capture Lincoln and spirit him south and use him to ransom thousands of Confederate soldiers languishing in Federal prisons. Much to their consternation, the president canceled his trip in order to attend a ceremony at the National Hotel in Washington, in which a Confederate flag would be presented to Oliver Morton, the governor of Indiana. In a bit of irony, John Wilkes Booth had a room in the same hotel.

On the night of April 14, 1865, Booth canceled his kidnap plot and instead, gathered his co-conspirators to inform them of his new plan; they were going to attempt to kill a number of high-ranking Union officials that night, including the president. The plot was an audacious one, which needed perfect timing in order to succeed. Booth would kill Lincoln when he attended the performance of *Our American Cousin* that was to take place at Ford's Theater that night. Lewis Powell was to kill Secretary of State William Seward who was recovering at home after a fall form a carriage accident, while

George Atzerodt would kill Vice President Johnson at his room at the Kirkwood House. In the end, only Booth succeeded. Atzerodt got cold feet and fled the scene. Powell inflected severe wounds on Sec. Seward but he would recover. After killing Lincoln, Booth and David Herold fled the city, made a stop at Mary Surratt's boarding house to pick up some arms and then headed to the home of Dr. Mudd where the doctor treated his broken leg which he suffered when he jumped from the presidential box after shooting the president.

The question that historians have asked is, did the Confederate government in Richmond play a role in the assassination or kidnap attempts on President Lincoln? The circumstantial evidence gathered in the past 150 years is yes.

Once Booth fled Washington after the assassination he was aided and abetted by a number of people who had direct or indirect contact with him, prior to and after the assassination. Here are a number of the people who helped Booth, and their roles in the Lincoln assassination plot:

*Dr. Samuel Mudd. He set Booth's leg at his home, had at least three previous meetings with Booth in Washington and at his home, and knew a number of people in the plot to kill the president including John Surratt, Samuel Cox, and Thomas Harbin.

*John Surratt Jr. He was the son of Mary Surratt who owned the boarding house in Washington as well as the tavern in Surrattsville, Maryland, which was a way station for Confederate agents and smugglers. He was well acquainted with Booth and was part of the kidnap plot against the president. He said that Booth and his coconspirators were acting under orders from the men who were as yet unknown.

*Thomas Harney. He was a member of the Confederate Torpedo Bureau in Richmond and was an expert in the use of mines and explosives. He was supposed to have been part of a plot to blow up the White House when Lincoln and his cabinet were in residence but the plot never took shape.

*Thomas Nelson Conrad. He was a member of the Confederate Secret Service and was to take part in a Confederate plot to kidnap President Lincoln. He arrived in Washington in September 1864 with the intention of capturing the president. The plot was directed from the office of Judah Benjamin, the Confederate Sec. of War. Conrad said that he scouted the route the president would take but decided it was too risky. Conrad received four hundred dollars in gold for the kidnap plot from the coffers of Sec. Judah Benjamin from his secret service fund.

*Thomas Harbin. Harbin was a Confederate agent who lived in Charles County, Maryland. He was once the postmaster Bryantown, Maryland, the home of Dr. Mudd. When Booth paid a visit to Bryantown to see Dr. Mudd, the doctor introduced Harbin to Booth. It was during this meeting, which took place on December 18, 1864, that Booth recruited Harbin into his scheme to kidnap Lincoln.

*Thomas Jones. Jones was one of the most important Confederate agents in the region of Charles County, and was an agent for the Confederate Signal Service who carried mail and Southern soldiers into Virginia. He played a pivotal role in the escape of Booth after the assassination. On April 20, 1865, Jones moved Booth and his friend David Herold to the banks of the Potomac River where a boat was waiting for them. Jones gave them a compass and a candle to navigate by. Seeking to find the Virginia side of the river, the men got lost and returned to the same spot where they started. Jones was later arrested but was soon released. The Union authorities never realized how important a role he played in the escape of Booth and Herold. He later wrote a book on his experiences called *J. Wilkes Booth.*

*Elizabeth Quesenberry. She was one of the few women who took part in the aftermath of the assassination conspiracy. She was a widow who lived in King George County, Virginia near Machodoc Creek. Both Booth and Herold arrived at her home and she reluctantly gave them food and shelter and then made arrangements with Thomas Harbin to move the men further down the escape route. Booth and Herold were passed along to William Bryant who took them to the home of Dr. Richard Stuart. Mrs. Quesenberry was subsequently arrested but was ultimately let got for lack of evidence.

While there is no smoking gun that links the assassination to the top leaders of the Confederate government, the paper trail linking Booth and the numerous agents who aided him and were ready to help in his escape from Washington after the assassination is undeniable.

The greatest conspiracy of the 20th century was the assassination of President John F. Kennedy on November 22, 1963. The president was gunned down while riding in an open limousine through the streets of Dallas Texas in the part of the city called Dealey Plaza. A short while later, Dallas police captured a young man who fit the description of a man who had shot a Dallas Police Officer named J.D. Tippit. The man, an ex-Marine named Lee Harvey Oswald was captured in a movie theater in Dallas and was subsequently taken into custody for interrogation.

The Dallas police were not the only ones who spoke to Oswald that day. There were representatives from the Secret Service, the FBI as well as other agencies. On Oswald's possession, there was an identification card in the name of A.J. Hidell, a fake name that Oswald used in the past. As the questioning of Oswald began, the authorities found out that he had left the Marines after serving in a super-secret Marine base in Japan which oversaw the flight of the U-2 spy planes over Russian and China. He then defected to the Soviet Union and stayed there for over two years, marrying a Russian woman and then coming back to the United States. Some people who have researched the many aspects of the Kennedy assassination believe that Oswald was on some sort of secret military mission for the United States, a fake defector who was sent to find out what he could about what the Russians were doing as far as their military was concerned. While under questioning, there was no secretary to take notes, nor was any of what the police or Oswald said put in writing.

As the terrible weekend of the assassination began, the Dallas Police and the FBI believed that Oswald was the lone assassin and that he had no confederates who helped him in his killing of the president. During his interrogations, it was revealed that Oswald had been in Mexico City for a short period of time right before the assassination and that he was in contact with certain members of both the Soviet and Cuban governments while he was in the city. The reason he was in Mexico City was supposedly to get a visa to get back to Russia via Cuba. Oswald was turned down and he the re-entered the United States.

On Sunday, November 24, 1963, while the body of the president was being viewed by a grieving nation, Oswald was shot in the basement of the Dallas Police Department by a local nightclub owner by the name of Jack Ruby. Ruby himself was a low-level member of organized crime in the United States and in the months before the assassination he was in touch with various members of the American Mafia. One of the assumptions for Oswald's killing by Ruby was to silence him before he could stand trial and tell what he knew regarding his role (or others unknown) in the plot to kill Kennedy.

In November 1963, days after Kennedy was killed, the new president, Lyndon Johnson, ordered a federal review of the Kennedy assassination and he chose Earl Warren who was the Chief Justice of the U.S. Supreme Court to head the investigation. The results of the Warren Commission came out in September 1964 and it blamed Oswald alone for killing JFK, along with Dallas Police Officer Tippit. Case closed. It said that neither the CIA nor the FBI had anything to do with the assassination. It could not prove a motive for Oswald's killing of the president, thus giving us the "lone nut" theory. They said that Jack Ruby had no relationship with Oswald (although there were some people who swore that Oswald was seen in Ruby's night club on a few occasions), and that neither the Soviet Union nor Cuba had participated in the Kennedy assassination.

The Commission said that there were three shots fired by Oswald from the Texas School Book Depository and that all the wounds suffered by the president and Texas Governor John Connelly who was riding with the president were struck by the gun owned by Oswald, an old World War II piece of junk with a broken sight.

In the middle of the 1960s, the public, eager to learn the truth about the murder of the president, begun to doubt the official version of events. Authors like the late Mark Lane and others, began writing books and going on radio talk shows dismissing the Warren Commission and told the public where the Commission had gone wrong.

It wasn't until 1976 that the congress of the United States approved a bill that would look into the assassination of JFK and Martin Luther King. The House and Senate created their own investigative panels and an eager nation looked toward them to answer the questions that the biased Warren Commission failed to pursue. The Senate created a panel chaired by Idaho Senator Frank Church (the Church Committee) to investigate domestic assassinations and illegal CIA abuses and the House established the House Select Committee on Assassinations (HSCA). For all their imperfections, the investigative panels, especially the Church Committee, were blessing as far as finding out about the darker side of the CIA in the 1960s. The committee revealed the CIA-Mafia plots to kill Fidel Castro, massive illegal CIA abuses at home, the revelation of the so-called "Family Jewels," a number of illegal CIA actions that hit the nation's newspapers like a bombshell.

One of the conspiracy theories was that the American mob put out a hit on the president because they believed he had broken his word that the president's father, Joseph P. Kennedy had promised to the mob that if they would back Jack Kennedy's run for president and if he were elected, they would back off any persecutions' of them. The president appointed his brother Robert Kennedy to be the new Attorney General and he quickly went after the same men who helped the president get elected, Jimmy Hoffa, Sam Gianciana, Johnny Rosselli, Carlos Marcello, and Santos Trafficante. It was also revealed in the Church Committee that some of these same Mafia leaders, Sam Gianciana, Johnny Rosselli were in league with the CIA in order to kill Fidel Castro. At one point, Robert Kennedy had Carlos Marcello deported, and he was possibly flown back to the United States by a man named David Ferrie, a rabid anti-communist and former airline pilot who hated the Kennedy's liberal social policies. Ferrie was part of the New Orleans contingent that included Guy Banister, a former FBI agent who operated out of a small office at 544 Camp Street in New Orleans. One of the people who worked for Banister in the summer of 1963 and passed out pro-Castro literature was none other than Lee Harvey Oswald.

Marcello and Hoffa were high-level mob leaders who had a deep hatred for the Kennedy family. Marcello, who was the head of the Louisiana mob, was said to have made this statement referring to the Kennedys: "Take the stone out of my shoe."

The HSCA wrote the following regarding the Kennedy assassination:

> The Committee believes on the evidence available to it, that President John F. Kennedy was probably assassinated as a result of a conspiracy. The Committee is unable to identify the other gunmen or the extent of the conspiracy.

Here are some of the theories on the Kennedy assassination:

The Cuban's did it.

Beginning in the last days of the Eisenhower administration, the CIA began a secret plot to kill Fidel Castro and used certain members of the American Mafia to go along with the hit. All of these attempts failed but Castro knew of the attempts on his life and he held the CIA responsible. In April 1961, the CIA attempted an invasion of Cuba using less than two thousand Cuban revolutionary fighters at a place called the Bay of Pigs in Cuba. The CIA told JFK that they were sure that once the brigade landed ashore, the Cuban people would revolt against Castro and the regime would collapse. This never happened and those remaining fighters who were lucky enough to escape to the U.S. had a deep hatred toward Kennedy for the invasion's failure, one, they kept alive for the rest of the life of the Kennedy administration.

Another black mark on the Kennedy White House was the 1962 Cuban Missile Crisis in which the Russians placed intermediate nuclear missiles in Cuba, threatening World War III. The Kennedy administration created a naval blockade of Cuba, threatened an invasion if the missiles were not removed and all waited for the showdown that was about to happen. In the end, the Russians removed their missiles and the threat of war was ended. However, some anti-Castro rebels in the United States saw Kennedy's actions as tantamount to treason for not finally getting rid of Castro once and for all. The Castro did it scenario was that in retaliation for the Bay of Pigs and the missile crisis, Fidel Castro ordered a hit on JFK an used the Cuban leaning Lee Oswald as the patsy.

The Russians did it theory.

This angle has fostered much heated debate in assassination circles, but like the Castro thesis, holds little water. Yes, Oswald was a believer in Marxist philosophy starting at a young age, was an admirer of Castro and Cuba, and read Marxist literature while in the Marines (a strange thing, to say the least). Some people say that Oswald's defection to the Soviet Union was his chance to become a part of Russian society, disclaiming his American nationality. There is also a crazy belief that the "Oswald" who was shot by Jack Ruby in Dallas was a Russian-born KGB agent who was a doppelganger of the real Oswald. But at the time of Oswald's defection to the Soviet Union, the United States had a false defector program going on. Was Oswald part of this program?

Another link to the Russians came in September 1963, when Lee Oswald made a trip to Mexico City where "Oswald" tried to get a visa to return to the Soviet Union. It was a common procedure for the CIA to bug the Cuban Consulate and the Soviet Embassy where "Oswald" went, in order to get the necessary travel documents.

Oswald made contact with Valery Kostikov in the Soviet Embassy. Kostikov was a high-level KGB agent who had been serving in the Soviet's Mexican compound since 1960. Kostikov was also a member of the top secret Department 13 that was responsible for assassination activity in the Western hemisphere. Using this highly tenuous link (it is unclear whether it was even the real Oswald who was in Mexico City) certain members of the CIA tried to paint Oswald as a member of the Communist Party (which he wasn't), and more important, as a Soviet agent in touch with Kostikov. Thus, they tried to falsely tie the Soviet Union to the president's assassination.

The Hoover did it theory.

The famous FBI director J. Edgar Hoover was no friend of the Kennedy family and had highly incriminating files on both Jack and Bobby Kennedy that he could have used at any time. However, he chose to keep them under wraps, using them as a "Sword of Damocles" over their heads. The FBI had a black eye after the assassination because it did not list Oswald as a possible threat to

JFK while he was in Dallas.

Also, FBI agent James Hosty had met several times with Oswald after his return from Russia. He was ordered by higher ups in the Bureau to destroy a note brought to Dallas FBI Headquarters by Oswald before the assassination. No one knows what was written in the letter. Hoover is also said to have ignored a telex that he received a few days before the assassination warning of a plot to kill the president.

Other theories involve Lyndon Johnson and elements within the Dallas police and underworld (including Jack Ruby) or aerospace conspiracies involving Werner von Braun and certain aviation and space companies (the military industrial establishment that President Eisenhower warned us of at the end of his presidency)—a comprehensive list would probably include a collaboration of many of these players.

The Kennedy assassination remains one of the greatest murder mysteries in American history and will remain so until all the documents that are still being withheld in the National Archives are finally released. (Note to readers. The National Archives released a portion of their withheld documents in October 2017, but withheld a large portion that is now to be released in March of 2018. There is no excuse for the government to withhold any of these historic documents if there was no conspiracy, as the Warren Commission postulated. At this time, the American people deserve the truth. Time will tell.

The closets conspiracy scenario to the plot to kill the pope lead by a few men was the event that took place in Philadelphia, Pennsylvania in July 1776 when a secret gathering took place to set the seeds for American independence over the tyrannical rule of Great Britain. When one studies the American Revolution, the thought of a conspiracy does not readily come to mind. But that was exactly what the founding fathers were doing that hot July day when they met to shed the cloak of British rule and set the cause of American liberty.

When the members of the 13 colonies met in Philadelphia they began writing a Declaration of Independence that would allow the colonies to form their own separate, independent nation. The men knew exactly what they were doing and it took a considerable amount of nerve and guts to go through what they were about to do. Benjamin Franklin, the oldest of the men in conclave set the mood, when he told his fellow delegates, "We must all hang together, or surely we shall all hang separately."

The list of names of those intrepid men who stood up to British rule were a collection of different people, of different backgrounds and education, some of whom did not even know each other. They came from different parts of the country, from cold New England to the sunny shores of Virginia, to the streets of New York and the Middle Colonies. Among them were Joseph Warren, John and Samuel Adams, George Washington, Alexander Hamilton, Benjamin Franklin, Thomas Jefferson, Patrick Henry, among others. Together, these men would unit and forge a new nation, one that would be the envy of the rest of the world for generations to come.

The major cause of the revolution was the imposition of taxes by the British government on the merchants of the colonies, especially those in Boston. The Stamp Act put taxes on all printed material consumed in the colonies without the say of the local population. The British then sent troops into Boston and the surrounding areas, sometimes taking the homes of innocent Bostonians who had no way to resist.

But resist they did. Samuel Adams, along with many other men of his ilk, formed a group to challenge British rule called the Committee of Correspondence to coordinate resistance among the people of Massachusetts. They also organized a fighting force called the Sons of Liberty who did all in their power to thwart British activity in New England. They used letters and proclamations to tell their fellow citizens what their grievances were, among them Adam's "State of the Rights of the Colonies," a "List of Infringements and Violations of those Rights of the Colonies," written by Joseph Warren, one of the least known, yet brilliant men of his generation, and a "Letter of Correspondence" which was written by Benjamin Church who later it turned out was a double agent working for the British during the Revolution. Within the next two years, all but two of the colonies would have their own version of committees of correspondence, thus, setting the seeds for independence.

The first real show of independence came on a cold night of

December 16, 1773 when a number of men dressed like Native Americans, boarded ships in Boston harbor and began dumping tea into the river. The so-called "Boston Tea Party," led the British to put severe punishments on the people of New England, which were called "The Coercive Acts" which led to the stationing of British troops in the city.

In retaliation for these despicable British moves, Paul Revere began a secret spy ring in Boston called the Mechanics whose job it was to follow the British as they made their rounds of the city and report back to their local leaders on the military capacity and strength in the city. The culmination of all these activities took place on the night of April 18, 1775 when British soldiers entered the sleepy town of Concord, Massachusetts to take arms and ammunition that was supposed to have been stored there. As the British entered the city, Paul Revere and his friend, William Dawes, road on in the night to warn the people that the "British were coming." The result was a gunfight at Lexington, and a British retreat back to Boston.

By 1775, the rebellion was in full effect in the colonies and the Crown took immediate notice. More and more British soldiers flocked into Boston and the other colonies, gearing up for a war that was inevitable. In 1776, the delegates from the 13 Colonies met in Philadelphia where the Continental Congress issued a formal declaration of independence from Great Britain. The delegates "pledged their lives, fortunes, and sacred honor" in the cause of liberty.

George Washington was chosen as the military commander of the new nation despite the fact that his military experience was limited to his service in the French and Indian War. He was also a member of the first Continental Congress and served as the first president of the United States after independence was won. He bravely led the fight against the enemy during the darkest days of the revolution when the outcome was always in jeopardy. He led the army from the retreat at Brooklyn to the victories at Princeton and Trenton and saw the war won at the battle of Yorktown.

John Adams was one of the most important figures of the Revolutionary saga and served in the First and Second Continental Congresses. He was on the committee to draft the Declaration of Independence and was one of its signers. Adams did not really want a standing army at the beginning of the revolution instead he looked to the people to do what was right for the entire nation as opposed to certain factions that were out only for themselves.

Alexander Hamilton at age twenty-one was to become George Washington's most trusted military aide and was with him through the thick and thin of the revolution. He was born in the Caribbean island of St. Kitts and came to the United States as a young lad. He was a thinker beyond his years and spoke out against slavery as part of the American fabric of life. After the war, Hamilton served as President Washington's first secretary of the Treasury and was killed in a duel with Vice President Aaron Burr on the New Jersey side of the Hudson River.

A conspiracy hatched by a number of men who saw the concept of freedom that was worth fighting—and possibly dying for—against the mightiest army and navy in the world at the time, succeeded beyond their wildest dreams.[6]

With the pope dead, the final chapter in the saga of the main protagonists in his demise was finally beginning to play out (much of the material in his last part of this chapter will be re-told and expanded in the following chapter).

Roberto Calvi opened a bank in Nicaragua called Ambrosiano Group Banco Commercial around January 1979. The bank was supposed to handle international banking transactions, but its ulterior motive was to move from the Nassau Bahamas bank in which Bishop Marchinkus had a large part "of his money stashed away, a large amount of the evidence that would reveal the fraudulent and criminal device used in the share-purchasing acquisition of the Milan parent bank. In this way, the evidence would be hidden even more securely from the Bank of Italy." To further this scheme, Licio Gelli paid off the ruler of Nicaragua, Anastasio Somoza with a bribe of many millions of dollars. Both Calvi/Gelli would now get a Safehaven for their illegal banking activities to proceed without any governmental interference. With the opening of the Calvi/Gelli bank in Nicaragua, Calvi received a diplomatic passport courtesy of the government whom he was now in bed with.

During this time there was a brewing insurrection going on in Nicaragua among the rebels who were trying to overthrow the

[6] Jeffers. H. Paul, *History's Greatest Conspiracies,* The Lyons Press, Guilford, Ct, 2004. Page 8-10.

government in Managua. Both Gelli and Calvi were playing both sides against each other and wanted to be on the side of the winner when the end came. When the government fell in 1979, all the banks were nationalized with the exception of the Gelli/Calvi Ambrosiano Group Banco Commercial.

For Licio Gelli, things were about to get much worse. In March 1981, Italian authorities arrived suddenly at his door looking for evidence surrounding the kidnapping of Michele Sindona. They found a list that Gelli kept of 962 members of his P-2 organization as well as many government documents. The Gelli sandal resulted in the downfall of the Italian government and the new prosecutors renewed their case against Calvi. Calvi's family turned to Bishop Marchinkus for help but the priest had no intention of helping his fellow crook and turned down all their entireties.

In August 1982, the Italian government along with Switzerland laid an intricate trap to ensnarl Licio Gelli. Gelli had a secret bank account in Switzerland and for some unexplained reason he was not able to transfer money out of his account as he had done in the past. The bank told him that if he wanted to see his money, he'd have to appear in person. He came to Switzerland using a fake Argentine passport and arrived in Geneva on September 13, 1982. He entered the bank, showed his bank account papers and was told that someone would be there to see him as soon as possible. Gelli never got to see his money. It seems that the government had started a sting operation, and as he was in the bank, the police nabbed him. The account had been frozen the by Italian government. The account had been created by Roberto Calvi for Gelli, and it consisted of $100 million.

Gelli was put in jail in Switzerland while he awaited the legal proceedings to get under way. It seems that Gelli had many friends in South American and when his arrest made news in Argentina, a member of the Argentine government, Emilio Massera said, "This country has much to thank him for and will forever be in his debt."

Gelli was put in Camp Dollon but he did not stay there very long. On August 10, 1983, with inside help, Gelli escaped. The authorities put the blame for Gelli's escape on a lonely corrupt guard by the name of Umberto Cerdana. Blame had to be put on some ones shoulders and Umberto Cerdana took it full in the face.

Once out, Gelli's son took him to France and then by helicopter to Monte Carlo. He was then transferred to a waiting yacht and was taken back to South America, this time to Uruguay. The new prime minister of Italy Bettino Craxi said of Gelli's escape, "The flight of Gelli confirms that the grand master of a network of powerful friends."

Before all this happened however, Gelli was involved in another scandal concerning an Italian petroleum product whose profits were funneled into the coffers of Michele Sindona's bank. The gist of the story is that an a muckraking newspaper in Italy called OP run by a man named Mino Pecorelli whose paper was well read, and concentrated on digging up dirt on many Italian politicians. Pecorelli was a member of P-2 and he had a feud with Gelli that put both of them at odds with each other:

> He [Pecorelli] obtained information about one of the biggest thefts in Italian financial history. The mastermind behind the theft was Licio Gelli. The scheme was responsible for robbing Italy of $2.5 billion in oil tax revenues.

The conspiracy was planned by two men, the oil magnet Bruno Musselli, also a P-2 affiliate and the head of the finance police Raffale Guidice, also of P-2, to falsify the records surrounding the taxes paid on the petroleum products at a lower rate than normal. The profits were subsequently funneled through the Vatican Bank to a number of financial institutions owned by Michele Sindona.

Pecorelli then began to publish the full account of the theft centering on Gelli and his henchmen. Some influential people in the government and the police put pressure on Pecorelli and he abruptly stopped his stories for his own personal safety.

Not to be outdone, Pecorelli began writing an exposé on the Freemasons who had infiltrated the Vatican, over one hundred in all. One of the people who received a copy of the list was Albino Luciani.

Feeling good about himself, Pecorelli met with Gelli, and asked him for more money if he didn't want him to reveal more of P-2's secrets. Gelli refused to pay and the editor went further into Gelli's past, writing that Gelli was at one time a right-wing fascist, and had spied for the Communists during World War II and worked for them after the war ended. Not to be undone, Pecorelli wrote that Gelli had ties to the CIA—something that Gelli did not want known.

Gelli then contacted Pecorelli and asked if they could meet. A site was set and on March 22, 1979 as he was leaving his office, gunmen shot and killed Pecorelli as he left his office and headed for his car. The assassins put their shots directly into his mouth, a typical Mafia way of saying that a person will never talk again. No one ever claimed responsibility for Pecorelli's murder but in 1983, Antonio Viezzer, who once worked in the SID, Italian secret service, was arrested and charged with suspicion for killing the editor. Viezzer it seems, was a member of Lico Gelli's P-2.

But Gelli was still not done with his secret machinations. In 1980 he offered to aid the candidacy of Ronald Reagan who was running for president of the United States against President Jimmy Carter. On April 8, 1980, Gelli wrote a letter to Phil Guarino, a friend of Reagan's. The letter ran as follows." If you think it might be useful for something favorable on your presidential candidate to be published in Italy, send me some material and I'll have it published in one of the papers here." After Reagan was elected, Gelli received an invitation to attend one of Reagan's inaugural balls that he attended.

Shortly before the death of Pecorelli another person who was linked to the papal death, Cardinal Villot died.

In 1979, Michele Sindona was in New York. Things were not going so well for him. On March 9, 1979, the U.S. Justice Department indicted him and charged him with ninety-nine counts of fraud, perjury, and misappropriation of bank funds. He posted $3 million and was released on bail. He had one stipulation—he had to report each day to the U.S. Marshall's office.

It seems that at this time Michel Sindona was having some sort of mental problems. One day when he was in his office in New York a man named Dr. Joseph Crimi came calling. Sindona never met the man but he told him that he carried a message from Licio Gelli and Sindona asked him to take a seat. Crimi then told Sindona a much outrageous story. He and the P-2 were going to organize a plot to overthrow the government of Sicily and he asked for Sindona's help. After Crimi left, Sindona called Gelli and told him what just happened. Gelli said that he knew Crimi and that he was "an honest man, though not very bright, no genius. But Crimi was a man of good faith."

Soon thereafter, both Gelli and Sindona met in New York where they discussed the plot to overthrow Sicily. Gelli said he was ready to mobilize his faction called Real Action. Gelli told him he was crazy and the only way the coup could be successful was to overthrow the entire Italian government and replace it with a presidential dictatorship in Rome.

Sindona, not wanting to distance himself from Crimi, told him that he was ready to finance the plot and that he'd contact him in the future. Sindona now turned to an old friend, a man who was in the OSS during World War II, Max Corvo. Sindona told him about the planned Sicilian coup and asked him if he could give him help in arranging men and material for the coup. Corvo told Sindona that he was crazy, that the planned coup was a fantasy and that neither the U.S. nor the Italian government would allow such a thing to happen. He also told Sindona that the Mafia leaders would never go along with the plot. Corvo told Sindona, "You're ill, Michele. Your mind is not working. Do yourself a favor and see a doctor. The stress has caused you to have delusions."[7]

Michele Sindona was not yet ready to abandon his Sicily coup plans. For whatever it was worth, he met with two members of the Mafia in Staten Island New York, Johnny Gambino and Rosario Spatola and told them of his plans. Johnny Gambino was the nephew of the Mafia crime boss Carlo Gambino and a cousin of Rosario Spatola. Spatola was the boss of the Palermo based Gambino, Inzerillo, and Spatola crime families. Sindona told them a story filled with lies and wishes on his part. He said that the U.S. military would aid them in their cause once the coup took place. He asked Spatola and Gambino if they could supply two hundred men with guns to aid in the coup. He told the men that if the Mafia helped them, he would grant all Mafioso amnesty for crimes committed before the coup. He also demanded that all drug trafficking be stopped. He said that if the mob went along with his plan he would give the Gambino family control of the orange export business.

Rosario Spatola met with the higher-ups in the mob and he told

[7] Di Fonzo, Luigi, *St. Peter's Banker: Michele Sindona,* Franklin Watts, New York, 1983, Page 236-7.

Sindona that the bosses of the Gambino family had agreed to his plans. They were going to work with Sindona in what he called the Time For Sicilian Action but there were certain conditions that had to be met. "In exchange for giving up the heroin factories in Sicily, however, the Gambino family wanted Sindona to assure them that any member of their family facing a long prison sentence in America would be able to flee to Sicily and live in freedom." Spatola also wanted to be able to build a casino in Palermo. They told Sindona that if he agreed to their terms they'd give him a false passport and a disguise. Sindona agreed. He was now in bed with the mob but his fantasy regarding a coup in Sicily never took place.

While Michele Sindona was making crazy schemes to take Sicily out of Italy, the last stanzas for both Roberto Calvi and Bishop Marchinkus were underway. With the scandal and final collapse of Banco Ambrosiano in which both men played a vital part, Italian authorities developed enough evidence to charge three of the most important prelates in the Vatican-Archbishop Marchinkus, the bank's chairman, Luigi Mennini, its managing director, and Pelligrinio De Strobel, its chief accountant, with being accessories to fraudulent bankruptcy. At the time that the indictments were handed out, all three men remained safely hidden in the bowels of the Vatican protected by its laws. During this period of time, the Vatican and the government of Italy did not have an extradition treaty and if the Italian officials wanted to get their hands of all three men they'd have to go through diplomatic channels to get them, a feat that was not easy to come by.

When Pope Paul II who was a friend of Bishop Marchinkus heard of his indictment he commented, "We are convinced that you cannot attack a person in such an exclusive and brutal manner, but we are taking the case with all seriousness, and we will have it studied by competent authorities."

Marchinkus took over the Vatican Bank in 1971 and Roberto Calvi became the managing director of Banco Ambrosiano and had worked in the bank since 1947. Their first directive was to make Banco Ambrosiano an international bank, doing finance with whom and wherever they could find willing accomplices. Their daily practice was to open up shell companies around the world who would launder the banks money, and the rigging of the Milan stock market. Associated with both men were Michele Sindona and Licio Gelli, the puppet master of P-2.

The Vatican Bank then took a stake in Banco Ambrosiano Overseas, in Nassau, Bahamas, and Marchinkus become one of its board members.

Calvi at that time was not widely known to many people but as time went on that was about to change. He was convicted of currency offenses in 1981, and was fined $10 million, and spent four months of a four-year jail term.

"The rub of the Ambrosiano scandal and the Vatican's part in it involved the setting up of ten shell companies in Panama by the bank's Luxembourg subsidiary, itself a shell holding company. It appeared that the Vatican Bank nominally controlled these companies; Marchinkus insisted that they were collateral for loans made to Banco Ambrosiano. Both Calvi and Marchinkus ran them during different periods, but the legal and responsible ownership remains an enigma."

The ever-present Calvi lent $1.3 billion to these various shell companies, and the money, some say, went to manipulate the stock of Banco Ambrosiano and make the company more profitable. Eventually, the stock in Banco Ambrosiano quickly fell, with the company suffering a hole of $1.3 billion, most of which was owned by these various shell companies.

For his part, the Bishop told anyone who'd listen that the Vatican Bank was totally unaware of any financial shenanigans when these companies were set up. However, it seems that only one year before, Bishop Marchinkus issued what was called "Letters of Comfort," or "patronage," showing that the Vatican Bank controlled these ten shell companies.

Banco Ambrosiano came crashing down in June 1982 and Calvi was now in the hot seat. The banks creditors were now clamoring for their money to be returned and in May 1984 a joint commission of inquiry was set up to aid the process. The members of the commission represented the Holy See and the Italian government. After reviewing many Vatican Bank documents, the Bank of Italy said in October 1984, "though the commission did not arrive at unanimous conclusions, it did demonstrate the objective involvement of the IOR (Vatican Bank), thus establishing the premise for the negotiation of a contribution from the IOR." The settlement to the creditors amounted to $250 million.

A further inquiry on the Ambrosiano matter took place in 1986 when a finance company (Liquidators) named Touche Ross recovered more of Ambrosiano's missing assets. It cost the company a hefty $25 million and in the end, the liquidators found an additional $40 million short of the losses.[8]

So, the final chapter in one of the most scandalous chapters in the history of Vatican had ended.

So, where do we stand at the end of the story? All the changes that Albino Luciani wanted to implement went to naught with his sudden and unexpected death. Matters at the heart of the church went on as usual with none of the prelates whom the pope wanted to replace losing their jobs.

In the end, all the main participants in the drama, Roberto Calvi, Paul Marchinkus, Licio Gelli, Michele Sindona, and Cardinal Villot got what they wanted-freedom to continue their illegal activities from money laundering, to shell companies hiding millions of dollars in Vatican Bank, money that was supposed to have been spent on legitimate church business, links to the Sicilian and American Mafia in who knows what schemes we know or don't know. Their later endeavors would catch the attention of the world in ways they could not image at the time the pope died. While none of these men were caught in the room the night (or morning) the pope died, his passing was a blessing in disguise. Their main nemesis, Pope John Paul I was dead and whatever plans he had for them was now mute. Many times in a criminal law case, circumstantial evidence is enough to convict a person. With all the evidence established in the death of Albino Luciani, Pope John Paul I, a good prosecutor, if allowed, would have made a solid case against all these men in the death of the pope. Who knows how much difference the operations of the Vatican would have been effected if the pope had lived. That is for the historians to decide.

---

[8] *A Thief In The Night*, Page 124-27.

Pope John Paul I.

Roberto Calvi.

Chapter 6

The Vatican Bank Scandal

By the late 1970s, the world woke up to a financial scandal that would soon be front page news across both the United States and Europe. By the time it all ended, the affair would engulf the Vatican, which was by all accounts, one of the most trustworthy institutions in the world, the Mafia, certain high- ranking prelates who managed the Vatican's finances, shadowy characters who would come to dominate the headlines, and the failure of certain banks in both the United States and Italy. At the heart of the affair was a high-ranking Priest from Cicero, Illinois, Archbishop Paul Marchinkus, who was the president of the Institute for Religious Works, the Vatican Bank.

The history of the Vatican Bank goes back to 1929 during the reign of the Italian dictator Benito Mussolini. During the 1920s, the Vatican did not have its own bank and was essentially broke. All this changed dramatically when in February 1928, the Lateran Treaty was signed by the Vatican and Mussolini and the Vatican became its own separate state, having full diplomatic rights as would any other nation. The Vatican was now given a huge fortune that amounted to three-quarters of a billion lire in negotiable bonds in compensation for the lands it lost when it became a nation-state. With the Vatican now cash rich, it set up an organization to administer what it called the Patrimony of the Holy See and the funds were administered by the Bank of Rome that was more than happy to look after the Vatican's finances. Soon though, the pope changed the name of its banking organization to The Institute for Religious Works, or IOR. He did this because he didn't want the Vatican to be seen as a banking institution that lent and borrowed money. In another deal with Mussolini, it was agreed that the IOR would not pay tax on its dividend income and the Vatican would now be cash full and not have to rely on other institutions for its money.

The original function of the Vatican Bank that was set up by

Pope Leo XIII in 1887, was to gather and administer money for religious purposes. In the modern sense, it was not a regular bank as we know it today but was rather to administer "the custody and administration of monies and properties transferred or entrusted to the institute itself by fiscal or legal persons for the purposes of religious works, and works of Christian piety."

The first person to actually run the bank was Father (later Cardinal) Alberto di Jorio who was appointed by Bernardo Nogara. With the aid of both Angora and di Jorio, the Vatican Bank spread it tentacles wide and it now had banking relationships with such institutions as the Rothschild's in London and Paris, Credit Suisse, Hambros, Morgan Guarantee Trust, Bankers Trust, Chase Manhattan Bank, and Continental Illinois, among others. The bank eventually branched out and was able to take interest in companies that produced food, insurance, cement, and real estate. They also bought buildings in such places as France, Canada, and the United States, including the Watergate building that would go down in infamy during the presidency of Richard Nixon. Bernardo Nogara's significance in the founding and leadership of the Vatican Bank was summed up by Cardinal Spellman of New York when he said, "Next to Jesus Christ the greatest thing that has happened to the Catholic Church is Bernardino Nogara."

It has always been the tenant of the Church to believe in piety and the shedding of monetary wealth, but under Nogara that went out the window. It was estimated that about $500 million was controlled by the Special Administration of the Church, $650 million controlled by the Ordinary Section of the APSA (Patrimony of the Holy See), and the total assets of the bank during that time was estimated to be about $940 million. There were also rumors that a large amount of this money went directly into the pockets of whatever pope happened to be in place at that time.

The man who was most responsible for taking the Vatican bank on the course that it ultimately took to ruin was Pope Paul VI. Backed by the Pacellis family whose member was Pope Pius, Pope Paul VI was the mainstay as far as how the bank operated and who was put in a position of power to run it on a daily basis. Paul brought in to the bank his own people, who were sometime referred to as the "black nobility." Some of the men who Paul brought in

336

with him were Cardinal Vagnozzi, who at one time was the Papal nuncio in Washington. Others included Cardinal Cody of Chicago (who was mentioned in the last chapter), Cardinal Sergio Guerri, who was appointed to the post of governor of Vatican City, Cardinal Giuseppe Caprio, who headed the Beni della Santa Sede (Bank of Holy Ghost), and Bishop Paul Marchinkus who'd play a leading role in the demise of the Vatican Bank.

Marchinkus first met the future Pope Paul in Rome and as the story goes, saved him from an unruly crowd by carrying him on his shoulders and out of danger.

Another man who was brought into the Vatican Bank story was Michele Sindona who'd play a prominent role, (along with Bishop Marchinkus) in the Vatican Bank scandal. If the future pope had twenty-twenty hindsight, he'd never have appointed either one of them to such a high post.

The pope turned to Sindona to make sure that the Vatican's tax exempt policy remained in effect despite the many attempts by the Italian government to end that status. It worked out perfectly for both Sindona and the Church when during financial troubles facing the Italian regime in 1964, Sindona threatened to sell hundreds of millions of dollars in stock on the open market. This would have completely ruined the government and they reluctantly agreed to keep the Vatican's no-tax policy in effect. The two parties both got what they wanted; the Italian regime was saved from default and the Vatican continued to have its tax-exempt status in place for some time to come. This was not the last time that Sindona would use his multi-faceted talents to help the Church. Over time, he'd make the Church rich beyond its wildest dreams, yet at the same time, sow the seeds for its final demise.

Sindona also helped the Vatican take control over a bank called Banca Unione (BU) by intimidating its major stockholder, Giangicomo Feltrinelli into selling all of his family's shares in the bank to Sindona's group and agreeing not to black ball the company further.

It was during this time that Sindona made friends with David Kennedy who was the former secretary of the treasury under President Nixon. Kennedy was by then the president of Continental Bank of Illinois and in time, they'd buy up 20 percent of Sandon's

Banca Privata Finanziaria in Milan. In 1972, Kennedy became the director of a company called Fasco, A.G. that bought the controlling interest in the Franklin National Bank. What both Sindona and Kennedy could not have known at that time was that the failure of the Franklin National Bank would have severe consequences for all of them in the future.

With Michele Sindona as the right hand man of the pope when it came to financial matters at the Vatican, Pope Paul only had to listen to his friend when he made recommendations when it came to any dealings he might have to offer. One day the pope met with Sindona in his Papal apartment to discuss future monetary policy. In a bold move, Sindona asked the pope for permission to move certain Vatican monies out of Italy and into, the tax-free Eurodollar market in order to make more money for the Church. This move would put the Church on par with other major lending institutions around the world and show the international bankers that they wanted to be seen as being one of the boys when it came to global finances. The pope was at first reluctant but in the end he acceded to Sindona's request. This was an incredible bit of luck for Sindona. He now had complete control of hundreds of millions of dollars in Vatican funds that he could spend as he liked. He knew that he'd have no restrictions placed upon him by the pope. After all, he was now "God's Banker," with all the respect that came with it. Along with Bishop Paul Marchinkus, the head of the Vatican Bank and other leading prelates that included Cardinal Giuseppe Caprio, and others, he now held a virtual monopoly over Vatican finances and he was ready to move forward, no matter what it took.

Who was Michele Sindona and where did his roots lie? He was born from a poor background in Patti, Sicily, where he was raised by his grandmother, Nunziati, along with his brother, Enio. Both were sickly children with Michele suffering from rheumatic fever and his brother from bronchitis. The town of Patti was located on the northeast coast of Sicily and was surrounded by mountains. On December 28, 1908, a huge earthquake hit Pattie and destroyed it. The casualties amounted to 160,000 people who were displaced between it and Messina. One of the victims was Don Michele Sindona, Michele's grandfather. By the time the quake ended more than 90 percent of the buildings had been destroyed and more than eighty thousand people were dead. The Sindona's were lucky and were spared the worst that their neighbors bore. His grandfather once worked in various jobs including the lumber trade, iron, and tools. In time the family became wealthy and were among the most respected in the Patti-Messina region. Of his grandfather, Don Michele, Michele said of him, "At thirty he was king of Patti, a descendant of the royal family of Aragon, the conquerors of Sicily." One day in the summer of 1914, Don Michele Sr. took a swim in the Tyrrhenian Sea, returned home and died in his sleep.

Nunziati knew the local bishop and she would take young Michele to see him often. The bishop would ply the boy with stories of the Church that Michele relished.

In 1938, he attended the University of Messina and graduated four years later with a degree in tax law. After school he got a job as a bookkeeper and also worked in real estate. But with the allied invasion of Sicily during World War II, young Michele's life would be forever changed.

On July 10, 1943, as allied armies landed on Italian soil, the local Mafia aided British and American troops in securing the beachhead. Michele Sindona drove a produce truck for the arriving Americans and British, and also supplied the local population with food. All of this was done under the direction of mob boss Vito Genovese. During the war, Michele was against the Dictator Benito Mussolini's government and while in school at Ginnasio, the high school in Patti, he refused to wear the uniform that was required of all students at that time and was given a demerit. While Sindona gave food to the allies following the invasion of Sicily, his actions were led by the local Mafia who aided him in his endeavors. Although Michele probably did not know that his benefactor, Vito Genovese was an international drug smuggler and head of the New York crime family founded by Lucky Luciano. One of the things he learned by his association with the Americans during the Sicilian invasion was, that if he was going to be something in later life, he'd have to make friends with important people, most of them Americans. He said at that time, "It was then that I realized, if I wanted to do something big, I would need to be friends with America."

Four years later, Michele moved to Milan where he was given an introduction to the pro-secretary of State for the Vatican, Giovanni

Battista Montini, later to be named Pope Paul VI. Michele quickly won over the prelate and he was appointed as the Vatican's first chief fundraiser, later to become the chief financial director of the Vatican.

While living in Milan, he worked for company that did business in the consulting and accounting fields. He was very talented in the art of keeping his clients away from paying large taxes on their income and that fact alone made him a prime asset for the Mafia that was so important in Italy at that time. Sindona soon was working for the Gambino crime family in Italy, keeping their ill- gotten gains from the tax man. The two main centers of the Gambino crime family were in New York and Palermo that was controlled by the Sicilian Mafia. Sindona was so well liked by the Mafia in Italy that on November 2, 1957, a meeting was held in the Grand Hotel de Palmes in Palermo and his Mafia bosses invited Sindona to attend. The meeting at the de Palmes was for Sindona, a huge opportunity to expand his relationship with them. The Mafia leaders asked him to manage their profits from the heroin trade in which they were engaged in. In reality, he was now their laundry man, able to hide their profits from the government and invest it in other illegal entities. Besides working for the Mafia, Sindona bought and sold various companies, hiding their profits and making huge sums of money for himself.

The meeting at the Hotel de Palmes that November day was a who's who of the top Mafia leaders around the world. Among those in attendance were Joe Bonanno, his top aide Carmine Galante, Lucky Luciano, the mob's top money man, and Thomas Buscetta and Frank Coppola, who were well-known heroin smugglers with connections to the Gambino crime family.

Less than two years after he began working for the mob, Sindona bought his first bank, Milan's Banca Privata Finanzaria, or BPP for the Vatican, but he had to hide the Vatican's ownership of the bank and used his connection in Switzerland to hide the transaction. Soon he had invested the Vatican's money in both legal and illegal enterprises, most of them not known to the pope. BPP was founded in 1930 and served as the conduit for the illegal transfer of money from Italy for a few rich investors.

In 1959, Sindona aided the Church when it wanted to raise

money for an old people's home. The Church brought him in and in time, Sindona was able to raise $2.4 million to fund the project. The prelate who opened the home was none other than Cardinal Giovanni Battista Montini, later to become Pope Paul VI. From that moment on, both men would become close friends and as the years passed, the pope would ask Sindona to aid the Church in funneling its money via the Vatican Bank that would eventually lead to its ruin. What was not known at the time was the money raised for the retirement home was given to Sindona by the Mafia and the CIA.

The renegade CIA officer Victor Marchetti wrote about this saying:

> In the 1950s and 1960s the CIA gave economic support to many activities promoted by the Catholic Church, from orphanages to the missions. Millions of dollars each year were given to a great number of bishops and monsignors. One of them was Cardinal Giovanni Battista Montini. It is possible that Cardinal Montini did not know where the money was coming from. He may have thought it was coming from friends.[1]

Sindona was now on a bank spending spree and with the money he'd made from his earlier investments he was able to buy two more banks, Banca di Messina and in 1964, a bank in Switzerland called Banque de Finacement (Finabank) in Geneva. The bank was partly owned by the Vatican and in time, it would come to own 29% of the shares in the bank.

In 1963, Sindona had made his first American purchase, the Libby, McNeil, Libby Company, a food processing company that had international distribution sales. Later that year, Sindona began his partnership with a secret society in Italy called the Masonic Lodge headed by a right-wing nationalist named Licio Gelli. Also called P-2, or Propaganda 2, and made up of Freemasons, people who throughout the centuries, took part in revolutionary activities against existing governments. P-2 was one of Italy's most secretive organizations.

As time went on, Sindona would invest some of the Vatican's money in P-2. By 1974, and using P-2's cash, Sindona had bought

[1] Yallop, David, *In God's Name,* Page 108.

6 banks in 4 countries, including the United States. From all his Vatican investments, many of whom the pope and his top aides did not know about, Sindona got the nickname as "God's Banker."

In the summer of 1974, he enlarged his financial empire by establishing an international money Brokerage Company called Moneyrex. Using Moneyrex as a cover, he transferred millions of lira out of Italy and placed them in secret Swiss accounts. He also transferred money from P-2's drug business into his own personal accounts.

Moneyrex was founded on February 5, 1965 and started out as a legitimate business. But as with all of Sindona's financial entities, this one soon became less than legitimate. Two years later, Moneyrex had a net profit of $2 million most of which was not taxed by the government due to Sindona's expert handing of the cash between his various companies.

As time went on, Sindona had a run-in with Carlo Bordoni who once worked for the Milan branch of Citibank as a manger before being fired for highly questionable business practices. Bordoni was now working with Sindona in Moneyrex and the two of them clashed over how to run the company. At one point Bordoni yelled at Sindona and told him that, "Your force is the Mafia and your power is Freemasonry. I don't intend to risk my good name and the success of Moneyrex just because a Mafioso asks me to."

Through the hard work of both Bordoni and Sindona, Moneyrex soon had a large following in the international banking world, with 850 client banks-including Westminster National Bank of England, First National Bank of Boston, and the Central Bank of Hungary. Other banks who did business with them came from all areas of the world including the Middle East, South America, Asia and Africa.

Moneyrex was not the only investment that Sindona was making. He allied himself with the Christian Democratic Party of Italy and gave them thousands of dollars from his accounts for their various political activities. In a bit of cloak and dagger, Sindona met in Rome at the Grand Hotel with two men, Raffaello Scarpetti and Fillipo Michele, both members of the Christian Democratic Party. Seated at a table, Sindona handed the men a suitcase full of money that they gladly accepted. Just like what he did with the Mafia and the Church, Sindona was now in bed with the ruling party in Italy.

The United States at the time also poured millions of dollars into right-wing causes in Italy, funneling $800,000 into the account of SID chief Vito Miceli, a member of P-2.

There has been persistent rumors that Sindona had covert ties with the CIA although he never said a word about it. There was also talk going around at that time that some of the $10 million dollars the CIA spent in Italy in that nation's 1972 elections were funneled through many of Sindona's banks. One of the results of the CIA funding was a possible link between Sindona and a man named John McCaffery, chief of the European resistance movement in Great Britain during World War II, to start a coup in Italy (this was part of the planned Sicily coup that was described in the last chapter).

The planned coup that now expanded to include the whole of Italy as well, was described in an affidavit signed by a lawyer for Sindona on February 3, 1981, written by John McCaffery in Ireland.

The statement said that the Communists and Leftists in Italy were ruining the country and bringing it into economic and political chaos and that one of the men who was leading the fight against them was Michele Sindona. McCaffrey said that in this fraught political climate, Sindona approached McCaffery and proposed plans for a nation-wide coup to end the threat of Communist/leftist expansion in Italy. Their aim was to create a new pro-American government in both Sicily and Italy. McCaffrey said that he met with Sindona and an unidentified Italian military officer in Rome to discuss the matter:

> At this meeting I presented a detailed plan for the takeover of the government and for the new administration's first year in office. In view of my background, my collaboration had not only the value of technical competence, but also could be considered as a guarantee of excluding any attempt at neo-fascist dictatorship. Neither the United States nor Great Britain could have accepted any such outcome, nor indeed would they have wanted a purely military take-over, even with the best intentions. The idea was to secure the backing of the

armed forces for orthodox democratic politicians who wanted a proper Parliamentary government and not a branch of the Kremlin. The military men involved were fully aware of this and did not aspire to any autonomous action but merely wanted to be the defenders of the Western democratic system.

Following this meeting, Sindona spoke to me on several occasions regarding the proposed coup. It was clear to me from these conversations with Sindona that he was the key to the entire operation. I am sure to a moral certainty that Sindona spoke about the proposed coup with important figures in the American CIA and with top level officials in the American Embassy in Rome. I would think it highly probable that the existence of the planned coup was known by Graham Martin, then American Ambassador to Italy. There is no doubt but there exist numerous documents in America which reflect the benevolence on the part of the United States towards the coup organized by Sindona.[2]

With his lame brained plans for a coup in Italy dashed, Sindona now set his sights on America and bought his first American bank, New York's Franklin National Bank. He paid $40 million for one million shares of the bank. Once in control of Franklin, Sindona transferred millions of dollars of Franklin's assets to his Swiss accounts, causing Franklin to collapse. Franklin's demise soon lead to the collapse of Sindona's other European financial holdings.

The collapse of Franklin National could be seen from the beginning. It was founded on Long Island, New York as a small institution with large expectations. It soon branched out to Manhattan where they could not compete with the large, established banks that had been in business for decades. The owners of Franklin bought a large office on Park Avenue and then sold controlling interest in the bank to Sindona. From the very start, Franklin was going bankrupt and Sindona knew it. But that did not stop him from making unsecure loans and doing business the way he did in Italy. People who knew Sindona, he said, would come back to him because of

2   *St. Peter's Banker*, Page 104.106.

his important business acumen he had in Italy. In the United States, the Federal Reserve, seeing how bad business was going at Franklin and who the owner was, decided to pour $2 billion into its coffers in order to stem the tide. It did no good. With the failure of Franklin now complete, a number of its top officers were arrested in the then largest bank failure in US history. Sindona left the United States in the wake of Franklin and was now safely back in Italy.

In 1974, with terrible luck of its own making, bad foreign currency transfers, and the swing in foreign exchange rates, the bank lost millions of dollars in assets. Franklin lost $63 million in the first five months of 1974, more than any other bank in American history up to that point. In the aftermath of the collapse of Franklin, the US charged Sindona with illegally transferring $40 million form banks he controlled in Italy to buy Franklin National, and then siphoning $15 million from it. Just as his trial was to begin, Sindona disappeared in what amounted to a fake escape plan on his part (more about this later). But in the world of American finance, the collapse of Franklin was one that would have long-range effects on the American banking system for years for come. When Franklin went bust, the US government helped it go under in order to prevent any more financial harm to its investors. This use of the Fed to help in the dismantling of Franklin was seen in 2009 during the great recession in which countless, large and well-known financial institutions went bankrupt. The US government then stepped in and helped save most of these institutions thus, preventing further damage from being done to the economy.

Franklin National was the 20th largest bank in the United States at the time of its collapse and the federal regulators were not going to let the failure go unnoticed. Until this time, Sindona had many friends in the Nixon administration and had even once tried to give a campaign donation to the president's re-election campaign. Now, in 1974 at the time of the collapse of Franklin, the political wind in the United States was moving against him. Watergate was consuming the Nixon presidency and his allies in the Republican Party had no interest in helping Sindona out of his financial problems. By the summer of 1974, Nixon would resign and the new president, Jimmy Carter was no friend of Sindona or the people whom he represented.

Sindona had to find a way out of his ever-growing predicament and he turned once again to his old friend, Roberto Calvi. This time, however, Calvi was not going to help Sindona, due to the circumstances surrounding the Franklin debacle. At least for Calvi, Sindona was now too hot to handle and he begged off.

There is little rhyme or reason as to the circle of events in our world. This proved to be the case surrounding Sindona and the Franklin collapse a world away that would have far reaching ramifications regarding Sindona and his financial empire. On a hot night in July of 1979, a man named Giorgio Ambrosiano who was tasked with the job of liquidating the Sindona fortune was gunned down near his home in Milan by an assailant who was waiting in ambush. As part of his investigation into Sindona's activities, Ambrosiano was looking into Sindona's actions regarding this hostile takeover of Franklin and was ready to testify in court when Sindona went to trail (more about Ambrosiano in this chapter). Ambrosiano had been giving US authorities as much information as he had on the Sindona/Franklin deal and the US feds were taking it all in. With the collapse of Franklin, the heyday of Sindona's time as "God's Banker" was slowly coming to an end.

Sindona also had ties with the CIA when he bought the Rome *Daily American,* a newspaper which the Agency covertly funded. Later, Sindona said that he bought the paper at the request of American Ambassador Graham Martin who feared that the paper would "fall into the hands of the leftists." Later, Ambassador Martin denied the charges and called Sindona "a liar." To say that Michele Sindona was well connected in business and financial banking circles is an understatement. He had on his side, Mafia dons, banking leaders such as the Hambros of London, Continental Illinois, the Rothschild family, David Kennedy, President Nixon's Treasury Secretary, the Vatican Bank and its president, Bishop Paul Marchinkus. He once said of his relationship with these powerful people thusly, "I prefer to deal with men like Somoza. Doing business with a one-man dictatorship is much easier than doing business with democratically elected governments. They have too many subcommittees, too many controls. They also aspire to honesty, that's bad for the banking business."

By 1973, however, Sindona's luck was beginning to run thin. In Rome, Bishop Marchinkus wrote a check for $307,000 for losses accrued by the Vatican Bank by Sindona as a result of illegal dealings on the American stock exchange in shares from a company called Vetco Industries. The Security and Exchange Commission found out that an investment broker in Los Angeles had acquired on behalf of Sindona and Marchinkus some 27% of Vetco. "The Vatican paid the fine, then sold its shares at a profit."

Things were about to get worse for Michele Sindona when, in 1974, the Italian judiciary set up a secret investigation of him, his links to the Vatican and his other nefarious operations worldwide. The man who was put in charge of the Sindona probe was Giorgio Ambrosoli who, by March 1975, sent a secret report on Sindona's actions to the attorney general of Italy. He soon had proof that Sindona was using a myriad of offshore lending institutions to launder his money, many of which belonged to the Vatican Bank. As his investigation went on, Ambrosoli was able to make a list of seventy-seven names of people who were doing illegal business with Sindona, including a number of people inside the Vatican Bank. During his investigation, Ambrosoli was threatened by unknown persons who hinted that if he did not stop his investigation then bad things were going to happen to him. Instead of surrendering to the threats, he continued to purse his leads wherever he found them. A banking colleague of Sindona's, Enrico Cuccia, overheard Sindona tell a friend while he was in New York that, "He wanted everyone who had done him harm killed, in particular Giorgio Ambrosoli." Unfortunately for Ambrosili, that horrible event was about to take place.

On September 29, 1974, attorney Giorgio Ambrosoli was appointed to be the liquidator of Sindona's Banca Privata Italiana, one of his crooked banks. Ambrosoli has been appointed to his position by the Treasury Ministry and the director of the Bank of Italy. He soon found a large amount of evidence leading to major crimes committed by Sindona and he reported up the chain of command. While proceeding with his investigation, Ambrosoli told his wife that, "Whatever happens, I'll certainly pay a high price for taking this job. But I knew that before taking it on, and I'm not complaining. It has been a unique chance for me to do something for the country. Obviously I'm making enemies for myself."

Giorgio Ambrosoli knew he was getting close to Sindona when Sindona tried to bring charges of embezzlement against him. These were of course, trumped up charges which never stuck, but Ambrosoli now knew the power of the man whom he was up against. In a rare move of arrogance, Sindona's son-in-law, Pier Sandro Magnoni, approached Ambrosili and asked him if he would like to become the owner of one of Michele's new banks, "once you have settled this tiring business of the bankruptcies."

By March 1979, the liquidator was able to put the figure on the size of Sindona's Banco Privata at a loss of $257 billion lira.

The closer he got to nailing Sindona outright, he began to get threatening phone calls. He even went as far as taping his phone calls in order to have a recording of who called and what they said.

Sindona now turned his attention to another man, Enrico Cuccia, the managing director of Mediobanca, a publically owned investment bank. Cuccia knew that Sindona was a crook and Sindona mistakenly believed that Cuccia could somehow have his arrest warrant that had been issued during his leave from Italy, rescinded. He also wanted Cuccia to someway find the staggering amount of 257 billion lira to bail out Banca Privata. When both men met, Sindona turned his attention to his new nemesis, Giorgio Ambrosoli. He told Cuccia that, "That dammed liquidator of my bank is harming me, and therefore I want to have him killed. I will make him disappear in such a way that he leaves no trace."

Enrico Cuccia had ample reason to fear Michele Sindona. In October 1979, a bomb went off near his home but somehow he escaped without getting seriously hurt. There was an investigation, and the person who probably sent the assassins to kill Cuccia was most likely Sindona, or people who worked for him.

These assassination attempts took place right after Sindona was indicted on ninety-nine counts of financial misconduct concerning the collapse of the Franklin National Bank by American authorities. As mentioned before, US investigators wanted desperately to talk with Giorgio Ambrosoli regarding his information on the Sindona case. The judge who was presiding at Sindona's New York trial, Thomas Griesa, arranged for Ambrosoli to make a deposition under oath in Milan. On July 9 in Milan, a number of US law enforcement officials including two special marshals sent by Judge Griesa, along with a number of lawyers, and an Italian Judge named Giovanni Galati, began hearing his testimony. Also in attendance were a number of lawyers representing Sindona.

Besides testifying before the judicial committee, Ambrosoli also met with Boris Giuliano, the deputy superintendent of the Palermo police force and head of the city's CID. Ambrosoli gave them the same testimony that he parted to the judicial panel, all concerning the misdeeds of Michele Sindona. In an incident that would have merit to the Sindona case, a mobster named Giuseppe Di Cristina, who was employed by the Gambino, Inzerillo and Spada families, was murdered in Palermo in May of 1978. "On his body Giuliano found checks and other documents that indicated that Sindona had been recycling the payments from heroin sales through the Vatican Bank to his Amincor Bank in Switzerland. Having compared notes on their separate investigations, the two men agreed to have a fuller meeting once Ambrosoli had finished his testimony to the American lawyers."

Ambrosoli was now a very busy man and he had a meeting with Lt. Colonel Antonio Varisco who was then investigating Lico Gelli's P-2.

Ambrosoli also told investigators of Sindona's relationship with both Roberto Calvi and Bishop Marchinkus in particular, regarding the sale of Banca Cattolica de Vento and how the bank changed hands.

He finished his testimony on July 11 and then prepared to sign his deposition and give any further information to American investigators as wanted.

On July 11, 1978, after Ambrosoli was leaving his office for his Milan home, he was approached on the street by three men who stopped him abruptly. They asked him if he was Doctor Ambrosoli and without any fanfare, they shot him three times in his chest. He was rushed to a hospital but was dead within hours. Before he died he managed to say that the person who shot him had an American-Italian accent. In the days following his death, two other Italian officials who were investigating the case were killed. One was Lt. Colonel Antonio Varisco, the same man whom Ambrosoli had previously met. The other victim was Boris Guilano, the chief of the Flying Squad who was killed as he left a local restaurant in Palermo. Guilano also met with Ambrosoli during the probe of Michele Sindona. The man who took over Ambrosoli's job, Emanuele Basile, was killed the next year while walking with his family on a crowded street.

In every murder investigation, the police look for those people who have the means, motive, and opportunity to carry out the deed. In this case, one need not look too far. The one person who had all of the above motives was Michele Sindona. Giorgio Ambrosoli, Colonel Antonio Varisco, and Boris Guilano all posed threats to Sindona and his empire. One needn't pull the trigger himself in order to be charged with a crime. If indeed, and all the circumstantial evidence points in the direction of Sindona in these horrible murders, than any good prosecutor would have had a solid case in bringing conspiracy and murder charges against him in a court of law. With all these three men gone, a large burden would have been lifted from Sindona's head and he could now sleep a little easier.

In the wake of the killings, the Italian government made a cursory investigation into the affairs of the looting of Banca Privata Italiana, and the allegation that Sindona, Roberto Calvi, and Bishop Marchinkus might have diverted $6.5 million among themselves. However, no further investigation was conducted and the matter died on the vine.

After the death of Ambrosoli, the Italian justice system fell silent. People who had once been an ally of the late Ambrosoli now forgot that they even knew him and decided it was wise not to have anything to do with any further probe of the Calvi-Sindona-Gelli-Marchinkus affair. Let sleeping dogs lie, was the new norm.

On March 9, 1979, Sindona was indicted on 29 counts of perjury, fraud, and misappropriation of bank funds. His trial was set for August 1, but on September 1, 1979, he was kidnapped from his New York home and taken to Palermo. After being interrogated by men in hooded masks, he was taken out of Italy to Salzburg, Austria, Munich, and Frankfurt and back to New York. On October 6 1979, Sindona's attorney, Marvin Frankel, received a phone call from Sindona himself saying that he'd been released and was in New York at 42nd Street and Tenth Avenue. He was picked up, and eight days later, he was in the courtroom of Judge Thomas Griesa. He told the judge that he'd been kidnapped by "leftists" and that he was supposed to be tried for "economic crimes."

In a huge twist that no one expected, the Italian police arrested John Gambino during a visit to Rome. When they searched him, they found a piece of paper on his person that read, "741, Saturday,

Frankfurt." All this had to do with an FBI investigation of a TWA flight with that number which left Frankfurt for New York's Kennedy Airport on October 13, three days before Sindona suddenly reappeared. One of the passengers on the plane was a man who said his name was Joseph Bonamico of Brooklyn, New York. It turned out that the street address he wrote on his customs declaration did not exist, and the agents sent the customs form to their forensics lab. The results of the exam were shocking; the handwriting on the form belonged to Sindona but his fingerprints were on the customs form that belonged to Bonamico. Is it possible that Sindona was lying about his own kidnapping and that it was all a hoax? That is a possibility that we have to consider when looking into Sindona's absence during that time. At the time of his so called kidnapping, the American FBI and Interpol also became involved in the case and the FBI put Carlo Bordoni, a co-defendant under police protection. While Sindona was missing, things began to get interesting, fast. His Rome attorney, Rodolfo Guzzi, "got an envelope postmarked from Brooklyn. It included ten hand-written questions about senior Italian politicians, prominent businessmen including Fiat's Angnelli family, and even the Vatican. A notation after the last one said," All written by me on precise orders, Sindona. "A picture accompanied the letter showing Sindona in not too good a shape. The note was signed by a group called the Proletarian Committee of Subversion for Better Justice."

Days later a letter came demanding money but the Italian police got a tip and the messenger was arrested. He turned out to be Vincenzo Spatola, a thirty-one year old contractor from Palermo who had ties to the Gambino crime family in New York.

In October 1979, he surrendered to US authorities. On March 27, 1980, he was convicted of 68 counts of perjury and mishandling bank funds. He was sentenced to a 27-year jail term at the Federal Correctional Center in Ottisville, New York.

Sindona was so eager to get the United States authorities off his back that he even put out feeler to a professional hit man named Luigi Ronsisvalle to assassinate John Kenney who was the Assistant US District Attorney who was heading his extradition case while he was still in Europe. Much to Sindona's displeasure, Ronsisvalle turned down Sindona's generous offer of $100,000 for the Kenney hit. Ronsisavlle knew too much about how the US Judicial system worked to be suckered into Sindona's wild and impractical scheme.

In 1986, justice was finally meted out for the murder of Giorgio Ambrosoli. An Italian court found Sindona guilty of the murder of Ambrosoli and he was given a life sentence. Michele Sindona died in prison while serving a life sentence under unusual circumstances (why not). After eating breakfast in his private cell, he suddenly collapsed yelling. "I've been poisoned. He was in a coma, dying two days later.

But like everything in the life of Sindona, his death left many more questions than answers. During the autopsy doctors found a lethal dose of cyanide in his blood stream (a gram of poison was found). While he was in jail, his movements were monitored by hidden cameras and his meals were prepared separately. A total of 12 guards monitored his cell on shifts during the day and night. "It took eight months for an investigating magistrate to reach a much contested but never disproven conclusion; the jailhouse poisoning was suicide."[3]

Besides Michele Sindona, the other main players in the Vatican Bank drama were Bishop Paul Marchinkus, Roberto Calvi and Lico Gelli, who headed a Masonic Lodge in Italy. The Masonic Lodge was also called P-2 or Propaganda 2, made up of Freemasons, people who throughout the centuries took part in revolutionary activities against existing governments. P-2 was one of Italy's most secretive organizations and was banned by the Italian government when an investigation revealed that it was linked to some of the highest members of the Italian parliament, military, and the press. There were also allegations that P-2 took part in assassinations, kidnappings, and illegal arms trading across the world. It was also rumored that P-2 was somehow involved with the death of Roberto Calvi in London. Gelli was well connected in Vatican circles due to his friendship with Cardinal Paolo Bertoli who worked in the Vatican's Diplomatic Corps. Cardinal, Bertoli even introduced Gelli to Paul Marchinkus.

Once the Vatican scandal erupted in plain sight, Gelli did not fare well. After the collapse of Banco Ambrosiano, the Italian police raided his private offices on March 17, 1981, and confiscated

---

[3] Posner, Gerald, *God's Bankers: A History of Money and Power At the Vatican,* Simon and Schuster, New York, 2015, Page 351.

a large amount of vital information which included lists of names of the P-2 members, which included members of the government, of parliament, of the armed forces, and heads of the Italian secret services, and information on both Roberto Calvi and Michele Sindona. Other members of the P-2 that were revealed were some high-ranking members of the Vatican who allied themselves with Gelli. P-2 was shut down by Italian prosecutors and after its fall Gelli went on the run and was captured in Cannes, some years later. As the scandal over the IOR or Vatican Bank erupted out into the open, Cardinal Agostino who was secretary of the Council of the Public Affairs of the Church, told Bishop Marchinkus that he would stay in his post until a replacement for him could be found. In April 1989 indictments were handed down on a number of former Banco Ambrosiano officials, among them was Lico Gelli. Bishop Marchinkus got off and was not indicted due to a ruling by the Church that he was exempt. When Marchinkus heard that he wasn't criminally liable for the collapse of Banco Ambrosiano he said, "I may be a lousy banker but at least I'm not in jail."

Another participant in the scandal was the Banco Ambrosiano of Milan that was owned by the Vatican Bank and became involved in a massive financial scandal causing $790 million run on "Ambro funds." Some conspiracy theorists and other mainstream writers who covered the Vatican Bank scandal, came to the conclusion that either one or more of the above mentioned people had something to do with the sudden death of Pope Paul I, Alberto Luciano who died in his papal chambers after serving as Pontiff for one month. During his brief tenure, the pope had serious doubts about how the IOR was running and he even sold one bank controlled by the IOR called Banca Cattolica de Vento, or "the priest's bank" to Roberto Calvi. Pope John Paul had no idea that the bank was laundering money and before his death he had a talk with both Roberto Calvi and Bishop Marchinkus to discuss possible changes in the way the bank was run and who would oversee it. It was rumored that the pope was thinking of replacing Marchinkus with Cardinal Giovanni Benelli of Florence. In an interesting plot twist, many members of the Vatican staff, some priests, nuns, and others, organized a lottery to see which day Bishop Marchinkus would be fired.

We are getting a little bit ahead of ourselves at this point but there was a huge connection between Roberto Calvi, the IOR and Banco Ambrosiano. At the time of his death in London, Roberto Calvi had been in charge of Ambrosiano's operations. The bank was then under imminent collapse due to huge debts and mismanagement that spanned years. The board of directors had fired Calvi only one day before his death.

It seems that only days before his demise, Calvi wrote a personal note to Pope John Paul II in which he wanted to set the record straight regarding the Banco Ambrosiano and the Vatican Bank. "In the letter, Calvi declared that he had been a strategic front man for the Vatican in fighting Marxism from Eastern Europe to South America. And he warned that upcoming events would provoke a catastrophe of unimaginable proportions in which the Church will suffer the gravest damage." He also said he had important documents for the pope to see but just what they were he didn't say.

What he probably meant by that statement was the imminent collapse of Banco Ambrosiano. The bank was in debt to the tune of $1.8 billion, most of which was guaranteed by the IOR, or the Vatican Bank.

Calvi was the former head of Banco Ambrosiano who had long-standing covert contacts with both Sindona and Bishop Marchinkus. The life of Roberto Calvi was one that would have made any Hollywood producer proud and the facts surrounding his death in London was even more bizarre. On June 12, 1982, Roberto Calvi left his home in Rome and using a fake passport, fled to London. Six days later a passerby walking from the Blackfriars Bridge in chat city, noticed a body hanging from one of the pillars. The police were called and the body was cut down. What the police found left them confused. The name on the man's passport read Glan Roberto Calvini. The body was weighted down with 7,400 British pounds and large amounts of Swiss and US currencies.

As the investigation proceeded, British and Italian authorities began to uncover one of the largest banking and political scandals in recent memory, and one that would reach into the portals of the Vatican. The very idea of a Vatican Bank is a strange phenomenon, yet such an operation had been going on just beyond the pastoral halls of the pope's balcony. By the late 1960s, the banks power and influence grew to the point where it controlled interests in thousands of local companies in Italy and owned considerable real estate in Rome. The Vatican Bank also heavily invested its money in the US. Germany, and Switzerland. But by the early 1970s, bad investments caused the Vatican Bank to go broke, and the man most responsible for the collapse was Michele Sindona, who by 1974, had squandered away somewhere between $120 million and $1 billion. But the story does not end there. Back in Italy, Banco Ambrosiano of Milan owned by the Vatican Bank became involved in a massive financial scandal causing a $790 million run of cash.

The president of the Vatican Bank, Archbishop Paul Marchinkus asked the Secretary of State to open an investigation of Banco Ambrosiano's dealings. The focus of the investigation centered on the bank's president, Roberto Calvi who was eventually tried and found guilty of taking $27 million out of Italy and was given a four year term (Banco Ambrosiano closed down on August 6, 1982).

Roberto Calvi was the intermediary for the Vatican as it began to invest its money in various offshore shell companies, some legal, some not, and began taking in a horde of cash. Bishop Marchinkus sat on the board of the Banco Ambrosiano's subsidiary in Nassau, Bahamas and he controlled the case that flowed out of the Caribbean-Lichtenstein-Luxemburg network. Calvi was responsible for these undercover connections-including those that were funneled from dummy corporations in such places as Panama and other areas around the globe. In 1963, Calvi and Banco Ambrosiano had acquired Banca del Gottardo in Lugano, Switzerland that, due to Calvi's illegal efforts, made Banca del Gottardo one of the key conduits for laundering Mafia money. Another bank that Calvi ran was called Banco Ambrosiano Overseas, Nassau that was founded in 1971 and in a rather unusual circumstance, had Bishop Paul Marchinkus as one of its board of directors. Not known to financial authorities in Italy and elsewhere during this time was that Calvi arranged that the Vatican Bank and Banco Ambrosiano were interconnected in their illegal money laundering activities. One example of their cooperation was when, in November 1976, Calvi bought 3.5 percent of Banco Mercantile of Florence and hid the fact that the purchase was made on behalf of the Vatican Bank. Throughout Calvi's wheeling and dealings, he made purchases on behalf of the Vatican Bank who gave a wink and a nod to his corrupt activities.

Calvi's downfall came when Italian authorities arrested Lico Gelli in March 1981 when they arrived at his home looking for evidence surrounding the kidnapping of Sindona. They found a list that Gelli kept of 962 members of his P-2 organization as well as many government documents. The Gelli scandal resulted in the downfall of the Italian government and the new prosecutors renewed their case against Calvi, and two months following the Gelli raid, the police arrested Calvi. Calvi's family turned to Bishop Marchinkus for help but the priest had no intention of helping his fellow crook and turned down all their pleas. The Vatican Bank was not going to be brought into a scandal of their own making and Calvi, for all intents and purposes was on his own. Bishop Marchinkus told Calvi's son Carlo that, "If we do, it's not only the IOR and the Vatican's image that will suffer. You'll lose as well, for our problems are your problems, too." To make matters more problematic for the Vatican, while Calvi was in his Lodi prison, he somehow continued as president of Banco Ambrosiano, leaving the banking world shaking their heads.

Throughout the Vatican Bank's secret dealings, the Bank of Italy had been quietly looking into Calvi's strange dealings and they took particular interest when Calvi wanted to make a deal with one of his clients, a Bahamian-based company called Artoc Bank & Trust. The bank was based in Nassau, the old stomping ground of Calvi's many shell companies. Banco Ambrosiano already owned 20 percent of Artoc and Calvi wanted to merge the two banks into one. The Bank of Italy found out about the Calvi-Artoc plans and they sent a long letter to Calvi asking that he explain the details of the proposed merger. They also wanted him to explain his $1.4 billion in loans to subsidiaries in the Bahamas, Peru, and Nicaragua. The Bank of Italy also demanded that the letter be read at the next board meeting of Ambrosiano and that each board member state that in their opinion, before the sale went through. At the meeting that took place on June 7, Calvi refused to produce the documents of his proposed sale and the board took swift action against him. After spending seven years in charge of the bank, the board of directors voted 11-3 demanding that the bank produce all necessary papers that the Bank of Italy wanted to see.

The Bank of Italy was not done with investigating Roberto Calvi.

In November 1978, after looking closely into Ambrosiano's books, they released a 500-page report regarding Calvi and his dealings with the Church via Ambrosiano. The report could not really verify what Calvi was doing or just where all his money was going but what they found out made them believe that Calvi was hiding something big and important as far as the bank was concerned. "The report—named after its chief inspector—Giullo Padalino—devoted 25 pages to questionable dealings between Ambrosiano and the Vatican Bank. It chided Calvi for failing to disclose the deals of his business with the Vatican."

A new line of inquiry regarding Calvi was set up by Emillo Alessandrini, of Milan police, who opened up a criminal case against Calvi. He got help from a part of Italian law enforcement that looked into white-collar crimes. Alessandrini wanted to get enough evidence to "to charge Calvi with manipulating the share price of public companies and passing any profits through different countries to circumvent taxes and restrictions on the export of the lira."

Like Giorgio Ambrosoli, Alessandrini shared the same, terrible fate. As he dropped his son off at school in Milan, an assassin shot and killed him, executing him as he was on his knees.

The case against Calvi was turned over to Luca Mucci of the white-collar crime division. But the case soon turned cold as lead after lead was not looked into. It seemed that the head of the division, Raffaele Gindice, Mucci's boss, was a member of Gelli's P-2 and Gelli had intervened with Gindice to drop the case.

It seemed that Calvi had friends in high places and despite his being investigated by the Bank of Italy, his pal, Bishop Marchinkus persuaded some large Vatican institutions such as Banca Nazionale de Lavor, as well as Ente Nazionale Idrocarburi, the nation's state-owned energy holding company to loan him money.

As the Italian Bank began looking deeply into Calvi's dealings, he now turned his attention to a man whom he thought would be able to help him avoid any further problems, Falvio Carboni. Carboni was a Sicilian property contractor who had met Calvi in August 1981. Before Calvi's flight out of Italy it was Carboni who was closets to Calvi and made plans for his departure for he and his family. Carboni was an influential man who was well connected in all aspects of Italian politics and business. They had first met in Sardinia when Calvi and his wife visited Carboni at his yacht in the city. Soon, both men began a friendship and Carboni would frequently meet with Calvi when Calvi was in Milan.

Calvi was now feeling threatened by the erupting scandal and in May 1982 he had his wife and daughter leave Italy for the United States.

It seemed that people who had some connection with Roberto Calvi were always getting into trouble and feared for their lives. One such person was Roberto Rosone who worked his entire career at Banco Ambrosiano. From 1981 on, he was the general manager and deputy chairman of the bank. He knew well what was going on as far as the debts occurred by the bank and he proposed placing the bank into the hands of the Bank of Italy to finally solve the problem. Rosone lived in Milan and on the ground floor of his home was a branch of Banco Ambrosiano. On April 27, 1982, as he was leaving his office, he was stopped on the street by a man holding a pistol and was shot in the leg, wounding him. The bank guards saw the attack and subsequently killed the attacker.

The man who attacked Rosone was a citizen of Milan named Abbruciati. It seem that this Abbruciati was well known to Carboni but in the initial stages of the investigation, the police did not know that fact. No one really knew the motives of why this petty crook attacked Rosone but later on there were rumblings that either Carboni or Abbruciati were the ones who put the hit out on Calvi. Calvi visited with Rosone after the shooting and tried to make him feel better. According to author Gerald Posner in his book *God's Bankers,* "It would be a couple of months before investigators tracked a $150,000 payment to the hit man."

It was later to be learned that Carboni was getting money from Banco Ambrosiano through Calvi. When Swiss investigators looked into the Calvi affair they found out that $14 million had wound up as part of $20 million held in personal accounts by Carboni and his girlfriend. Carboni later said that the money was payment for a loan that he made to Calvi. A second theory of where the money came from was to pay for a large shipment of stolen jewels passing through the hands of Carboni and then to Calvi.

Carboni had the crazy idea in which $80 billion lire would be paid out to purchase a solution the trouble that Calvi was having with the Bank of Italy and others who were after him. Another part of the scheme was even more bizarre. It involved the use of the secretive Catholic organization called Opus Dei who would pay some of the money of the debts of the IOR (Vatican Bank) owed to Ambrosiano. In return for Opus Dei's assuming the IOR's debt, pope John Paul would elevate Opus Dei into a personal prelature. That never happened.

So, what was Opus Dei and how did the Church feel about them? Opus Dei was founded in 1928 in Spain and it 72,000 members were once called "executive class Catholics. Pope Paul VI was no friend of Opus Dei and did all in his power to curtail its movement. When John Paul I1 took over as pope he had a different view of Opus Dei and gave them the status of "a person al prelature," giving the more autonomy in Church affairs.

In 1992, Falvio Carboni was placed in a rather difficult circumstance. In that year Italian prosecutors indicted Pavel Hnilca, a Slovak bishop who was then living in Rome, along with Calvi's buddy, Flavio Carboni "over a convoluted shakedown of the Vatican concerning the contents of Calvi's missing attaché' case. Another person charged was a man called Giulio Lena, a local mobster. When the police raided Lena's house in an unrelated operation, they found unsigned checks from Hnicla's Vatican Bank account. "Investigators believed the seventy-two-year-old bishop had written Carboni $2.8 million in checks from his IOR account, hoping to buy Calvi's case. Rome's Public Prosecutor, Francesco De Leo, said that Lena and Carboni hoped to get upwards of $40 million from the Vatican for Calvi's case."

But there was more to the Calvi-Hnicla story. Both men met before the death or Calvi to discuss a delicate matter. The matter was the cover transfer of money to the Poland to help the ever-growing Solidarity movement that wanted to bring democracy to that nation,

The Calvi- Sindona link was more than anyone could imagine and after Sindona was charged with ordering the murder of Giorgio Ambrosoli, who was investigating Sindona's illegal activities, Calvi tried to commit suicide by taking an overdose of barbiturates.

On July 20, he was sentenced to four years in jail for taking $27 million out of Italy and fined 16 billion lira. His lawyers managed to get him released on bond and to everyone's surprise (or not) the board of Banco Ambrosiano unanimously reconfirmed Calvi as chairman. One wonders how many hands he had to pay off in order to make that happen?

The circumstances of just how Roberto Calvi died are as mysterious as his life and entire books have been written on that subject. Now out on bail but not out of the clutches of the law, Calvi sought out his contacts in the Mafia, most notably the above mentioned arms smuggler and Mafia don, Flavio Carboni. Carboni got Calvi a fake passport in the name of Gian Roberto Calvini, the same one that would be on his body at the time of his death. With time running out, Calvi, still in Milan, told his daughter Ann to be prepared to leave the country, with or without him. She then proceeded to Switzerland. Now, Calvi left Milan bound for Rome where upon landing, he met up with Carboni and stayed at his home. In swift order, Emilio Pellicani, who worked for Carboni, under mysterious circumstances took Calvi out of Rome bound for Trieste.

Once in Trieste, Calvi met up with a man named Silvano Vittor, a petty crook and border smuggler who agreed to help Calvi on his next move. Calvi next went to Austria using a fake passport to leave the country. The passport number was G116847, which was issued in Rome on March 12, 1981. The name on the passport was Gian Roberto Calvini. He was then taken to a remote region in Switzerland called Ticino.

By now all the relevant authorities in Italy had been notified that Roberto Calvi had fled the country and immediately alarm bells began to sound. The man who with Michele Sindona and Bishop Marchinkus had concocted the most outrageous bank scandal in Italian history had now escaped the jaws of the law.

The Calvi curse, as it was beginning to be called by people who was associated with him, took another, tragic turn while Calvi was on the run. The person in question was a 55-year old woman named Graziella Corrocher who was Calvi's personal secretary. She was a single woman who devoted her entire life to the Bank as well as Roberto Calvi. She must have had some reason to allow herself over the years to be at Calvi's side even if she did not know exactly what her boss was doing at Banco Ambrosiano. Shortly after the Bank of Italy took over the operations of Banco Ambrosiano, Miss Corrocher wrote a note summing up how she felt as the last stages of the Calvi drama played out. She wrote, "I stand by the decision taken by the board, but I cannot stand by Calvi any longer. What a disgrace, to have run away. May he be cursed a thousand times for the harm he has done to everyone at the bank, and to the image of the group we were once so proud of."

Shortly after penning this note, she threw herself out of a window to her death. Later, investigators found the note she left prior to her suicide. Conspiracy theorists have long disputed the actual cause of her death. Some say that she was pushed out of her window, others say she was so melancholy over the events surrounding the predicament she found herself in that suicide was the only way out.

For Roberto Calvi, the next few days were hectic. He left his temporary home on June 13 with his accomplices bound for Innsbruck, Austria. Calvi and company then travelled to a small town called Bregenz, a small village near the Swiss-German border. Calvi was helped on his way to London by a mysterious man named Hans Kunz. Six days later, a passerby walking along the Blackfriars Bridge in that city, noticed the body of a man hanging from one of the pillars. The name on the man's passport read Gian Roberto Calvini. The body was weighed down with 7,400 British pounds and large amounts of Swiss and US currencies. Also in his body were 7,400 in sterling, plus 58,000 Italian lire. They also found two watches which had stopped at 5:52 a.m.

Here are the basic facts surrounding Calvi's mysterious death. As described above, Calvi sought help from various people as he made his way across Europe towards London, especially, his frieind Flacvio Carboni.

The official coroners inquest in London where he met his fate was the Calvi had committed suicide by strangulation. But if so, how could he have climbed down a busy London bridge, attaached a rope to his head, and committe the final act without anyone seeing him? To make matters more confusing for the police, they found on Calvi's body four pieces of brick and concrete and a separate piece had been lodged in the front of his pants, all of these items weighing twelve pounds. Did they just happen to be on his person when he died? Sounds fishy, don't you think?

The likelihood of Calvi's death being ruled a suicide is impractical. For instance, he had to climb down a paraphet to a scaffold and then onto a ladder to a level where he could then somehow, weigh himself down with twelve pounds of rock and hang himself. The most likely alternative is that he was killed by persons unknown, and then taken in the pre-dawn hours and left on the bridge for others to find him.

Deputy Superintdent John White of the London police told writer Edward Jay Epstein in an interview that, "We don't even know how he got from his hotel, for one half mile away, to Blackfriars Bridge." After his death, the London police canvased taxi drivers in the city and no one admitted to have taken Calvi anywhere near Blackfrirers Bridge that day, nor could they find anyone who could tell them about his activities in the city in the three days prior to his death. Calvi had been smuggled to London by a conspiracy that involved arranging three false indentities, eight separte plane flights around Europe, a speed boat, four different cars and 14 temporary residences including the Baur Au Luc and Holliday Inn in Zurich, the Amstel in Amsterdam, the George in Edinburgh and the Hilton, Sheraton and Chelsea in London. The conspirators included Flavio Carboni, a Sardinian contractor, Silvano Vittor, a cigarette smugglr and their girlfriends, the Austrian sisters Manuela and Micheala Kleinszig. They all denied seeing Calvi the night he disappeared.

For conspiracy theorists the type of Calvi's death is important. Death by hanging is one of the penalties used by the Masons for someone who had voilated their oath. Was Calvi's death a warning by Mason's not to fool with them in any way? Over time, Calvi would cryptically say to others that he was associated with the Masons, even if he did not produce any evidence. There was in London a Mason office which Calvi could have used while he was in residence in London. There were stories going around that Lico Gelli had put Calvi in touch with certain people associated with the London Masons but there was no concrete proof in that matter. In an intersting bit of informaton, there was even a "Blackfriars" lodge in London, number 3,722 in the list of Lodges Masonic.

Calvi spent most of his time upon his arrival in London in his room and he even shaved off his mustache which he had always worn. He also contacted his daughter Anna who was then in Zurich pleading with her to leave Switzerland for the United States. He told Anna that, "Something really important is happening, and today and tomorrow all hell is going to break loose." What he meant by that is not known. He also told Anna that someone whom he knew would fly to Zurich and give her the money for her travel expenses.

One of the last persons whom Calvi was in contact with in London was Flavio Carboni who checked into the Sheraton Hotel. Carboni tried to have a meeting with Calvi at Calvi's hotel but Calvi refused to come down to see his old friend. Calvi's associate, Silvanoi Vittor, who helped Calvi get to London, left England for Vienna by plane. The sisters Kleinszig also departed London and wound up in Austria. Carboni, the man whom Calvi trusted the most in his last days of his life also left London and arrived in Austrial by private plane. He was later arrested by police in Lugano that July. Calvi was now a man truly alone in London, all his friends and acquaintances having fled the scene.

Once the body of Calvi was found on June 18, the police contacted Teodoro Fuxa, the Italina consul to inform him that one of his fellow countrymen had been found dead near Blackfriers Bridge. When Fuxa learned all the details that the police told him, and identified him as Gian Roberto Calvini, Fuxa put two and two together and figured out quickly that the man whose body was found was probably Roberto Calvi. The scandal involving the default of Banco Ambrosiano was front page news in London and it didn't take a rocket scientist to figure out that Calvi probably fled to London in order to escape justice.

When the body was searched, the police found notes that were stuffed in his pants pockets with certain names on them which included Rino Formica, the Socialist Finance Minister, Alberto Ferrari, who once worked for the Banca Nazionale del Lavoro, and the P-2, and Hilary Franco from the Vatican. Why the names of these people were in his notebook is not known or their association with Calvi.

Consul Fuxa cabled Rome and told them what had happened. He also went to see the body at the morgue and soon got a message back from Rome saying, " You've got your banker."

The finding of the body of Roberto Calvi soon took on the attention of London's higher ups and one of the men who was notified was William Whitelayk the Home Secretary. Why would the Home Secretary have been notified if the case was something other than a random person having been found dead in a London bridge? Something out of the ordinary would have been going on to have such a high rankinbg official being notified of the incident. It is obvious that when the Home Secretary leanrned of the true identity of the boy that was found on Blackfriers Bridge, alarm bells must have sounded in London. Anyone who had been following the goings on in Vatican City regarding the down fall of Banco Ambrosiano surely kinew the players inovlved; Roberto Calvi, Michele Sincona, and Bishop Marchinkus. That one of them was now dead in London must have made the top-men in Whithall stand up and take notice. Just what was the wanted fugitive Roberto Calvi doing in England and why was he there? The British ministers probably knew right from the start that they had the makings of scandal on their hands and did not know how to contain it.

On July 13, an official inquest was convened to look into the circumstances regarding all aspects of Calvi's death, five weeks after the body was found. A jury was appointed under the care of Dr. David Paul, the coroner. They came up with a verdidct of "strangulation by suicide."Dr. Paul used the help of Professor Keith Simpson, who was the dean of the British medical examiners who had performed the autopsy on Calvi. Professor Simpson said after he examined the body that he found no cause for foul play and that ,"there was no evidence to suggest that the hanging was other than a self-suspension in the absence of marks of violence." When Calvi's brother Lorenzo told the inqust in a written statement that his brother had once tried to kill himself some time before. When the jurors began their deliberation Dr. Paul said that they did not have to come up with an unanimous verdict. Seven of the nine jurors would be all it would take to come up with a decision, he said. When the jury came back their verdict was suicide. Case closed.

If the British government was willing to close the case, the famlily of Roberto Calvi did not. They decided to open up their own invesitgation of the case even though the family was in Washington, thousands of miles from the crime scene. Calvi's wife Clara spoke loudly against those whom she preceived as having anything to do with her husband's death, the Church, Italian politicians of all stripes, and threatened law suits for one and all.

Soon, conspiracy theorists on both sides of the Atlantic began looking deeper into the events surrouding Calvi's death. First of all, Calvi suffered from vertigo and could not have climbed 25 feet down a ladder from the embankment parapet, without falling. Then there is the question of where he found the stones that were on his body? Did he actually put the stones on his person and walk or was taken to the bridge from his hotel without anyone seeing him (he probably could not have walked with all the stones in his body all the way to the bridge). And why did he not kill himself in his hotel room which would have been more private if he wanted to end his life that way? Inside his hotel room the police found a large amount of barbiturates and also learned that Calvi had bought a $3 million life insurance policy with his family as the sole beneficiaries.

It was learned later that Calvi gave an interview to *La Stampa* on June 15,1982 in which he gave cryptic remarks to the interviewer. He said, "The climate was that of a religious war. Now, it's almost the order of the day to attack me, and in this sort of atmosphere, any barbarity is possible. A lot of people have a lot to answer for in this affair. I'm not sure who, but sooner or later it'll come out."

Clara Calvi "maintained that her husband's murder was sponsored by the anti-Opus Dei faction, alarmed at the consquences for the Vatican's carefully nurtured dealings with Communist Eastern Europe. Calvi told his lawyers that he had channneled $50 million to Solidarity, and that there was more to follow. If the whole thing comes out, it'll be enough to start the Third World War."[4]

When Michele Sindona heard of Calvi's death he said those responsible were "left-wing South American freemasons."

The writer mentioned the lost suitcase belonging to Roberto Calvi and what might have been in it. Author Rupert Cornwell writes regarding the missing suitcase that, "Did Calvi destroy his most senstive papers himself, or was their destruction the completion of the cover-up which began with his murder?

In Italy, a second investigation regarding Calvi's death had begun and they ruled it a suicide. In March 1983, three Italian forensic experts concluded that, "On the basis of exhaustive examination, that it was probable, although by no means certain, that Calvi had taken his own life."

Months later both Silvano Vittor and Flavio Carboni were under questioning by Italian police. Both men were charged in circumstances regarding Calvi's disappearance but did not extend

[4] Cornwell, Rupert, *God's Bankers,* Page 202.

beyone organizing his flight from Europe to London.

But it seems that all was not lost in the Calvi drama. On March 29, 1983, Lord Chief Justice Lane ordered a new hearing to be held regarding the circumstances that took place on Blackfriars Bridge. He ordered that the original verdict be quashed on the grounds that it was not properly held at the time and that Carboni should have been called as a witness. He ordered that a new trial be held later that year to hear new evidence. The experts said that a certain amount of drugs could have been used to put Calvi to sleep before he was hung.

After the British decision was reached, the Italian press and others in high places in Italy began to write that the British decision of suicide was wrong. When the British began their investigation a number of Italian's representing the government were sent to England to aid in the probe. One Italian said of Calvi, "Why bother to go to London to do that.?

The new probe was not like the first one. The man who ran it was Dr. Arthur Gordon Davis, who impanled another jury of nine people. The new panel took two weeks to hear the evidence and deliberated three hours before coming up with their new findings of an "open verdict," which meant that they could not find any positive reason for Calvi's death or how it happened and the original verdict of suicide was thrown out.

The Calvi family, now living in the United States, hired a well-known private security comnpany called Kroll Security Group to mount their own probe into Calvi's death. After digging into all aspects of the affiar, Kroll said that, "the British inquests were incomplete at best and potentially flawed at worst."

The family also hired two former Scotland Yard forensic scientists and they reported that "water staining on Calvi's suit and unexplained marks on the back of his jacket were found. It was almost inconceivable that Calvi alone had climbed to the spot on the bridge's scaffolding from which he was hung."

In 1998, the Calvi family convinced a Roman judge to exhume Robert Calvi's body for further examination. The team of doctors who performed the autopsy said that Calvi's wrist had possible bruises and also said that they found traces of another persons DNA on his body. They said that in their opinion that murder was probably the reason for his death.

To add to the confusion regarding Calvi's death, when boxes containing parts of Calvi's body were located when the Institute of Forensic Medicine was moving to new location and were examined, they found no microscopic iron filings under his nails or shoes or socks which would have been on his body if he had climbed over the bridge's scaffolding. From what they discovered it seems that Calvi had been strangled *before* the cord was placed around his neck.[5]

It took another three years for the judicial process to work itself out and at that time authorities had enough evidence to indict people, including the former chief of the secret Masonic lodge of which Calvi was a member, and also Flavio Carboni, his earstwhile friend. The trial for the defendants took place at Rome's Rebibbia Prison which was constructed especially for the trial. It started on October 6, 2005 and ran for twenty months before all the testimony was completed and the jury got to decide their fate. The jury deliberated for a day and a half and then came back with a verdict of not guilty on all charges. In 2010 and 2011 two Italian appelate courts upheld the verdict.

The interest among the public in general did not stop the deep attention of just what happened to Roberto Calvi. In 2002 a movie about Calvi was made but a judge ordered it out of the theaters because Falvio Carboni filed a defamation suit. Years later attention as to who killed Calvi centered on four mobsters as the prime suspects. Twenty-one years after Calvi's death, a "formal declaration that foul play was involved came out. The press again paid attention to the old case and among those written about in the plot to kill Calvi were the ususal suspects, the Vatican, who might have wanted to cover up their part in the IOR scandal, the Mafia who had their own reasons for possibly killing Calvi, or the Masons.

Of all the remaining people involved in Calvi's death, the man most people wanted to hear from was Flavio Carboni for he had most of the answers that he never gave up. There is the fact that payments were sent to him before and after Calvi's death, including $100,000 that was deposited in the bank account of his mistress, Laura Concas, and a payment of $530,000 to his underworld friend Ernesto Diotallevi whom he had met in Switzerland before leaving for London on June 16.

Who was the most likely to have taken part in Calvi's death?

[5] Posner, Gerald, *God's Bankers,* Page 7.

The major culprits were probaly Bishop Paul Marchinkus and/or Michele Sindona or their henchmen (Carboni, et al). Both men had no love for Calvi and it is entirely possible that they may have pulled strings with their Mafia associates to have Calvi rubbed out.

Who was the Amercan who took part in the Vatican Bank scandal and was associated on a close level with both Calvi and Sindona?

Paul Marchinkus was at times the papal bodyguard called "the Gorilla" and an Arcbishop of the church at the time the Vatican Bank scandal erupted. He was born on January 15, 1922 in Cicero, Illinois, the center of Al Capone's criminal network. He came from a Lithuanian family who were working class and spoke poor English. He studied to become a priest and was ordained in 1947. He then went to Rome where he studied at the same school as that of the future pope, Albiano Luciano, called Gregorian. He later got his doctorate in cannon law and his star in the church was now on the rise. He was a large man, over 220 pounds, not your typical looking priest. He later went back to Chicago where he worked as a parish priest and a member of the local diocese. He caught the attention of Cardinal Sameul Stritch who was the head of the archdiocese in Chicago and he had Marchinkus transferred to the English section of the Vatican secretary of state's office in 1952. He also served the church in Bolivia and Canada before returning to Rome.

One of Marchinkus' most notable fans was New York's Cardinal Spellman who often told Pope Paul VI that Marchinkus was someone who could aid the church in the future. He saved the pope from harm when the Pontiff was in Rome and an overeager crowd suddenly barred his way. Marchinkus elbowed the pope to safety and a star was immediatley born. When the pope travelled on overseas trips to such places as India and the United Nations, it was Paul Marchinkus who served as his bodyguard.

In 1974, the pope made a decision that would have a profound effect on how the Vatican Bank would be run for years.; he appointed his trusted advisor and friend, Paul Marchinkus as head of the IOR, or the Instutute for Religious Works (he would stay in that position until 1989). One of Marchinkus' favorite phrases was, "You can't run a church on Hail Mary's."

In 1971, the year that Marchinkus was appointed to head the IOR, he first met Roberto Calvi through Michele Sindona and from that first introduction, the seeds of the Vatican Bank scandal, with all three men participating, were laid, with fatal consequences for all of them. By his own admission, Marchinkus had no knowledge of banking and it was only by his intimate friendship and support of the pope that he was selected to become head of IOR.

Another thing that the pope did not know as that Bishop Marchinkus was involved up to his neck with members of the Mafia. According to a mobster named Vincenzo Calcara who was being investigated by the Italian police, he said that when Marchinkus ran the IOR, the institution helped to launder $6.5 million in Mafia cash. He told inestigators that he flew from Sicily to Rome carrying two large suitcases containing $100,000. When he landed at the Rome airport, he was met by Marchinkus and an unnamed cardinal and was driven to a lawyer's office in the city where Calgera turned over the cash. The money eventually wound up as "clean" money with the IOR taking a service fee for their work. A second Mafia member named Rosario Spatola, testified that he heard Marchinkus "bragging" that he had high contacts in the Mafia.[6]

Marchinkus also made a secret deal with Roberto Calvi when it came to the IOR's relationship and loans to various other banks with whom they did business (mostly undercover). In August 1981, Marchinkus met with Calvi at IOR's headquarters and gave him what was called "letters of patronage" or "letters of comfort," which assured the parties that the Vatican stood behind Banco Ambrosiano. The letters went on to say that the IOR "directly or indirectly" controlled banks in Panama, Luxembourg, and Liechtenstein. The letterts were so vaguely written that the receiver would be led to understand while the IOR would not assume debt, it would let the participant know that it was endorsing the loan. Marchinkus also asked Calvi to give him a counter-letter which was backdated to August 26, absolving the Vatican of any obligation to repay the loans. For a man who had no knowledge or interest in banking, Bishop Marchinkus was learning fast.

While Marchinkus was involved with Calvi and Sindona in their money laundering schemes using the IOR as their conduit, he was making friends with high-level Amercan officials in Washington, providing them with valuable information coming from the Vatican. Marchinkus's contact in Rome was the US envoy to the Holy

[6] Ibid, Page 377.

See, William Wilson, a friend and advisor of President Ronald Reagan. Upon arriving in Rome in Februrary 1981, Ambassador Wilson counted Marchinkus as a friend and the two men met many times officially and unofficially. Soon, Marchinkus was providing Ambassador Wilson with classified information on the activities of the pope and he even tried to persuade the Pontiff to take pro-American positions when it came to foreign relations. Marchinkus's information was passed on to other American ambassadors with the warning that, "Please be sure to protect the source." The State Department soon learned of Marchinkus's illegal involvement with Calvi and Sindona but they did not press Wilson for further information on what he was up to. The thought in Washington was the less they knew about what Marchinkus was up to, the better.

The Bishop was now in the cross hairs of an FBI investigation relating to the possible defrauding of the United States government relating to a company called American Trading Services, "by concealing millions of dollars in the Instutute of Religious Works (Vatican Bank). A total of $7.7 million dollars was supposed to have been concealed in two accounts owned by the Instutute Per Le Opera di Riligione that had been opened five years previously by the ATS. The matter got the attention of the US Deputy Presidential Envoy to the Holy See who delivered a three-page telex to Marchinkus by Benjamin Civiletti, the Deputy Attorney General. Civiletti asked Marchinkus for details of the American Trading affair and he replied one month later saying that he he'd gone through the facts of the case but could not find anything wrong that the Vatican Bank might have been accused of. He had the nerve to tell Civiletti that, "the IOR is not a bank in the ordinary sense of the word." Speaking of the questionable $7.7 million he said, "Ours is a modest organization and any question involving large sums would not go unnoticed."

In 1973, two FBI agents and a federal prosecutor visited Marchinkus in the Vatican as part of their investigation into counterfeit bonds and securities and believed that he had some part in running it. He said that the Vatican was not responsible in any way for the sale of $900 million worth of stock and bonds which were made up of counterfeit money. The IOR, he said, had gotten involved "because of the stories told by some confidence people." The FBI came away from that meeting confident that Marchinkus

370

was somehow involved in the confidence scheme but had no solid evidence to prove their point beyond a reasonable doubt.

In a stuning development Ambassador Wilson told the US Attorney General that the accusations against the Bishop were "based on innuendo and possibly, even by association." He also had the gall to ask the Justice Department to let Marchinkus read the contents of any FBI files they had on him (this request was refused). It seemed that certain high-level members of the Reagan administration were trying to protect the bishop at all costs, even if it meant covering up his crimes.

While all this was going on, Marchinkus was facing further scrutiny from a book that was to be released by the noted writer, Richard Hammer, "with the first ever account of the 1973 fraud and counterfeit investigation that prompted the FBI to interview Marchinkus at the Vatican. Ambassador Wilson even got former New York Mayor Robert Wagner to intercede on behalf of Marchinkus and he approached the publisher, Holt Reinhart to allow Marchinkus the opportunity to read the manuscript before publication (it was refused). The book, called *The Vatican Connection,* was released early, due to the major publicity it received in the press. The publisher wrote of the books contents as, "The astonishing account of a billion-dollar counterfeit stock deal between the Mafia and the Church."

In the end, Marchinkus was forced to resign his job as head of the IOR. The Vatican paid out $224 million to its creditors of the Banco Ambrosiano in what it called "recognition of moral involvement" in the bank's default.

Paul Marchinkus died on February 22, 2006, age 84, in Sun City, Arizona.

Roberto Calvi was found dead hanging from Blackfriars Bridge in London in June 1982.

Michele Sindona died in prison under unusual circumstances while serving a life sentence. After eating breakfast in his private cell, he suddenly collapsed yelling, "I've been poisoned." He was in a coma, dying two days later.

Roberto Calvi hung at Blackfriars Bridge in London.

Paul Marcinkus.

Chapter 7

Death of the Swiss Guards

On May 13, 1981, as Pope John Paul II was riding in his "pope mobile" around St. Peter's Square a gunman opened fire and wounded the pope several times, almost killing him. He was immediately rushed to a nearby hospital were doctors were able to save his life. As the pope fell, he was helped by one of the Swiss Guards who were riding with him, a man named Alois Estermann, 43-years old. His heroic action that day helped save the life of the pope and he was rewarded years later by the pope when he appointed him as Commander of the Swiss Guards, the men whose job it was to protect the life of the pope in the Vatican and when he traveled abroad.

However, on May 4, 1998, seventeen years later, Alois Estermann was killed in a violent shootout with a fellow Swiss Guard named Cedric Torany, 23, a corporal in the halls of the Vatican. When the deed was done, both Estermann, Torany, along with Estermann's wife, Gladys Meza Romero, were killed. The killing of the three people were unheard of inside the halls of Vatican City where murder was not a common occurrence. In the immediate aftermath of the killings, the Vatican hierarchy went into overdrive to hush up any hint of scandal or other nefarious reasons for the three deaths. But as time went on, rumors of sexual actions between one or more of the parties, especially in the part of Corporal Torany, the relationship between the secret Opus Dei organization, rumors of connections to the East German secret police during the cold war, the Stasi, all came to the front.

In February 1998, the Vatican officially closed down its investigation of the killings, issuing a four-page letter that was sent to journalists and other interested parties by the Vatican press office.

The letter tried to stamp down the stories that were published in a book called *God's Word, Gay Word,* a made up story about the love affair of a senior officer in the Swiss Guards and one of his sublanterns. The book was inspired by Colonel Estermann, and Cedric Tornay, who shot the colonel and his wife and then killed himself." The Vatican statement read as follows, "We do not accept the slightest suspicion about presumed hypotheses about tormented love stories or espionage with which some have tried to stain Alois. We would be grateful if people would stop adding to the pain that we feel."

Right after the deaths, some reporters in the Italian press wrote that Colonel Estermann was an East German spy, headed by the infamous East German spy chief, Markus Wolf. No one could prove that allegation but it had the lurid feeling of something out of the ordinary, adding to the already curious course of events.

The Vatican report said that Corporal Tornay carried out the killings of his boss, Colonel Estermann and his wife because he was passed over for a decoration he thought he deserved.

Allegations of sexual misconduct between Estermann and Tornay were alleged by author Massimo Lacchei in his book in which he said that he attended a party at the home of an "elderly and important gay politician, where Colonel Estermann and Corproal Tornay were also guests. He said that they were lovers, and that he had doubts about the Vatican version of events."

Rumors immediately began to swirl in the Italian press who were always looking for a good, juicy story, that Colonel Estermann and Corporal Tornay were gay lovers.

The gay-lover angle got the attention of Maria Meza Romero, the younger sister of Colonel Estermann's wife, and she flew to Rome to try and set the record straight. She told the press that, "At first, we paid no attention to these news stories, but then they started up again recently, with such lies and perversity. We decided we had to do it. None of the people who wrote about my sister and my brother-in-law had the slightest knowledge of them as a couple. If they did, they wouldn't write such unjust, false accusations."

Mr. Lacchei, the author, stood up for Mrs. Meza Romero but in the end admitted that he had no solid proof that either man was involved in a gay relationship.

The lawyer for Mr. Lacchei wrote in the newspaper *La Repubblica*, that Corporal Tornay might have been killed because "he knew too much, had met too many important people."[1]

Who are the Swiss Guards and how did they come into being? The Swiss Guards are under the leadership of the pope and are solely responsible for his safety. It is a military organization that has certain rules and regulation. All Guards have to be unmarried, Roman Catholic males of Swiss citizenship, between 19 and 30 years old, be at least 5 feet, 8 inches tall and must have a professional diploma (like high school) and must have completed basic training in the Swiss military. They are noted by their colorful attire consisting of blue doublets, berets and, sometimes, steel helmets. On ceremonial occasions they wear colorful Renaissance-era uniforms for which they are known. Their tunics are striped in the colors of the Medici family, red, dark blue, and yellow, who ruled Rome in generations past and were one of the most powerful families in Europe at that time. When greeting foreign visitors or heads of state, the Swiss Guards are seen wearing white ruffs and high plumed helmets with ostrich feathers colored to reflect different ranks, and sometimes wear armor. While on duty they carry pikes and swords, but a large arsenal of weapons is stored beneath the Vatican in case they are needed.

The Swiss Guards live in their own quarters at the eastern part of the Vatican north of St. Peter's Square. Their chapel is that of Saints Martino and Sebastiano, and the Campo Santo Teutonico, near St. Peter's Basilca.

The first use of the guards took place in the late 14th and 15th centuries and Swiss mercenaries were used in such countries as Spain and France during that time. In 1505, the Swiss bishop Mattaus Schiner, who was acting on behalf of Pope Julius 11, proposed the creation of a permanent Swiss contingent that would operate under the direct control of the pope. On January 22, 1506, the first members of the Swiss Guard made up of 150 men, led by a Captain Kaspar von Silenen, arrived at the Vatican. They fought bravely during the sack of Rome in 1527 when all but 42 of the 189 guardsmen were killed defending Pope Clement VIII.

____In 1914, the__ Swiss Guards were reorganized consisting of a

[1] Stanley, Alessandra, "Despite Vatican, Case of Swiss Guard's Murder Remains Alive," *New York Times*, February 18, 1999,

commandant with the rank of Colonel, 5 other ranking officers, 15 lesser officers, a chaplain, and 110 pikemen. Subsequent reorganizations took place in 1959 and 1976, and in 1979 their number was fixed at 100.

The Swiss Guards are oftentimes referred to as the Vatican City police, but a separately administered police force is charged with the overall security of the nation-state (except St. Peter's Square) which is under the jurisdiction of the Italian police."[2]

Immediately after the bodies of the three murdered people were found inside the Vatican halls, an investigation was started. The Vatican spokesman, Joaquin Narvarro-Valls told reporters that, "the preliminary information allows us to hypothesize a moment of madness by the vice corporal (Tornay)." He said that Colonel Estermann, his wife and Corporal Tornay had been killed by firearm, and that a service revolver had been found under the corporal's body. The Vatican ordered one of its own, Gian Luigi Marrone, the Judge of Vatican City to investigate the case. Right after he was appointed to investigate the crime, and without further clarification, Judge Marrone told the waiting press that, "There are no elements to make us believe that Italian judicial assistance will be requested."

As mentioned before, killings inside the Vatican are rare indeed. Besides the attempt on the life of Pope John Paul II by Ali Agca, the last death occurred outside of Vatican walls in January 1998 when Enrico Sini Luzi, 67, a descendant of a minor nobility with the title of Gentleman of His Holiness, was found dead in his apartment in Rome, wearing only his underwear with a cashmere scarf wrapped around his neck, a victim of a homosexual tryst that turned violent.

Before his murder, Colonel Estermann served for 18 years protecting the pope and was well respected by most who knew him.

The last commander of the Swiss Guards was Roland Buchs, retired in October 1998 for what was called "family reasons" and his deputy, Colonel Estermann, took over on an acting basis. It took the Vatican seven months to replace Commander Buchs and Alios Estermann was chosen in his stead. Colonel Estermann was sworn in, two days before the May 6th swearing in ceremony of the guards that was attended by the pope. Why did it take 7 months before the Vatican made the official announcement that Colonel Estermann would be chosen as the new commander of the Swiss Guards?

[2] Swiss Guards. www.britannica.com.

There were rumors swirling around Rome that the Vatican knew something about Colonel Estermann's background that would embarrass the Vatican and so they kept the process of naming him to the top post a long, drawn out affair. One person who knew Colonel Estermann, a writer named Mario Biasetti, said that, "I spoke to him this afternoon, and he was just delighted with his appointment." Prior to his being selected as Guards commander, Colonel Estermann said, "I love being a soldier and I am a practicing Catholic. To serve as a soldier to the Holy Father is a beautiful combination for me."

The "official" version as put out by the Vatican was that Corporal Tornay killed Colonel Estermann and his wife because of some sort of grievance that he felt was harming his career as a Swiss Guard and then once the deed was done, he then killed himself. Tornay, before the incident took place said, "After three years, six months and three days, they haven't given me the good service medal, so I've just got to stop other injustices... That which I am about to do, I'm forced to do for the good of the Corps."

No sooner had the controversy concerning the events surrounding the deaths of the Estermann's and Corporal Tornay began to rumble, another, more provocative allegation concerning Colonel Estermann hit the daily press. This bombshell came via a German newspaper called the *Berliner Kurier* that alleged that Colonel Estermann was once employed as a spy for the East German secret police unit called the Stasi that was run by the famous spy chief, Marcus Wolf. If this allegation could have been proven, it would have rocked the Vatican to its core and no one could then have predicted what would have happened next. No sooner had the allegations of Estermann being an East German spy hit the press than the Vatican spokesman, Dr. Joaquin Navarro-Valls once again tried to dismiss the charges. He held a press conference in which he said, "Here in the Vatican we're not even considering such a hypothesis. Unfortunately, this is not the first time that lies have been written about an honest man." The German newspaper wrote that Estermann had worked for the Stasi between 1979 and 1984 "during which time he filed at least seven extensive reports to the Stasi under the codename "Werder. The reports were filed via a postbox on the Rome-Innsbruck night train and then picked up by Stasi operatives based in Austria."

To add to the already explosive charges, the Polish tabloid *Super*

Express reported that Wolf said in an interview that Estermann "had unremitting access to the Holy Father, and so did we." Wolf was further to have said that Estermann was recruited in 1979 while he was applying for a job with the Swiss Guard. The reason for Estermann's work for the Stasi was purely monetary.

Who was the man who allegedly recruited Colonel Estermann? Marcus Wolf was born in 1923, the son of Jewish doctor, playwright, and a communist. The Wolf family left Germany in the 1930s just as Adolf Hitler was seizing power in Germany. Marcus then lived in Switzerland for a while and then in France. He traveled to Moscow in 1934 to attend a party convention. For many years he was known as "The Man Without A Face" as there was no picture of him in anyone's files. He also worked for a time as a journalist and covered the Nuremburg trials in which Nazi leaders were tried for their wartime crimes.

After the end of World War 11, Wolf aided the Soviet Union in setting up the East German government and entered the East German diplomatic service. He rose fast in the German pecking order and in 1958 he became the Chief Administrator, Intelligence (HVA), the foreign intelligence arm of the Stasi. His main accomplishment was to put a number of spies right under the noses of the West German government, even placing one inside the office of Chancellor Willy Brandt. The name of this mole was Gunter Guillaume and his identity was only uncovered in 1974. In the wake of the Guillaume scandal, Chancellor Willy Brandt was forced to resign. One of his top agents that he ran had a code name called "Topaz" who worked for two decades inside the halls of NATO headquarters. He also ran the highest-ranking woman in the West German intelligence service, the deputy head of its Soviet bloc division, who sent her reports directly back to Moscow headquarters. He finally sought asylum in the Soviet Union and also claimed that he had been offered a fulltime job by the CIA if he would tell them all he knew about his role as East Germany's top spy master. He refused.

Wolf retired from the Stasi in 1987 but if he thought his controversial role as head of the Stasi was over, he was mistaken.

Upon the unification of the two Germany's in 1990, the crimes committed by Marcus Wolf came to light. He was tried and found guilty in 1993 and sentenced to six years in jail. He had a change of luck when Germany's Constitutional Court ruled on May 23, 1995 that former Stasi officials could not be prosecuted for conducting Cold War espionage against the West. The court ruling was 5-3 that in effect, admonished many of the East German spies for their crimes against their own people. It was at this point in his life that Marcus Wolf thought about moving to Isreal because of his Jewish roots but after talking with many of his friends, they convinced him not to go that route because they told him that Israeli officials would not welcome him into the country. He was also tried in 1997 for kidnapping.

"The charges concerned the secretary of an American military attaché to West Germany who was driven by one of Wolf's agents in 1955 to an investigation for the purpose of recruiting her. A friend in the CIA told me that a charge like that would turn all off the intelligence officers in the world into criminals," Wolf said regarding the attempt to convict him. He alleged that the man behind the kidnapping plot was Klaus Kinkel who was the head of the BND (West German intelligence service), and later the foreign minister of Germany.

At one point, after his espionage charges were dropped by the government of West Germany, Wolf spoke out on various aspects of his life as a spymaster. He said that when he ran the Stasi, he never spied on Israel:

> The KGB approached me on several occasions and asked me to send agents and spies to gather information about Israel and in Israel. As Germans, it was easier for us to enter and operate in your country than it would be for Russians, Poles, or Czechs. But I always turned them down. In retrospect, I am happy to say that my Jewishness may have contributed to my lack of desire to operate against Israel, but it was mostly due to professional considerations. I preferred to concentrate all the effort on gathering information in West Germany and in NATO.

In the later part of his life, Marcus Wolf was a man who was sought after for his vast knowledge of intelligence and he made the most of it. He was frequently on television, giving his opinion of the days news and he later wrote a book on his espionage life called *A Man Without a Face.*

In an interesting turn of events, in 1997 Wolf went to Israel where he met with certain officials in the Israeli intelligence services to discuss topics of mutual interest. One of the people whom Wolf met on his trip to Israel was the former head of the Mossad, the Israeli intelligence service, Rafi Eitan. One of the topics they discussed was the relationship between the Stasi and the PLO-Palestine Liberation Organization that was run by Yasir Arafat. "He claimed that contact with terror organizations was maintained by another division of Stasi, known as "Number 22." He also told Rafi Etan about the Stasi role in the deadly Palestinian terror attack on Israeli athletes during the 1972 Munich Olympics. He said the PLO terrorists entered West Germany via East Berlin. "They did it without our knowledge, or at least without our knowing what the real plan was, and we were, of course, very embarrassed by the event. After the affair, we made it clear to the PLO that we would no longer agree to them using East Germany as a way station to conduct acts of terror."

Wolf also expanded on his knowledge of Carlos the Jackal. He said that Carlos stayed many times in East Berlin before heading out on his terror sprees. He said that Carlos "was a wild man and never listened to us. He would make the rounds at nightclubs and bars, and invite girls to his room. We finally had to kick him out and he was transferred to Hungary where he continued with his escapades."

Wolf told about his relationship with Dr. Wadia Hadad, the operations commander of the Popular Front for the Liberation of Palestine who spent many months in East Berlin (just like Carlos the Jackal). Hadad was responsible for the skyjacking of an Air France plane to Entabbe, Uganda under the control of the dictator, Edie Ammin, among other operations. He also suggested that Mossad agents might have been responsible for the death of Hadad, although he would not go into that story any further.[3]

From what we know about the reputation of Marcus Wolf over the years, almost all of the things he said and did regarding his espionage activities during the cold war were never disputed. The only time the powers that be in the Vatican and elsewhere took exception to what Wolf had to say was in respect to a possible Stasi-

[3] Melman, Yossi, "After East Germany Fell, I Considered Escaping to Israel," *Haaretz*, October 16, 2017.

Estermann connection. While we have no smoking gun as far as the Estermann-Stasi link is concerned, why would Wolf lie when he made that statement? He had noting to hide at the time he made the declaration; the cold war was over and he could suffer no retribution if any one was inclined to do so.

Another conspiracy theory regarding the deaths of Colonel Estermann, his wife, and Corporal Tornay was a result of an internal strife of a group of disgruntled priests inside the Vatican. One theory going around was that certain evidence into the murders were tampered with in order to fit the hypothesis that the murder of Estermann was the result of a moment of sudden madness on the part of Corporal Tornay. These claims were first introduced into the public realm by a book that was published in 1999 called *Blood Lies in the Vatican,* which was published by a book company based in Milan.

The book further alleges that Colonel Estermann and his wife who worked in the Venezuela Embassy to the Vatican were somehow involved in financial dealings with the secretive Opus Dei religious organization. The authors also say that there was a lot of opposition to the appointment of Colonel Estermann and the fact that he was appointed to his post only nine hours after his selection as head of the Swiss Guards, he was killed.

Just like in the aftermath of the death of Pope John Paul I, the apartment where Estermann was found dead was quickly sealed by Vatican officials. A hurried-up autopsy was done by Vatican doctors who were held to a pledge of secrecy. The rush to judgment regarding the activities of Corporal Tornay was soon in full gear. Shortly after the murders, Cardinal Alfons Stickler said that "Tornay was an individual suffering from the psychological disorder of paranoia" even though he had not met him before. Some one had told the Cardinal what to say about Tornay and he did so as ordered.

One interesting point of the autopsy results on Corporal Tornay was that small amounts of cannabis were found in the urine, but not the blood. The amount of cannabis was not enough in a person to describe he or she as a constant user. The autopsy also revealed that Tornay had a "benign subarachnoid cyst," 4.0 by 2.5 centimeters, which had "depressed the anterior part of the left frontal cerebral lobe, partially eroding the bone." The story of Tornays's so-called "tumor" took another turn when a second autopsy was done in Switzerland and it was determined that he had no such tumor. So why did the Vatican come up with the story in the first place? It seems that they wanted to smear him for some reason, to make him out to be the "lone gunman" (sound familiar?) in the murders of Colonel Estermann and his wife.

There were also two fundamental differences in the last rights given to both Estermann and Tornay. Colonel Estermann's and his wife's funeral service were overseen by Cardinal Secretary of State Angelo Sodano in St. Peter's Basilica in a Requiem Mass attended by many church officials. This was unusual because Colonel Estermann was a layperson, not affiliated with the church as a member of the clergy. Even if there were suspicions regarding the circumstances of Estermann's death, the church wanted to see him off in regal style, as if one of their own had been killed. As for Corporal Tornay, a funeral was held for him in a Church called the Church of St. Anne that was a private affair.

We now have to wonder just was going through the minds of the Vatican officials when they tried to explain just who Corporal Torany was and how he became a guard in the first place. If he had mental problems as they had alleged, why was he allowed to become a Guard in the first place? He had served as a Swiss Guard for the previous three years with a stellar reputation. His duties was being in charge of all the guards deployed in the Apostolic Palace, the place where the pope lives, and monitoring St. Anne's gate, the "key entry point into Vatican territory."

In contrast, the Vatican put out quite a respectful story when it came to Colonel Estermann after his death. He was the chief bodyguard of Pope John Paul II, and saved his life in the assassination attempt in 1981. At one point, Church officials asked him to research the life of Nicolai Wolf, a Swiss layman being considered for canonization.

If the Vatican wanted to be done with the entire affair after the burial of Colonel Estermann, his wife, and Tornay, they were mistaken. They now had to deal with the distraught mother of Cedric Tornay, a woman of many passions, Muguette Baudat. Mrs. Baudat had a rather hard life, being married twice and twice divorced. She was abandoned by her first husband and beaten by her second, but she was able to raise her children in the Catholic faith even though she herself was a Protestant. Cedric was young when his mother remarried and one can only wonder how he must have felt as his family was being torn apart. After her son's death, Mrs. Baudat wrote to the pope asking him to look into the circumstances of her son's demise but she got no reply.

She wrote of her frustrations with the way the Vatican was stonewalling her by saying, "From the start, I was the victim of pressures, manipulation, dissimulation, and lies." She alleged that Vatican leaders tried to persuade her not to come to Rome after her son's death. She was told by Monsignor Jehle, the chaplain of the Swiss Guards, that supposedly her son's head had been ripped off of his body. It was said that Chaplain Jehle made that statement on the orders of Cardinal Sodano.

Mrs. Baudat made further comments on the above-mentioned subject by saying:

> He (Cardinal Sodano) wanted to find out how much I knew and what I planned to do about it. He gave me a rosary, but he also threatened me in the name of his superiors, telling me I should stop asking about Tornay's death and think of my surviving children. He said he was sure I wouldn't want anything bad to happen to them. That's a threat, isn't it?[4]

Ms. Baudat went even further to prove her son's innocence. When Cedric's body was taken back to Switzerland for burial, she had the body taken from a Swiss morgue for a second autopsy conducted by Dr. Thomas Crompecher, a professor of forensic medicine at the University of Lausanne. Based on his conclusions, Baudat hired two French lawyers, Luc Brossolet and Jacques Verges, who had previously defended Slobodan Milosevic before the World Court at the Hague. Meeting the press, the two lawyers issued a seventy-five page report that disputed the Vatican's version of the murders and called for another investigation. Among the contradictions in the official report they found were that Tornay's pistol used 9 mm. bullets, but the exit wound in his head measured 7 millimeters. Second, "Tornay apparently suffered a fracture of a cranium bone,

---

[4] Arcee, Moina, *The Swiss Guard Murders*, www.infobarrel.com/ TheSwissGuard Murders, June 15, 2013.

which was not on the bullet's trajectory. His lungs contained a large amount of blood and saliva which could not have been caused by suicide, but could have been caused by internal bleeding due to blows on the head before he died."

In an interesting twist to the story, Mrs. Baudat said that one year before her son's death, he told her that some of the Swiss Guards were investigating Opus Dei but when she asked him further questions about the matter, he told her, "The less you know about it, the better." "Later, said Baudat, "I found out from some friends of Tornay that Estermann was close to Opus Dei and had tried to recruit guards into it."

According to the article in *Infobarrel,* an unnamed Vatican monsignor observed, "There's one common thread running through this, and it's the Opus Dei movement. The Estermann's were both close to it. Navarro-Valls is a member, and he was very fast in getting to the scene of the crime when he was alerted. And the Holy Father's shadow, Dziwisz, is said to be supportive of Opus Dei. Given the movement's taste for secrecy, all these people are going to follow the principle that the less said the better."

With all the negative publicity swirling around the actions of Cedric Tornay, one of his friends in the Guard had this to say about him," He had a heroic side to him. I have absolutely no doubt that he believed in the oath. Tornay really would have given his life to save the pope." Another ex-Guard said, "Tornay was a victim, He wasn't of a violent nature, but he was the victim of bullying for three years… for the Swiss Germans he was the devil in person." Another Guardsman said that, "Tornay was a great guy, and the Vatican blackened his name when he could no longer speak for himself. The truth is that he was no better and no worse than others as far as discipline went. Estermann was always hounding him."

Shortly after the death of Cedric Tornay, the Vatican had in its possession a letter that he had written right before his death. The Vatican did not want, for whatever reasons, to have Tornay's letter stay put, but somehow it was released to the press. It is not known who leaked the letter, either the Vatican, which seems unlikely, or the family of the deceased corporal. The letter was written in French and is translated as follows:

Mummy.

I hope you will forgive me because what I have done but they were the ones who drove me on. This year I was due to receive the benemerenti and the Lieutenant Colonel refused it to me. After three years six months and six days spent here putting up with all the injustices. The only thing I wanted they have refused it to me. I must do this service for all the guards remaining as well as to the catholic church. I have sworn to give my life for the pope and this is what I am doing. I apologize for leaving you all alone but my duty calls. Tell Sara, Melinda and Daddy that I love you all. Big Kisses to the Greatest Mother in the World."

Your son who loves you.[5]

As mentioned before in this chapter, a number of Tornay's fellow guardsman had nothing but good things to say about him after his death. A man named Colonel Roland Buchs, who was Colonel Estermann's predecessor as the commander of the Guards, spoke at Tournay's funeral and had only praise for him. He said he loved life, loved the work he did at the Vatican. "His first step as a young adult was to put himself at the service of the Chruch, and that way to make his contribution to the common good. Commander Buchs told as many people who'd listen that in his opinion, the words coming out of the Vatican regarding the accounts of the murders were not to be believed and that Corporal Tornay was not being fairly treated.

Enter into the mix is the secretive organization known as Opus Dei which has been a conspiracy theorists bane of contention for years. The story as it relates to the deaths of Colonel Estermann, his wife, and Corporal Tornay comes in the person of a Vatican intelligence official named Yvon Bertorello. There is not much known about Yvon Bertorello in the written record but according to the literature regarding the events in Rome was that his assignment was to spy on the Swiss Guards and to find out how deeply Opus Dei had infiltrated that organization. If one is to believe that scenario, Bertorello made friends with Corporal Tornay and possibly recruited him as a spy. Both men spoke French and it was that, among other reasons, that Bertorello recruited Tornay.

[5] Follian, John, *City of Secrets: The Truth Behind the Murders at the Vatican,* William Morrow, New York, 2003, Page 23.

It was rumored that Colonel Estermann was himself a member of Opus Dei and if he were, he probably wouldn't have wanted any one else to know about it. Reports swirled around the Swiss Guards that Colonel Estermann was a member of that secret organization, and one person who knew him said, "Many people in the Vatican feel that Opus Dei has got its finger in too many pies. There's so much intrigue in the Vatican, so many factions."

An historical aside on just how much intrigue gathered around the Vatican in years past comes during the decades of the 1970s and 1980s. It was discovered during that time "the Kremlin also had an ear in the Vatican, in the shape of a listening device hidden in the apartment of John Paul's right-hand man, the then secretary of state, Cardinal Agostino Casaroli. The bug was in a glass-cased statuette in the dining room, its signal picked up at the Villa Abamelec, the Soviet ambassador's residence not far away on the Gianicolo Hill."

Bertorello also claimed that the real reason for the pope's taking so much time in appointing Estermann to the commander of the Guard were the rumors of Colonel Estermann's possibly being a homosexual. Bertorello claimed that Tornay was heterosexual, but at times tried his hand in the homosexual underworld, possibly with other Guard members, possibly including Col. Estermann.

For the conspiracy theorist interested in just why Opus Dei would want to infiltrate the Vatican, what better path would be then the Swiss Guards? Msgr. Vladimir Felzmann, an ex-Opus Dei member, believed that "Estermann would be of great interest to Opus Dei." An Opus Dei member at that high level inside the Guard would be in an unique position to spy on the goings on inside the pope's inner circle and report back on what he learned. When asked if the pope himself was involved with Opus Dei, Msgr. Felzmann replied, "Of course he is. In all sorts of ways. We used to bank with Banco Ambrosiano, I used to deposit money in our account there. When the pope had to find two hundred million that Calvi, "God's Banker," owed the Vatican in 1982, Opus Dei came up with it.

Speaking of Corporal Tornay's relationship with Opus Dei, he said, "Opus Dei is like a fire. If you get close you can get warm; if you get inside you can get burned. Tornay didn't stand a chance."

One of the most highly disputed conspiracy theories surrounding the Estermann-Tornay affair is the belief among many interested parties that Colonel Estermann, contrary to the public perception, was not the savior of the pope after he was shot by Ali Agca but was a participant in the plot to begin with.

As written earlier in this book, Ali Agca alleged that the Soviet's and the Bulgarians were somehow involved in the attempted assassination of Pope John Paul II and that they used Soviet bloc agents to try and kill the pope. If we take that direction of reasoning one step further, then is it so outlandish to propose that Estermann, if he was indeed a member of the Stasi, as alleged by Marcus Wolf, was part of the assassination conspiracy? People who have questioned this new line of reasoning say that it was possible that Estermann knew of the impending attack on the pope but did nothing to prevent it until the pope was wounded, and then he sprung into action. No new information on that allegation was ever put out in the open, so it will still remain one of the outstanding issues in the whole, sordid chain of events.

There were also allegations that Colonel's Estermann's private residence was burgled on a number of occasions and that files were removed but all his personal valuables were left untouched. He complained to his superiors in the Vatican that he felt he was under surveillance and had CCTV monitors set up in all areas that fell under the jurisdiction of the Swiss Guards. If that were true, then wouldn't there be some sort of footage on the night the murders took place, and if there was, what happened to it?

Since the assassination attempt on the pope in 1981, John Paul II had a huge debt to pay regarding the actions of Colonel Estermann. The two men became close and that is probably one of the reasons that he promoted him to be head of the Swiss Guards.

One of the household workers inside the Vatican made these remarks following the Estermann-Tornay murders. "I can't imagine there was anyone in the pope's life dearer than Alios; he looked at him as his own son; John Paul was a regular visitor to the Estermann apartment next to the palace. His Holiness was devastated when he heard the news."

If we take the conspiracy foundation one step further regarding any possible role of Colonel Estermann in the pope's shooting in 1981, could Estermann have told Tornay anything relating to the events regarding Agca's attempt on the pope's life, and if he did, what might that have been? If indeed Tornay knew something about the attempted assassination of the pope, could he have used that information as leverage against Estermann in any way? All these things have to be considered if we truly try to understand what happened in the Vatican the night the murders took place.

Researchers who have closely followed the Swiss Guards murder case saw a parallel to that of the alleged assassin of President John Kennedy, Lee Harvey Oswald. When looking at the case in detail, some conspiracy theorists came to the conclusion that Cedric Tornay, like Lee Oswald in 1963, was being set up as a patsy in the crime in order to deflect the blame on others.

Let's looks at both cases. In Tornay's situation, high Vatican officials spent a considerable amount of time trying to besmirch his reputation, despite the fact that he was well liked by his fellow Guardsmen and had a stellar record in the Guards before the fatal incident that took all their lives. They tried to tell the public that he was upset for not getting the decoration he thought he deserved and that let him to slip into madness and kill Colonel Estermann, his wife, and finally himself. Then there were the blatantly false charges that he had a head tumor, and the fact that he had small amounts of cannabis in his body, led officials to further attack his credibility. Then there was the official campaign to attack his mother, Mrs. Baudet because of her insistence that her son had been blackballed by certain Vatican officials who wanted to put the blame directly on his shoulders. The Vatican acted in its own defense after the incident and to this day, they never apologized to the family of Cedric Tornay or to anyone else who was connected to the horrible incident. The sense in the Vatican at the time, and now, was to let sleeping dogs lie and not provoke anything that might upset the status quo.

In the case of Lee Harvey Oswald, it would take a book just to provide the reader with all the relevant information on the falsifications that were put out by the American government after the president's assassination. The FBI stated that Oswald was a Communist, (a fact that was not true-he read Marxist literature as a young man), and said he was anti-Kennedy (in fact, people who knew Oswald said he admired the young president). In the weeks prior to the assassination, there were false Oswald sightings around Dallas and the surrounding area. Some people said they saw him at a rifle range making anti-Kennedy remarks, others said he was seen at a car dealership and took out a car for a drive at high speeds (Oswald did not have a drivers license), and he was also supposed to have been at a draft board in order to try and change his discharge papers.

There were also unconfirmed reports that Oswald was seen in the company of a CIA officer named Maurice Bishop in Dallas prior to the assassination. The person who was known as Maurice Bishop was said to have been David Atlee Phillips—a high-ranking CIA operative who worked covertly in Latin America and the Caribbean during the decades of the 1950s and 1960s. At that meeting, Oswald and Phillips were supposed to have been talking to an anti-Castro leader named Antonio Veciana who was in charge of an organization called Alpha 66. After the president's assassination, US officials tried to pin Oswald to many radical internal groups, as well as Russia and Cuba. However, as in the case of Cedric Tornay, the Warren Commission who investigated the Kennedy assassination never came up with a conclusion as to the motive of Oswald in his killing of the president.

More information on different fronts regarding the assassination of the Swiss Guards came from author John Follain in his book *City of Secrets: The Truth Behind The Murders At the Vatican,* which came out in 2003. In the book, the author tells the story of his investigation into the murders and tells the account of a meeting he had with an unnamed Italian Catholic Monsignor who had information to partake to him. They met outside the Finnish embassy to the Holy See on the Villa Borghese near the Roman Colosseum. The clergyman was in his late fifties or early sixties, and was a likable fellow. Over ice cream that the clergyman liked, Mr. Follain told the priest that he wanted an introduction into the Swiss Guards and that he was also looking into the murders at the Vatican that dominated the news cycle for a number of months. The priest told Follain that after the deaths took place, the guards were lined up and told not to speak about what happened on orders from Jehle, who was the chaplain. "He said that in the name of unity they shouldn't accuse or blame anyone in the Guard for what happened… other than Tornay, obviously. Some swearing-in ceremony."

The priest said that the man most responsible for trying to keep the murders inside the Vatican a secret was Secretary of State Sodano who tried to silence Tornay's mother. He said that Sodano wielded a huge amount of power inside the Vatican and went so far as to not criticize the Pinochet regime in Chile that jailed a number of priests, sometimes torturing and jailing them (Pope Paul did nothing to stop this action).

The priest said that there was a cover-up between Sodano, Monsignor Gianbattiste Re, the deputy at the Secretary of State, Navarro-Villas, and Judge Marone who was to investigate the murders. "It took them just a half an hour to decide what to say about the deaths, and who should say it. By the way, Sodano and Re are also the ones who prevented Tornay's mother-and anyone else for that matter-from getting access to the files of the inquiry after it ended."

Follain asked the priest about the pope's reaction to the deaths. He replied by saying the following, "You must be joking. His Holiness just went along with what Sodano cooked up. The Holy Father is so ill he's become a prisoner of the Curia. There's a Vatican saying: popes never fall ill, they just die. So, Dziwisz, his secretary, does all he can to make John Paul appear in control, but at night, he's woken up by his boss, struggling to get up and pray when he is in pain."

Follain then tried to get the priest to come forward regarding any information he had on the security of the pope during those days. The priest made a very interesting comment in that regard. "Well, there's something else which springs to mind. If you think about it, there's one common thread running through this, and it the Opus Dei movement. The Estermann's were very close to it. Navarro-Villas is a member, and he was very fast in getting to the scene of the crime when he was alerted. And the Holy Father's shadow, Dziwisz, is said to be supportive of Opus Dei. Given the movement's taste for secrecy, all these people are going to follow the principle that less said the better."[6]

He also expanded on his views of the influence that Opu Dei had inside the halls of the Vatican by saying," I'm no snob myself. But its true that many people in the Vatican feel that Opus Dei has got its finger in too many pies. There's so much intrigue in the Vatican, so many factions, sometimes I get the impression the Holy Spirit never

[6] Ibid, Page 69.

got past St. Anne's Gate."

The second topic that John Follain tackled in his book, regarded the allegation that Colonel Estermann was a member of the East German Stasi during the cold war era. To that effect, Mr. Follain traveled to Berlin to meet with a writer named Peter Brinkmann who wrote a newspaper article called *Dead Bodyguard was a Stasi Spy.* Mr. Follain wanted to get as much information as he could from the writer in order to try and find out the real story of what Colonel Estermann did or did not do in the Stasi. Peter Brinkmann told Mr. Follain that his article was based on an anonymous letter he received in the mail.

The source was a former Stasi major identified only as "H. Sch (age 57), "said to be the officer in charge of Werder (possibly Colonel Estermann). The newspaper that Peter Brinkmann worked for, contacted this mysterious person and he was quoted as saying, "I had nothing to do with it."

The article did say that Colonel Estermann contacted the East German commercial affairs section and not the East German embassy. When Follain asked him if he could see the original article he wrote, he told him that he threw it away. When Follain asked him if he thought the article was a made up story he replied in the negative. "It was definitely not an outsider, and not a crazy guy. That's the way the Stasi worked; it was so compartmentalized. So these guys give you just a tidbit, a teaser. Then it's up to you to to get extra details from the other people in the know. For me, that's what happened in the Estermann case: one guy knew a small part of the story and wanted it to come out." Brinkmann told Follain that he believed the reason that Estermann took the job as a Stasi spy was for money.

When asked by Follain if he believed that the letter was a fake, Brinkmann said possibly. He gave no real answer, just said that sometimes the ex-Stasi people wanted to see how stupid the newspapers were and that could have been a reason for the letter to him. He said that his newspaper, the *Berliner Kurier,* shut down any further reporting because it was going no where and was getting too expensive.

Follain then went to a place called the Gauck Academy, a repository of all the old cold war era files that had been collected from the Stasi records.

The files were part of a collection of old cold war era documents that were stored for further research. The collection were rumored to include more than 40 million index cards and that the files ran more than a hundred miles long (who could find anything in that mess?). Follain met with a worker named Rudiger Stang, a senior researcher at the Academy with whom he made an appointment with. Stang opened a box that Follain asked to see. The title on the cover was labeled "Vatican."

The box contained whatever information they had on Werder. "It's a copy of the index card that bears the agent's cover name, in this case, Werder. It's part of a catalog know as F22. There's another index, F16, which is the most important one. Everything is in it. The real names of anyone whom the Stasi has a file. That's means all the agents, and all of the victims of the Stasi's spying. Plus the details of what the Stasi did to these people."

Follain was sure he had a winner but then, suddenly it all came crashing down. Stang told him, "I'm sorry. The F16 reference to Werder is missing. It was probably destroyed when the people of East Berlin stormed the headquarters."

There was one more puzzling piece of evidence that Follain asked Stang about. On the card file was a number that read XV/3764/79. "That number was the registration number under which all of Werder's output was classified," he said regretfully since those files were gone.

The card did though, have some useful information. It described Werder as an IM, or unofficial collaborator. The date of his recruitment was August 29, 1979 (however, the article in the *Berliner Kurier,* said it was October 29, two months earlier). "The card also showed that Werder had initially been attached to a section that looked after East Germany's central bank and other financial and economic institutions." Stang said that this section had noting to do with military intelligence or religious institutions. When asked if there was any connection between Estermann and Werder, Stang said, "We looked for Werder and we looked for Estermann. The only thing we found on Werder was on this index card. We found nothing on Estermann. So we can't check anything out. We can't establish, on the basis of our files, whether Werder was Estermann."

Stang then gave Follain the names to two ex-Stasi agents who might be able to help him in his probe, Hans-Peter Schippmann and Walter Lucke. There was file that had the name of Schippmann which was marked "Most Secret: For Internal Use Only!" There was his date of birth and had the reference of H. Sch (age 57) written on it.

Stang then gave Follain a most important file about an asset the Stasi had inside the Vatican called "Lichtblick." He said he didn't know his real name but it might have been a Benedictine monk named Eugen Bammertz, who was dead. Stang said this person sent reports to the Stasi from Rome but the reprots were destroyed.

Stang then told Follain that there were some other files on "Litchblic" that he could have. Stang gathered them up and made Follain pay for them. After leaving the building, he began studying the papers that included "Lictchblic's" reports on the Vatican's policy towards the two Germany's, and the policies of the Polish Pope, John Paul II, the ties between the Church and the Reagan administration, and the relationship between the Church and the CIA. There were also two reports on the May 1981 assassination attempt on the pope, but nothing regarding Estermann. It turned out that Eugen Bammertz had been a former POW in Russia, was fluent in Russian, and worked until 1986 as a translator for the German-language edition of the official Vatican newspaper, *L'Osservatore Romano*. Follain said that he concluded that Lichtblick and Estermann were not the same person. But were Estermann and Werder the same?[7]

Using the information that Stang gave him, Follain began his search for the two, ex-Stasi men. The first person they tried to see was Hans-Peter Schippmann, whose residence he was able to locate. Schippman spent two years in the Komosomol youth movement then joined the Communist party at age nineteen. His first job in the Stasi, like many others of his age, was that of a collaborator. In time, he was sent to the Soviet Union for further training and received medals along the way. He lived in an old building in East Berlin, one he had resided in for years. The first person whom Follain and his guide met was Schippmann's son Olaf who showed them inside. He said his father was out but he took a message from the two men who said they'd be back later.

[7] Ibid, Page 130-31.

While waiting for Schippmann to return, they located the other ex-Stasi agent, Werner Lucke. After speaking with Lucke for a few minutes, he reluctantly let them in, and while Lucke was reluctant to speak to them, his wife took over the discussion. They asked Mrs. Lucke if she remembered anything about the killings of the Swiss Guards and she said yes. She said her husband believed the official story put out by the Vatican was "rubbish," "that Werder worked in Section XVIII/4, that dealt with economic and industrial espionage, and that it had nothing to do with religion." She also said her husband only worked with East Germans while in the Stasi, not any foreigners.

Later, Follain left the Lucke home and returned to his hotel. Some time later, he phoned the Lucke's again and this time was able to speak with Lucke himself. Follain got down to the point quickly. He asked Lucke if he had any information regarding either Estermann or Werder. He told him that the section he worked in had nothing to do with the Vatican, that it was a domestic agency only, and that they were forbidden to work with anyone from outside the country. Lucke said that he had no idea who Werder was and could not be of further help in that area.

In time, Follain was able to get in touch with Schippmann and he too told him that he had no idea who Werder was "and that he could rule out any link with Estermann and the Vatican. When asked if he knew if Werder was still alive, Schippmann made the following comment, "I'd rather not give you his real name. But I can tell you he had nothing to do with any foreign country. He used to live in a town of Gosen near Berlin, and I came across him when I was in charge of overseeing security for a training center being constructed by the Stasi. Werder was restaurant manager; he helped us solve a small problem, something to do with disclipine among our construction workers."

The one thing that Follain took away from his meeting with both Schippmann and Lucke was that neither man knew who the real Werder was.

Back in Rome, Follain, once again on the trail of the mysterious Werder, met up with Yvon Bertorello, the man who spied on the Swiss Guards and was a friend of Tornay's. Bertorello told Follain a little about his background. He said he was an "international consultant" for the sale of gold and jewelry for heads of state and their VIP's. He said he carried three passports, but did not say why he needed them. He also said he was a deacon, not a priest, as others had said he was. He said he had long running problems with certain people in the Vatican who suspected him of being a member of the SIMI, the Italian military secret service. He said he was put on trial, that he was accused of illegal transfer of millions of dollars, and of drug trafficking. He said he was acquitted, but the whole affair left a bitter taste in his mouth. Bertorello declared that in the 1970s and 1980's, SIMI agents spied on the Vatican, and that they had help from people inside the Holy See. They were able to learn all sorts of political information right under the nose of the pope. He also claimed that Russia had planted listening devices in the office of Cardinal Agostiono Cassaroli, who was then secretary of state. He said the bug was placed in the Cardinal's dining hall and that it was received in the Soviet ambassador's home, nearby.

Bertorello did not confirm that he worked for SIMI as a spy, but refused to say if he worked for the Vatican in that same capacity.

Follain then asked his friend to comment on any relationship that Tornay might or might not have had with Opus Dei, and that Tornay might have been investigating that organization when he was killed. Bertorello then said, "It would make a great thriller. But I won't talk. Are you playing devil's advocate with me" Did the Vatican send you to me?" He said that if he talked about the case, the Vatican would never stop coming after him. It was better if he not say anything more. Follain asked him if he believed that Torany killed Estermann and his wife, and then killed himself. His reply was, "If the Vatican says so, it must be so." He continued by saying, "I've got a dossier on Tornay, with photographs of him. The dossier is my bargaining chip while I wait for the letter clearing my name." Bertorello was a man who had many secrets regarding the Guards shooting and his relationship with Cedric Tornay. In the end, he wasn't talking.

Much speculation has been made regarding what role Col. Estermann played during the assassination attempt on the pope in May 1981. The official version is that Estermann shielded the pope's body after Agca fired the shots. That scenario was played up by the Vatican after the shooting, trying to make Colonel Estermann to be the hero in the entire affair. However, there were chinks in the armor of that story, as will be explained here. The story about what happened that day was relayed by a man named Francesco Pasanisi, who had served for some time as the Italian chief of police acting as the liaison with the Vatican for the pope's security. Pasanisi was in the caravan when the pope was shot, walking by the jeep the pope was riding in.

In the car at the time was the pope's driver, along with the pope's secretary, Dziwisz. Pasanisi, who said there were a few Swiss Guards walking along with Colonel Estermann alongside the jeep while it made its way around St. Peter's Square. When the shots were fired, Pasanisi shielded the pope's body with his own, with Dziwiz and another man named Gugel who were also in the car. Pasanisi said that he had no idea where Estermann was when the shots were fired but he was certain he wasn't in the car. Pasanisi told author Follain that, "I didn't see him (Estermann); he must have been behind me. Anyway, there weren't any more shots, so how could Estermann have shielded the pope from them?" He reiterated that during the whole shooting episode, Colonel Estermann was behind him, of that he was sure. Pasanisi also said that Estermann was not at the hospital when the pope arrived there, something that he probably should have done because of the important position he had. Pasanisi likewise said that he was not armed that day because he didn't feel that there was any security risk for the pope.

The car the pope rode in that day, an old, black Mercedes, license plate SCV-1, was not bulletproof. The car wasn't bulletproof because the pope wanted to stand in the back and wave to the crowds as their car passed by. He said that the bullet that hit the pope was later sent to the town of Fatima in Portugal so that it could be mounted at the crown of the statue of the Virgin Mary.

It was sometime later that Follain met again with his ex-spy friend, Bertorello. Bortorello said that he had finally gotten the letter from the Vatican absolving him of any wrong doing in the case being brought against him. He said the man who signed the order was Jean-Louis Tauran, the foreign minister.

Follain again asked him if he could tell him more about the assassination case but he clamed up. He wanted to be paid five million francs for his information, something that the author refused to do. He also demanded that he be placed in a witness protection program, something a civilian like Follain could not be expected to do. Whether he was boasting or not, Bortorello said that he, "knew sixty percent of what happened. That's what I know, there's what I've been told, and there's what I think."

Bertorello related that Tornay got in touch with him shortly before he was killed. He said he was on a plane heading back to Rome and that Tornay tried to call him twice, saying that it was urgent that he get back to him. What Tornay wanted to tell Bertorello is not known. Maybe it was something important, maybe not.

Bertorello said that Estermann was closet homosexual and that there was some kind of sexual relationship going on between him and Tornay, but what that was, he wouldn't say. Bertorello also said that some of the Guards were homosexual, and that fact was well known among the higher-ups in the Vatican, but that they didn't want to make that known in order to avert a scandal. Could that fact alone have been the reason he killed Colonel Estermann and his wife?

Throughout this chapter, the name of Opus Dei and its relationship with Colonel Estermann keeps coming up. Another former Swiss Guard named Steve Kellenberger gave his fair share of information on that subject. He said that it was no secret among the Swiss Guards that Estermann was one of Opus Dei's members and told of a story when a Spanish monsignor who was a member of Opus Dei came to the Vatican asking for Colonel Estermann. The monsignor said they were organizing a trip to a villa for a party but that he did not attend. The place where the dinner was to be held was the headquarters of Opus Dei. Kellenberger said that the Guards chaplain, Monsignor Jehle, told Estermann to stop trying to recruit guard members into Opus Dei. During one of these sessions, when confronted by Monsignor Jehle, Estermann hotly denied that he was a member of Opus Dei.

While many people who knew Cedric Tornay, inside and out of the Vatican, had nothing but good reports about him, one prominent clergyman had a different view, Cardinal Schwery. Schwery had been a physics teacher before joining the church, and at the tender age of fifty-nine, became the youngest bishop of the Church. During his tenure at the Church, Cardinal Schwery served on boards that oversaw the Church's finances, along with the discipline of the sacrament, among others. He was interviewed by author Follain and he told him there were certain differences between the members of the French and German guards. Most of it had to do with discipline, with some members sticking to strict rules and procedures, while others were less inclined to the rigors of being a Swiss Guard.

Follain then asked Cardinal Schwery about what he knew of Cedric Tornay. He explained that he was shocked to learn of the deaths of Colonel Estermann, his wife, and the corporal. He then said, "But if there was one guard who was going to do such a thing, it was him." The Cardinal said he had a one-on-one meeting with Tornay at one point and the corporal opened up to him. He said that Tornay told him he was angry with Estermann, and with Monsignor Jehle. Tornay said he hated the strict regulations that he had to put with on a day-to-day basis. He expanded by saying about Tornay, "What I can say is that there had been no sign that he'd do what he did. I would never have guessed that he'd be willing to go to such lengths."

Cardianl Schwery then said something interesting as it pertained to the events on the night of the murders. "You want my opinion? I think that when he went up the staircase of the officer's building, he was out to get Jehle, not Estermann. Jehle wasn't at home, but I think he'd have gotten a bullet if he'd been in." The cardinal expanded more by saying that many of the Swiss Guards hated Monsignor Jehle, and that they told him (Schwery) on more than one occasion. He said that Tornay hated Monsignor Jehle more than anyone else in the Guards. "The main reason for Tornay doing what he did is everything he had experienced before, and the shock of seeing Estermann promoted."[8]

Cardinal Schwery said that at one point, he had a meeting with Col. Estermann in which he upbraided him on certain things that were going on with the guards. One of the topics they discussed was the cultural prejudice "the French speakers were having to put up with." He also mentioned the retreat that Colonel Estermann had gone to some time back in which Tornay refused to go.

Follain writes that he met with an unnamed retired senior officer of the guard who would talk to him on the condition that his name not be used. "Tornay was very depressed. He told me that Estermann had summoned him to his office and had detailed the punishment: three days confined to barracks, a day's leave canceled, and three hours of extra work."

Estermann then sent another letter to Tornay, saying that he was

[8] Ibid. Page 266-268.

adding two more penalties—no benemerenti medal and immediate expulsion. It was mean and narrow-minded, a pure vendetta on Estermann's part. The officer stated that when Tornay complained to Estermann, the colonel relented concerning the granting of the medal and rescinded the expulsion order.

The source ended the conversation saying, "But Tornay had made up his mind to leave in July. Basically, Estermann always had it in for Tornay. He kept Tornay in his sights."

With all this going on one can only sympathize with how Tornay felt. He had been sought out on purpose by Colonel Estermann for various reasons regarding his duties as a Swiss Guardsman. He must have believed he was being singled out by Estermann for some slight he did not know about. What must have been going through his mind in the last days of his life is unknown, but one can only sympathize with the young corporal during that time. But were all these slights enough to have taken his revenge on Estermann in the final analysis?

In order to learn more about Tornay's state of mind before the killings, Follain met in London with a man named David Canter, a professor of investigative psychology and a leading expert on the science of criminal profiling. Carter had previously advised Scotland Yard, the FBI, and the US Army on offender profiling for about a decade. His biggest success was his work on the so-called "Railway Rapist" case, in which he drew up a detailed profile of the killer who was eventually captured. Follain sent all the material he had on the Swiss Guards murder to Canter for his perusal. Mr. Canter said that in his opinion, the Vatican officials had no reason to follow up on any other leads, other than Cedric Tornay was responsible for the killings of Estermann and his wife. He, Tornay, had a fit of madness, as the Vatican officials had said, case closed. Canter expanded on what he meant by a fit of madness of Tornay's part by saying, "Quite frankly, I don't know what the Vatican means by that expression; it's not a scientific phrase. It's wrong to assume that what Tornay did was irrational to him. In any case, I think you'd have a hard time finding any reference in any text on homicide to a fit of madness."

Canter said that in his opinion, there were a number of reasons why Cedric Tornay might have killed Estermann and his wife. He had a great deal of resentment towards the colonel for some time, and that Estrmann handled Tornay's resentment improperly. "It all gets out of control, "he said. "I can see all the frustrations, the problems, coming together in a particularly vulnerable individual, and in a particularly unsupportive environment."

The one person who knew probably more than he was willing to speak about was Chaplain Jehle. Author Follain tracked him down in the Vatican and he reluctantly spoke to him about what happened the night of the three deaths. He said that on the night he was killed, Tornay came to see Chaplain Jehle but for some reason decided not to talk to him. When asked why the corporal backed down from talking with him, Jehle had no answer. Chaplain Jehle then put the blame for the circumstances surrounding the deaths strictly on the shoulders of Colonel Estermann. "In any case, it was Estermann's fault. He did wrong. You can't let Tornay know just two days before the ceremony that he won't get the medal he's been expecting. Estermann should have told him before. That was wrong."

When asked if Estermann had any links to Opus Dei, Jehle shot back, saying that he would not comment on that subject. He did however, say that it was the policy of the Swiss Guards not to participate in any political order, and that Opus Dei was in that category. Jehle was then asked to give his opinion on the so-called homosexual relationship between Estermann and Tornay. He deflected by saying that, "That's old hat. In any case, bear in mind that the Church tolerates homosexuals, as long as they are chaste."

Follain then asked the Chaplain why the Vatican tried to make Tornay out to be a bad person, why wasn't he dismissed from the service. He replied by saying, "Both Estermann and I were in favor of Tornay's promotion because he had good qualities. We tried to offer him responsibility, but he took advantage of it. And he interpreted everything as a slight. He suffered from paranoia."

"The pope said he couldn't understand the deaths," he said, "and neither can I. It was a situation in which two worlds clashed. It was the work of the Devil. But a man of God does not despair. He cannot despair. God must have sown a seed in Tornay, but you cannot expect to see it sprout so quickly."

There are so many unanswered questions regarding the circumstances surrounding the deaths of Colonel Estermann, his wife, and Corporal Tornay that have still not been explained. Like the Warren Commission's investigation of the assassination of President John

F. Kennedy in 1963, the Vatican investigation of the Swiss Guards deaths was not thorough enough. Like any other powerful institution, be it religious or lay, there are certain people in high places whose primary job it is to protect the status quo. There are secrets that have to be kept, no matter the truth. Sometimes it is more important to keep a secret rather than give it the light of day.

Let's review some of the mysteries about the incident involving the major players in this drama.

There is the connection of the religious order Opus Dei and its possible relationship with Colonel Estermann. Did he belong to the group, and was Corporal Tornay trying to investigate Estermann at the time of his death? Were there other members of the Swiss Guards who were members of Opus Dei at that time? Why did the Vatican allow Tornay's last letter to his mother be published in which he told her of his problems in the Guard and the circumstances regarding not getting his medal? Then there is the story regarding Colonel Estermann's supposed relationship with the East German intelligence service, the Stasi, and Wolf's allegation that Estermann was the mysterious agent named "Werder." Another factor in the investigation was the so-called homosexual relationship between Estermann and Tornay and did it really exist?

Then there was the widespread campaign on the part of the Vatican to smear the reputation of Tornay, from the allegation that he was a poor Guardsman, from the charge that he smoked pot and had a so-called brain tumor, and the charge that he killed the Estermann's out of a "fit of madness." The Vatican tried to intimidate Tornay's mother into dropping her investigation of her son's actions and the fact that they tried to stop her from coming back to Rome after her son's death.

Another point of contention was the exact role Estermann played in the after math of the assassination attempt on the pope in May 1981, and whether or not he actually shielded the pope's body from Agca's bullet, as the Vatican story implied. One more problem was the story that Tornay was so upset about Estermann's trying to stop him from getting his medal that he freaked out and killed him in revenge.

Like so many other contemporary conspiracy theories, the case of the murder of the Swiss Guards will probably never be fully explained.

One of the Vatican's Swiss Guard.

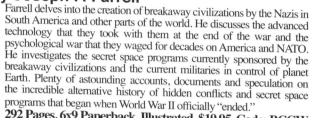
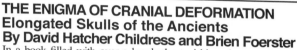
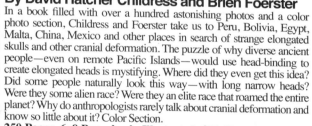

HESS AND THE PENGUINS
The Holocaust, Antarctica and the Strange Case of Rudolf Hess
By Joseph P. Farrell
Farrell looks at Hess' mission to make peace with Britain and get rid of Hitler—even a plot to fly Hitler to Britain for capture! How much did Göring and Hitler know of Rudolf Hess' subversive plot, and what happened to Hess? Why was a doppleganger put in Spandau Prison and then "suicided"? Did the British use an early form of mind control on Hess' double? John Foster Dulles of the OSS and CIA suspected as much. Farrell also uncovers the strange death of Admiral Richard Byrd's son in 1988, about the same time of the death of Hess.
288 Pages. 6x9 Paperback. Illustrated. $19.95. Code: HAPG

HIDDEN FINANCE, ROGUE NETWORKS & SECRET SORCERY
The Fascist International, 9/11, & Penetrated Operations
By Joseph P. Farrell
Farrell investigates the theory that there were not *two* levels to the 9/11 event, but *three*. He says that the twin towers were downed by the force of an exotic energy weapon, one similar to the Tesla energy weapon suggested by Dr. Judy Wood, and ties together the tangled web of missing money, secret technology and involvement of portions of the Saudi royal family. Farrell unravels the many layers behind the 9-11 attack, layers that include the Deutschebank, the Bush family, the German industrialist Carl Duisberg, Saudi Arabian princes and the energy weapons developed by Tesla before WWII.
296 Pages. 6x9 Paperback. Illustrated. $19.95. Code: HFRN

THRICE GREAT HERMETICA & THE JANUS AGE
By Joseph P. Farrell
What do the Fourth Crusade, the exploration of the New World, secret excavations of the Holy Land, and the pontificate of Innocent the Third all have in common? Answer: Venice and the Templars. What do they have in common with Jesus, Gottfried Leibniz, Sir Isaac Newton, Rene Descartes, and the Earl of Oxford? Answer: Egypt and a body of doctrine known as Hermeticism. The hidden role of Venice and Hermeticism reached far and wide, into the plays of Shakespeare (a.k.a. Edward DeVere, Earl of Oxford), into the quest of the three great mathematicians of the Early Enlightenment for a lost form of analysis, and back into the end of the classical era, to little known Egyptian influences at work during the time of Jesus.
354 Pages. 6x9 Paperback. Illustrated. $19.95. Code: TGHJ

ROBOT ZOMBIES
Transhumanism and the Robot Revolution
By Xaviant Haze and Estrella Eguino,
Technology is growing exponentially and the moment when it merges with the human mind, called "The Singularity," is visible in our imminent future. Science and technology are pushing forward, transforming life as we know it—perhaps even giving humans a shot at immortality. Who will benefit from this? This book examines the history and future of robotics, artificial intelligence, zombies and a Transhumanist utopia/dystopia integrating man with machine. Chapters include: Love, Sex and Compassion—Android Style; Humans Aren't Working Like They Used To; Skynet Rises; Blueprints for Transhumans; Kurzweil's Quest; Nanotech Dreams; Zombies Among Us; Cyborgs (Cylons) in Space; Awakening the Human; more. Color Section.
180 Pages. 6x9 Paperback. Illustrated. $16.95. Code: RBTZ

TRUMPOCALYPSE NOW!
The Triumph of the Conspiracy Spectacle
By Kenn Thomas

Trumpocalypse Now! takes a look at Trump's career as a conspiracy theory celebrity, his trafficking in such notions as birtherism, Islamofascism and 9/11, the conspiracies of the Clinton era, and the JFK assassination. It also examines the controversies of the 2016 election, including the cyber-hacking of the DNC, the Russian involvement and voter fraud. Learn the parapolitcal realities behind the partisan divide and the real ideological underpinnings behind the country's most controversial president. Chapters include: Introduction: Alternative Facts; Conspiracy Celebrity–Trump's TV Career; Birtherism; 9/11 and Islamofascism; Clinton Conspiracies; JFK–Pro-Castro Fakery; Cyber Hacking the DNC; The Russian Connection; Votescam; Conclusion: Alternative Theories; more.

6x9 Paperback. 380 Pages. Illustrated. $16.95. Code: TRPN

MIND CONTROL, OSWALD & JFK
Introduction by Kenn Thomas

In 1969 the strange book *Were We Controlled?* was published which maintained that Lee Harvey Oswald was a special agent who was also a Mind Control subject who had received an implant in 1960. Thomas examines the evidence that Oswald had been an early recipient of the Mind Control implant technology and this startling role in the JFK Assassination. Also: the RHIC-EDOM Mind Control aspects concerning the RFK assassination and the history of implant technology.

256 Pages. 6x9 Paperback. Illustrated. $16.00. Code: MCOJ

INSIDE THE GEMSTONE FILE
Howard Hughes, Onassis & JFK
By Kenn Thomas & David Childress

Here is the low-down on the most famous underground document ever circulated. Photocopied and distributed for over 20 years, the Gemstone File is the story of Bruce Roberts, the inventor of the synthetic ruby widely used in laser technology today, and his relationship with the Howard Hughes Company and ultimately with Aristotle Onassis, the Mafia, and the CIA. Hughes kidnapped and held a drugged-up prisoner for 10 years; Onassis and his role in the Kennedy Assassination; how the Mafia ran corporate America in the 1960s; more.

320 Pages. 6x9 Paperback. Illustrated. $16.00. Code: IGF

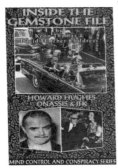

ADVENTURES OF A HASHISH SMUGGLER
By Henri de Monfreid

Nobleman, writer, adventurer and inspiration for the swashbuckling gun runner in the *Adventures of Tintin*, Henri de Monfreid lived by his own account "a rich, restless, magnificent life" as one of the great travelers of his or any age. The son of a French artist who knew Paul Gaugin as a child, de Monfreid sought his fortune by becoming a collector and merchant of the fabled Persian Gulf pearls. He was then drawn into the shadowy world of arms trading, slavery, smuggling and drugs. Infamous as well as famous, his name is inextricably linked to the Red Sea and the raffish ports between Suez and Aden in the early years of the twentieth century. De Monfreid (1879 to 1974) had a long life of many adventures around the Horn of Africa where he dodged pirates as well as the authorities.

284 Pages. 6x9 Paperback. $16.95. Illustrated. Code AHS

PROJECT MK-ULTRA AND MIND CONTROL TECHNOLOGY
A Compilation of Patents and Reports
By Axel Balthazar

This book is a compilation of the government's documentation on MK-Ultra, the CIA's mind control experimentation on unwitting human subjects, as well as over 150 patents pertaining to artificial telepathy (voice-to-skull technology), behavior modification through radio frequencies, directed energy weapons, electronic monitoring, implantable nanotechnology, brain wave manipulation, nervous system manipulation, neuroweapons, psychological warfare, satellite terrorism, subliminal messaging, and more. A must-have reference guide for targeted individuals and anyone interested in the subject of mind control technology.

384 pages. 7x10 Paperback. Illustrated. $19.95. Code: PMK

ANCIENT ALIENS & SECRET SOCIETIES
By Mike Bara

Did ancient "visitors"—of extraterrestrial origin—come to Earth long, long ago and fashion man in their own image? Were the science and secrets that they taught the ancients intended to be a guide for all humanity to the present era? Bara establishes the reality of the catastrophe that jolted the human race, and traces the history of secret societies from the priesthood of Amun in Egypt to the Templars in Jerusalem and the Scottish Rite Freemasons. Bara also reveals the true origins of NASA and exposes the bizarre triad of secret societies in control of that agency since its inception. Chapters include: Out of the Ashes; From the Sky Down; Ancient Aliens?; The Dawn of the Secret Societies; The Fractures of Time; Into the 20th Century; The Wink of an Eye; more.

288 Pages. 6x9 Paperback. Illustrated. $19.95. Code: AASS

AXIS OF THE WORLD
The Search for the Oldest American Civilization
By Igor Witkowski

Polish author Witkowski's research reveals remnants of a high civilization that was able to exert its influence on almost the entire planet, and did so with full consciousness. Sites around South America show that this was not just one of the places influenced by this culture, but a place where they built their crowning achievements. Easter Island, in the southeastern Pacific, constitutes one of them. The Rongo-Rongo language that developed there points westward to the Indus Valley. Taken together, the facts presented by Witkowski provide a fresh, new proof that an antediluvian, great civilization flourished several millennia ago.

220 pages. 6x9 Paperback. Illustrated. References. $18.95. Code: AXOW

LEY LINE & EARTH ENERGIES
An Extraordinary Journey into the Earth's Natural Energy System
By David Cowan & Chris Arnold

The mysterious standing stones, burial grounds and stone circles that lace Europe, the British Isles and other areas have intrigued scientists, writers, artists and travellers through the centuries. How do ley lines work? How did our ancestors use Earth energy to map their sacred sites and burial grounds? How do ghosts and poltergeists interact with Earth energy? How can Earth spirals and black spots affect our health? This exploration shows how natural forces affect our behavior, how they can be used to enhance our health and well being.

368 PAGES. 6x9 PAPERBACK. ILLUSTRATED. $18.95. CODE: LLEE

LIQUID CONSPIRACY 2:
The CIA, MI6 & Big Pharma's War on Psychedelics
By Xaviant Haze
Underground author Xaviant Haze looks into the CIA and its use of LSD as a mind control drug; at one point every CIA officer had to take the drug and endure mind control tests and interrogations to see if the drug worked as a "truth serum." Chapters include: The Pioneers of Psychedelia; The United Kingdom Mellows Out: The MI5, MDMA and LSD; Taking it to the Streets: LSD becomes Acid; Great Works of Art Inspired and Influenced by Acid; Scapolamine: The CIA's Ultimate Truth Serum; Mind Control, the Death of Music and the Meltdown of the Masses; Big Pharma's War on Psychedelics; The Healing Powers of Psychedelic Medicine; tons more.
240 pages. 6x9 Paperback. Illustrated. $19.95. Code: LQC2

TAPPING THE ZERO POINT ENERGY
Free Energy & Anti-Gravity in Today's Physics
By Moray B. King
King explains how free energy and anti-gravity are possible. The theories of the zero point energy maintain there are tremendous fluctuations of electrical field energy imbedded within the fabric of space. This book tells how, in the 1930s, inventor T. Henry Moray could produce a fifty kilowatt "free energy" machine; how an electrified plasma vortex creates anti-gravity; how the Pons/Fleischmann "cold fusion" experiment could produce tremendous heat without fusion; and how certain experiments might produce a gravitational anomaly.
180 PAGES. 5x8 PAPERBACK. ILLUSTRATED. $12.95. CODE: TAP

QUEST FOR ZERO-POINT ENERGY
Engineering Principles for "Free Energy"
By Moray B. King
King expands, with diagrams, on how free energy and anti-gravity are possible. The theories of zero point energy maintain there are tremendous fluctuations of electrical field energy embedded within the fabric of space. King explains the following topics: TFundamentals of a Zero-Point Energy Technology; Vacuum Energy Vortices; The Super Tube; Charge Clusters: The Basis of Zero-Point Energy Inventions; Vortex Filaments, Torsion Fields and the Zero-Point Energy; Transforming the Planet with a Zero-Point Energy Experiment; Dual Vortex Forms: The Key to a Large Zero-Point Energy Coherence. Packed with diagrams, patents and photos.
224 PAGES. 6x9 PAPERBACK. ILLUSTRATED. $14.95. CODE: QZPE

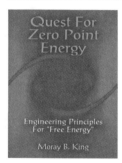

AMERICAN CONSPIRACY FILES
The Stories We Were Never Told
By Peter Kross
Kross reports on conspiracies in the Revolutionary War, including those surrounding Benedict Arnold and Ben Franklin's son, William. He delves into the large conspiracy to kill President Lincoln and moves into our modern day with chapters on the deaths of JFK, RFK and MLK., the reasons behind the Oklahoma City bombing, the sordid plots of President Lyndon Johnson and more. Chapters on Edward Snowden; The Weather Underground; Patty Hearst; The Death of Mary Meyer; Marilyn Monroe; The Zimmerman Telegram; BCCI; Operation Northwinds; The Judge John Wood Murder Case; The Search for Nazi Gold; The Death of Frank Olsen; tons more. Over 50 chapters in all.
460 Pages. 6x9 Paperback. Illustrated. $19.95 Code: ACF

ORDER FORM

10% Discou...
When You Ord...
3 or More Items!

One Adventure Place
P.O. Box 74
Kempton, Illinois 60946
United States of America
Tel.: 815-253-6390 • Fax: 815-253-6300
Email: auphq@frontiernet.net
http://www.adventuresunlimitedpress.com

ORDERING INSTRUCTIONS

✓ Remit by USD$ Check, Money Order or Credit Card
✓ Visa, Master Card, Discover & AmEx Accepted
✓ Paypal Payments Can Be Made To:
    info@wexclub.com
✓ Prices May Change Without Notice
✓ 10% Discount for 3 or More Items

SHIPPING CHARGES

United States
✓ Postal Book Rate { $4.50 First Item / 50¢ Each Additional Item
✓ POSTAL BOOK RATE Cannot Be Tracked!
    Not responsible for non-delivery.
✓ Priority Mail { $6.00 First Item / $2.00 Each Additional Item
✓ UPS { $7.00 First Item / $1.50 Each Additional Item
NOTE: UPS Delivery Available to Mainland USA Only

Canada
✓ Postal Air Mail { $15.00 First Item / $2.50 Each Additional Item
✓ Personal Checks or Bank Drafts MUST BE
    US$ and Drawn on a US Bank
✓ Canadian Postal Money Orders OK
✓ Payment MUST BE US$

All Other Countries
✓ Sorry, No Surface Delivery!
✓ Postal Air Mail { $19.00 First Item / $6.00 Each Additional Item
✓ Checks and Money Orders MUST BE US$
    and Drawn on a US Bank or branch.
✓ Paypal Payments Can Be Made in US$ To:
    info@wexclub.com

SPECIAL NOTES

✓ RETAILERS: Standard Discounts Available
✓ BACKORDERS: We Backorder all Out-of-
    Stock Items Unless Otherwise Requested
✓ PRO FORMA INVOICES: Available on Request
✓ DVD Return Policy: Replace defective DVDs only
ORDER ONLINE AT: www.adventuresunlimitedpress.com

**10% Discount When You Order
3 or More Items!**

Please check: ✓

☐ This is my first order   ☐ I have ordered before

Name
Address
City
State/Province   Postal Code
Country
Phone: Day   Evening
Fax   Email

Item Code	Item Description	Qty	Total

Please check: ✓

☐ Postal-Surface	Subtotal ▶	
	Less Discount-10% for 3 or more items ▶	
☐ Postal-Air Mail	Balance ▶	
(Priority in USA)	Illinois Residents 6.25% Sales Tax ▶	
	Previous Credit ▶	
☐ UPS	Shipping ▶	
(Mainland USA only)	Total (check/MO in USD$ only) ▶	

☐ Visa/MasterCard/Discover/American Express

Card Number:

Expiration Date: Security Code:

✓ SEND A CATALOG TO A FRIEND: